PARTICULAR FRI

The Correspondence
SAMUEL PEPYS and JOHN

Contents

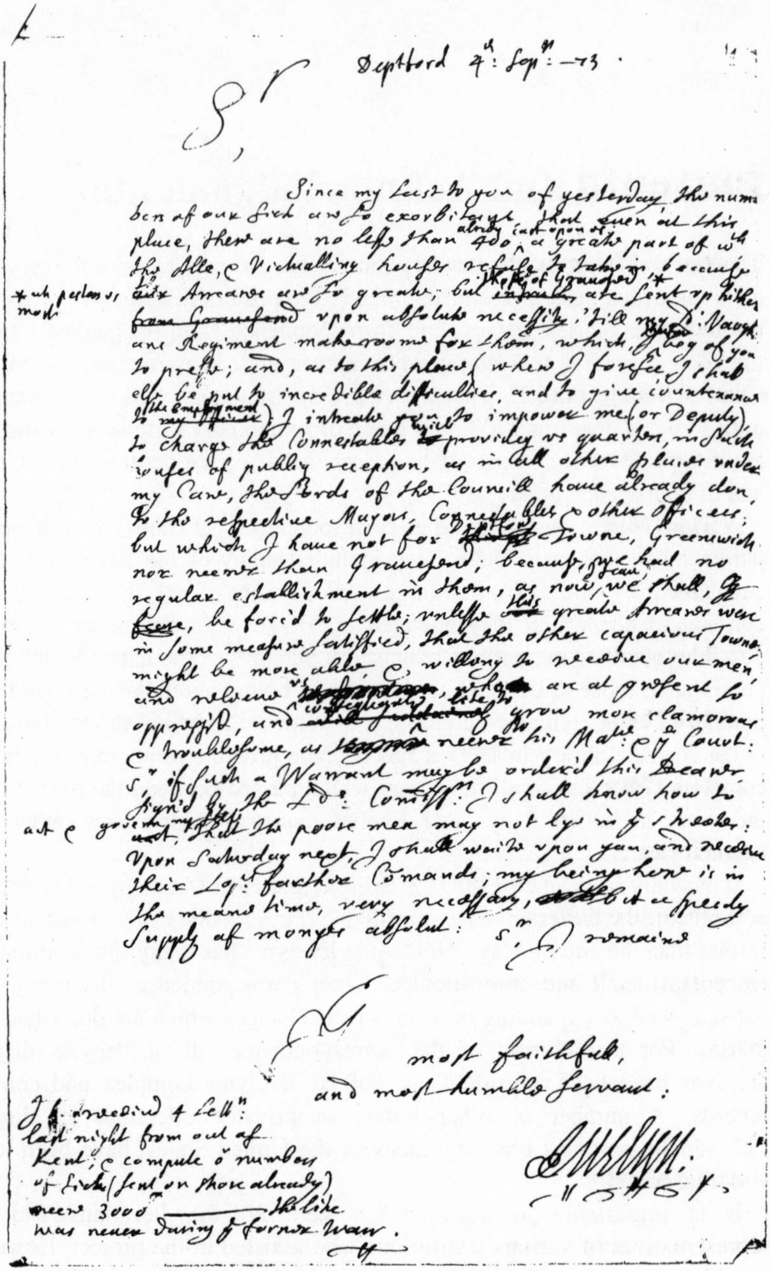

Deptford 4th: Sep^r: –73

Sr,

Since my last to you of yesterday the number of our sick are so exorbitant that even at this place, there are no lesse than 400, already cast upon us, a greate part of which the Alle, & Victualling houses refuse to take in, because their Arreares are so greate; but those of Gravesend are sent up hither upon absolute necessity: 'till my Ld: Vaughans Regiment make roome for them, which I beg of you to presse; and, as to this place (where I foresee, I shall else be put to incredible difficulties, and to give countenance to the employment) I intreate you to impower me (or Deputy) to charge the Connestables to provide us quarters, in such houses of public reception, as in all other places under my Care, the Lords of the Councill have already don, to the respective Mayors, Connestables & other Officers; but which I have not for Deptford Towne, Greenewich nor neerer than Gravesend; because, we had no regular establishment in them, as now, we shall, I feare, be forc'd to settle; unlesse this greate Arreares were in some measure satisfied, that the other capacious Townes might be more able, & willing to receive our men and relieve us, who are at present so oppressd, and unwillingly likely to grow more clamorous & troublesome, as so neere his Majestie & the Court: Sr if such a Warrant may be order'd this Bearer, sign'd by the Lds: Comissrs: I shall know how to governe myselfe, that the poore men may not lye in the streetes: Upon Saturday next, I shall waite upon you, and receive their Lops: farther Comands; my being here is in the meane time, very necessary, but a speedy Supply of mony is absolut: Sr, I remaine

Sr

most faithfull,
and most humble Servant:

J Evelyn:

I received 4 letters last night from out of Kent; & compute the number of Sick (sent on shore already) neere 3000 — the like was never during the former Warr.

Fig. 1 John Evelyn to Samuel Pepys
draft letter of 4 September 1673 (**B6**, pp.84–5)
Reproduced by permission of
Princeton University Library (Robert H. Taylor Collection)

Foreword and Acknowledgements

The diaries of Samuel Pepys and John Evelyn are only parts of the remarkable archives which these two unusual men left to posterity. Both have provided us, through their diaries, papers, and correspondence, with unequalled images of the second half of the seventeenth century and, in particular, the reigns of Charles II and James II. That the two were friends as well, and remained so until Pepys's death in 1703, is a piece of remarkable fortune for it means we are in a position to compare their descriptions of personalities, places, events, and of course each other.

Various selections from the correspondence of both men have been published in the past. These have included many of the letters which were exchanged by the two, the largest proportion of all the very extensive correspondence which they engaged in. However, it has never before been possible to collate the various manuscript versions of the letters which include letters-sent, loose drafts, and copies kept in bound letter-books; in addition, a number of letters remained unpublished. With the arrival of the Evelyn archive at the British Library in 1995 it has become possible to attempt to compile a complete collection of all the letters which passed between them. In so doing the ways in which Pepys and Evelyn managed their correspondence has become clearer.

It has only been since 1955 (for Evelyn) and 1971 (for Pepys) that definitive editions of the diaries have been available. Pepys's diary of course takes us no farther than the end of May 1669, while Evelyn's has many shortcomings with respect to detail and completeness. Their correspondence fills many of the gaps, as well as expanding on events or exchanges which are described in the diaries. For this edition of the correspondence, all of Pepys's dispersed archives have been consulted, as well as Evelyn's complex and confusing records. A number of other letters in private collections or dispersed individually amongst libraries, many in the United States, have been located and transcribed.

It is impossible to acknowledge here all the librarians and other representatives of various institutions who assisted in the project. However, I would like in particular to express my thanks to Dr Frances Harris of the British Library for her unfailing kindness and enthusiastic help with making available John Evelyn's manuscripts now stored there, and for reading the entire manuscript making many valuable comments. Professor Michael Hunter of Birkbeck College, London, read the whole manuscript in draft and made many immensely useful corrections and comments. Robert Harding of Maggs Brothers, London, provided invaluable assistance with access to certain manuscripts and information about many old catalogues. In New York Eric Holzenberg of the Grolier Club provided some vital clues to the whereabouts of some of the letters lost since they appeared in an 1889 sale catalogue. The respective staff of the Bodleian, Clark (Los Angeles), Guildhall (London), Houghton (Harvard), Huntington (Pasadena), Maine Historical Society, New York Public, Pennsylvania Historical Society, Pepysian, Princeton University, Ransom Institute (University of Texas) libraries all provided assistance with access to copies of manuscripts. I would also like to make special mention of: William H. Fern, who responded to my advertisement in *The Book Collector* magazine, and Mary, Lady Eccles, both of whom made available copies of letters in their private collections; Professor Douglas Chambers of the University of Toronto, and Professor John T. Harwood of Penn State University, who made many minor and major contributions to the project; and Adrian Carey, my father-in-law, who translated most of the Latin and Greek passages quoted in the letters.

The letters have all been accorded equal treatment, regardless of length and content. No cuts have been made to any of the texts, and endorsements and addresses are recorded in full. With a very small number of exceptions the letters have all been freshly transcribed from the originals. The transcriptions, annotation, typesetting, design, and camera-ready copy of the book have been made by myself and therefore any errors are entirely my responsibility. Every effort has been made to make this as definitive an edition as possible; however, in time, some of the missing letters may surface and revised readings of some of the passages in the others may be suggested. Nevertheless, the exercise has been an instructive experience in reconstituting dispersed archives, utilising everything from a fax machine to *The Rough Guide* to the United States.

Guy de la Bédoyère
Savannah, 20 December 1996

Introduction

The existence of the correspondence of Evelyn and Pepys has been widely known ever since their respective diaries were first transcribed and published in the early nineteenth century. Not only had Evelyn and Pepys recorded many of their personal experiences but they had both enjoyed significant contemporary reputations. Their friendship, and their relationships with others, recorded in the diaries and in the letters, give us an exceptional opportunity to experience something of life at the heart of Restoration England and the remainder of the seventeenth century.

Almost any discussion of Pepys and Evelyn invites a comparison of their origins. This is not the place to embark on detailed biographies but it is worth looking at how they came to be who they were, and the origins of their friendship. Biographers of either man have always looked at this relationship in some degree. It has become almost customary to contrast Pepys's background as the son of a tailor, and his ambition for financial wealth and personal status, with Evelyn's inherited means, his upbringing as a member of the educated gentry, and his instinctive aesthetic tastes and cultivated manners.

ORIGINS

The origins of the Evelyns are now obscure but they were not much clearer to the diarist. He believed that the name came from the French family Ivelin of Eveliniere[1] but this is unproven. The English Evelyns first appeared in written records in 1476 when William Evelyn of Harrow died. His descendants were farmers in Stanmore and Harrow, but through marriage may have obtained other farms in or around Claygate in Surrey. William Evelyn's great-grandson George (1526–1603) was the source of the Evelyn family's subsequent wealth and status. Elizabeth I awarded him the royal monopoly on the manufacture of gunpowder. The lucrative industry required substantial amounts of fuel. This was amply supplied by the woodlands of north-eastern Surrey, and George Evelyn was able to acquire a number of estates on the proceeds. They included Wotton, near Dorking. It was just as well that making gunpowder brought him wealth for his two marriages left him with several sons and daughters to provide for. His youngest son Richard (1589–1640), and the only one by his

---

[1] Diary, 26 May 1670.

second wife, was bequeathed the Wotton estate. Richard's second son, the diarist, was born there in 1620.

The Evelyn family wealth was new and its members had few connections with the peerage or other old families of England. Its senior male members served as magistrates or MPs, and as the local squires of their estates. By investing his wealth in land, George Evelyn was one of numerous Elizabethans who sought social elevation by the most traditional of routes. If this stimulated a sense of proprietorial hostility from the old nobility, it made little practical difference to the Evelyns. Their absorption into polite society as members of the gentry was complete by the time the diarist was born. Even so, John Evelyn the virtuoso was a family phenomenon in almost every respect. He declined honours, titles, and even some appointments. But he retained a powerful sense of loyalty to the obligations and duties of kinship. His diary is peppered with news of relatives, however distant. When the Wotton estate passed to Evelyn and his heirs in 1699 his other interests were largely subordinated to securing his grandson's prospects.

Evelyn spent much of his childhood in the care of his indulgent maternal step-grandmother. Thanks to his diary we have some details of his early life whereas with Pepys we are more dependent on circumstantial information or retrospective comments in his own diary. Evelyn frustrated his father's attempts to send him to Eton and declined the opportunity to study law after he had finished his time at Oxford. Crucially, by the end of 1640 both his parents were dead. The combination of unconditional means, and the lack of responsibility enjoyed by a younger son, gave him the opportunity to spend the next few years travelling abroad while his elder brother George took care of the family estate and lands.

Evelyn is best seen as a product of his own personality rather than anything else. Like most of his educated contemporaries he had no sense of intellectual boundaries. His approach was enthusiastic and dedicated, but characteristically haphazard and unfocused. From July to October of 1641 he made the first of three journeys into Europe and seems also to have found this a convenient way to avoid what he called 'the ill face of things at home'. While Evelyn was thus part of the English Civil-War generation, it was not a period which he experienced at first-hand beyond a brief foray in late 1642 when he attempted to join the Royalist army. He was easily dissuaded and instead left for a second, and more protracted, journey in 1643, not returning until 1647. This not only gave him the opportunity to see the architectural and artistic consequences of the Renaissance, but also brought him into contact with the exiled court of Charles II. In this circle he established many of his most important intellectual and social contacts. He also began to accumulate books on all subjects and this formed the basis of his enormous, and celebrated, library.

Evelyn's archive, despite extensive depredations, shows that he noted on paper everything of interest emulating, probably deliberately, the habits of

Pliny the Elder.[1] He corresponded widely, and his literary output was an important ritual consolidation of his own reading and interests as analysis of his texts has shown.[2] This was not unusual but he was relatively prolific even for an age when an ambition to gain knowledge and authority in a wide range of disciplines was realistic. Evelyn was creating himself in his own image as a virtuoso but his literary and intellectual contributions to his age were, in truth, minimal. Had his remarkable private archive and diary not survived he would almost certainly exist in our perception as a peripheral, but productive, eccentric of the most honourable kind. Nonetheless, his contemporaries admired him and respected his company and contributions even if, perhaps, the more creative and able members of his circle were politely aware of his shortcomings, not least of which was his prolix literary style.

Pepys became one of these admirers. Born in 1633, he was a little over twelve years younger than Evelyn. Pepys's family had also once been farmers. His great-grandfather, John Pepys of Cottenham (d. 1589), married an heiress and became wealthy enough to increase his lands in Cambridgeshire. He was thereby able to finance advantageous marriages for his daughters, and careers for his sons. By the seventeenth century there had been landed gentlemen, lawyers, and tradesmen amongst the Pepyses but large families and marriage settlements dispersed the Elizabethan family wealth. As a result John Pepys's grandson, also John (1601–80), father of the diarist and ten other children, was a modest tailor in London. Even if the Pepys family's connections with trade were more thinly-disguised than those of the Evelyns Pepys himself was, however, ready to take advantage of the opportunities which existed in London for men of intellectual and ambitious substance with useful connections.

Of Pepys's childhood we know little but his occasional references, and other documentary information, supply some facts. He was educated in Huntingdon to begin with, a reflection of his family roots but probably because it was considered safer during the Civil War. After the hostilities he was brought back to London to continue his education at St Paul's where he won an Exhibition to Cambridge.

Evelyn's account of his time at Oxford is limited. It seems that apart from establishing friendships, and experimenting with music and debating (which hardly marks him out as exceptional amongst students), this was not a particularly influential phase of his life. We know even less of Pepys's time at university. Family connections may well have lain behind his decision to go to Cambridge. Unlike Evelyn who left Oxford to travel, Pepys was dependent on the patronage of his cousin Edward Mountagu for his subsequent employment. In 1654 Mountagu, at the time sitting on Cromwell's Council of State, gave

---

[1] Pliny the Younger, *Epist.*, III.5 *passim*.

[2] See *Writings of John Evelyn* (1995). E, like many of his contemporaries, followed the pattern for study recommended by Quintilian (*Institutio Oratoria*, X.ii.1ff) that one should model one's own work on that of the greatest authorities.

Pepys a job, later describing him as having been his 'secretary'. This was a crucial step in Pepys's progression but in 1655 he made what would have been considered an inappropriate marriage, or at any rate one which would bring him little advantage. Evelyn's marriage in 1647 to Mary Browne (then about twelve years old), daughter of Sir Richard Browne, the King's envoy to the French court, was a conventional statement of loyalty to his social equals and betters. It also brought him indirectly the estate of Sayes Court at Deptford. Pepys, in contrast, married the fifteen-year-old Elizabeth St Michel whose father was a Huguenot refugee. She brought him nothing but herself and obligations to her family which Pepys observed throughout the rest of his life, long after her death in 1669.

Mountagu's appointment as General-at-Sea in 1660, and his choice as the man to bring the King home gave Pepys a convenient entrée to the new administration. He was even invited to accompany the fleet to the Hague to fetch Charles. By June 1660, with his cousin and patron ennobled and made Vice-Admiral of the Kingdom, Pepys found himself promoted to Clerk of the Acts for the Navy Board.

In this job Pepys excelled. His responsibilities during the Second Dutch War, which was declared in 1665 (though hostilities and preparations had begun the previous year), brought him into direct association with Evelyn. When they first met is uncertain. Both heard the same church services at Exeter House from at least as early as 1 January 1660. On 23 January 1661 Pepys attended his first meeting of Gresham College, later to become the Royal Society. He does not mention Evelyn, who was certainly present. Instead Pepys admiringly referred to the 'great company of persons of Honour there.'[1] That he was instinctively drawn to the society of like-minded men who shared his interests and a fertile, open-minded fascination with all that was new goes without saying. It was appropriate that a man like Pepys be accepted. But it is equally evident that he regarded his presence as a privilege; being welcomed into the company of men such as Evelyn elevated his self-esteem, even if he felt initially humbled.

Pepys's first diary description of Evelyn does not come until 9 September 1665, by which time they had already corresponded. Pepys was impressed by Evelyn's self-discipline, dignity, and integrity, qualities which had encouraged the King to request his service on royal commissions. Evelyn was usually pleased to agree because he had a powerful sense of loyalty to the person and office of the king (though he once declined a request that he serve as a magistrate). By 1665 Evelyn had something of a reputation as a virtuoso, writer, and public servant. His extended treatise on the cultivation of trees, *Sylva*, and his translation of Fréart's *Parallel of the Antient Architecture* had both appeared in 1664, and followed a number of earlier works. Like most of

---

[1] Diaries, 23 January 1661 (see also Latham and Matthews, II, 22, n.1).

his books they exemplify his skill in accumulating information, but show just as clearly that he had a limited capacity to be selective and analytical.

As an experienced member of earlier commissions Evelyn had been appointed a commissioner for the sick and wounded seamen and prisoners of war in late 1664. He maintained a conscientious adherence to the responsibilities of his job. Pepys had the powers to process some of the problems which faced Evelyn but had other preoccupations of his own, one of which was victualling the fleet. His trips on business to see Evelyn included visits to female friends, and he was easily distracted by Evelyn's garden, library, and other interests.

Although they belonged to the same circle Pepys was conscious of their difference in rank. So was Evelyn who omitted Pepys from his diary until 1669, but expressed a desire that they should know each other better in his letter of 3 October 1665. Pepys was already quite certain that Evelyn was someone in command of 'all manner of learning' (diary, 27 September 1665).

Pepys came to recognise that Evelyn enjoyed his role. 'A most excellent person he is, and must be allowed a little for a little conceitedness; but he may well be so, being a man so much above others', he noted on 5 November 1665. Pepys was gradually replacing his initial admiration with a more genuine affection. With the cessation of his diary on 31 May 1669 we must trace their relationship through Evelyn's occasional, and sparse, accounts of their meetings and their much fuller correspondence. The quality of their mutual affection was expressed by Evelyn when he recorded in May 1703 the passing of Pepys who 'had ben for neere 40 years, so my particular Friend'.

THE DIARIES
Pepys's diary was kept only from 1 January 1660 to 31 May 1669. Its vitality and lucidity serve to diminish the rest of his life, reflected in the biographies which focus on the diary period. In contrast Evelyn's diary, though it covers almost his whole life, has long been noted for its self-conscious tone and an air of moral contrivance. It is thus of great importance as an historical record but sterile as a portrait. Evelyn was writing for an audience, and on more than one occasion indicates that he expected it to be read. He wrote it in longhand, revising it retrospectively where he felt necessary. Pepys seems to have written solely for himself and this seems, apart from the convenience, to have been why he wrote it in shorthand.

Both diaries create impressions (and the letters show they are only that) of being comprehensive records of the men's lives but in quite different ways. Pepys recorded a great deal of daily detail. Evelyn was much more erratic; he often omitted to make entries for odd days or even weeks. A large proportion of the shorter entries are confined to notes of sermons or names of dinner guests. Much of the first section of Evelyn's diary is taken up with a retrospective account of his travels in Europe, parts of which were written up from published guidebooks. Towards the end of his life he relied increasingly on newspaper accounts of contemporary events, interspersing summaries of these with lengthy accounts of sermons.

The publication of Evelyn's diary in 1818 in a bowdlerised and edited form led to the publication of Pepys's diary. The existence of the latter had been known to scholars for rather longer than Evelyn's which had only come to the attention of non-family members in 1814.[1] That Pepys had written his in shorthand contributed to it not appearing until 1825 (in an equally bowdlerised form). Once in print though it has always been more popular for obvious reasons. Evelyn's personal standards appealed to the Victorian literary market but despite the publication of a definitive edition in 1955 he has remained in Pepys's shadow ever since 1825.

THE CORRESPONDENCE

One of the reasons so much correspondence survives is that both men sometimes made drafts, and also additional copies in a letter-book. Some letters are (or were) thus represented by several manuscripts which obviously increases the chances of survival. They also kept much of their incoming correspondence. But there are problems with differences between the various versions and these are discussed in the following Note about the Texts.

It is perhaps surprising how little of the information in the letters accords with the diary entries. This is not a question of contradictions but simply because the diarists hardly ever recorded in their diaries business or encounters which are discussed in the letters. As we have seen Evelyn makes no mention of Pepys until 1669 in his diary and therefore their relationship is known only from the correspondence and Pepys's diary references. Even Pepys's far fuller daily accounts, particularly during the Second Dutch War, hardly ever refer to the precise subject matter of the letters. He does not mention a face-to-face meeting with Evelyn until 9 September 1665 but had been corresponding with him since at least 27 April. The contrast between the content of Evelyn's letter of 3 October 1665 and the meeting which followed on 5 October, recorded in Pepys's diary is a further example.[2] So there is no doubt that the surviving correspondence not only fills out much detail missing from the diaries but also demonstrates that even the most apparently comprehensive diary may be less complete than it seems. However, the two do not make a whole. Robert Hooke's diary survives, and on 23 and 24 May 1678 he records meeting Evelyn and discussing the latter's plans for his 'Paradise' of which Pepys is to

---

[1] For Evelyn's diary see de Beer (I, 53–5). For Pepys see Latham and Matthews (I, lxviiiff; especially, lxxiv).

[2] See below, p.38, note 2.

be patron.[1] The occasion and arrangements pass without mention in Pepys's and Evelyn's correspondence, and Evelyn's diary.

The opening letters contain harrowing and vivid accounts of the business of the Dutch Wars. Evelyn's letters to Pepys are compelling in their vivid portrayal of a desperate state of affairs and his frustration with an inefficient and parsimonious bureaucracy which left him stranded with sick and crippled men and nowhere to billet them. But as early as 1669 Evelyn was seizing the opportunity to give Pepys detailed advice on contacts and sights in France. They increasingly exchanged information on a variety of subjects with particular emphasis on Pepys's collection of engravings and his projected definitive naval history.

For the most part Pepys's letters are matter-of-fact with occasional exceptions. In old age bladder problems stimulated his curiosity and eventually he found a barley-water cure which he passed on to Evelyn in the poignant letter of 7 August 1700. On 24 December 1701 he tried passionately (but without success) to persuade Evelyn that his grandson should be allowed to travel abroad. A larger number of Evelyn's letters survive and, perhaps as a result, they are more varied. Despite his predilection for using his correspondence to consolidate his own reading, it is in the letters to Pepys that Evelyn emerges as a far more rounded human being than the one in his diary. He veers from frustration at the lot of the prisoners of war in 1665 to bewildered fury at his daughter's elopement in 1685, while on happier occasions he was both chatty and humorous, clearly taking delight in passing on dockyard gossip. Evelyn took considerable trouble over writing his letters. They represented a specific medium of expression for him; in comparison Pepys's letters seem sometimes relatively perfunctory.

HOMES

The bulk of Evelyn's letters were written at Sayes Court in Deptford. These bear either 'Sayes Court' (in a variety of abbreviated forms such as 'S: Court' and 'Sa: Co:') or 'Deptford'. Sayes Court was a royal manor leased to Evelyn's wife's family. During the Commonwealth, while Evelyn's father-in-law, Sir Richard Browne, was in France it was requisitioned and sold. Evelyn was urged to move in on Browne's behalf which he did during 1652, and at the same time began negotiating to purchase the house and land. He sealed the transaction at the beginning of 1653.[2] The house presented Evelyn with a number of long-term structural problems but the location and the land, which he developed into his celebrated gardens, were ample compensations.

---

[1] Probably an ornamental garden. *The Diary of Robert Hooke*, ed. H.W. Robinson and W. Adams, London 1935, 359.

[2] The process was a complicated one. De Beer provides a useful summary of the sequence of events (II, 537, n.6; and III, 59, n.1).

Nonetheless, in the severe winters of the seventeenth century, the route from Deptford to London was often arduous or even impassable so Evelyn took to wintering in central London. These sojourns produce the occasional appearance of Whitehall, Soho Square, or Dover Street on the letter heading. Evelyn's son John had rented a house in Dover Street and Evelyn stayed there once his son had gone to Ireland as a commissioner for the Revenue in 1692.

In 1694 Evelyn gave up Sayes Court to rent-paying tenants (though he occasionally returned there) and moved to the Evelyn family seat at Wotton. His sense of family duty, coupled with what appears to have been a shortage of capital, thanks in part to his son's financial embarrassment, had led him eventually to accept his elder brother George's invitation to go and live there. George's sons were all dead, leaving Evelyn, his son, and grandson, as the only direct male line of descent. But a quarrel over provision for George's grand-daughters caused acrimony. Evelyn was also bored, something which is particularly obvious in his letters to Pepys in the latter years; even so, he took some pleasure in modelling himself on retired Roman senators working their estates in the late Republic. He returned to London whenever he could, taking over the lease in Dover Street following his son's death in early 1699. Old age concentrated his mind on the interests of the Wotton estate and the prospects for his grandson. He died at Dover Street in 1706 with these mostly settled.

Pepys was a little more consistent though he moved more frequently. He had neither the opportunity or inclination to move too far away from London. In the 1660s he wrote to Evelyn from the Navy Office and his home in Seething Lane. The death of Elizabeth Pepys in 1669, following a trip to the Continent, contributed perhaps to his willingness to leave in 1673 when, following a fire at the Navy Office, he moved to Winchester Street. It is at around this time that his housekeeper, Mary Skinner (or Skynner), appears as a regular feature of Pepys's life. There seems no doubt that she became his wife in all but name and, as Richard Ollard has observed, the fact that Pepys did not actually marry her remains a mystery, unless it was out of some kind of abiding respect to the memory of Elizabeth. Evelyn and his wife certainly came to regard Pepys and Mary Skinner as man and wife which, considering Evelyn's sense of propriety, indicates that the relationship must have been otherwise both respectable and decorous. In a letter to Pepys of 15 March 1687 Evelyn refers to a 'Mrs Pepys' and this can only be Mary Skinner.

By January 1674 Pepys had moved to the Admiralty's temporary offices in Derby House, a site now marked by New Scotland Yard. In 1679 he moved again, this time to York Buildings by Villiers Street, to live with his former servant Will Hewer. A single letter from Portsmouth was sent in 1683 marking his voyage to Tangier but, oddly, he seems not to have written subsequently to Evelyn from Tangier, or even about the journey. It is difficult to be certain how much they saw each other after 1688. It seems likely that Pepys never visited Evelyn at Wotton. The pleasure which he had taken in the gardens of Sayes Court in the 1660s seems not to have encouraged him to go even there more than very rarely.[1] He did hold regular Saturday-evening gatherings for his friends, and Evelyn implies he was a regular participant (letter, 7 January 1695) but how often he actually attended is quite unknown. Hewer later moved to Clapham; Pepys followed him in 1700 to recuperate after bouts of serious illness. Evelyn visited him on 23 September 1700 and was impressed by the house, and especially by Pepys's 'Indys and Chineze Curiositys'. Pepys died at Hewer's house in Clapham in May 1703.

THE DISPERSAL AND PUBLICATION OF THE LETTERS

The discovery that Pepys and Evelyn had corresponded extensively with one another was a source of considerable interest to the early editors of their respective diaries. Unfortunately, the idea that such archives were best kept together was of little concern either to the diarists' descendants or the scholars.

Evelyn's archive was first trawled by the antiquarians William Bray and William Upcott. Upcott's description of the 1814 Evelyn household's use of old letters for making dress patterns[2] makes it fairly clear how some gaps in the surviving correspondence occurred and why there is little chance of filling them. Bray's editions of the diary carried Upcott's transcriptions of some of the letters contained in Evelyn's copy-letter books. The selection, extended for the 1852 and later editions, also included one loaned by the Pepys-Cockerell family, some of the letters at the Bodleian in Oxford (the Rawlinson manuscripts), and letters from Pepys to Evelyn acquired by Upcott from the Evelyn archive. Upcott stated that anything he had from there had been a gift of the diarist's great-great-grandson's widow (his albums were purchased by the Evelyn family at his sale in 1846 and are now at the British Library).

Pepys's library and papers were inherited by his nephew John Jackson. Unlike the library, there was no requirement that the papers all pass eventually to Magdalene College, though some did. The antiquarian and collector Thomas Rawlinson (1681–1725) acquired a substantial quantity, which Richard, Lord Braybrooke, Pepys's first editor, believed may have been left at York Buildings when Pepys moved to Clapham in 1700. Happily, they found their way to the Bodleian after Rawlinson's death with a selection of them being published by R.G. Howarth in 1932. Most of the remaining papers stayed in family hands and became known as the Pepys-Cockerell papers.[3] Braybrooke's (principally 1825 and 1854) and Smith's (1841) editions of Pepys's diary carried transcriptions of letters drawn from this source, the Bodleian, and Upcott's albums. They seem to have been allowed to acquire some of the manuscripts, which thereafter disappeared. Some turned up during

---

[1] For example 24 July 1691 (E's diary) but the visit is implicit rather than stated.

[2] Quoted by de Beer (see above p.12, note 1).

[3] P's nephew John Jackson's daughter, Frances (d. 1769), married John Cockerell (d. 1767), and part of the family thereafter adopted the name Pepys-Cockerell.

the work for this book, for example Evelyn's letter of 10 May 1700, now at The New York Public Library.

A previously-unknown group of letters appeared for sale in 1889 (see a Note about the Texts below, pp.22–23). Corresponding to gaps in the extant Pepys-Cockerell papers (1680–1, and 1685–89) it seems likely that they came from there but as neither Braybrooke nor Smith appear to have known about them it is likely that the Pepys-Cockerell papers had been split up before 1825. Much of what did remain in the family was published by J.R. Tanner in 1926 and 1929. These papers, contained in five volumes, were all sold at Sotheby's on 1 April 1931; apart from one (forming the basis of Tanner 1929), which went to the National Maritime Museum, the rest were bought by a collector, Gabriel Wells, changing hands again at Christie's, London, on 11 June 1980.

Apart from small numbers of letters in private ownership, the only remaining large assemblages of letters are those retained in official records, and at the Pepysian Library. These were largely transcribed, though unreliably, by Clara Marburg and published in 1935. She also made a concerted effort to produce lists of previously-published letters, and of those which she had seen in private collections or advertised in sale catalogues. Unfortunately, she was unable to examine many of them with the result that there are so many duplications, omissions, and errors that the lists are effectively useless.

Of 136 letters identified for this book, 131 are presented here in full, 28 of which have never been published before, even from drafts or copies. The missing five are represented by extracts or descriptions taken from sale catalogues. Every effort was made to locate them but since being sold variously in 1889, 1900, and 1919, they have apparently disappeared. Of the rest, the vast majority have been freshly-transcribed from originals, though it has occasionally been necessary to utilise printed texts, or Pepys's and Evelyn's retained copies.

The efforts of some earlier editors made the whole task much easier for there is no doubt that two or three pairs of eyes are better than one when dealing with some of the damaged, or barely-legible, texts. As a general observation it may be said that Tanner's and Howarth's texts are reliable. Upcott's and Smith's are less so but fall within the better standards of their time. The efforts of Braybrooke and Marburg leave more to be desired. In Braybrooke's case texts were sometimes telescoped or rewritten as convenient, without any indication of what had happened. Marburg seems occasionally to have been the victim of unfamiliarity with the handwriting and terminology of the period, perhaps compounded by limited opportunities for repeated checking against the dispersed manuscripts. The following Note about the Texts expands in much more detail on the problems encountered during the transcriptions, and the treatment of the texts for this book.

A Note about the Texts

It is not surprising that the correspondence of Pepys and Evelyn presents us with a number of problems. These arise principally from the existence of more than one version of some letters, and the dispersal of various parts of the assemblage over time.

The letters fall into several main groups. First are the letters now stored in libraries or other public collections. These are mainly the British Library and the Public Record Office in London, the Bodleian in Oxford, and the Pepysian Library at Magdalene College, Cambridge. The letters concerned arrived by various different routes, some having remained in official archives, those in the family collections, and others which had circulated in private hands.

The second group is known collectively as the Pepys-Cockerell papers. They are now substantially in private ownership, following their sale in 1931.

The third group probably originally formed part of the Pepys-Cockerell papers but was offered for sale in a catalogue published by Samuel Davey of Great Russell Street, London in 1889, and part again by the Langham Company (Davey's successors) in 1900. The letters are now divided amongst the Evelyn archive at the British Library, the Guildhall Library in London, and various American private and public libraries. Some, however, have disappeared, never resurfacing on the market, and could not be traced.

The fourth group is made up of individual letters which have surfaced one or more times in salerooms, but how and when they entered the market is unknown. Letters such as these were in some cases certainly extracted individually from the Pepys-Cockerell papers (for example several published beforehand by Braybrooke in 1825, and Smith in 1841) and the Evelyn family archives, and possibly also from official archives, in the nineteenth century.

Finally there are letters which are apparently referred to in the surviving correspondence, but are otherwise entirely unknown. A list of these is appended to the Catalogue (p.305). It is extremely unlikely that any of these have survived though the possibility that some may surface exists. There are also the 'phantom' letters (p.306). These are listed in earlier sale catalogues or published editions of texts but on closer examination have turned out to be misdated references to letters which are already known. The mistakes are due largely to Evelyn's habit of giving his copies different dates from the equivalent letter-sent, or the errors of editors and sale catalogue compilers.

DRAFTS AND COPIES

The letters in this book are only a small portion of Pepys's or Evelyn's total correspondence. Nonetheless this is the first modern compilation which has taken into account as many of the different sources as possible. Although some of Pepys's correspondence has appeared in reasonably modern editions, its editors did not always have the opportunity to collate texts available to them with those from other sources. The manuscripts take a variety of forms: letters-sent,[1] drafts, and copies made by the writer or the recipient. A surviving letter may exist in only one, or any combination, of these.

The work for this book began by compiling a list, based on date, of letters which passed between Pepys and Evelyn, using every possible published and unpublished source. As the texts and dates were compared patterns of letter-writing practices began to emerge, as well as the consequent problems for scholars which have hitherto perhaps not been fully recognised. The texts of the letters-sent form the principal source and I have invariably preferred them where available; they include a small number now only available in published editions. However, it has still been possible to collate some of these against original drafts or copies. It has occasionally been necessary to use only a draft or copy text simply because the corresponding letter-sent was lost before its text could be published in full.

Evelyn often began with a draft, written on loose blank sheets, or even on the sheets of the letter to which he was replying. Most of his surviving drafts are in the Evelyn archive at the British Library, and many can be matched with letters-sent. Conversely, the letter to Pepys of 4 September 1673, now at Princeton, exists today only as a loose draft. The equivalent letter-sent does not survive so we cannot be certain either that it ever existed, or, if it did, whether what was sent had the same date and wording.[2]

Having written a draft Evelyn wrote the letter for sending, but not necessarily on the same day. The letter-sent to Pepys of 22 July 1700, now amongst the Pepys-Cockerell papers, is matched by a draft in the Evelyn archive dated 21 July 1700. This draft, and other examples, show that Evelyn marked passages and words to be moved about, or for deletion. Generally these changes correspond with the text of the letter which Pepys received.

Subsequently, Evelyn copied selected letters he had sent. He transcribed them into a numbered series, in what he believed to be chronological order, in bound volumes, now his 'Copy-Letter Books I and II' (British Library Evelyn MS39a and b).[3] Evelyn said, in a note dated 15 November 1699 in volume II, that his purpose was to make copies 'for my own satisfaction and to look now

---

[1] 'Letter-sent' here means the manuscript or text actually received by the addressee. They were delivered in person, by servants, friends, or left with postal agents, such as shopkeepers, for carriage (see the letter of 30 May 1694, p.244).

[2] See above, p.4, and below, p.84, note 1, and p.85, note 5.

[3] MSS numbers used while they were deposited at Christ Church have been retained.

and then back upon what has past in my private Concerne and Conversatione'. Of 34 copies of letters to Pepys 33 belong to the period 1680–96. Continuity of presentation and handwriting suggests the copying was done on long sittings, though occasional marked changes (for example on p.184 of volume II) suggest breaks in the work. It is probable that the copying was done several years after the letters had originally been written. If so, Evelyn would have needed the drafts because the letters-sent would no longer be readily available. This was certainly the case with the letter of 6 December 1681 where, exceptionally, the letter-sent, draft, and copy all survive. Phrases and order of words show that the copy was made from the draft, and not from the letter-sent which differs from both in many respects. The last complete copy he made was of a letter (not to Pepys) dated 6 February 1698, followed by one more, undated, and abruptly incomplete.

Only ten drafts of letters to Pepys survive, half of which belong to 1700 and 1701 thus post-dating the end of the copy-letter books. Out of 34 letters to Pepys entered in the copy-letter books, just two can be associated with surviving drafts. This suggests that Evelyn usually discarded drafts he had copied. The lack of drafts, and copies, of a number of letters to Pepys known to have been sent, like almost all those of the 1660s and 70s, may be explained either by Evelyn not writing a draft in the first place (and thus having nothing to copy from); or, by him rejecting the letter for copying, and destroying the draft. In view of Evelyn's record-keeping habits the latter is very unlikely.

Twenty-two of the copies of letters to Pepys also survive as letters-sent. When compared, it can be seen that all these copies diverge from the letters-sent to a greater or lesser degree. The variations range from single words to whole passages. Fifteen copies bear dates which differ from the letter-sent from a day to a year. A copy which predates the corresponding letter-sent can be explained by Evelyn writing the draft and setting it aside for a day or more before preparing a letter for sending. It is harder to explain how a copy could postdate the letter-sent, though several do.

The letters of 29 and 31 July, and 3 August 1685 are represented by a single copy, dated 3 August, which itself contains some phrases only present in the letter-sent of 29 July. The letters of 2, and 8, January 1686 are matched by copies dated 31 December 1685, and 1 January 1686 respectively. Evelyn's letter of 25 September 1690 is a special problem. In it Evelyn told Pepys he was about to visit his brother in Wotton. Pepys replied later that day, referring to the trip (confirming this was the text he had received). Late on the 26th, the next day, Evelyn wrote to his brother to cancel the visit. Evelyn recorded his letter of the 25th to Pepys in his copy-letter book but seems to have revised it in view of the change of plan. This copy is dated 2 October 1690 and while the first half is almost identical to the letter-sent of 25 September the second part is completely different, with no mention of a trip to Wotton. Evelyn had perhaps rewritten the 'copy', though it barely merits the description, or had used a draft composed before a trip to Wotton had been mooted. Either way it is difficult to understand why Evelyn should have entered such a text, half of which had never been sent, into his copy-letter book.

It is logical then that where one of Evelyn's letters is *only* represented by a copy the date and content of that copy must be regarded as unreliable. Evelyn himself knew this: one copy of a letter to the Earl of Ossory, has no date and Evelyn has added 'This is misplaced' (vol. II, no. 448). The 'copies' may contain revealing information about Evelyn's views but it cannot be assumed that Pepys read what was written in the form Evelyn recorded, as the letter of 25 September and its copy show.[1] Evelyn also perhaps either could not read his own handwriting and mistook dates; or, the text of some drafts was so abbreviated that expansions for a copy would inevitably differ from the letter-sent (the draft of 3 October 1687 bears no date). There is a possibility that some of Evelyn's letters which only exist now as copies were made from drafts for letters which were never sent, especially where there is no confirmation such as a reply or subsequent reference to the content. The copy-letter of 19 September 1682 bears signs of being no more than a private statement of conscience composed in the style of a letter to Pepys.[2]

Pepys was also selective about the letters which he wished to record, calling them those 'which I have a mind to keep'.[3] These copies, including some addressed to him rather than just being from him, were made in chronological order by himself, or assistants, into letter books.[4] Pepys also made drafts on loose sheets or other letters but these were often in shorthand, for example that of 30 August 1689 which was written on the bottom of the manuscript of Evelyn's letter of 26 August. In this particular case he then had a copy made, probably by his former clerk Will Hewer,[5] which as written, corresponds to the shorthand draft but an insertion shows that it was amended to match the letter-sent to Evelyn, in Pepys's own hand, which also survives. This indicates that all three manuscripts were together at one time and made consecutively in short order. In most of the other cases where Pepys's letters to Evelyn are matched by surviving copies, for example 23 January 1674, there is no discernible or significant difference in date or content.[6] This even applies to

---

[1] See also the remark at the end of a copy dated 20 January 1689/90, absent from the letter-sent (17 June 1690), p.219, note 5. For other examples of noticeable textual differences see p.153, note 5 (3 August 1685), and p.175, note 2 (15 March 1687).

[2] See p.136, note 1, p.140, note 3; and also p.240, note 4, and pp.256–7.

[3] 'I... entered some letters in my book'. P's diary, 10 January 1661.

[4] P also made copies of some of E's letters containing lengthy discourses on naval history and other subjects. However, these are not all in chronological order and seem to have been compiled retrospectively. In one instance E made alterations in his own hand to P's copy of his letter of 21 August 1669 (see p.72, note 3).

[5] P's diary entry for 17 November 1666 describes the process of drafting and transcribing, and Will Hewer's participation in the routine.

[6] Except 14 August 1694, copy dated 10 August but with no textual variation. Even in this instance the date on the letter-sent seems to have been altered from '10'.

loose copies such as that of 24 December 1701. The varying hands in the letter book(s) for 1662–79[1] indicate day-to-day updating as his diary entry of 10 January 1661 implies. Thus it seems that Pepys, unlike Evelyn, collated his copies so that they were a faithful record of his correspondence.

Pepys was not given to extensive retrospective record-keeping, whereas this was one of Evelyn's favourite activities. Pepys clearly felt no need to maintain a substantial log of his private correspondence, but it was an accurate one. While this has deprived us of the chance to substitute copies for some letters which are lost, it has also meant that there is less opportunity for confusion. Pepys's diary was written up on a daily or weekly basis but much of Evelyn's was composed from memoranda decades after the events; this is evident from Evelyn's references to future events. There is no reason why we should not see his copied letters as being equally susceptible to revision.

Until now Evelyn's letters have not been collated, largely due to their extensive dispersal. This has accorded a degree of implicit, but unmerited, reliability to his copies, and also created the impression that rather more letters existed than ever really did. The present book started out with a total of around 160, largely reduced by collating the dates of Evelyn's copies with letters-sent. The analysis of his letters to Pepys clearly has implications for how all of Evelyn's correspondence should be treated.

Other problems have contributed to the confusion, for example misread dates. Evelyn's letter of 2 January 1686, also represented as we have seen, by a copy dated 31 December 1685, appeared in a 1930 Philadelphia auction catalogue dated 2 June 1685, a 1934 New York catalogue dated 2 January 1685, and in *American Book Prices Current* for 1945 once more dated to 2 June 1685.[2] Clara Marburg listed a letter dated 15 March 1686/7 which appeared in the 1889 Davey Catalogue (see below). It appears as a clearly-dated facsimile, associated with an undated catalogue entry. Marburg's transcription of the facsimile and its date is largely correct (though she mistook '15' for '14'). She entered the letter in her list but failed to connect it with the undated Davey Catalogue entry, which she also inexplicably recorded twice, then adding a fourth reference dated '14 March 1666/7' (there is no such letter in the Davey Catalogue). The letter of 15 March 1687 was thus inadvertently awarded four entries by her, three of them spurious. Evelyn's retained copy is, just to make matters worse, dated 19 January 1687.

PAPER AND HANDWRITING

The size of the paper used varies according to the length of the letter. Large sheets were often torn in half for shorter letters. Evelyn's letters normally survive in their original folded form with address on the outside and text

---

[1] National Maritime Museum LBK/8 (see Tanner 1929); in fact three bound together.
[2] See p.306 for how this, and other examples, happened.

within. They not infrequently bear traces of a wax seal bearing an impression of his ring intaglio.[1] Pepys's letters to Evelyn very rarely retain the address leaf, probably because Evelyn detached it in order to write a draft reply on it. He certainly did this with some other letters and it is occasionally possible to associate the separated sections, for example with a letter to him from Sir Thomas Peyton, dated 14 February 1676; only by comparing the handwriting was it possible to associate the separated sheets.[2]

Confirmation of the addressee, date, and contents is normally in the form of an endorsement written on the letter manuscript. In the earlier part of the period Evelyn and Pepys generally endorsed the letters themselves. Later on the endorsements occasionally appear in different hands, for example that of Pepys's nephew John Jackson. In these cases the endorsements may well be posthumous, and were the result of sorting and filing papers. The endorsements are not always accurate, but in some instances are the only source of the letter's date. It is not always certain who was responsible.

Despite fears for his eyesight (see p.275, note 2), Pepys's hand is usually large and clearly-formed with well-spaced lines and consistent spelling. Evelyn, however, made careless use of an array of abbreviations, and ran letters together, saying himself it was an 'Arabic not to be endur'd' (see p.68). The prefix *pres-*, for example, is often formed as a single flourish in which the *r* disappears and the *e* is represented by a superscript loop carrying on to the top of the long ʃ (*s*). His lower-case *a* and *g* are often unclosed, allowing them to resemble *u* and *y* (or vice-versa). Suffixes to words, such as *-tion*, are frequently just indeterminate squiggles, making the spelling difficult to discern. An undotted *i* may also resemble an incomplete *o*. Words ending in *-ed* are spelled thus, or -'*d*, or *-d*, all in the same letter. The suffix *-te* is barely distinguishable from *-le*, and likewise *-ie* and *ic*. It is thus difficult to make transcriptions which are spelled exactly as Evelyn intended. Happily, there are few cases where different readings make substantive changes to the meaning.

DISAPPEARANCE AND SALES OF LETTERS

Damp, family demands for scrap paper, and appropriations from the Evelyn archive prior to its deposition at Christ Church Library and subsequent sale to the British Library, have led to the disappearance of an unknown quantity of material which must include correspondence. As described in the Introduction the archives of both diarists have been broken up in various different ways. The most important group which has not found its way *en masse* to an institutional home, or otherwise remained intact, was probably taken from the Pepys-Cockerell papers. Its contents were offered for sale in 1889 by the London autograph dealer Samuel John Davey (1863–90). Davey told his

---

[1] Usually a classical figure standing left holding a shield depicting a gryphon passant.
[2] Address leaf in BL Evelyn S & W folder II; letter at BL.1093.

customers that for 'several generations these Manuscripts have been carefully preserved as family relics, and until within the last few months they have been regarded by the late owners as papers of purely private interest'. A few reappeared in the Langham Catalogue of 1900, issued by Davey's business successors. Most vanished into various private hands. Happily, they included those of the Evelyn family and some are now at the British Library in the Evelyn archive (this can be verified from the endorsements and other details which tally with the Davey Catalogue). It is known that William John Evelyn M.P.[1] purchased from sales and auction houses books and other manuscripts connected with the diarist. It seems that he chose to add material which became available including letters that had been sent by Evelyn and had therefore never originally been in the Evelyn archive.

Some letters from the Davey Catalogue entered the collection of Carl Pforzheimer of New York. In the 1930s Clara Marburg was not allowed to examine them closely (1935, p.84); she seems to have been misled about their dates, being told that they all belonged to 1699. There is no evidence at all that Pforzheimer ever possessed letters of 1699. The only certain letter of 1699 (14 January) has been known since 1825. The Pforzheimer letters, of which there are seven, all belong to the period 1680–9 and can be traced back to the Davey Catalogue via the collection of Alfred Morrison, sold at Sotheby's in 1919. They were published in the Pforzheimer catalogue in 1940 and have since been transferred to a permanent home at the University of Texas in Austin.

Other Davey Catalogue letters have also now turned up, for example, at the Pierpont Morgan Library in New York, the Huntington Library in Pasadena, the Maine Historical Society, and the Historical Society of Pennsylvania. That of 8 September 1685 surfaced in 1968 at Sotheby's and was later presented to London's Guildhall Museum by a descendant of a relation of Pepys. Those which remain missing are probably either still in similar private collections or have been lost. Sometimes individual letters, previously 'unknown', appear at sales, for example that from Evelyn of 1 May 1665 which was sold in June 1869. His letter of 12 October 1665 emerged as recently as 1995 at Sotheby's when a private collection accumulated in the 1800s was sold.

THE PRESENT EDITION

This edition includes the full text of every letter identified, regardless of sources which include original manuscripts, photographs and photocopies of manuscripts, and previously-published transcriptions. The total is 136 out of which the full texts of 131 appear here. A full Catalogue at the end identifies each letter, its different versions, and their locations if known. Where the original was accessible it has been consulted. Of the letters given in full only

---

[1] 1822–1908. He was not Evelyn's direct descendant but had inherited the Wotton estate and was loyal to his forbear's memory and reputation.

three have had to be taken from printed sources only; the rest have been newly-transcribed from the manuscripts, or facsimiles of, or compared against an original draft or copy. Otherwise drafts and copies have only been used where the letter-sent is unavailable or lost, or in a few instances of difficult readings. For reasons of space differences between letters-sent, and drafts or copies are only noted for substantive changes of meaning, or points of interest.

Of the remaining five letters known to have existed, but which could not be traced, part of one is available from sale catalogues. That leaves four where the exact content is unknown; I have substituted sale catalogue descriptions of the manuscripts. These *do not* include letters whose contemporary existence is implicit from references in surviving letters but which are otherwise unknown. I have dealt with these separately in the Catalogue (p.305).

The letters are classified by decade. Letters prefixed 'A' represent the 1660s, 'B' the 1670s, and so on. The source of the text used in each case is made clear in footnotes. Any visible endorsements on the manuscripts have been included in full but it is not always possible to identify the hand.

Original spelling and punctuation have normally been retained within the limits of what can be read with reasonable certainty. I have, however, generally ignored Evelyn's underlining of occasional words, a form of emphasis usually interpreted in print with italics which is tiresome to the eye; his misplaced commas have been amended when sense is affected; and, his omitted, or misplaced, closing brackets have been corrected.

Abbreviations, though, have been expanded, except where they are in common modern usage. Thus *Mr* or *Dr* have been retained but *Ld:* for *Lord* has not. Where an expansion has been required I have used spelling indicated by the abbreviation; so *Maties* becomes *Majesties* even though we would use *Majesty's* in the context (the possessive apostrophe is rarely employed by either writer). The archaic *y^t* for *that* is not easily recognisable to a modern reader, nor was it ever pronounced *y*, so the policy has been to present these words in a modern form reflecting their seventeenth-century and modern pronunciation. Other conventions, such as *l.* for *£*, *m̄* for *mm*, *ff* for *F*, or *-con* for *-tion*, have been modernised or expanded. Personal names have been treated similarly, thus abbreviated first names have been expanded. Conversely where they are absent, and the identity is ambiguous, a footnote identifies the individual. This reflects the commonsense idea that typeset text requires different treatment from handwritten text.[1]

Dates of the letters have been modernised not only for consistency but to make them absolutely clear. It will have been evident from the preceding discussion that the dates of some letters have created enormous confusion. This was partly due to Evelyn's, and to a lesser extent Pepys's, inconsistencies, and also the fact that New Year was regarded as beginning on 25 March. Dates between 1 January and 24 March were thus awarded the transitional dual year,

---

[1] Hunter (1995a). See also de Beer (1955, I, 50–1) on Evelyn's writing habits.

for example *14 January 169⁸/₉* for 1699. Where retained copies were
concerned this practice was not always followed. I have noted therefore the
exact form that the date takes on the manuscript as well as any corroborating
information. This is of importance where the year is clearly wrong (see p.98,
notes 2 and 5) or where Evelyn used a numeral to abbreviate the month; *7br*
and *Xbr* for example, mean *September* and *December*, and not July and
October for which they have occasionally been mistaken in the past. Dates
were 'Old Style' and are thus ten days behind the continent (see p.146, note 2).

Every effort has been made to identify any sources, individuals, events, or
books which are mentioned but this has not always been possible. Latin
phrases and words are accompanied by translations.

The shortcomings of Evelyn's handwriting have been discussed above
(p.22); as a result there are instances of doubtful readings throughout. This
affects the draft of the letter of [11] September 1688 more than any other.
Pepys's more widely-spaced hand (or those of his clerks) and generally neater
presentation mean that his texts present very few problems.

Pepys and Evelyn have been abbreviated to 'P' and 'E' throughout in the
footnotes. References to Latham and Matthews, and de Beer, are to the
definitive editions of the respective diaries. *Writings* indicates my 1995 edition
of Evelyn's published texts. Other abbreviations are listed at the beginning of
the Catalogue of Letters (pp.299–300).

APPENDICES AND LISTS

Appendix 1 includes some letters or documents associated with the main
correspondence (other than brief ones, already included in footnotes).
Amongst these are letters or papers which Evelyn enclosed with his letters to
Pepys, for example one to Sir George Carteret attached to his letter of 30
September 1665. A small number of unpublished but relevant letters or
documents in the State Papers or the Evelyn archive have been added, for
example Evelyn's letter to his wife of 22 August 1685.

Individuals mentioned by either Pepys or Evelyn are listed in Appendix 2
with brief biographical details and a note of the letters in which they appear.
The list is not exhaustive as not all the personalities could be identified with
certainty. Points about them which are relevant to specific references in the
actual letters are covered in footnotes.

A List of the Letters follows overleaf indicating number, date, sender,
content, and page number of each letter. The Catalogue (pp.299–306) provides
full details of all versions of each letter, provenance, previous publications,
present locations, letters now unknown but whose existence is implicit from
the content of others, and spurious or 'phantom' letters.

Illustrations are listed on p.335. Of Pepys's letters most could not be copied
to a high-enough standard, and others were not available for reproduction.

List of the Letters

List of Figures

(For captions to Figures 2–6; and, details of published illustrations of letters from Pepys, see p.335)

1 The 1660s

Most of the letters written by Pepys and Evelyn to one another during the 1660s were concerned with the practical difficulties of dealing with sick and wounded seamen. With Pepys as Clerk of the Acts in the Navy Office and Evelyn a newly-appointed commissioner for sick and wounded seamen and prisoners-of-war they were bound to encounter one another. The correspondence opens with a letter from Pepys which is the earliest letter located between the two.

Very few of these early letters remained in the archives of either diarist. The main sequence belongs to the second half of 1665 and early 1666. Entirely concerned with the Second Dutch War most were written by Evelyn, sometimes on consecutive days and with a mounting sense of urgency. It is clear that his personal anxiety was intense as the problems of looking after hordes of sick men with totally inadequate financial resources plagued him night and day. For Pepys though Evelyn's troubles were only a small part of the administrative headaches which made his life so complicated. Glancing through the pages of his diary we can see that Evelyn's problems were hardly a preoccupation, 13 December 1665 being a case in point.

Evelyn regarded his relationship with Pepys on a professional basis, raising points which were relevant to the latter's concerns. He was often franker in his letters to others. The additional material included in Appendix 1 and in the footnotes here makes it clear that for a while Evelyn was in a precarious financial position. Not until the end of this period does Pepys feature in Evelyn's diary, perhaps a mark of his marginally-inferior social status. They had also socialised on a number of occasions, Pepys's accounts of which contrast markedly with the harsh realities of their professional responsibilities. In his letter of 3 October 1665 Evelyn reciprocated some of Pepys's admiration by expressing an apparently genuine desire that they become better acquainted.

Once the War was over their relationship took a new turn. Pepys was planning a trip to Europe and Evelyn, ever the informed expert, was only too happy to produce a detailed list of suggested sights and contacts. By June 1669 Pepys had closed his diary. Ironically it was only then that Evelyn refers to him in his own, describing how he took his younger brother Richard to see Pepys to give him courage to undergo surgery for the removal of a kidney stone. But the 1660s close with a letter from Pepys, returned from his trip, telling Evelyn of his wife's serious illness. She died shortly afterwards. In the 1670s the two men turned once more to a naval war with the Dutch.

A1. SAMUEL PEPYS TO JOHN EVELYN[1]

Sick men set ashore in Ireland

Mr Evelin

[Navy Office]
27 April 1665[2]

Sir,

From a letter this day come to my hand from a Shipp of ours (the little *Guift*)[3] that in a Conflict with a Hollander on the Irish Coast (wherein shoe though much over matched hath acquitted her selfe very well) hath had severall Men wounded, who are putt on shoare for care at Galloway, give me leave to aske you whether any Provision for sick and wounded men is made in Ireland, not with respect to theis Men only, but to the future ocasions in Generall which wee may Probably have of useing it there. You will Pardon this enquiry from one that hath soe little Right to offer you trouble as

Your humble servant
S:P

---

[1] Source: NMM Letter-Book 8, 199 (copy in P's hand). Used by permission of the National Maritime Museum. This is the earliest letter in the sequence of correspondence which could be located, and was oddly omitted by Tanner (1929; it perhaps went unnoticed because E's name is tucked tightly into the bottom left corner of the page). It is implicit, though, from the content of this letter that P had some personal knowledge of E. P had certainly witnessed and recorded E's paper on bread-making at the Royal Society on the preceding 1 March (diary) but does not mention E by name. Prior to that both had recorded their presence (diaries) at the launching of the double-bottomed *Experiment* at Deptford on 22 December 1664.

It may also be noted that Evelyn, Clifford, Reymes, and Doyly signed a document dated 24 November 1664 addressed to the Commissioners of the Navy, in which they requested details of ships at sea to restrict claims for relief of the sick and wounded to those 'as shall really suffer in His Majesties service'. The document was endorsed by P (Sotheby's Catalogue for 24 July 1995, Lot 488).

[2] MS: '27 Aprill 1665' in lower left margin. P was at the Navy Office all day (diary).

[3] Sic. This is almost certainly the *Gift*, also known as the *Gift Minor*. It was a 16-gun vessel, originally the Spanish *Bon Jesus*, captured in 1658 and sold in 1667. Its name distinguished it from the *Gift Major*, a 40-gun French ship captured in 1652 (Colledge 1987).

A2. JOHN EVELYN TO SAMUEL PEPYS[1]

On the sick and wounded in Ireland

For Samuel Pepys Esqr:
at the Navy Office
London

Sayes Court
1 May 1665[2]

Sir,

My absence neere 30 miles from my house, when your Letter[3] came thither, will, I hope, excuse the slow returne of this answer: Sir, there is neither in our Commission, or Instructions the least mention made of any provision for Sick and Wounded-men in Ireland; our Districts reaching no farther then Plymouth towards the West, and Yarmouth North-East; and the intermedial ports reduc'd to as few as could be, for sundry important reasons: Notwithstanding I conceive it were very fit there should, for the future, be some courses taken for the settling of some Correspondence there for this effect; but our Commission dos take no Cognizance of it: Sir, when my Collegues in Office meete, I will not faile to Communicat this particular to them, and what his Majestie shall be pleas'd to superadd to his other Commands, I know they will be ready to undertake as far as lyes in their power; this comeing onely from

Sir,
Your most humble servant
JEvelyn:

---

[1] Source: BL.1469. Endorsed by P, '1st: May 1665 Mr Eveling About want of Provision made for sick and wounded in Ireland.' The letter also bears: a handwritten note that it was purchased in June 1869 from 'Sotheby and Hodge'; and, a clipping from the sale catalogue describing the letter (Lot 364). It was probably purchased by, or on behalf of, William John Evelyn of Wotton who expended much energy on recovering books and manuscripts connected with the diarist.

[2] MS: 'Says-Court May.1:65.' P visited Sayes Court in the evening ('it being dark and late' – diary) on this day, perhaps in response to the letter though he does not mention it (ibid). E was not there and states in his own diary only that he went to London on 1 May. He had presumably departed before P arrived.

[3] See letter of 27 April (A1), above.

A3. SAMUEL PEPYS TO JOHN EVELYN[1]

Pepys seeks advice for the sick and wounded in Ireland

Mr Evelyn

Navy Office
9 August 1665[2]

Sir,

I am once more to trouble you with my old question concerning the provision made for the sick and wounded seamen in Ireland,[3] for that a charge is and hath for a good while beene running on at Kinsale in expectation of paiement from this office; which we have yet no authoritie to make nor is it fitt the care of it should be put upon persons soe little at leisure to look after it as the Officers of the Navy; besides that, I have been told, That it hath beene by the King and Councill left to the Lord Leiuetent of Ireland to give directions in: I beseech you Sir what advice you can give me in any part hereof, be pleased to let me receive, for that what is disburst must soone or late be paid some where, and the longer it's left unsettled 'tis likely the King will be soe much the more Sufferer.

Sir I have looked after when you woulde thinke fitt (in pursuance of our last discourse,[4] and Sir William Coventrie's advice) to intimate at what ports, and what number of recovered men are ready to be called for, That soe as we have Ships in the way they may be directed to take them in. I remaine

Your affectionate and most humble
Servant
SPepys

---

[1] Source: BL.1080. Endorsed by E, 'Mr Pepys 9 Aug 1665 Navy-office.'
[2] MS: 'Navy Office 9 August 1665 Mr Evelyn' at foot of letter.
[3] See letter of 27 April 1665 (**A1**).
[4] Although P records visiting E's house on 1 and 5 May 1665, he does not record a face-to-face meeting until 9 September (diary). This letter and the previous one suggest that his diary is unintentionally misleading in this respect. It seems clear that they must have met before this letter and very probably before that of 27 April.

A4. JOHN EVELYN TO SAMUEL PEPYS[1]

Evelyn in despair for want of cash

For Samuell Pepys Esqr
One of the Principall Officers
of His Majesties Navy at Greenewich:

Sayes Court
23 September 1665[2]

Sir,

There are divers miserably sick prisoners at Wollwich, especialy in this bearers Ship: If they could be conveyd downe to our Fly-boates before Gravesend, Our Chirurgeon there might looke after them; and they have also a Guard; but you know I am prohibited realiving any at Wollwich, even of our Owne men: They might be, I suppose, at Eryth; but how shall we (when recoverd) secure them from running away? At Gravesend we are forc'd to make stay of one of the Flie-boats on purpose, for the numerous Sick-prisoners which we could not march with their fellows to Leeds; therefore I beseech you order them by some meanes or other to be sent (viz, the sick onely) to those Vessels at Gravesend, where there will be care taken for them:

Sir, Since I saw you yesterday, comes notice to me that of the £5000 I was to touch by promise this Weeke from Mr Kingdome[3] by order of my Lord Ashley, no lesse then £3000 of it is diverted for other purposes from Oxford:[4] consider with indignation, the misery, and confusion all will be in at Chatham, and Gravesend, where I was threatnd to have our sick all expos'd, if by Thursday next I do not send them £2000; and in what a condition our prisoners at Leeds, are like to be: If my Lord of Albemarle (to whom I am now hailing)[5] do not this day helpe me by an high hand;[6] dreadfull will be the consequences, and I will leave you to consider, at whose doores, this dealing at Oxon is to be layd;[7] I am almost in despair, so you will pardon the passion of Sir,

your most faithfull Servant:
JEvelyn:

---

[1] Source: PRO S.P. 29/133, f.28. Endorsed, '23 7ber 65 Sayes Ct Mr Evelyn'.
[2] MS: 'Says-Court 23d:Sbr:–65'.
[3] Captain Richard Kingdon. Neither E nor P record the previous day's meeting.
[4] The King had arrived in Oxford on 25 September (de Beer, III, 423, n. 7).
[5] Or 'heading'.
[6] See E's diary for 23 September. Albemarle told E to attend for an instalment of cash (9 October; BL Evelyn S & W folder II). Brouncker wrote to E saying '£10000' was to be paid to E by Kingdon (11 October; HMCR IX [Morrison], Pt II, 446b).
[7] See E's letter to Sir Richard Browne, 14 October 1665, Appendix 1.

A5. SAMUEL PEPYS TO JOHN EVELYN[1]

Pepys has done all he can

Greenwich[2]
26 September 1665[3]

Sir,

as I will in every thing else, soe I have in your request this afternoone done
what you with any moderate reason can expect of mee. But I beseech you
consider that what I have done reaches but for foure days, and therefore pray
you to hasten some other expedient to serve your selfe at theyr determination;
what wee have done herein being very irregular, and not excusable I thinke to
bee done twise. Sir I would have been glad to have kissed your hands before I
returne to the fleete which will bee to morrow afternoone.[4] I will endeavour it
if possible and rest

Your most affectionate humble
Servant
SPepys

---

[1] Source: BL.1081. Endorsed by E, 'Mr Pepys: 26: September Greenwich 1665.'
[2] Pepys had stayed the night before at the Crowne Inne at Rochester, leaving at 5am
for Greenwich (diary). Once arrived he went straight to the office there, presumably
writing this letter, before setting off to requisition East India Company ships at Erith.
[3] MS: 'Greenwch Sept 26 1665'.
[4] P travelled in E's coach on the 27th to see Albemarle and later 'had most excellent
discourse of Mr Eveling touching all manner of learning; wherein I find him a very
fine gentleman, and perticularly of Paynting...' (diary, 27 September 1665).

A6. JOHN EVELYN TO SAMUEL PEPYS[1]

Evelyn obliged to repeat a request

For my most honord Friend
Samuel Pepys Esqr
at the Navy-Office in Greenewich

Sayes Court
29 September 1665[2]

Sir

This being but an iteration of what was Orderd on Thursday, when we were with his Grace,[3] I cannot divine how it comes to be repeated; But being told it was brought hither by two Captaines (in my absence this day at Erith)[4] who it seemes applyed them selves to my Lord for the conveying of their Sick-men (and indeede I have no quarters neerer then those places his Grace mentions Graves-end and Chatham being full) I suppose it was written to pacifie their importunity, and quicken the raising of the monyes to be assign'd me: There was a Copy of the letter, left at my house with it, which causes me to write thus confidently of the Contents: Sir, I am

Your most humble
and obedient Servant:
JEvelyn

The bearer hereoff (one of our Chyrurgeons) whom I sent to see the state of our sick, will give you an account[5] of the extreame misery of both our owne and Prisoners, for want of bread to preserve[6] them perishing

---

[1] Source: PRO S.P. 29/133, f.58. Endorsed by P, '29 7ber. 65. Says Court. Esqr Evelin.'

[2] MS: 'Says-Court 29th:–7br –65'.

[3] Thursday was the 28th. E reports that he met Albemarle on the 28th (diary). P records a meeting with Albemarle and E on the 27th (diary, see p.34, note 4). De Beer (III, 420, n.1) suggested that two meetings were unlikely and that P was more likely to be right. However, de Beer does not refer to this letter which appears to confirm E, or that there were two meetings.

[4] E had spent the day there organising the sale of East India 'prizes' which, it had been agreed on 23 September by Albemarle, would help finance care of the prisoners (E's diary 23 and 29 September).

[5] MS: 'accoūt'.

[6] Clumsily formed ($p_{[r]}^e\int$erue) where 'p[r]es' is formed as a single character.

A7. JOHN EVELYN TO SAMUEL PEPYS[1]

Evelyn cannot do miracles

For my honor'd Friend
Samuell Pepys Esqr at
the Navy Office or Else Where:[2]
For his Majesties Special Service
in all speede:

Sayes Court
30 September 1665[3]

Sir,

The inclos'd had kiss'd your hands before this,[4] had not the most infinite
trouble of other dispatches in order to your Commands, hindred mee, and the
present necessities of sending Orders to Woolwich and the places adjacent, for
the Quartr[in]g of more Sick-men obtruded on us, but refuse to be entrtaind: I

---

[1] Source: PRO S.P. 29/133, f.63. Endorsed by P, '30 7ber. 65 = Says Court. Eqsr
Evelin.' The MS is scrawled, obviously written in a state of anger and frustration.
[2] P sailed to Woolwich on the 30th on the *Bezan* (a 4–6 gun, 35-ton, yacht, 'the
King's new pleasure-boat' – P's diary, 12 September 1661) leaving the following
evening to sail on to Gillingham arriving on the morning of 2 October. From there he
walked to Chatham, and on to Rochester where he dallied with three local women in
the castle ruins. He left on horseback for Gravesend and then took a boat to Woolwich
for the night before returning to the Navy Office, then at Greenwich, late on the 3rd
(diary).
[3] MS: 'Says-Court 30th: 7ber: 65.'
[4] A letter to Sir George Carteret, see Appendix 1. It describes the horrific conditions
in which the sick and wounded seamen and prisoners were suffering. There is no
suggestion in P's diary that he responded immediately. However, he wrote to
Coventry on 3 October 1665 (NMM LBK/8; Tanner 1929, no. 48), bemoaning the
'Want of money, numbers of prisoners (which the Commissioners for Sick and
Wounded have flung upon us) to be fed' amongst 'our present burthen'.
E had also written a letter to Sir William Coventry which described the desperate
situation: 'Sir William D'Oylie and my selfe have near ten thousand upon our Care,
whiles there seems to be no care of us; who, having lost all our Servants, Officers, and
most necessary Assistants, have nothing more left us to expose but our Persons,
which are at every moment at the mercy of a raging pestilence... Our prisoners... beg
at us, as a mercy, to knock them on the head; for we have no bread to relieve the
dying Creatures...' (BL CLBI.257, dated 2 October 1665, published in various Bray
editions of E's diary with correspondence). A further copy of this letter, dated 30
September 1665, in two unknown hands, and not signed in E's name, is at NMM MS
AGC20 51/064/11. Probably a Navy Office copy, and as such its date is more likely
to be correct because it will have been made from the letter-sent.

have sent for a Martiall to Chel[sea]¹ to send downe to Erith, and thence to Graves-End for Guards for the prisoners, but I heare not yet of him; nor can I heare of Assistants that will undertake to gouverne that affaire, if he faile me from London; One of my men, this afternoone, desiring to be dismissd in regu[ar]d of the Contagion: I inclose you the letter[s?] you desird, and you must forgive the dissorderly writing, There is plainesse, and truth in the particulars, and I am not solicitous of any mans censure of the forme, when I discharge my Conscie[nce]² I know I shall be thought impertinent, unlesse you back me with your attestation, and that with some zeale, which therefour I humbly supplicate of you: In the interim, I bes[eech]³ you not to look on me as sluggish in my station, or indiligent as far as my talent reaches; nor of so slavish and disingenuous a nature to be tyd to impossibility and servitude: I cannot do miracles, nor know I how to sell goods and treate with the Merchant;⁴ but I can dispence such effects as shall be put into my hands for the discharge of what is intrustd to me; and if I should pretend to other excellences, it were to abuse you; But I am at all moments ready (in accknowledgme[n]ts of these deficiencys) to resigne the honor his Majestie has don me, to greate[r candi]date[s]:⁵ I beseech you inter[pret]⁶ this to myne advantage,⁷ who am

> Sir,
> Your most obedient Servant:
> JEvelyn

10 o'clock⁸ at night
    I have not eaten one bit of bread to-day.
    Be pleasd to seale [this?]⁹ when perusd;
    Look on Sir William Doolye last:
    [.....]

---

¹ MS torn.
² MS: 'Conscie'.
³ MS torn.
⁴ E is perhaps being a little insincere here in his anxiety to distance himself from trade and commerce, a socially-inferior occupation. In fact he was reasonably familiar with the practical financial realities of life. On 9 December 1657 he bought East India Company stock; in 1666 he began to look into the possibilities of a commercial brick-making enterprise, and in 1668 purchased a mill close to the Sayes Court estate.
⁵ Reading here is extremely uncertain due to a hole in the MS.
⁶ MS torn.
⁷ P's diary entry for this day suggests he was aware of the depth of the problem.
⁸ MS: 'Xᵏ'.
⁹ MS: 'yᵗ'.

A8. JOHN EVELYN TO SAMUEL PEPYS[1]

What I shall do with these miserable Creatures?

For Samuell Pepys Esqr

Sayes Court
3 October 1665[2]

Sir,

I was in some doubt whither those Letters you commanded me to prepare, ariv'd timely enough to accompany yours to Court on Saturday-night;[3] For finding divers Chyrurgeons, and Sick-persons at my dores who had come from Several places with sad complaints that they could not procur quarters for them. I was forc'd to dispatch Warrants to the Connestables and other Officers to be ayding and assistant to my Deputyes, and some of these concernd me as far as Deale and Sandwich, where we are so overlayd, that they send them back upon us, and they perish in the returne; so that I had not a moments leasure to finish my letters, till it was neere 7 of the Clock; and I would be glad to know whither [any][4] came to your hands at all. Sir, I have had earnest intreaties from Severall of the Commanders (riding before Woolwich) to dispose of their Sick- and wounded-men on shore, but the Clearke of the Cheque[5] there reproches our Chyrurgeon, and obstructs the effect of the Warrant I sent to the Connestable, upon a pretence, of bringing the Contagion amongst them; whiles in the meane time, I am sure, they suffer others to tipple in the Ale-houses; And Sir Theophilus Biddulph was with me to spare Greenewich, because of your sitting there, and Deptford in reguard of his Majesties Yard: I would be glad to know (Since Chatham, and Graves-End can

---

[1] Source: PRO S.P. 29/134, f.23–4. Endorsed by P, '3 Octobr 65 Says Court Esqr Evelin.'
[2] MS: 'Says-Court 3:Octo:–65'. P's diary entry for the 5th gives a flavour of his approach to the problem, '...so away to Mr Evelings to discourse of our confounded business of prisoners and sick and wounded seamen, wherein he and we are so much put out of order.' (5 Oct 1665). Pepys was not so concerned about the subject that on his way to Evelyn's he had overlooked the opportunity to 'pass some time with Sarah', moving on to visit Mrs Bagwell and 'there did what I would con ella' (ibid). He and E then spent the rest of the evening discussing trees and gardens which contrasts markedly with the subject matter of the letters.
[3] Saturday, 30 September. See previous letter.
[4] MS torn but enough survives to make the reading fairly certain.
[5] MS: 'Cheq'.

hold no more,) and that I have peopld all the intermedial Villages, what I shall do with these miserable Creatures, who are not able to move? Though had halfe of these but bread to eate (I speake not here of the Prisoners, but our owne men) we should not have neere the multitudes, which are impos'd upon us. Sir, I do not tell you these stories out of any designs to engage or trouble you with other folkes buisinesse, as you have lately seem'd to impute it to me; because without monnye I could not feede two-thousand Prisoners; but to let you see, that it is not without reason I have made my Complaints nor at all my crime, if his Majesties Subjects perish for want of harbor. It was also tr[eat]ed as a failure in my Industry, that I had not receiv'd the Prisoners into my c[are][1] and assisted towards the raising the £5000 to be assign'd me; But upon my pa[rticular][2] applications to my Lord Broncker and Sir John Mennes (according to his Graces direction) a[bout?][3] my Yesterdays dispatching two very able Officers to take their names, receive them out of the[4] respective prizes and shipps; there were none of those Vessells ready you were pleas'd to name, nor roome in them for a quarter of the number; so as my Martials return'd *re infecta*,[5] and could not fall downe with them to Graves End when I had also provided Guards to secure[6] them: For this service Sir, I therefor yet attend your Commands, and am ready, when the Vessels are so; and more then so, to take them quite off your hands, and the Vessels too when I have touch'd the mony which must make them live; having since I saw you contracted with my Lord Culpeper (fourty miles from this place,) for Leeds-Castle, where I am repairing, and fitting things for their safty, that I may not seeme to be indiligent, because I am unhappy, and have no talent[7] to rayse monnye, though I can tell where it may be had, when I know the Commodity: Sir, I have at this moment* [*which belong to all 4 Commissioners and not to my care alone.][8] Chelsey College, two Hospitals in London and Nine other townes, besides Villages, where I have Deputys, Physitians, Chyrurgeons, and Martials, who employ me with buisinesse sufficient to take up any one persons time, but to reply to their Letters, make them Warrants, send them Medicaments, Mates, Monye, if I had not the importunity of a thousand Clamors at my dores which neither lets me rest day nor night: Sir, in a Word, I have studied my Commission,[9] and the Instructions annex'd to them, and I hope shall be able to

---

[1] MS torn.

[2] MS torn.

[3] MS torn.

[4] MS: 'their'; 'ir' struck out.

[5] 'With the task unfinished'.

[6] Replaces 'take' (struck out).

[7] Replaces 'skill' (struck out).

[8] Note in the margin; the * is E's.

[9] A copy of this, dated 8 June 1665 and endorsed by E, is amongst P's papers, now Bod MS Rawl. A289, f.89.

justifie every article, though I cannot compare my faces[1] and abillities with others: Nor did I in the least obtrude the importunity which I am sensible[2] the Prisoners have been to you; but upon his Grace's certaine knowledge of our wants of monyes to feed them, and without any provocation of mine (more then what you heard of our poverty) he was pleased to Order what was so very necessary, and I have not I hope presum'd to any favour upon my own Score; for I no where find, by my Commission, that I was to provide monyes,[3] but to dispense it when I had it, and to give a just accoumpt of its application which I am ready to do with joy: Nor have I yet been wanting in giving notice to the Greate-ones at Court, from post to post-day (long before this as having prospect sufficient of what is befallen us) in a style more zealous and peremptory, than perhaps becomes me; and as I continu'd to do this very morning in a letter I writ to my Lord High Chancellor[4] which I sent by Sir Richard Browne; having alarm'd all the rest (not one excepted) with my continual representations of our miserys: And if (as I could tell you from a Person that best knowes in England) I should shew you from whence this neglect of us proceedes, it would not add a Cubite to your stature: Be assur'd Sir, from me, that I shall be most tender of adding to your trouble, (whose burthen I find is already so insupportable) and I hope I shall not be esteem'd remisse, when I also keepe within my owne Sphære. What has come collateraly on you (not through my fault) ought[5] not be imputed to me; And I hope when you do know me well (as I am greatly ambitious of that honour) you will find I have taken too exact a measure of your reale merits, and personal Civilities to me, then to forfaite them by my impertinencies; as I beseech you to believe, that I have not in this paper exaggerated any thing of mine Owne Sufferings, to magnifie the poore Service I have hitherto don (as by little acts we are prone to do) but that you would looke on me as a plaine-Man, who desires to serve his Majestie (till he is pleas'd to release me) in the station I am assigned to the best of my abilities; and which I shall be sure to improve, if you still allow me a part of your Esteeme, who cannot eclipse the brightnesse of your Example from

Sir
Your most faithfull, and
most obedient Servant
JEvelyn

---

[1] MS reading uncertain. Appears to read 'faces', perhaps using 'face' as an analogy for the various offices E was having to perform.

[2] 'Which I am sensible' is inserted.

[3] I.e. out of his own pocket.

[4] Edward Hyde, Earl of Clarendon. It is not extant, and E did not retain a copy.

[5] Replaces 'I hope will', struck out.

A9. JOHN EVELYN TO SAMUEL PEPYS[1]

Some inconvenience, mischiefe, and another Cheate

For my most honord Friend
Samuell Pepys Esqr:
at Greenewich:

Sayes Court
12 October 1665[2]

Sir,

This Enclos'd from his Grace[3] concernes the whole Fleete so neerely: that (after our former attempts) we are even forc'd to renew our Petition for prevention of the mischeife which now threatens more then ever, and especialy at Chatham.

I do also take the liberty on this opportunity to informe you of some inconveniences which concerne the honourable the Principal Officers, in relation to the Chest;[4] and to supplicate their advice in order to the redresse: First, Our men in the London Hospitals steale downe to Chatham before they are Cur'd, and then returning back, with their gratuity, inflame themselves with drinke and dissorder, which exceedingly retards their health: They all this while concealing their having pensions, enjoy the Kings Super-allowance in the Hospitals, which formerly was not continud; when if their weekely allowance was more then their annual pension; the over-plus was only paid them, and the pension defaulked.[5]

The remedy of this (under submission) may be, a restitution of the former practise; that the pay-master to the Hospital be ordered to difalk[6] out of the additional allowance, as much as their pensions at the Chest amounts to

---

[1] Source: MS, collection of William H. Fern, Connecticut (ex-Sothebys 24 July 1995 sale catalogue, Lot 487). Endorsed by P, '12.8br:65 Commissioner for sick and wounded. Some observations of his how the chest is abused by seamen, and propounds remedy for it'. The letter came from a collection accumulated in the 1800s, but was probably once in official records, where the others of this period still are.

[2] MS: 'Says-Court 12th: 8br–65'.

[3] Albemarle. He had written to E on 9 October (see p.33, note 6), advising E about where to collect money and also to instruct him to forward an enclosure to Brouncker and Mennes. It is probable that this is what is referred to here. The MS also bears, by the address, a pencilled note (by E?) 'with to read'. P went to see Albemarle on 13 October (diary).

[4] A welfare fund for disabled and wounded seamen (see Latham and Matthews, X, 59). The actual chest is on display at the National Maritime Museum, Greenwich.

[5] Defalk: reduce by deductions.

[6] See previous note.

weekly: This, will be our part to reforms: Whilst the Principall Officers and Comissioners of his Majesties Navy are desir'd to order the Clearke of the Chest to give our pay–master of our Hospital– Sick– Seamen etc an abstract of all Pensions and Gratuities settld at the Chest, and bestowd on any this yeare past; and alsoe that the sayd Clearke might once every fortnight transmitt our Officer a list of such as are from time to time addmitted into Pensions:

They of late also practise another Cheate; which is, when they are discharg'd our Hospitals as cured, to conceale the Chirurgeons Certificats that they are in part, or totaly dissabl'd (which is a caution we have chargd our Chirurgeons to insert) and come ranting and swearing to us for Conduct-mony to returne to their Shipps, when the next newes we hear, is, that they goe to the Chest, and no farther: For prevention whereoff you may be pleas'd to order that none be admittd from any our Infirmitories into Pensions, but such as have the hand of the Pay-Master of our Hospitals etc to their Certificates:

Upon view of these abuses, I thought fit to offer them to your Consideration, it being an Article frequently repeatd in our Instructions, to be as frugal, and circumspect as we could in the mangement of our Trust; and these coming under my particular cognizance, as I have had (to the greate increase of my Trouble) the Hospitals of London to look after during the absence of my Brother Commissioners (to whom the care equaly belongs), I recommend those to your more careful[?] addresses[1] who remaine Sir

Your most humble and faithfull servant
JEvelyn:

Sir

Our small pittance at last in prospect, I am marching away with the Prisoners as fast as I can, and hope in short time to cleere the shipps; after which, (unlesse prevented by something very effectul) I resolve for Oxon,[2] where if I see no evident assurance of some solid fonds[3] to carry on the Worke, without exposing us to such another plunge, and accidental subsistance; I shall cease for the future to continue the trouble to you and resigne to some more fortunate Person.

---

[1] Pepys was impressed by E's assiduous pursuit of the corruption and his rigorous record-keeping. He wrote to Coventry to tell him that, 'Mr Eveling (to instance one port) showed me his accompt of Graves-end where for every penny he demands allowance for and for every sick man he hath had under his care he shews you all you can wish for in Colloms of which I have here for your satisfaction enclosed an Example which I dare say you will say with me he deserves greate thanks for, I have since wrott to him [letter unknown] to cause transcripts of these accompts to be sent to us and hope our people will see the King here have the benefit of it in the payments of shipps and adjustment with pursers...' (letter to Coventry, 14 October 1665, NMM LBK/8, 256; published by Tanner 1929, no. 52).

[2] E apparently never made this threatened journey.

[3] An obsolete, pre-18th century, form of 'funds'.

A10. JOHN EVELYN TO SAMUEL PEPYS[1]

A guard for the money, and some pestiferous men

For my most honor'd Friend
Samuel Pepys Esqr his
house in Greenewich

Sayes Court
13 October 1665[2]

Sir,

I am this afternoone to send away £1000 to Deale and Dover with a Guard, not having been able to find any opportunity of returning the mony otherwise; which will make me so unmanerly, as not to be able to waite on you as I ought: There is likewise another Calamity on me, from the negligence of others; therefore (though the occasion be very instant, as to those Vessells for our pestiferous men) I must defer the kissing of your hands til to morrow, unlesse you resolve to do me the honor of refreshing your Selfe in our poore Garden any time this evening when you have best leasure, where I shall be to receive your Commands, who am[3]

> Sir
> Your most obedient
> and faithfull Servant
> JEvelyn:

---

[1] Source: PRO S.P. 29/134, f.85. Endorsed by P, '13 October 65 Says Court Esqr Evelin.'

[2] MS: 'Says-Court 13:Octr:65'.

[3] Such a meeting, if it occurred, is not recorded. E has no diary entry from the 11th to the 14th October inclusive. P seems to have spent most of the day at the office engaged on its 'infinite business' (diary, 13 and 14 October).

A11. JOHN EVELYN TO SAMUEL PEPYS[1]

The unconscionable bills of the Apothecaries

For Samuel Pepys
Esqr etc at the Navy Office:
Greenewich:

Sayes Court
14 October 1665[2]

Sir,

By what I have sent you, you will have a Specimen of the Method observed where I have any-thing to do.[3] If the heads[4] be not particular enough, be pleas'd to give me your instructions where I may pertinently add: Take notice also, I pray, how few have miscarried [Most of those who dyed perished for want of covering],[5] the last winter consider'd, notwithstanding our agreement at a certainety with our Doctors and Chirurgeons for 3s[6] per head; to avoyd the unconscionable bills of the Apothecaries, with one article alone would have been double all the expense, as by experience in the last Warr we learn'd: The Certificates answer to every individual person, which after you have perus'd, and are satisfied in, pray returne by this bearer; because they onely are my Vouchers; The other Accoumpt, keepe by you as long as you please, I having a duplicate; and call to us for the Whole when ever you please; because I long to give it in, and be discharg'd of so much of my Burthen: The two printed papers are an invention I have particularly practis'd in my owne Circle onely, which I hope you will not reprove, because it dos a little obviate the quærie of Sir William Coventry, to whom (if what I transmitt, prove satisfactory to you) speake your just thoughts of my Duty in the particulars he mentions and add to your former favours, that of including these Letters in your Packett for

Sir,
Your most obedient,
and faithfull Servant
JEvelyn:

---

[1] Source: PRO S.P. 29/134, f.93. Endorsed by P, '14:8ber.65 Says Court. Esqr Evelin.'

[2] MS: 'Says-Court 14th:8br:–65'. See E's letter of the same day to his father-in-law, Sir Richard Browne for a more graphic account (Appendix 1, no. 3).

[3] E attached a copy of the printed form (see Appendix 1, no. 2).

[4] I.e the headings.

[5] Marginal note.

[6] Abbreviation *s* is a probable reading, though *l* for £ is a possibility.

A12. JOHN EVELYN TO SAMUEL PEPYS[1]

Pepys is seeking comprehensive records

For Samuel Pepys Esqr:
One of the principall Officers
of his Majesties Navy at Greenewich

Sayes Court
23 October 1665[2]

Sir,

Yours of the 17th Instant[3] I found at my returne from Leades,[4] and Kentish Circle, requiring an accoumpt of what Sea-men have been sick on shore? the ships whence they came? and the place to which? with other particulars to encounter the fraud of the Pursers etc. Sir, for mine owne concerne, I sent you that of Deale, and am ready to present you with the rest of mine to the 5th June last [from November to June];[5] since which we have not yet altogether finished the last quarter; but I presume may be ready with it to a day, by that time you have examin'd these: For those of my other Breathren, I presume they are also prepard for you: But I can give no positive account of it, they being all of them many miles distant from our place of meeting: In the meane time I have sent your Letter to Sir William Doily, that he may know what your Commands are: I verily believe his are in very good order, having lent him my Clearke[6] so long, though to mine owne prejudice: With what concernes my Selfe as to this particular, I shall to morrow (God willing) waite on you,[7] who am   Sir,

Your most obedient and humble Servant
JEvelyn:

---

[1] Source: PRO S.P. 29/135, f.44. Endorsed, '23 October 65. Says Court. Esqr Evelin'.
[2] MS: 'Says-Court 23d:Octr:1665'. E wrote more freely to Sir Richard Browne, the same day: '...The King will not have a man to serve him shortly... Do they believe 12000 Sick-men can be maintained with nothing?... The Major of Rochester, swore to me, they would throw our sick-men in the streetes if I did not send them mony, their poore miserable Landlords who quarter them clamoring so to the Court there, and exclaiming, not to say cursing, with dreadful imprecations, comparing the tymes, with former. But of this, more when I see you, and may speake freely...' (BL.1480).
[3] Not known – it is evident from later in this letter that E had sent it on to Doyly and presumably never made a copy. P made no copy in his letter book (NMM LBK/8).
[4] Leeds Castle, Kent. E marched 500 prisoners there from Maidstone on 18 October, returning to Deptford on the 22nd (diary).
[5] Marginal note.
[6] Probably William Barbour (see Latham and Matthews, X, 19).
[7] He did (P's diary, 24 and 25 October 1665).

A13. JOHN EVELYN TO SAMUEL PEPYS[1]

The cost of ulcerate sores of inveterate malignity

Sayes Court
4 November 1665[2]

I have six or seaven men who have spent us a greate deale of mony, and care at Deale, who are likely never to be cured, having some of them been dissmembrd,[3] others dissabl'd by ulcerate sores of inveterate malignity, totaly unfit for any service: I once made it my suite to you (and you seemd to consent) that such persons might be discharg'd: be pleas'd to signifie what my Deputy, and Chirurgeon (who are both ready to certifie this) shall do with them to

Sir, Your
most obedient Servant
JEvelyn:

---

[1] Source: PRO S.P. 29/136, f.31. Endorsed by P, '4 9ber. 65 Says=Court. Esqr Evelin.' The letter is included by Marburg (her M8) who did not note that the surviving manuscript seems only to be the second half of the original letter. For this reason no destination address survives. The missing text probably amounted to at most around six or seven lines. However, the clear space immediately above the first line suggests that there is a possibility that only an opening 'Sir' may be missing. The letter, like most of those from this period, is not represented in E's copy-letter book and its original length cannot therefore be verified.

[2] MS: 'Says-Court 4th:9br:–65' at foot of letter. The following day the men found time to relax as Pepys described in remarkable and memorable detail (diary, 5 November 1665). E, typically, restricts his own diary entry for 5 November to a notice of a sermon.

[3] E's diary entry for 24 March 1672 during the Third Dutch War is a particularly graphic account of the misery such amputations created:

'I din'd with Mr. Commissioner Cox having seene that morning my Chirurgeon cut off a poore creaturs Leg, a little under the knee, first cutting the living and untainted flesh above the Gangreene with a sharp knife, and then sawing off the bone in an instant; then with searing and stoopes stanching the blood, which issued aboundantly; the stout and gallant man, enduring it with incredible patience, and that without being bound to his chaire, as is usual in such painefull operations, or hardly making a face or crying oh: I had hardly such courage enough to be present, nor could I endure to see any more such cruel operations.'

A14. JOHN EVELYN TO SAMUEL PEPYS[1]

A hospital ship indispensable

For Samuel Pepys Esqr
on[e] of the principall Officers
of his Majesties Navy
at Greenewich

Sayes Court
[23 November 1665][2]

Sir,

I am but just now ariv'd;[3] of which I will give you no farther account at present, because the post shall not goe without the direction you require, though it be not so particular as I could wish it: The last I receiv'd was from Mr Fillingham,[4] and since that he is gon very sick home to his owne house to which I have no other addresse then by Mr Fillingham; so that the most expeditious will be to enclose Sir Williams Letter in a paper to him with this superscription

> *For Mr Fillingham at Mr Loverans's in Hadleigh to be left at Stratford*
> *beyond Colchester*   *Suffolk:*

Sir,
Mr Conny[5] (who is now with me) informes me of the indispensable necessity of having an Hospital Ship, and therfor conjures me to put you in mind of the favour: Pardon dear Sir, this abrupt scribble of

Sir,
Your most humble Servant
JEvelyn:

Says-Court at
7 the Clock.

---

[1] Source: PRO S.P. 29/137, f.84. Endorsed by P, '23.9br.65 Mr Evelyns direction how to send to Sir W[illia]m Doyley'.

[2] MS: 'Says-Court at 7 the Clock' below. Date given by P's endorsement. E had been at Wotton, returning to Deptford this day (diary). In his own diary P reports a meeting with E the following day (24 November 1665) in which they looked at old manuscripts. There is no reference to official business, or this letter.

[3] From a meeting with Albemarle (diary, 23 November 1665).

[4] Bartholomew Fillingham. A number of letters of this date from E to him exist as loose MSS in the Evelyn archive at the British Library.

[5] John Conny, a surgeon at Chatham.

A15. JOHN EVELYN TO SAMUEL PEPYS[1]

Unclothed miserable Creatures and unserviceable Old-Men

For Samuel Pepys Esqr
One of the principall Officers
of his Majesties Navy at Greenewich

Sayes Court
7 December 1665[2]

Sir,

Forgive me that I[3] beg the favour of having these Letters convey'd to the Post
by your Ordinary Messenger this Evening: And that I do not let slip this
opportunity of bespeaking your assistance and advice where I am to apply
myselfe, that some effectual Course be taken with divers miserable Creatures
under our Chirurgeons hands (at Deale especialy) to furnish them with
Clothes, that so they may at last be sent on board; since it is not health, but
Covering which they have long wanted; and whilst they suffer this Calamity,
spend his Majestie five times the value in quarters: There are likewise more
then 50, who being Old-Men, tabid, inveteratly Ulcer'd and universaly
infirme, will never be render'd serviceable to his Majestie but have layne at
prodigious expenses for Cure: As many as I have been able to convey, I have
removed into the London Hospitals (since the abating of the Contagion
amongst them has again opned their doores) but some that are remote I cannot
stir (for you have never allow'd us any boates to call as we beggd you would,
and wh[ich] would have aboundantly borne the charge[4] of it) unlesse I should
cart them: This[5] I the rather mention because I have been frequently not onely
promis'd they should have their Ticketts, and be totaly discharg'd; but been
injoynd to signifie their names to you: which both my Deputys and
Chirurgions have don, with all necessary attestation: Yet still they remaine
upon our hands: Sir, I depend very much upon your addresse in representing
how much his Majestie suffers by these two Inconveniences, whilst I can but
give notice of them according to my duty, and as they occurr to Sir,

Your most humble and
faithfull Servant
JEvelyn:

---

[1] Source: PRO S.P. 29/138, f.60. Endorsed, by P, '7 December 65 Says Court Esqr
Evelin'.
[2] MS: 'Says-Court 7th:Dr:–65'.
[3] Inserted.
[4] Replaces 'cost', deleted.
[5] 'Wh[ich] some cannot' deleted before 'This'.

A16. JOHN EVELYN TO SAMUEL PEPYS[1]

Evelyn fears he will be forgotten

For Samuell Pepys Esqr
On[e] of the principall Officers
of his Majesties Navy
at the Navy Office
Greenewich

Sayes Court
9 December 1665[2]

Sir,

Your Letter of the 7th[3] concerning our Prisoners in the *Golden-hand* [4] and *Prince William* [5] came not an houre since to me; by what neglect I know not: I have sent to my Martiall at Leeds,[6] to be here on Moneday (if possible) and to march away with them; so that those Vessells shall speedily be cleared: Sir William Coventry gives me hopes our Lazers[7] shall be cloathed, but you must coöperate or we shall be forgotten: I am Sir, *Stylo Læconico*[8]

Your most faithfull Servant
JEvelyn:

---

[1] Source: PRO S.P. 29/138, f.77. Endorsed by P, '9 December 65. Says Court. Esqr Evelin'.

[2] MS: 'Says-Court 9th:Decr:–65'. P saw E at dinner on 10 December (diary) but makes no record of the conversation.

[3] Not known. There is no copy in NMM Letter-Book 8.

[4] This is probably the *Golden Hand*, a storeship referred to in *The Journals of Sir Thomas Allin 1660–78*, ed., R.C. Anderson for the Navy Records Society 1939–40, vol. II, pp.98, 116, *et alia* (for 1667). For Allin, see DNB, Allin, Sir Thomas (1612–85).

[5] MS: 'Pr: W:llm'. It can probably be identified as the 'flyboat' (a flat-bottomed coaster) *Prince William* captured from the Dutch in 1665 but recovered by them in 1666 (Colledge 1987).

[6] Leeds Castle, Kent.

[7] Variant of 'Lazar' from 'Lazarus', a diseased person.

[8] 'In the manner of a sweat-bath' – presumably a reference to the haste and intensive work involved.

A17. SAMUEL PEPYS TO JOHN EVELYN[1]

Evelyn's ships are needed to fetch coal

Mr Evelyn

Navy Office Greenwich
12 December 1665[2]

Sir

His Royal Highness hath commanded, that the *Golden hand* and *Prince William* [3] be imediatly sent to New Castle to fetch Coales for the poore of the Citty of London:[4] I doe therefore entreat you that if they have any Dutch[5] prisoners now onboard them as I am told they have you will please to thinke of some fitt place for the removal of them unto, and to cleare the shipps of them that we may in obedience to his Royal Highness's comands see the said shipps imediatly proceed on the forenamed service: I am

Your affectionat Servant
SPepys

---

[1] Source: Pierpont Morgan Library (catalogued as: '[No MA number]. *Collection*: Rulers of Europe' under Pepys). Endorsed by E, 'Mr Pepys Navy-Office 12 Decr –65'. An oddity of the MS is that the date of both letter and E's endorsement have quite clearly been altered, and by the same hand; it now reads '12' in both cases but may have originally read '7' or '17'.

[2] MS: 'Navy Office Greenwich 12 December 1665' at foot of letter. Notwithstanding the observation in note 1 above, Pepys recorded writing his letters late this day, just before going home for supper but not too late for them to be dispatched as E seems to have replied the next day (diary).

[3] MS: 'Wm'. See p.49, note 5.

[4] 'The weather setting in cold' (P's diary, 12 December 1665). P had also recorded, on 13 October preceding, that he encountered Albemarle, William, Earl of Craven, and Alderman Sir John Robinson, Lord-Lieutenant of the Tower 'talking of ships to get of the King to fetch Coles for the poor of the City, which is a good work. But Lord, to hear the silly talk between these three great people...' (diary; see Latham and Matthews, VI, 264, n.3, for additional references on this topic).

[5] Inserted.

A18. JOHN EVELYN TO SAMUEL PEPYS[1]

Evelyn will empty the ships but needs substitutes

For Samuell Pepys Esqr.
One of the principall Officers
of his Majesties Navy
at the Navy Office in Greenewich

Sayes Court
13 December 1665[2]

Sir,

Being now willing to remove not onely the Prisoners out of the *Golden-hand*, and *Prince William* [3] (according to the Command) but likewise to Cleere all the Shipps at once, that so you may be at full liberty for the future to dispose of them: I most humbly make it my request that you will facilitate the Worke by gratifying my Martial with your Warrant, impowering him to presse some tiltboate or other, as there shall be occasion, for the transporting them to Gravesend, in order to their march: This, Sir, if you shall do, you will much oblige

Sir,
Your most humble Servant
JEvelyn:

My Martials name is Mr John Rowlandson
   Martiall at Leeds-Castle. Kent
Be pleasd to send the Order to me by the Bearer hereoff.[4]

---

[1] Source: PRO S.P. 29/139, f.11. Endorsed by P, '13 December Says Court. Esqr Evelin.' This letter bears the text of a shorthand letter or memorandum in P's hand on the verso. Also dated 13 December 1665, it appears to be concerned with a bill of imprest (a cash advance) to Captain George Cocke, part of which Cocke was to use to pay a debt to P. E's letter does not appear to be mentioned. The negotiations with Cocke, conducted in the Pope's Head tavern in Chancery Lane, are discussed in P's diary (13 December 1665). The present letter was addressed to Greenwich. It seems that having collected, or been delivered, his post P found E's letter a convenient scrap of paper to use in the tavern to make a record of the deal with Cocke.
[2] MS: 'Says-Court 13:Dr:–65'.
[3] See p.49, notes 4 and 5.
[4] Although undoubtedly in E's hand this letter, and particularly the postscriptum, is written in a larger, and better-defined, hand than normal.

A19. JOHN EVELYN TO SAMUEL PEPYS[1]

Plan for an infirmary at Chatham

For Samuell Pepys Esqr:
One of the principall Officers
of his Majesties Navy,
at the Navy Office in Seething-Lane London
With a roll of paper

Sayes Court
31 January 1666[2]

Sir,

I do, according to your Commands, transmit you an hasty Draught of the Infirmary, and Project for Chatham;[3] the reasons, and advantages of it, which challenges your Promise of promoting it to the Use design'd: I am, my Selfe, convinc'd of the exceeding benefit it will every way afford us: If, upon examination of the Particulars, and your intercession, it shall merit a recommendation from the rest of the Principall Officers, I am very confident the effects will be fully answerable to the pretence of the Papers which I send to accompany it: In all Events, I have don my Endeavor; and, if upon what appeares even Demonstrable to me (not without some considerable Experience, and frequent Conference with our Officers, discreete, and sober Persons) I persist in my fondnesse to it, from a prospect of the many advantages would be reaped by setting it on foote; I beseech you to pardon the honest intentions, and to passe-by the Errors of

Sir, Your most obedient
and faithfull Servant
JEvelyn:

Sir, I must beg your excuse, if my desire to comply with your commands as soone as might be, and having severall avocations,[4] I could not delineate the Plot so accurately as I intended; but I hope it may suffice to explaine the Designe: neither had I one to write so fairely, as the paper inclosd in the rolle should have ben written:

---

[1] Source: PRO S.P. 29/146, f.73. Endorsed by P, '31 January 65 Sayes court Mr Evelen'.
[2] MS: 'Says-Court Jan:31: –65/6'.
[3] See P's diary, 29 January 1666 and below, p.336 (Figure 3). The draft shows a four-winged building surrounding a quadrangle. The MS drawing is now in the Bodleian at MS Rawl. A195, f.255, following E's letters of 26 March 1666 (**A24** and **25**).
[4] Distractions.

A20. SAMUEL PEPYS TO JOHN EVELYN[1]

Pepys passes the Chatham infirmary idea to the Duke of York

To Mr Evelyn

[Navy Office][2]
17 February 1666[3]

Sir

To tell you a litle more perticularly then I could in the middle of much businesse this morning my proceeding towards the advancement of your soe laudable designe of publique Infirmarys I did the very next meeting after your Honouring me with a coppy of your Project offer it to my Fellow-Officers, whoe concurred instantly with me in the haveing it presented as the vote of this Board that your sayd proposition should be layd before his Royal Highness[4] as a matter worthy his Royal Highness's recomending to his Majesty and to be put in present execution.

This I did in the name and presence of our whole board to his Royal Highness at my Lord Treasurers[5] on Wednesday last,[6] giveing him for memory sake the Following abstract of your proposall, vizt

Mr Evelyns Infirmary for 500 men

	£
1st to be built and furnished for	1400
2 to be mayntayned at the Monthly Charge of	471
3 the like number of men stand the King monthley (as it is now mannaged)	840
4 Which saves the King monthly in each 500 Men	370
Which is Yearely	4817

And reimburses the King his £1400 in 15 weekes.

Besides these additional Conveniencys:–

---

[1] Source: NMM Letter-Book 8, 369. Used by permission of the National Maritime Museum. The letter probably crossed with E's of the same date (A21, below).
[2] No place, but in the diary P records he was busy there in the morning.
[3] MS: '17 Febry 65', for 1665/6, at foot of letter which is in sequence following letters of December 1665.
[4] The Duke of York.
[5] Thomas Wriothesley, Earl of Southampton.
[6] Pepys's diary, 14 February 1666.

1 .... The present unavoydable neglect of Sick men, through the distance of thyre Quarters, will be[1] remooved.

2 .... They will be kept from Intemperance and consequently from thyr frequent relapses

3 .... Accounts will be more regularly kept

4 .... The Building will dureing peace serve for a worke house or other Uses.

5 .... The Clamours of landladys etc to the reproch of the service will be taken away.

6 .... Lastly, the Seamen will more regularly be entred and discharged and (if recovered) with more certainty be secured for further service.

You will forgive me if I omitted any of the considerable advantages intended to his Majesty in this proposall. But these were enough to move his Royal Highness to promise the reminding[2] of his Majesty about it which he did with great sence of the vallue of it, and comanded us to speake with you about the method of proceeding towards the doeing it, and how we might cast to have another erected about Harwich

If it thwart noe occasions of yours it might be usefull that you would let us see you heere on Tuesday morning about 10 where we shall be all together and perhaps may determine on some thing to offer to his Royal Highness the next day, when (in course) we attend him. my good will to further what you have with soe much paynes and Goodness intended will excuse the length of the Trouble I now give you whoe am[3]

Your most affectionat and most Humble Servant

SP

---

[1] MS: 'wilbe'; 'will be' is substituted here and later in this letter.

[2] Amended from 'recomending' or vice-versa.

[3] E's diary for 20 February (Tuesday): 'To the Commissioners of the Navy, who having seene the project of the Infirmary, encouragd the worke, and were very earnest it should be set about speedily: but I saw no mony, though a very moderate expense, would have saved thousands to his Majestie and ben much more commodious for the cure and quartering our sick and wounded, than the dispersing of them into private houses, where many more Chir[ur]giones, and tenders were necessary, and the people tempted to debaucherie etc:'.

P's diary for 20 February: '...to the office... Mr Evelyn's proposition about public infirmarys was read and agreed on, he being there. And at noon I took him home to dinner, being desirous of keeping my acquaintance with him; and a most excellent-humourd man I still find him, and mighty knowing'.

On 13 March E 'went to Chattham to take order and view a place design'd to take an Infirmarie' (diary). He then sent P an estimate in the letter of 26 March (see below).

A21. JOHN EVELYN TO SAMUEL PEPYS[1]

His Majesty well pleased with the Chatham plans

For Samuell Pepys Esqr
One of the principall Officers of
his Majesties Navy at
the Navy-Office in
Seething Lane London

Sayes Court
17 February 1666[2]

Sir,

His Majestie was well pleas'd with what I shew'd him of our Infirmary for Chatham, which he gave me leave to explaine to him at large:[3] If you have thought it worthy your recommendation to his Royal Highnesse I would be glad to heare of the successe; being still as assur'd of its effects to all the purposes I pretend in the annexed papers, as ever: It were tyme something were resolv'd on before the Spring advance upon us, that we may apply it to the designe of

Sir,
Your most affectionate and
humble Servant
JEvelyn:

---

[1] Source: PRO S.P.29/148, f.51. Endorsed by P, '17th Feby 65. Says-Court Esqr Evelin.'

[2] MS: 'Says-Court 17: Feb: 65/6'.

[3] This interview took place on 8 February when the King 'call'd me into his bed-chamber, to lay-before, and describe to him my project of an *Infirmarie*, which I read to him, with greate approbation, recommending it to his Royal Highness' (E's diary, 8 February 1666).

A22. JOHN EVELYN TO SAMUEL PEPYS[1]

Evelyn dare not show his face till he has more money

For Samuell Pepys Esqr
One of the principall Officers of
his Majesties Navy at
the Navy Office:

Sayes Court
28 February 1666[2]

Sir,

I had immediately yealded obedience to your Commands in going downe to
Chatham, and prepard what was necessary to put that affaire in some
forwardnesse, if I could have receiv'd the monyes which I have long expected
that must enable me to appeare there; not for the carrying on of that Worke,
but the discharge of our Sick-mens quarters there, my arreare being so greate,
that I dare not shew my face, 'till I can bring them some refreshment: but so
soone as I shall be enabld (and I am daily promisd monye) to appeare amongst
them, I shall not retard my journey a moment, and so soone as I have (with the
advise of Mr Commissioner Pett) made choyce of a fitting place; I shall either
waite on you with the account of it, or transffer the particulars to you, if I find
it necessary that my aboade there may more conduce to your Service: Sir, I
beseech you be pleas'd to make part of this to the rest of the Principall
Officers from[3]

Sir,
Your most humble and faithfull Servant
JEvelyn:

---

[1] Source: PRO S.P.29/149, f.59. Endorsed by P, 'Says Court 28:Feb:65 Mr Eveline'.
[2] MS: 'Sayes-Court 28:Feb:65/6'.
[3] P makes no reference to this letter in his diary but records his concern that the
Additional Aid Act of 1665 was 'putting us out of a power of raising money' (diary,
28 February 1666). He had already outlined the financial shortfall in a letter to
Coventry on 19 February (Tanner 1929, no. 94; NMM LBK/8, p.371). There was a
deficit of more than £0.8 million, 'besides the charge for the sick and wounded,
widows and orphans...' (ibid).

A23. JOHN EVELYN TO SAMUEL PEPYS[1]

Evelyn prepares accounts as fast as he can

For my honord Friend
Samuell Pepys Esqr
one of the principall Officers,
of his Majesties Navy:
at the Navy Office:

Whitehall
16 March 1666[2]

Sir,

That I may by degrees observe your Commands, I do by this Bearer send you the Dover Accompt for your present occasion, and the rest as fast as they are return'd me;[3] this day and every day expecting those of Deale and Gravesend etc: Be pleasd to returne me by this hand, the Particulars, or paper of the estimate I gave you of our proposd Infirmary, that it may direct me to draw up and calculate what I am to laye before you upon this expedition to Chatham[4] which I shall do, so soone as I have an houre to spare from my present miseries and care how to get a little monye to relieve your sick flock in my district: I am Sir, with all affection

Your
most humble and obedient Servant
JEvelyn:

Sir,
Since the writing hereof, I have certaine tidings of our Deale Accompt: and am promisd it shall be given you in tomorrow.

---

[1] Source: PRO S.P. 29/151, f.35. Endorsed by P, '16 Mar. 65 Esqr Evelin'.
[2] MS: 'White-hall 16 Mar:65/6'.
[3] On the 19 March P sat down with Brouncker, Penn, and Coventry to deal with the accounts for 'most of the morning' (diary); but, there is little of the sense of urgency which characterises E's letter on the subject.
[4] It took place on the 13 March (E's diary).

A24. JOHN EVELYN TO SAMUEL PEPYS[1]

Despite the work an estimate for Chatham is prepared

To Samuell Pepys, Esqr
One of the principall officers
of his Majesties Navy at Navy Office

Sayes Court
26 March 1666[2]

Sir,

I know not with what successe I have endeavourd to performe your
Commands; but it has ben to the uttmost of my skill, of which you are to be
my judges: The favour I bespeake of you is, your pardon for not sending it
before: I have not enjoy'd one minutes repose since my returne (now a
fortnight past) 'till this very morning; having ben ever since soliciting for a
little monye to preserve my miserable flock from perishing:[3] On Saturday,
very late, I dispatch'd Mr Barbour towards[4] my Kentish Circle where our sick
people are in quarters; and at his returne, I hope to present you a compleate
Accompt but 'till this instant morning I had not written one line of these
tedious Papers; so that if through hast (the parent of mistakes) there may
happly appeare some Escapes, give Pardon to your Servant; or let me purchase
it with this small Present of Fragments (such as yet you have ben pleasd to
accept) and a little Booke,[5] that I also recommend to excuse my expense of
such Leasure as I can redeeme from the other impertinences of my life. As to
the Report which I send you, I would receive it as a favour; however your
resolutions of putting it in execution may succeede (the tyme of yeare being so
farr Elaps'd, in reguard of Action, and more immediate use) it might yet be
gracefully presented to his Royall Highnesse, or rather indeede, to his Majestie

---

[1] Source: Bodleian MS Rawl. A195, f.249. No endorsement. This letter is associated
with a Report by E on the projected Chatham Infirmary, presented as a further letter of
the same date to P (see next letter, **A25**). Both were originally published by William
Bray in editions of the diary with correspondence, presumably from this source, but
this is not stated.
[2] MS: 'Sayes-Court 26 Mar:66'.
[3] E had 'sent away 2000 pounds to Chattham' (diary, 24 March 1666).
[4] MS: 'to', altered to 'towards'.
[5] Probably E's (anonymous) translation of *Les Pernicieuses Conséquences De la
nouvelle Heresie des Jesuites contre le Roy et contre l'Estat*, by Pierre Nicole, and
published in 1666 by E as *The Pernicious Consequences of the new Heresie of the
Jesuites, against the King and the State* (diary, 1 March 1666; and Keynes, no. 79).

himselfe, who has so frequently ben pleas'd to take notice of it to me as an acceptable Project; because it would afflict me to have them thinke I have either ben remisse, or trifling in my proposall.

This obligation I can onely hope for from your Dexterity, Addresse and Friendship, who am,

Sir,
Your most affectionate, and humble servant
JEvelyn:

Sir,[1]
There is nothing in the other Paper which you commanded me to returne; but what is included in these, with ample, and (I hope) considerable improvements.

I must beg a Copy of these Papers when your Clearkes are at Leasure, having never a duplicate by me; and it may happly neede a review.

Sir,[2]
The Bearer hereoff Roger Winne, being our Messenger (and without whose service I cannot possibly be, having so frequent occasions of sending him about buisinesse belonging to my troublesome Employment) dos by me supplicate your protection, that he may not be Pressed, of which he is hourely in danger as he travells about our affaires, without your particular indulgence, which I therefore, conjure you to let him have under your hand and signature.

---

[1] Footnote on the MS.
[2] Marginal note on the MS.

A25. JOHN EVELYN TO SAMUEL PEPYS[1]

A very thorough estimate

Sayes Court
26 March 1666[2]

Sir,

If to render you an account of the progresse of my late Proposal, be any testimony of my obedience to your Commands; be pleas'd to believe, that I most faithfully present it in these papers according to the best of my talent. And if you find the Estimate considerably to exceede the first Calculation, you will remember it was made to the meridian of London; that the Walles were, both by his Majestie and the directions of the Principall Officers to be made thicker, and higher; that the Materials, and Worke-men were presum'd to be found much cheaper in the Country; and that the Place and area to build on was suppos'd a Level: But it has fall'n out so much to our prejudice, and beyond all expectation in these particulars; that to commence with the ground, we could not in 4 or 5 miles walking about Chatham and Rochester, find one convenient spot that would bear a level of 200 foote square, unlesse it were one Field beyond the Dock, in the Occupation of Mr Commissioner Pett neare the bogg and marsh, which has neither solid foundation, nor fresh-water to it. There is a very handsome greene Close at the end of the Long Rope-house towards Chatham; but the declivity is so suddaine and greate to the West, that lesse than a ten-foote raising will not bring it to such a rectitude as that we can lay our plate upon the Wall, which will be a considerable trouble and charge to reforme, as may easily be demonstrated: For either the earth must be so much abated towards the East, or the Wall advanc'd to the height of neere 20 foote, whiles one Extreame of the roofe will touch the superficies of the earth: Besides, the field is not above 150 feet wide: But supposing all this might be encounter'd (as indeede it might with charge) it bordures so neere to the Rope-houses, the Dock, and that ample way leading to it from the Hill-house and Chatham, as might endanger his Majesties people in case of any Contagion; because it will be impossible to restraine them from sometimes mingling amongst the Worke-men and others, who have Employment in the Dock, when the Convalescent-men shall be able, or permitted to walk abroad. This, and

---

[1] Source: Bodleian MS Rawl. A195, f.251ff. Endorsed in E's own hand, 'Mr Evelyns Report touching Erecting an Infirmary at Chatham 1666'. This accompanied the previous letter of the same date (p.58) but was presented as a separate letter. The document is extremely complex and has required substantial adjustment of the layout.
[2] MS: 'Sayes-Court 26:Mar:1666'.

some other difficulties made us quit the thoughts of that otherwise gracefully situated place. After many other Surveyes, we at last pitch'd on a Field call'd the Warren, just beneath the Mill, and reguarding the North towards the River. The Accesse is commodious; it has a well of excellent Water, ready dugg, and wanting only repaires; and though this ground be likewise somewhat uneven, yet, with helpe, it will carry about 240 feet in length, and 150 in breadth, allowing the filling up of some Vallies and depressures of about 4 or 5 foote deepe, to be taken from severall risings: This, for many reasons, I conceive to be the fittest for our purpose, it having also a solid foundation on the Chalke, and being at a competent distance from all dangerous commerce with the Towne, which will greately contribute to the health of the sick, and protection of the Inhabitants; but being at present in Lease to the Chest, leave must be obtayn'd, and the Tennant, who now rents it, satisfied; in all which Mr Commissioner Pet (whose direction and assistance I tooke, according to your injunctions) informes me, there will be no difficulty:

Upon examination of the Materials on the Place:

	£	s	d
Bricks will not be deliverd at the place under	00:	18:	00
Lime, per Load, containing 32 Bushels, per thousand	00:	16:	00
Drift Sand, by Tonn	00:	00:	14
Tyles, per thousand deliverd	01:	01:	00
Heart-Lathes, per Load, containing 36 bundles	02:	10:	00
Sawing, per hundred	00:	03:	04
Workmen sufficient (in which was our greate mistake)	00:	02:	06

Upon these Matirials we conceiv'd thus of the Scantlings.

Walls, at 1 Brick	½		
Wall-plates	9 in.	5	
Parallel rafters	9	6 middle 16½ feet long	
	11	7 ends	
Single rafters	4½	3½	
Purlins	9	6	17
Binding-beames	12	12	
Windoe-frames	4½	3½	4 2
Dore-cases, in brick-Worke: single-doores	7	6	6 2 8in
The two outward double, with Architrave	7	6	9 9 4
Ground-floor gist	4	4	18

And if stone-floores to the 4 Corner-roomes, as has been since judg'd more commodious, the

Gists	8	3
So'men	14	11

Besides Partitions, Posts, Interstise, Quarterage.

At these scantlings, together with the alteration of the Walles for height and thicknesse, etc.

Every rod of square Brick-worke, solid, at 1½ thick: containing in bricks of 9 Inch: about 12 bricks Long, to 16½ in height: 15 bricks to every 3-feet high, which to 16½ is about 83: so that 83 by 21 is 1743 bricks superficial: This, at the design'd thicknesse, is every square-rod 5229 bricks, which I suppose at 17 (the lowest we can expect) deliver'd at the place, is every rod square, £09 08s 01d. The total of brick-worke then, contains about 118 square rodd, without defalcations of doores, Windows (being 8 doors at 6 and 3-feet; windows 114 at 3 and 2-feet, reduc'd to measure, contains doores 24 feet by 48, which is 1152 square foot; windows, 342 feet by 228 feet is 77,976 feet square); both these reduc'd to square rodds, are almost 30 rodds square; whereof allow 10 square rods for inequality of the foundation and Chimnies (if upon the Warren ground), and then the Bricks of the whole (without lime and sand) will cost for 98 square rods, at £04 08 01

	431	12	02
And every rod after the rate of of 18d for one foot high, in workmanship, to	01	04	09
Which for 98 rod, is	122	06	00
So as the Brick-worke for the whole will come to	650	00	00
Tyling, at 30s per square	450	00	00
Timber, at 40s per square	600	00	00
Glasse about 684 feet, at 6d per foote	17	00	00
Windoe-frames, at 4s each	22	00	00
Single doores and Cases, at 20s each; Double doores and Cases (for the more commodious bringing in of the sick, being frequently carried), at 36s with the casements, locks, hinges, etc	30	00	00
Stone-floores	32	00	00
Stayres, per step, 3s., 76 in all	11	08	00
Levelling the ground, as computed upon view	46	10	00
Total:–	1859	18	00

But this Erection reduc'd to 400 Bedds, or rather persons (which would be a very competent number, and yet exceedingly retrench his Majesties Charge for their maintenance) and the whole abated to neere a 5th part of the Expense, which amounts to about	371	00	00
The Whole would not exceede	1487	18	00
Whereoff the Timber and roofe	480	00	00
The Timber alone to	360	00	00
Which, if furnish'd from the Yard, the whole charge of the building will be reduc'd to	1127	18	00
So as the number of Bedds diminish'd, Cradeles, and Attendance proportionable, the Furniture compleate will cost	480	00	00
Total–	1607	18	00

according to the formerly-made estimate, and which whole charge will be sav'd in quarters of 400 men onely, within 6 monethes, and about 15 dayes, at 6*d* per head, being no lesse than £10 per diem, 70 per Weeke, 280 per Moneth, 3640 per Annum;

Which is more then double what his Majestie is at in one yeares quarters for them in private-houses; besides all the incomparable advantages enumerated in the subsequent paper, which will perpetually hold upon this, or any the like occasion: The quartering of so many persons at 1*s* per diem amounting to no lesse than £7280 per annum.

If this shall be esteem'd inconvenient, because of disfurnishing the Yard, or other-wise a temptation to imbezill the Timber of the Yard:

All the Materials bought as above	1487	18	0
Furniture	480	0	0
Total–	1967	18	0

The whole Expense will be reimbours'd in 8 monethes:
viz. in 400 men's diet alone, by 6*d* per diem   £378 per Month
                                                        4536 per Annum

Whereas the same number at his Majesties ordinary entertainement is	627	04	00	per month
	7526	08	00	per annum
So as there would be saved yearely	2990	08	00	

Note, that the Sallary of the stuard (who buyes in all provisions, payes, and keepes the Accompts, takes charge of the Sick when set on shore, and discharges them when recover'd, etc.) is not computed in this estimate: because it is the same which our Clearks and deputies do by the present Establishment:

Thus I deduce the particulars:

Chirurgeons 7: viz 3 Master-Chirurgeons, at 8*s* per diem each; Mates
    4: at 4*s*; diet for 400 – £280; one Matron, per week, 10*s*; 20
    Nurses, at 5*s* per week; Fire, Candles, Sope, etc, 3*d* per week
                                280
                                 56
                                 42
                               £378   per Month

Cradle-Bedds, 200, at 11*s* per Cradle, at 4½ feet wide, 6 long	110	00	00
Furniture, with Bedds, Rug, Blanquet, Sheetes, at 30*s* per bed	300	00	00
Utensils for Hospitals, etc	70	00	00
	£480	00	00

But I do farther affirme, and can demonstrate, that supposing the
whole Erection, and Furniture (according to my first and largest
project, and as his Majestie and the Principall Officers did thinke
fit to proportion the height and thickness of the Walles), for the
Entertainement of 500 men, should amount to

Entertainement of 500 men, should amount to	1859 18 00
Furniture to	582 10 00
Total	2442 08 00

Then would be saved to his Majesty £332 18*s* per month, £3994 16*s* per Annum.

So that in lesse than 8 moneths time there will be saved, in the quarters of 500
men alone, more monye than the whole expense amounts to; Five hundred
mens quarters at 1*s* per diem coming to £25 per diem, 175 per week, 700 per
Month, 9408 per Annum.

Upon which I assume, if £3994, by five-hundred men, or £3640 in foure-
hundred men, or, lastly, if but £2990 be sav'd in one Yeare in the quarters of
400 sick persons, etc., there would a farr greater summ be saved in more than
6000 men; there having ben sent 7000 Sick and Wounded men to Cure in my
district onely, and of those 2800 put on shore at Chatham and Rochester, for
which station I propos'd the Remedy. Now, five-hundred sick-persons
quarter'd at a Towne in the Victualers and scattered Ale-houses (as the
Costome is), will take up at least 160 houses, there being very few of those
miserable places which afford accommodation for above 2 or 3 in an house;
with, frequently at greate distances, employ of Chirurgeons, Nurses, and
Officers innumerable; so as when we have ben distress'd for Chirurgeons,
some of them (upon computation) walked 5 or 6 miles every day, by going but
from quarter to quarter, and not ben able to visite their patients as they ought:
Whereas, in our Hospital, they are continualy at hand: We have essay'd to hire
some capacious empty houses, but could never meet with any tollerably
convenient; and to have many, or more then one, would be chargeable and
very troublesome: By our Infirmary, then we have these considerable
advantages.

At 6*d* per diem each (in the way of Commons), the sick shall have as good,
and much more proper and wholesome diet, than now they have in the Ale-
houses, where they are fed with trash, and Embezil their monye more to
inflame themselves, retard and destroy their Cures out of ignorance or
intemperance; whiles a sober Matron governs the Nurses, lookes to their
provisions, Rollers, Linnen etc. And the nurses attend the Sick, Wash, Sweepe,
and Serve the Offices, The Coock and Laundrer comprehended in the number,
and at the same rate, etc. By this Method likewise are the almost indefinite
number of Chirurgeons and Officers exceedingly reduc'd; The Sick dieted,
kept from drinke and Intemperance, and consequently from most unavoydably
relapsing: They are hindred from Wandering, Slipping-away, and dispersion:
They are more sedulously attended; the Physitian better inspects the
Chirurgeons, who neither can nor will be in all places, as now they are

scattered, in the nasty Corners of the Townes: They are sooner, and more certainely cur'd (for I have at present neere 30 bedds employ'd in a Barne at Graves-end, which has taught us much of this experience). They are receiv'd and discharg'd with infinitely more ease: Our Accompts better and more exactly kept: A vast, and very considerable Summ is saved (not to say gain'd) to his Majestie: The materialls of the house will be good if taken downe; or, if let stand, it may serve in tyme of Peace, for a Store, or Worke-house: The Furniture will (much of it) be useful upon like occasion; And what is to be esteem'd none of the least Virtues of it, 'twill totaly cure the altogether intollerable clamor and difficulties of rude and ungratefull people; their Landlords and Nurses, rays'd by their poverty upon the least obstruction of constant and Weekely payes; for want of which they bring an ill repute upon his Majesties Service, Incense the very Magistrates and better sort of Inhabitants (neighbours to them) who too frequently promote (I am sorry to speake it) their mutinies; so as they have been sometimes menacing to expose our Men in the streetes, where some have most inhospitably perish'd: In fine, This would encounter all Objections whatsoever; is an honorable, Charitable, and frugal Provision; Effectual, full of Encouragement, and very practicable; so as, however for the present it may be consider'd, I cannot but persist in wishing it might be resolv'd upon towards Autumne at the farthest; Chatham and Rochester alone having within 17 or 18 monethes cost his Majestie full £13,000 in cures and quarters; halfe whereof, would have neere ben saved had this method ben establish'd: Add to this, the almost constant station of his Majesties shipps at the Buoy in the Noore, and river of Chatham; the Clamor of that place against our quartering these, this crazy tyme, and the altogether impossibility of providing else-where for such numbers as continualy presse in upon us there, more than any where else, after Action, or the returne of any of his Majesties fleete: which, with what has ben Offer'd, may recommend this Project, by your favourable representation of the premises, for a permanent Establishment in that Place especially, if his Majestie and Royal Highnesse so thinke meete. This Account, being what I have ben able to lay before you, as the Effects of my late Inspection upon the Place, by Commands of the Honourable the Principal Officers, I request through your hands may be address'd to them from,

Sir,
Your most obedient servant,
JEvelyn

We might this Summer burne our owne Bricks, and procure timber at the best hand, which would save a considerable charge.

A26. JOHN EVELYN TO SAMUEL PEPYS[1]

A Scheme of the Dutch Action in 1667

For my honor'd Friend Samuell Pepys Esqr
Clearke of the Acts etc:
at the Navy Office with,
a little Roll of Paper. London.
        encl:

Sayes Court
20 January 1668[2]

Sir,

I am heartily asham'd I could not performe your Commands before now: It was friday[3] 'ere I could possibly get home, and since I am here, I have ben so afflected with the Griping of the Gutts,[4] that I was not able to bestow the paines I intended on the Scheme[5] I send you, which will onely serve you to preserve our reproch in memory, and my little skill in designing; But I have don it as I could, and as it appear'd to me from the Hill above Gillingham. The draught which I follow for Chatham River is from an old paper lying by me, and not from any printed Mapp, and some of the flexures I have presumed to reforme (as I thinke at least) as the River then presented itselfe to my Eye: You must excuse the defects of Sir,

Your most humble servant
J Evelyn:

The extreame whiteness of my Inke also deceived me etc

---

[1] Source: Bodleian MS Rawl. A195, f.77. No endorsement.

[2] MS: 'Sayes-Court 20th:Jan:–67/8'.

[3] Friday, 17 January.

[4] A constriction of the bowels; not an uncommon complaint of E's but, curiously, there is no mention of the ailment in his diary, as there often is.

[5] The drawing is bound with this letter at MS Rawl. A195, f.78, endorsed by E, 'A Scheme of the Posture of the Dutch-Fleete, and Action at Shere-nesse and Chatham 10th, 11th and 12 of June 1667 taken up on place by JE'. A reproduction was published in Braybrooke's editions of Pepys's diary and correspondence in 1825 and 1854. An earlier version, also in E's hand, is in Texas (Pforzheimer MS 35B). It seems to have been sent originally to P with the letter of 6 December 1681 (**C10**) and was sold as Item 2862 in the Davey Catalogue. It was described as the draft sketch made on site, forming the model for the fair copy above. A modified and clarified copy is reproduced here on p.337. Both drawings depict the lower reaches of the Thames and Medway, and the location of numbered ships marked with a table of their names and fates.

A27. SAMUEL PEPYS TO JOHN EVELYN[1]

Praise for Evelyn's draughtsmanship

Esqr Evelin

[Navy Office][2]
8 February 1668[3]

Sir

You will not wonder at the backwardness of my thankes for the Præsent you made mee soe many days since of the Prospect of Medway, while the Hollander rode Master on't,[4] when I have seriously told you, that the sight of it hath ledd mee to such reflections on my perticuler Interest (by my employment) in the reproach due to that Miscarriage, as have given mee litle lesse disquiet then he is fancyed to have who found his face in Michaell Angelo's Hell.[5]

The same should serve mee allso in excuse for my silence in the celebrating your Mastery shewen in the Designe and Draught, did not Indignation rather then Court shipp urge mee soe farr to commend them, as to wish the furniture of our House of Lords changed from the Story of 88 to that of 67,[6] (of Evelins designeing) till the pravity of this were reformed to the temper of that Age, wherein God Almighty found his Blessing more operative, then (I feare) hee doeth in ours his Judgements. Adieu

Your most affectionate and humble Servant
SP

---

[1] Source: NMM Letter-Book 8, 526. Copy in P's hand. Used by permission of the National Maritime Museum. Howarth published this letter, incorrectly stating his source to be Tanner 1929: the only previous edition of this letter is Braybrooke's. It is possible, however, that Tanner made his notes available to Howarth. Howarth's text is certainly slightly more accurate than Braybrooke's.

[2] He was at the office all day (diary).

[3] MS: '8 Febry 67', for 1667/8, at foot of letter. The letter is in sequence following December 1667).

[4] See p.66, note 5.

[5] This is a reference to Michelangelo's *Last Judgement* (1534–41). One of its detractors was Biagio da Cesena whom Michelangelo punished by portraying him as Minos in the composition.

[6] Tapestries depicting the Armada in the House of Lords.

A28. JOHN EVELYN TO SAMUEL PEPYS[1]

A brief guide to Paris

Directed thus
For my noble Friend
Samuel Pepys Esqr, One of the Principal Officers
of his Majestys Navy etc

Sayes Court
21 August 1669[2]

Sir,

I send you my Rhapsodies; but know, that as soon as I had set pen to paper, I was diverted by a thousand accidents; then follow'd Mr Cowley's Funeral,[3] but I sneak'd from Church, and when I came home (which was near 5 a Clock) an Army of Work-men (your Wall-builders) and others, besiege me for money, and to reckon with them;[4] so as what I send you is snatches and night-work, and unconnected, which you must pardon; and if you judge worthy it, cause to be transcrib'd; for my Running Hand is an Arabic not to be endur'd: But yours is a Running Voyage and desultory; and therefore you will the easier pardon me. There may be likewise diverse gross Omissions, which you will best judge of when you come to Paris, and begin to traverse the Town; so as it is from you I shall expect to be payd with fresh and more material Observations. I could have sett you down Catalogues of many rare Pictures and Collections to be seen in that City, but you will every day meet with fresher intelligence. It is now many years since I was there, *et mutantur tempora, et mores, et homines.*[5] Pray forget not to visit the Taille-Douce shops, and make Collection of what they have excellent, especially the Draughts of their Palaces, Churches, and Gardens, and the particulars you will have seen; they will greatly refresh you in your Study, and by the fire-side, when you are many years return'd. Israel, Sylvestre, Morin, Chaveau, are great Masters, both for things of the kind extant, and Inventions extreamly pleasant. You will easily be acquainted with the best Painters, especially Le Brun, who

---

[1] Source: PL.2237 (1–12), copy by P. E seems to have examined P's copy and made a number of insertions in his own hand. These are marked <>. The extensive description of Paris frequently matches E's diary in order and it is evident that he used it (or the same source) to write this letter (de Beer, I, 72ff).

[2] MS: 'Sayes-Court 21 Aug.1669'.

[3] Thomas Cowley (d. 11 August 1669), not his brother Abraham Cowley (d. 1667).

[4] A section of dockyard land had in 1667 been leased to Sayes Court (see plan, p.338; and, E's diary, 14 August 1668). The effect was to distance E's house from the dockyard. The reference here is probably to the erection of a new dividing wall.

[5] 'And times, customs, and men are changed.'

is the Chief of them; and it would not be amiss to be present at their Academie, in which Monsieur du Bosse (a principal Member) will conduct you. For the rest, I recommend you to God Almighty's Protection, augure you a happy Journey; and kissing your Lady's Hands, remain,

Sir, Your most humble and obedient Servant,

J Evelyn

These 3 Letters I enclose to be presented according to the Directions; with many more I could burthen you; but your short Stay at Paris will not require it; and besides, being Persons of great Quality, much of your time would be consum'd in making and repaying but impertinent Visites, in which I believe you would not willingly engage. I send you the Letters open for you to seal when you please.

P.S.

Sir,

When you are arriv'd at Paris, the best Service [which][1] can be done you, will be to address you where you may immediately repose your self, till you are provided and settled in a Lodging suitable to your Company. Therefore you may please to enquire for One Hughs an Englishman, who lives in *la Rue de la Boucherie, au Fauxborg St Germain*, a Friend of Sir Samuel Tukes, who will send for Dr Fitz-Gerrard (to whom you have a Letter) and he will assist you both to find out a fit Lodging, and whatever else you shall require.[2]

Sir,[3]

If you make your Journey through Picardy (which I believe you may resolve to do in regard of the Contagion) if you could so contrive it as to see Monsieur de Lion-Court's Seat at Lion-Court, the Gardens and Water-works would much please you; at least, if they are continu'd with that Care we have knowne them. But because I cannot tell you how inconvenient it may prove to deviate so far from your direct Road, I do only mention it *en passant*.

Calais.[4] You will find a strong Town by the new Fortifications and by two adjoyning Forts, besides the Citadelle and the Sluces, by which they can environ it with water at pleasure. The Market-place and Magazine, which was once a Staple for English Wool is observable; and so is the Architecture of an Altar-piece (as I take it) of black marble. I us'd to lodge at the Silver Lyon. Hence you have 7 Leagues to *Boulogne* a small Town; but famous for our

---

[1] MS: 'w^{ch}', possibly deleted.

[2] Pepys referred to this recommendation of (correctly) Fitzgerald by E in a letter of 29 September 1679 to his brother-in-law Balthazar St Michel 'when your poor Sister and I were in France' (Heath 1955, 106). None of E's introductory letters is extant.

[3] The copy now continues on a fresh leaf at PL.2237.3.

[4] These and other towns here italicised appear in the margin of the MS.

Henry 8's Expedition. The Lower Town has a large Street, and there I suppose you may lodge *au Bras d'or*. The Fortifications are not considerable. After 7 Leagues riding you will come to

Montreuil, where you will see an irregular Citadel; but the Town situated on a strong Eminence; and towards Paris-side the Fortification is very considerable by an Horn-work, and most noble Bastions, which are worth Remark, and will give you an idea of the Strength of such Places as they fortify abroad.

Abbeville – is 10 Leagues, a reasonable pretty Town; and though it be well fortify'd, there is nothing very observable in it. Here they used to offer us Pistols and Guns to buy. I think you will lodge there, or proceed 4 Leagues further to

Pont Dormis. A Little strong-Place regularly fortify'd. Thence to Crevecoeur 4 Leagues: And thence to

Poix Where you come into wretched Places, till you arrive at

Beauvais 9 Leagues (as I remember) a pretty large Town, and Market-place, and well-water'd: The Houses built of Wood. The Bishop's House is of Stone, and has some good Appartments in it. The Church is imperfect; but the Architecture good, though plain, and with handsome Sculpture behind the Quire. Pray observe the measures of the Town for their Serges,[1] and the Standards of them by Iron-Chains of different Lengths. After 8 Leagues you come to

Beaumont. Here, and before you will enter among the Vine-yards, I know little more observable, except it be the House and Garden of the President Nicolais, as you draw near Paris; which I esteem much for the Avenue and Fountains. But your mind will be so set on Paris, which is now but 4 leagues distant, that you will hardly stay. And indeed this whole Journey will render you little satisfaction, being for the most part, through a Frontier and miserable Country, and where you will see part of the Calamity of a Tyrannical Government, and the Effects of a continual War, such as has afflicted all that Tract for diverse Years. When you are arrived at

Paris, My Counsel is, that you take *Chambre garnie*[2] (as they call it). Sir Samuel Tukes addresses you to a Friend of his, an Irish Doctor of Physick (unknown to me) who he assures will be so honest, humble, and necessary to you, that you shall need no other to conduct you to all the considerable Places, and to introduce you both at the Courts and other Assemblys, which it is necessary for you to see. He will likewise find you out a convenient place for your Lodging, and do the Offices of a Guide in all that you can desire; and which will therefore much shorten the trouble I was going to engage you in, by giving you any large Directions of my owne–

That yet, this Paper may serve to put you in mind of some Particulars, which happly the shortness of your Expedition may otherwise indanger you to omit. I

---

[1] Lengths of woollen cloth.

[2] 'A furnished apartment'.

would in the first place climb-up into St Jacques Steeple to take a synoptical Prospect of that monstrous City, to consider the Situation, extent, and Approaches; so as to be the better able to make Comparisons with our London; which you will do with pleasure, by imagining it extended to a Length which you will find in a Circle.[1]

The principall Places where Persons of Quality dwell are in the Sub-urbs, especially that of St Germains, and in that the Abbey, an old Foundation, but nothing much remarkable in it. But the Hospital of *La Charité* is worthy your seeing, for the worthy Charity which is every day there exercis'd in so full, so cleanly and devout a manner, as must needs much affect you; especially when you shall have seen the rest of those admirable Foundations, among which you must not forget the *Hostel-Dieu* near *Notre-dame*, though it be not altogether so neat and comp[ac]t; yet for the Number and manner of it, very considerable.

There are diverse noble Houses in these Fauxbourgs; but none comparable to that of

Luxembourg call'd *le Palais d'Orleans*; which for the Fabrick and Garden (now I hear much neglected since the Decease of the best Gardiner in the World, the Duke) is exceedingly worthy your frequent Visite. Consider the Building well, and the Extent of the Ground about it, as within so great a City; The Fountains, Walks, Eminency on which it stands; and you will judge it almost as fine as Clarendon-House, whose situation somewhat resembles it. The Duke's Library and Gallery well furnish'd with Books, and incomparable Medals (of which he was the most knowing and curious Person in Europ) together with the Gallery painted by the Hand of Rubens (so as we have none in England, and therefore our Painters know not what belongs to Historical Works) will exceedingly please You, if these Curiosities remain still in the Lustre they did at my Sojourn there.[2]

In the City, the first Place of note is the Louvre, or Court of that Great Monarch. The Galleries, *Salle* of Antiquities, Printing-house, *Monnoye*,[3] Gardens of the Thuilleries, Furniture, Architecture, and ten thousand Particulars will take you up a good time here. Besides that you ought to kiss the King and Queen's Hands; to see some publick Audience; Observe his Table, his Guard, Council, and what else will be suggested to you by your Conductor. As you go to Court, you will pass over *Pont-neuf*, and wish ours of London had no more Houses upon it, but instead thereof a Statue, such as you will there find erected, the Work of the famous Giovanni de Bologna, greatly esteem'd.[4] At the foot of this Bridge (for the River is not considerable) there was a Water-work called the *Samaritaine*, and in my time such a curious and rich Piece of Artificial Rock-Work, as was hardly to be seen in Europ. But the

---

[1] See E's *The State of France* (1652), quoted in de Beer (1955, III, 637–8).
[2] E's diary, 1 April 1644 (de Beer, II, 128–31).
[3] Mint.
[4] Of Henri IV; see also E's diary, 24 December 1643, and below, p.74, note 1.

curious Person that then was Master of it, is since many years dead, and perhaps the Rock demolish'd and sold: It is but asking the Question. However one would see the Machine.[1]

Notre-Dame is the Chief Church of Paris, built (as Tradition goes) by the English, but infinitely inferiour to St Pauls, or Westminster. You will do well to consider it, if the Giant at the Entry do not forbid you.[2] There are some Pictures in it considerable.

Near this is the *Pont au Change*, which though but short, is for the uniformity of the Houses and Bass-relieve of Brass at the front of it, pretty in perspective.

You will be much entertain'd in visiting the several Convents of the <Orders of Fryers and other Religious Men: One would therefore see the>[3] Convents of the Franciscans, Capucines, Fathers of the Oratory, and above all the Jesuites, both that of the Novitiate in the Suburbs near Luxembourg, for the trueness of the Architecture, and though plain, yet very excellent and that of St Louis, more splendid and costly. And you must not only behold the Outside, but procure Admission within to see their manner of living, which will bee wholly new to You; especially that of the Carthusians, which I conjure you not to omit; and to visit likewise a Nunnery or two, not forgetting Sion, and the Monument of Sir Samuel Tukes's Lady.[4]

When among the several Churches and Oratories you shall have once contemplated the *Val de Grace*, your Eyes will never desire to behold a more accomplished Piece.[5] There it is you will see the utmost effects of good Architecture and Painting, and heartily wish such another stood where once St Pauls was, the boast of our Metropolis; for than this, you will never see a more noble (though not great Fabrick;) the Co[n]vent and other Buildings about it are very compleat, especially the Carmes over against it.

After the Churches and Hospitals, remember the University, particularly the Sorbonne: The Schools are a plain Building, but the Church is a noble Structure, and the melancholy Situation of it within the Court, has some what (methinks) of particular in it, which affects me. Here, be sure to be at some publick Scholastical Exercise, and love our owne Universitys the better after it.

There is *le College des quatre Langues* founded by Cardinal Mazarin, but not yet finish'd, worthy your Enquiry after: And if his Majesty have done any thing for the Virtuosi (our Emulators) in designing <them> a Mathematical College, seek after it, and procure to be admitted into their present Assembly, that you may render our Society an Account of their Proceeding. You will

---

[1] It depicted the Samarian woman washing Christ's feet. See de Beer (II, 93, note 3).

[2] Perhaps the 'huge Colosse of St Christopher' (diary, 24 December 1643).

[3] Insertion in E's hand. Further insertions by E are indicated <> and not foot-noted.

[4] His first wife, Mary, née Guldeford. She had died in Paris in 1666.

[5] Built 1645–66 (de Beer, I, 84, note 1). Evelyn could not have seen it.

easily obtain that by the assistance of some Friend: But Mr Oldenburg being in the Country, (for I went to his House) you will miss of an infallible Address.

Now you must be sure to be early at some famous Aacdemy to see the Gentlemen ride the Great Horse, and their other Exercises, that you may be astonish'd a great Kingdom as ours, and so great a City as London, should not afford one *Cavalerizio* for the noblest Institution of Youth; there being so many in Paris, and in almost all the considerable Citys of France, which daily ride near an hundred managed Horses.

When you visit *le Palais Cardinal*, You will find many things worth your seeing, especially the Galeries and the Paintings; the King and Queen's Bathing-Rooms, Chambers of Audience; Theater for the Comedies, Gardens, and near it Cardinal Mazarin's Palace, at my being in Paris, and in his Life-time, doubtless the most richly furnish'd in the World.

I suppose the Library is yet extant: You must by all means see it, as one of the most considerable things in Paris <but the King has a Library well worth your seeing near Monsieur Colbert's house>. But what is of greater Antiquity, and to be reverenc'd for being so, is, the *Abbey de St Victoire* whose Bibliotheque is very remarkable. But infinite are the Collections of rare Books, Pictures, Statues, Curiositys etc, which the Noblemen and many private Persons have in Paris; which daily augmenting and diminishing, according to the genius of the Possessors of them, you must enquire after upon the Place, and procure means of seeing: For which I transmit you the 3 Enclos'd Letters to Friends of mine (though of the lower Rank) who will abundantly satisfy your Curiosity; and you will do well to purchase of them what they have of most rare of their own Works, as well Books as Tailles-Douces; the One being the most famous Artist for things in Graving with the Burin, and the other in Etching. Monsieur Du Bosse's Books of Architecture and Perspective etc are worthy your Collections.[1] And if you stayd so long to have your Lady's and your own Pictures engraven by le Chevalier de Nanteuille you would bring home Jewels not to be parallel'd by any Mortal at present, and perhaps by none hereafter. He is the greatest Man that ever handl'd the Graver, and besides, he is a Scholar and a well-bred Person.[2] And Monsieur Du Bosse (the other) is a plain, honest, worthy, and intelligent good man; both my Singular Friends and Correspondents for those Matters of Art etc.

The King's medicinal Garden and Laboratory with all the Apparatus, is at no hand to be omitted, because it is so well furnish'd and so rarely fitted for the Design, as having all the affections of Ground and Situation desirable. If you stayd a whole Winter in Paris, I would invite you to see a Course of Chimistry, which is both there and in several private Places shew'd to the Curious to their wonderful satisfaction and Benefit of Philosophic Spirits.

---

[1] E had Abraham du Bosse's *Maniere Universelle de Mr Desargues...* (1648). This and others by him in E's possession are now at the British Library (Eve.a.114–6).
[2] He had engraved portraits of E, his wife, and parents-in-law (diary, 13 June 1650).

Near to this is the *Gobelins*, where was wont to be the Manufacture of Tapestry; pray enquire it out most diligently, and by no means omit the visiting of all those Particulars; no, not Monsieur Colbert's late Silk-Worm-Work, or whatever there be of that Nature. <At these *Gobelins* are all the King's Manufactures: Pray therefore visit it most studiously.>

You must likewise see the *Hostel de Ville*, being their Guild-Hall, the *Palais* (which is their Exchange) and there the Hall of Justice; answerable to ours of Westminster, neater, but not so large, especially the Parliament-Chamber, and other Tribunals, which you will find to be much more august and splendid than most of ours. Here you will take notice of the Habits of their Advocates and Men at Law, and be curious to hear a Pleading, as well as a Masse and other Ceremomies at some of the Churches, that you may love your own Religion the better.

The *Place Royal* is our Piazza of Covent-Garden; but in my judgement nothing so chearful. The Brazen Horse in it is considerable.

By some especial Favour you may be admitted to take a View of the Bastille (which is their Tower) and Arsenal joyning to it. There you will see in what Equipage for Strength they are; for there they cast their great Guns, and there is the Repository of Stores. There are many noble Houses and pretty Oratories here-about, especially St Louis belonging to the Jesuites, with a Noble Frontispice.

For once you would be at the Preach at Charenton, and for once see a publick Comedy at *l'Hostel de Bourgogne*, and even the Mad-men at the *Petites-Maisons*: For all these Places and Humours are instructive; but none more *Divertissant* than the Mountebanks and prodigious Concourse of Mankind *au Pont-Neuf*,[1] which I would therefore have you frequently to traverse, and contemplate, as a lively Image of that Mercurial Nation.

In the *St Chappel* are some Reliques[2] which you may also see, when you are at the *Palais*; and be sure to bring home with you some good French Books, which you will encounter in you visiting their Shops.

The *Cours* you should likewise see, to compare it with our Assemblys of Gallants and Faire Ladys at Hide-Park: And then I know not what to say more; for by this time you will be willing to take some air perhaps abroad, and make a Journey about the Town, to see how they live in the Countrey, and how they make their Wine (for the Vintage almost meets you) among their Villa's. The Places I recommend to your view are chiefly,

St Cloud, those noble Gardens, where you will kiss the Hand of Madame la Duchesse d'Orleans.[3] Ruel, formerly a most elegant Villa.[4] *St Germain-en-Laye*, one of the King's Countrey-Houses, nobly situated, and where there

---

[1] 'Possessd by Montebankes, Operators and Puppet Players' (diary, 3 February 1644).

[2] The 'almost intyre Crowne of Thornes' (diary, 3 February 1644).

[3] Henrietta Anne (1644–70), sister of Charles II.

[4] Richlieu's villa at, correctly, Rueil (diary, 27 February 1644).

were the most Artificial Water-Works and Grotts in France, now I hear run exceedingly to decay. *Maisons* in my poor Judgment for the Architecture, Situation, cutt into the River, Forest, Gardens, Stables, etc, one of the most accomplish'd and sweet Abodes that ever I saw: But it is not perfect. Madrid is not very considerable; but one *Appartment* at Bois St Vincennes is worth your view, with the Park; of which you will find none comparable to ours in England. St Denys, I suppose, you might see in your Journey going or returning; and there, besides a venerable Church, the Dormitory of the French Kings, a Treasury of Reliques emulating even that of our Lady's of Loretto, and you must not omit it.

I would have you also make a step to Arcueil, which Mary of Medicis built for an Aquæduct; because it will furnish you with an Idea what those stupendious structures were extended to many miles, and of greater Altitude only.

Chantilly, Melun, Verneuil, Monceaux, Villers Cotteret, Limours, Bois le Vicomte,[1] Bisestre, an Hospital, are Countrey-Palaces and Gardens of great Fame, if your time serve you may do well to visit. <Many of these Places will be too far for you.> But at no hand must you forget to take a th[o]rough Survey of their renowned Fontainebleau; which when you have seen you will not judge comparable to Hampton-Court; nor can the French Monarch shew such a Castle, Palace, and Church, as our Windsor in all his wide Dominions. Yet here the Canal, and plenty of Water, with the Forest <about it> is stupendious; and there are some good Paintings in the House; but especially that Gallery, the Work of the famous Prima Titia.

Versailles will much please you; and Veau, the House of the late President Fouquet, amaze you for the infinite Cost both in Building and Gardens, august even in its very Ruines, and absence of its magnificent Founder.

I had forgott to acquaint you that the Church-yard of St Innocents in Paris is observable for the Quality of the Earth, which by the innumerable Buryings there, is become Sarcophagus; and there it is you will see the Hieroglyphics of the Philosophie Works of Nicolas Flamel; but in nothing beautifull or considerable.

I should not have so slightly mention'd *les Carmes*, a Church near Val de Grace, because it is most worthy your seeing, and particularly the Tabernacles upon the High Altar.

In the English College of Jesuites, Clermont, you will see the Systems of Copernicus, and the new Astronomers, moved by Water; For the rest, the Place is nothing observable.

Sir, Had I anything more to add, I should weary you; it is already late, and I almost blind: So as I am perfectly asham'd at my wretched Character.

J E[2]

---

[1] Sic; Michael Hunter (pers. comm.) points out this is a mistake for Vaux-le-Vicomte.
[2] P adds here further notes (in French) on Paris following his nephew's 1698 visit.

A29. SAMUEL PEPYS TO JOHN EVELYN[1]

On the death of Mrs Pepys

Mr Evelyn

Navy Office
2 November 1669[2]

Sir,

I begge you to beleive that I would not have beene ten daies returned into England without waiting on you,[3] had it not pleased God to afflict mee by the sickness of my wife, who, from the first day of her coming back into London,[4] hath layne under a fever soe severe as at this houre to render her recoverey desperate. Which affliction hath very much unfitted mee for those acts of civillitie and respect which, amongst the first of my friends, I should have paid to yourselfe, as hee to whome singly I owe the much greater part of the satisfaction I have met with in my late voyage. Next to you, I have my acknowledgements to make to Sir Samuel Tuke; to whome (when in a condition of doeing it) I shall beg your introducing mee, for the owneing of my obligations to him on the like behalfe. But Sir, I beg you heartilie to dispence with the ceremonie, till I am better qualified for paying it; and in the meane time receive the enclosed, which I should with much more satisfaction have delivered with my owne hands.

I am, Sir,
Your most obliged and obedient Servant,
SPepys

I most humbly kiss your ladies hands, and pray my service be presented to Sir Richard Browne.[5]

---

[1] Source: BL Upcott Antiquaries II. Endorsed by E, 'Mr Pepys 2 November Navy Office'.

[2] MS: 'Navy Office November 2 1669'.

[3] MS: 'without waiting on you' inserted.

[4] Elizabeth Pepys. She had been taken ill in Flanders while travelling with her husband in autumn 1669. She died on 10 November. The funeral took place on 13 November at St Olave's, Hart Street, where her monument remains. E attended the funeral and noted the fact in his diary entry for 14 November.

[5] A letter from P to Richard Browne, dated 26 March 1670, is at BL Up AnII. It was published by Braybrooke in 1825, and is included in various other editions, and that of Howarth (no. 36).

2 The 1670s

The letters from the 1670s are relatively few in number compared to the other decades. Although this might just be the result of chance, Evelyn's apparent reticence may in part have been due to his intense spiritual friendship with Margaret Blagge, afterwards Mrs Godolphin. This was manifested in a series of regular meetings between Evelyn and her which dominated his life for much of the 1670s until her death in 1678. The friendship was explored in some detail by W.G. Hiscock (1951) but it remains the most enigmatic episode in Evelyn's life.

On 16 May 1675 Margaret Blagge married Sidney Godolphin. Evelyn was kept unaware of the event, which suggests that his relationship with her had become one which she found overwhelming. When Evelyn discovered what had happened in April the following year he was bewildered by what he interpreted as an incomprehensible act of betrayal. It is sad that we have no idea what Pepys thought of the friendship.

During the early part of the 1670s Evelyn and Pepys were professionally involved with another Dutch War, Evelyn as a commissioner for sick and wounded seamen again and Pepys as Secretary of the Admiralty (from mid-1673). The subject matter of most of the letters is therefore similar to those of the 1660s. An additional letter, addressed to the Navy Commissioners and Pepys, is included in Appendix 1.

Pepys was moving towards the climax of his career. He entered Parliament in 1673 and also became Master of Trinity House and a governor of Christ's Hospital. Evelyn's star was perhaps a little on the wane. His prolific literary output of the 1660s was not repeated. However, in 1670, at the request of the King, he did embark on extensive research for a history of naval power and the Dutch Wars designed to demonstrate England's natural supremacy. Intended as a blatantly anti-Dutch treatise its purpose had expired when the end of the Third Dutch War came in 1674 and only its preface, *Navigation and Commerce*, was published. To Evelyn's annoyance it was rapidly suppressed to avoid causing offence to the new allies. However it is evident from the content of a number of his letters in the 1680s that he had already accumulated a substantial amount of background material.

It seems likely that both men had too many distractions, personal and professional, to engage in regular correspondence. However, the possibility remains that this period is one from which little has survived. The decade ended with a bitter blow for Pepys who was forced to resign his Secretaryship of the Admiralty. Evelyn's unswerving loyalty to him marked a pivotal point in their relationship, setting the tone for the next 23 years.

B1. SAMUEL PEPYS TO JOHN EVELYN[1]

A favour and a promise of money

Friday morning at Mrs Turner's[2]
17 February 1672[3]

Sir

to supply my not wayteing on you (which truly I purposed, when I first thought of comeing hither) give mee leave to tell you this way, that I have made provision for paying you the Sum you expect.[4] Soe as if you shall please to send your receipt upon Sir Dennis Gaudin's letter on Monday morning next to mee or in my absence to my servant Will Hewer your messenger shall bring you the Mony. I kisse my Lady's hands and Sir Richards[5] and am

Your most obedient and affectionate
Friday morning   Servant
at Mrs Turner's   S Pepys

Pray do not thinke it to arise from any value I putt upon this small cast[6] of my Office (for I'm allready pay'd for all I can ever hope to serve you in) that I adde this Postscript to bespeake your suffering mee to name a Person whom I can with all assurance recommend to your Service at Deale, when the businesse of Sick and Wounded comes to a settlement.[7] But not to interrupt you if otherwise præ-engaged.

---

[1] Source: BL.1082. Endorsed by E, 'Mr Pepys 17 Feb 1671/2.'

[2] This is Mrs Elizabeth Turner, wife of the Deptford storekeeper Thomas Turner (see below 27 February 1679, **B12**). P socialised with her throughout the diary period, and enjoyed casual sexual relations (diary, 20 September 1668). He thought her husband 'silly' (ibid, 31 January 1667). She lived in Deptford and P corresponded with her there (for example, NMM LBK/8, 702, 23 February 1675), and stayed with her. It is clear that P is apologising for not calling on E despite being in the vicinity.

[3] MS: 'Friday morning at Mrs Turner's [at end of letter]/17 February 1672'. The 17th was a Saturday. Presumably, therefore, the letter which bears both the date and the day must have been begun on Friday and finished or posted on Saturday; or, the date is wrong and was written on the 16th. The 17 February 1673 was a Monday (1672 having been a leap year) making it unlikely that the date given here means 1672/3.

[4] The money will probably either have been in connection with sick and wounded seamen, or related to property leases concerning Gauden's victualling premises and Evelyn's estate, both of which were adjacent to the Deptford dockyard.

[5] A letter from P to Sir Richard Browne of 'Feb. 1672' is recorded in the Davey Catalogue, Item 2897, concerning a new repository for royal papers at Trinity House.

[6] P means that he holds in little regard the power of his badge of office.

[7] If there was a response from E, it has gone unrecorded.

B2. JOHN EVELYN TO SAMUEL PEPYS[1]

Poore Creatures stark naked and mortified

For Samuel Pepys Esqr
Cleark of the Acts, and
one of the principall Officers
of his Majesties Navy at
the Navy Office:

Rochester
27 August 1672[2]
10 at night:

Sir,

I suppose you have ben told of a greate deale of noise that was made at
Gravesend when the Commissioners (your Colleagues) pass'd by: But they
could not informe you, how difficult a thing it will allwayes be, to quarter 800
people in a towne that can hold but 500, and where we had neere 200 before:
But this is the condition of Gravesend, and Mr Pearse the Chirurgion Generall
had advertisement of it: I came hither on Sonday,[3] and found not a man but
was decently quarterd, or provided for; nor has there ben dead above 5 of all
this number, whereof 2 were brought dead out of the Vessell, and maliciously
exposd in the Streete to improve the Clamor, which will never be appeas'd till
monye be sent, to discharge the arreares, notwithstanding that I have engagd
my selfe for no inconsiderable sum: I have ben visiting Chatham, Rochester,
and the Fleete and put all things in perfect order, save my selfe who have
never ben in bed since Saturday last:[4] But when all imaginable care is taken,
as to our part, unlesse you be pleasd to allow some Covering to the poore
Creatures, who are (many of them) put stark naked and mortified, on the
shore: multitudes of them must perish; and therefore (presuming on your
Charity, and indeede humanity) I have adventur'd to give way, that some of
the most miserable should have shirts or stockings (according to their needes)
to preserve them from perishing; and I do by these, beg of you, to Order your
Slope Sellers[5] to send a Competent number of such necessaries to our

---

[1] Source: PRO S.P.29/328, f.114. Endorsed by P, '27 August 72 Esqr Evelin shewes
the great want of necessaryes for the wounded and sick men put on board.' Bears a
visible posting mark 'AV/28' for 28 August in the form described on p.261, note 1.
[2] MS: 'Rochester. 27 Aug:–72'.
[3] 25 August. E's diary entry for that day includes, 'I was sent for to Gravesend, to
dispose of no fewer than 800 sick men etc:...'
[4] Three days before, Saturday 24 August.
[5] 'Slope' = 'slop', ready-made but substandard seamens' clothing supplied from

Deputies at Gravesend and Rochester: or to any other Person, whom you shall think fit to trust: That his Majestie may not loose his Subjects for want of so slight, and yet necessary supply: I do assure you Sir This is a very material thing, and therefore I do againe implore you to take it to heart: We have neere 2200 sick people in quarters in this province, amongst which divers are sadly ulcerated for want of cloathes and change: Such as are in any tollerable Condition, a few daies will perfect, though at present every tide increases the numbers: But those cursed people of Gravesend have no bowells and sweare they will receive not a man more, till their arears are discharg'd: We are above £2000 indebted in Kent, where our daily charge is £100 per diem for quarter onely; Judge by this how comfortable a station I am in, and whither all this clamor, has ben comparable to the occasions of the poore Inhabitants who give us Credit:[1] But enough of this, from Sir

I beseech you remember the Sloope[2] etc   Your most humble and
                                               faithfull Servant JEvelyn:

[N.B. see Evelyn's letter to the Navy Commissioners and Pepys of 12 June 1673 (Appendix 1, no. 4) and news from Gravesend (Appendix 1, no. 5) which show that over the succeeding year no improvement in conditions occurred at all.]

---

stores. P also uses the term, for example, 'the business of Slopps, wherein the seaman is so much abused by the pursers' (P's diary, 16 March 1663). Marburg (her M19) misread this term as the meaningless 'Shop Tellers'.

[1] E also wrote to Brouncker on his return from Rochester to describe the situation, '... I do againe fore-see, that not onely these but in severall other places under my Inspection, there will be Clamors, and perhaps real exposures of our sick flock without my power to remedy, 'til I have monyes assign'd me sufficient to discharge the greate Arreares owing in all those places, and for the carrying-on that chargeable service: I am at present £3000 indebted to miserably poore people, and have neere 3000 sick Creatures dispers'd amongst them; the Charge of whose reception being (without computing Sallaries to Chirurgions and other officers) £150 per diem (nor reckoning what the numbers are in the North, under Sir William D'Oylies care, which I think exceedes it) is not to be supported with a bare £1000, which is realy, the onely summ, which he and I have receiv'd, since the 21 of July last, and £2000 now assign'd us last Saturday, but of which we have not as yet touch'd one peny: I had the honor to serve his Majestie during 3 yeares of the Late War, and amidst many difficulties of the Contagion (as your Lordship knows) without reproch; which made me not un-willing to undertake this: but, if any man (who has better Credit than I have in Kent) will undertake to quarter 1000 men in Gravesend, and in those Circumstances of the 800, lately put to shore there, without monyes to discharge arreares already due, I will cherefully resigne him my Commission:...' (2 September 1672; PRO S.P. 29/328, f.140).

[2] Sic, = 'Slope' for 'Slop'. See p.79, note 5.

B3. JOHN EVELYN TO SAMUEL PEPYS[1]

Absconders from the fleet

For Samuell Pepys Esqr etc:
One of the Principall
Officers of his Majesties
Navy at the Navy-Office:

Star Chamber
20 September 1672[2]

Sir,

The Letter directed by your Board to the Commissioners for Sick and Wounded,[3] I shall take care to communicate to all my absent Breathren; and have in the meane time, sent it to the severall Ports; and Places within my precincts, with expresse Order to our Officers, that they do immediately set upon the Worke, and transmitt to you the effects of their dilligence with all expedition, beginning with those ships specified in the margent: There is no question but there will be many found to have faild of their duty in returning to the Fleete,[4] not-withstanding all the Care which could be apply'd to prevent it; and that it will cost some time to methodize the Lists as you are pleas'd to direct, but it shall be hastned with all the speede which may be from

Sir,
Your most humble and
faithfull Servant
JEvelyn:

---

[1] Source: PRO S.P.29/329, f.33. Endorsed by P, '20th Septr 72 Starr Chamb Esqr Evelin shall take care of directing the fee for the sick and wounded Commissioners and has in the interim sent it to all the Ports and places in his Precincts who will take care it bee obserbed'.
[2] MS: 'Star-chambr: 20th:Sepr: –72.'
[3] Not identified.
[4] E had been dealing with returning men who had recovered to the fleet earlier in the month (diary, 1 September 1672) but thereafter makes little detailed reference to anything other than his social activities for the rest of the month.

B4. JOHN EVELYN TO SAMUEL PEPYS[1]

In perpetual drudgery

For Samuell Pepys Esqr
One of the Principall Officers
of his Majesties Navy etc at the Navy-Office:

Star Chamber
7 October 1672[2]

Sir,

I received the letter[3] which was your reiterated exception, that the lists transmitted to your board from severall of our districts were not subscrib'd by the respective Deputies: In your first Instructions to us, that particular was not (as I remember), mentiond; and as soone as you were pleasd to renewe your directions; I tooke care that the Officers within my Circle should not omitt it: It is true, they have not as yet, all of them, dispatch'd what you desire: but it has not ben for want of all imaginable incitement, and which I have againe renew'd: You may please to call to mind, that you rejected that of Chatham and Feversham (which were the most considerable in my Circle) upon account of another omission, which they are now rectifying, and I do every moment expect it, together with that of Gravesend: In the meane time, as to those which came lately to you from Sir William Doylies District, I am very well assur'd that they are Authentique, being accompanied with the Letters of his Agents in those parts, whose hands we are acquainted withall; If your commands be positive, that I should returne them back againe for their subscription onely, It will require time; but if you shall be pleased to dispence with that omission, (upon my presumption that Sir William Doyly dos owne them) there neede be no interruption in your proceeding to pay-off the men: In all events, I am writing to Sir William, and shall advertise him of it –

Sir, I am oblig'd to write to you in the singular number, there being onely my selfe in Towne of the rest of my Collegues, to my very greate trouble: I had else made a journey my selfe to have set all this right in my quarters long before this time; and my Solicitude for monye (being indebted at Chatham alone neere £4000, besides what is owing in five or six other places) keepes me in perpetual drudgery: But, I hope you will receive all Satisfaction as to what you require about the Lists in a very few dayes. I remaine

Sir, Your most humble Servant
JEvelyn:

---

[1] Source: PRO S.P.29/329, f.94. Endorsed by P, '7.8.72 Star Chamber Esqr Evelin about his agents sending the account of sick and wounded.'

[2] MS: 'Star-chambr:7:8br:–72'.

[3] Unknown, but may be that mentioned in the previous letter (p.81, note 3).

B5. SAMUEL PEPYS TO JOHN EVELYN[1]

An invitation to the Admiralty

Whitehall
29 August 1673[2]

The Lords Commissioners of the Admiralty[3] meeting to morrow morning at the Robes Chamber,[4] I am Commanded by their Lordships to desire you to attend them there about 9 of the Clocke,[5] remaining

Your humble Servant
S P[6]

---

[1] Source: PL 2849.98 (P's copy). Endorsed, 'To attend the Lords'.

[2] MS: 'W.hall 29 Aug.73. Evelin Esq'. Marburg gives 9 August for this letter, having apparently mistaken the numeral '2' for a hyphen. The letter is catalogued as 29 August in the Pepysian Library. However, in his diary, E notes a visit to the Commissioners of the Admiralty 'about buisinesse' for 6 August 1673, and again on the 15th. The 30 August was a Saturday but E makes no reference to a meeting that day. He does, however, refer to such a meeting on Saturday, 6 September. It is quite possible that the diary entry is wrong and he means the previous Saturday. An indication of the business may be found in E's letter to the Navy Commissioners of 12 June 1673 (Appendix 1, no. 4).

[3] The Earls of Shaftesbury and Arlington, Sir George Carteret, and Henry, Baron Coventry (as listed in a copy-letter of 29 August 1673 at PL.2849.98). The Admiralty had been transferred to the control of commissioners on 9 July 1673 following the Duke of York's resignation as Lord High Admiral on 15 June.

[4] From 1669 at the old Savoy Palace. A hospital in the palace, founded in 1556 by Queen Mary (renewing an earlier one founded by Henry VII), had been used intermittently to house wounded soldiers and sailors. It was again in 1675.

[5] The preceding copy-letter, also dated 29 August 1673, summons the 'Victuallers' to attend the Lords of the Admiralty at exactly the same place and time 'in order to the discoursing you, about the Victualling the Fleete'.

[6] P had, in mid-June 1673, been promoted to Secretaryship of the Admiralty.

B6. JOHN EVELYN TO SAMUEL PEPYS[1]

Evelyn faces incredible difficulties

Deptford
4 September 1673[2]

Sir,

Since my Last to you of yesterday,[3] the numbers of our Sick are so exorbitant, that even at this place, there are no lesse than 400 already cast upon us: a greate part of which the Alle,[4] and Victualling houses refuse to take in, because the Arreares are so greate, but those of Gravesend where pester is most,[5] are sent up hither upon absolute necessity, 'till my Lord Vaughan's Regiment make roome for them, which, I therefore beg of you to presse; and, as to this place, (where I foresee I shall else be put to incredible difficulties, and to give countenance to the Employment) I intreate you to impower me, (or Deputy), to charge the Connestables with providing us quarters, in such houses of publique reception, as in all other places under my Care, the Lords of the Councill have already don, to the respective Mayors, Connestables and other Officers; but which I have not for Deptford Towne, Greenewich nor neerer than Gravesend; because we had no regular establishment in them, as now (I feare) we shall, be forc'd to settle; unlesse this greate Arreares were in some measure satisfied, that the other capacious Townes might be more able and willing to receive our men, and releeve us, who are at present so oppress'd,

---

[1] Source: Princeton University Library (Robert H. Taylor Collection). Endorsed by E, 'To Mr Pepys: Secretary to the Admiralty: Copy of my Last concerning the numbers of Sick, and Arreere 4th:7br:–73'. The letter is a loose draft (that it is a draft rather than a 'copy' is evident from the textual alterations), probably once in the Evelyn archive. It first appeared on the open market in a Maggs of London 1932 catalogue, and was previously unknown. Very few letters-sent of this period from E to P survive, a strange contrast with the substantial number in official records on the same subject from the 1660s. The letter is reproduced in this book on p.4 by permission of Princeton University Library.

[2] MS: 'Deptford 4th:Sepr:–73'. Despite the urgent nature of this letter it is interesting to note that E's sole entry for the first five days of September is a note that Margaret Blagge (later Mrs Godolphin) had come to stay.

[3] Not known.

[4] = 'Ale', i.e. 'Alehouses and Victualling Houses', see OED 'victualling-house'.

[5] Marginal insertion: 'wh[ere] pester is most'. 'Pester' = overcrowding.

and consequently like to grow more clamorous and troublesome, as neerer to his Majestie and the Court:

Sir, if such a Warrant may be order'd this Bearer, sign'd by the Lords Commissioners I shall know how to act on it and govern my selfe[1], that the poore men may not lye in the streetes: Upon Saturday next, I shall waite upon you, and receive their Lordships farther Commands;[2] my being here is in the meane time, very necessary, but a speedy supply of monyes absolut:[3]

Sir, I remaine
Your most faithfull,
and most humble Servant
JEvelyn:

I received 4 Letters[4] last night from out of Kent; and compute our numbers of Sick (sent on Shore already) neere 3000 ————: the like was never during the former Warr.[5]

---

[1] Marginal insert: 'on it and govern my selfe'.

[2] On Saturday, 6 September, E met with the Commissioners of the Admiralty (diary).

[3] On 15 September E was granted £4000 from the Lord High Treasurer 'and rectified divers matters, about the sick and wounded' (diary; from Sir Thomas Osborne, but see de Beer, IV, 24, n. 2).

[4] From the various ports. These letters could not be identified amongst those in the BL Evelyn Sick and Wounded folders (I–III) which are individual reports by E's assistants and colleagues. There is something of a gap for the month of September 1673, not perhaps surprising considering the present location of this MS, which must at some stage have been amongst the other Sick and Wounded papers. However, an example of the type of letter concerned is included in Appendix 1 (p.312, Robert Birstall to E, 11 June 1673, from Gravesend).

[5] P's letters of 8 September and 15 October 1673 (**B7** and **B8**) make no reference at all to the contents of this draft. It is possible that P had not received this letter when he wrote to E on 8 September or was too busy to take account of the contents. Equally, it is possible that this draft was in fact never made into a letter to be sent (see above, p.18ff).

B7. **SAMUEL PEPYS TO JOHN EVELYN**[1]

Mr Pierce to see the sick and wounded

Mr Evelyn

[No place]
8 September 1673[2]

Sir

This comes onely to acquaint you that his Majestie haveing directed James
Pierce Esq., Chyrurgeon etc to go down to the Burgess's House in order to the
informing him selfe of the true state of the Sick and wounded men on board
the Fleete, the *Buck Dogge*[3] appointed to attend the businesse of Sick and
Wounded is appointed to carry downe to the Fleete and bring up againe the
said Mr Pierce and there to be at your dispose, In the meanwhile it would not
be amisse to send at present well Men [who][4] are now ready[5] to the Fleete by
her. I remaine

Your most humble Servant
S P

---

[1] Source: PL 2849.118 (P's copy). Labelled by P: 'Acquaint him of the Chyrurgeons
going to the Fleete in the *Buck Dogge* appointed for the sick and wounded business
and thinke it not amisse to send the well Men men [sic] downe with her'. The copy-
letter seems to have been written in haste; it is difficult to read and words are omitted.
[2] MS: '8th:7:73' at foot of letter. Note that Marburg (her M25) erroneously gives
'October'.
[3] This is probably the Dutch vessel *Buck*, captured in 1672 and sold in 1674. It was a
dogh (Dutch = fishing boat), a term which seems to have been anglicised to create a
suitably imposing canine name for the ship.
[4] Not in MS but required to make sense.
[5] Perhaps 'who are not ready' should be assumed as the meaning.

B8. SAMUEL PEPYS TO JOHN EVELYN[1]

A request for the Buck Dogge's *services*

Mr Evelyn

Whitehall
15 October 1673[2]

Sir

This comes only to observe to you, that both by the dayly Lists from the Downes, and by Letters I have this day read from the Commander of the *Buck Dogge:*[3] it doth not appeare that you either have for some time past or are now designeing to make any use of that Vessell: If I am in an error pray rectify me; if otherwise, I shall desire you will let me know it that the Vessell being at Lib[erty][4] from your service, I may[5] make it my care [to][6] see her either usefully employed, on some other part of His Majesties Service, or called in and discharged. I remaine

Your most humble Servant
S.P.

---

[1] Source: BL.1083 (and copy at PL 2849.224). This is the letter-sent. Endorsed by E, 'Mr Pepys concerning the *dogge* Whitehall 15 October 1673'. Copy labelled, 'Desiring to know when the Buck Dogg is at liberty to give service'.

[2] MS: 'Whitehall 15th:Octor:73'.

[3] See note in previous letter.

[4] MS torn – copy supplies.

[5] In the copy-letter 'and attending to my Late, I since' has been struck out (so reading is uncertain) and replaced with 'I may'.

[6] MS torn – copy supplies.

B9. SAMUEL PEPYS TO JOHN EVELYN[1]

Orders to take care of sick soldiers

Mr: Evelyn

Derby House
15 January 1674[2]

Sir,

I have lately received a letter from one of the Officers of the Duke of Albemarle's Regiment from Dover, wherein hee acquaints mee that Severall of the Souldiers of that Regiment Shipped on board the *Marygold* [3] in the Downes, were sick so that they were necessitated to putt them on Shore, and that there being no order for providing for them, your Agent att Dover had att the instance of the Officers taken care for sending them up to convenient quarters. But in regard he had no directions therein from the Commissioners for Sick and wounded Seamen, he did desire that the same orders might be given concerning these Souldiers in the *Marygold*, as was for those in the *Blessing* [4] for the indempnifying your Agent in what he has done. Whereupon I have procured the like order from his Majesty in this Case as was in the former, and send the same to you inclosed.[5] Remaining

Sir: Your very humble Servant.
S.P.

---

[1] Source: PL 2850.37 (copy). Labelled by P in the margin: 'to send Orders to his [E's] Agent at Dover to take care for sick Soldiers'.

[2] MS: 'Derby House 15th Jany. 1673', for 1673/4. Dated to 1673 by Marburg (her M23) but the letter is in the early 1674 sequence in the copy-letter book in the Pepysian Library; moreover P did not date his letters from Derby House until January 1674 (Ollard 1991, 228). The move had become necessary following a fire at the Navy Office in Seething Lane a year before, on 29 January 1673. However, see note 3 below.

[3] The only ship of this name in naval records is the fireship *Marigold*, purchased in 1673. It was, however, reputed to have been destroyed in action in August 1673 (Colledge 1987).

[4] A fireship, purchased in 1673 and expended in 1674 (Colledge 1987).

[5] Apparently not extant. But see Appendix 1, no. 6, for a similar royal order, also to E and now in the Evelyn archive at the British Library. It concerns treatment of soldiers sick with smallpox and, in P's hand, relays royal instructions for their care which is delegated to the commissioners.

B10. SAMUEL PEPYS TO JOHN EVELYN[1]

The pressure of arrears

Derby House
23 January 1674[2]

Sir

Before I durst think it fitt for me to write any thing to Deale to the effect you desired, I thought it expedient to satisfy my selfe from my Brother as particularly as I could, whether the refractorines of the Persons hee complaynes of [3] might not arrise either from the pressure of the arreares due to them for Charges past, or apprehention (by the example of their Neighbours) of the uncertainty of their being better used for what is to come. And as I foresaw, I doe find from him, that this is the ground of that unwillingness with which the poore people there, doe receive any new burthens by the putting upon them as any fresh numbers of Sick Men from the Fleete, which being soe, and led thereto from the reason of the thing, noe less then from the captiousness of the tyme wherein wee now are, I am of opinion, that it is neither fitt with regard to the honour of his Majesties Service, nor the Safety of any of us his Servants, that any thing like Severity or Threates should be used upon any of the Persons complayned of, without good advice and express Order, either from his Majesty or those of his Ministers who are better able, both to advise and justify, what shall be fitt to be determined concerning them. Therefore lett me advise you, not to expect or to depend upon any single interposition from me in the Matter; but consider whether it may not be more advisable, both with regard to your selfe and the efficacy of it to the King's Service, that you make a representation of the Matter to his Majesty or my Lords of the Councill, and receive their Directions for your further proceedings. In which as farr as any Solicitation of myne can be either usefull to the Thing, or gratefull to you, you shall Command

Your most affectionate humble Servant
SPepys

---

[1] Source: BL.1084 (and copy at PL 2850.55–6). Endorsed by E, 'Mr Pepys Derby-house 23 Jan 1674/5' in error (see note 2). Copy labelled, 'about the necessitous condition of the people at Deale with Sick Seamen'.

[2] MS: 'Derby House 23rd Jany 1673/4'. But see E's incorrect endorsement (note 1).

[3] Balthazar St Michel (P's brother-in-law); see Heath (1955, nos. 18 and 19, P's letters to him about this, dated 19 and 23 January 1673/4; MSS at PL.2850.44, 56). St Michel, serving as muster-master at Deal and sub-commissioner for the Sick and Wounded, had written to E.

B11. SAMUEL PEPYS TO JOHN EVELYN[1]

Hopes for Evelyn's son

Derby House
1 March 1677[2]

Sir,

You'l allow one soe much in want as I am of what you soe much abound with, to be sollicitous in the getting all that he can raise any pretence of Right to from you. Therefore, pray remember the notes you shew'd me a Specimen of when last I had the honor of seeing you here.[3] For as full of Parliament-Causes as one would think a Man in my Circumstances should at this time be I have kept roome for the thoughts you are to inspire me with upon the Subject wee then discoursed of, and should have worse born my want of them thus long, but for the Entertainment you then left me with of the most hopeful Gentleman your sonn's preparing.[4] In whose early proofs of his Ingenuity and Stile, I will not now goe about to tell you how much I either value him or congratulate you, but leave it to my next waiting on you.

Your most Faithfull and most humble Servant,
SPepys

---

[1] Source: BL Upcott Antiquaries II. Endorsed by E, 'Mr Pepys. Derby House – 1 Mar 76/7'.
[2] MS: 'Derby House March 1, 1676–7'.
[3] E's last preceding reference in his diary to seeing P is for 26 August 1676.
[4] John Evelyn the younger. His principal talents were as a linguist.

3 The 1680s

The number of letters now known from this decade exceeds one third of the total, with seventeen alone belonging to the years 1685 and 1686. This high proportion should not pass without more detailed comment, and neither should the subject matter which is the most varied of all the correspondence of Pepys and Evelyn. There is a marked transition from the essentially professional nature of the letters of the 1660s and 1670s to subjects of a more personal and intellectual variety. This seems to have contributed to a higher number of letters actually being written in the 1680s, though of course the quantity which survive may be partly a matter of luck.

A glance at the Catalogue (below, pp.300–2) shows that after 1672 there are no more letters in official records, like the State Papers. That leaves the Evelyn archive, Pepys's archives, split amongst the Pepysian Library, the Bodleian Rawlinson manuscripts, and the privately-owned Pepys-Cockerell papers, and letters scattered amongst private and institutional owners. Very few of the letters from the 1680s are represented amongst the Pepys-Cockerell papers, the principal source of Pepys's correspondence for the latter part of his life; in fact there are noticeable gaps in that source between 1680–1, and 1684–90. Most of the letters located for this book from those periods appeared in the remarkable catalogue issued by Samuel Davey in November 1889 (see pp.22–23 above), with a handful reappearing in the Langham Company's catalogue in November 1900. That some of the letters from this source are sequential in date, for example July 1685 to September 1686, suggests that they were obtained as a single bundle. It is probable therefore (but not certain) that they originated in the Pepys-Cockerell papers. Even some of the letters now in the Evelyn archive at the British Library can be identified as manuscripts sold in Davey's catalogue, and were presumably purchased by the Evelyn family at the time. Others have been widely dispersed with the majority now in the United States. Although it has not proved possible to trace all the letters involved, those that have been located, along with the catalogue entries of those that remain 'lost', have made available some of the most memorable sequences in the entire correspondence.

Only eight of the letters of the 1680s are from Pepys though it is evident from the texts that another six at least originally existed, and we may assume that there were once even more than that. The unaccountable presence of Pepys's letter of 19 April 1687 at the Historical Society of Pennsylvania, for example, suggests the wide and early dispersal of some of his letters from the

Evelyn archive, particularly of this period. This is supported by his letter of
4 July 1685 (**C20**), now identified as being to Evelyn on the grounds of
content and a corrected reading of the date. It is bound in isolation in the
Additional Manuscripts at the British Library, having been purchased in 1874.

THE LETTERS

During the 1680s Pepys was the target of a campaign to oust him. It had
developed out of the alleged involvement of his clerk Samuel Atkins in the
Popish Plot. However, it was Pepys's participation in a privateering venture
with Sir Anthony Deane which gave his enemies hard evidence. The ship
which he and Deane had leased from the crown during the Third Dutch War
had, it turned out, also been used to attack English ships. Pepys was
imprisoned from May to July 1679. By mid-1680 the case had been dropped
but his experiences had caused him to give renewed consideration to writing a
history of the navy, something he had been gathering material for since the
1660s. He turned to Evelyn for assistance by sending him detailed questions
about naval history and records.

Evelyn responded with outpourings of historical and classical quotations,
and allusions, gathered together in epic compositions. Evelyn had drawn on his
notes for the abandoned history of the Dutch War and many parallels can be
drawn between the texts of his letters and that of his *Navigation and
Commerce* of 1674. Not only that but he repeated himself in the letters on
occasion, and was apparently oblivious that he had done so. It is a matter of
interest that this should have happened. The parallels are especially obvious
between the letters of 7 July 1680 (**C7**) and 19 September 1682 (**C15**). Evelyn
was particularly fond of accumulating elaborate notes on any subject which he
was researching. On these occasions he had probably used the same set of
notes to write the letters. The subject of naval history recurs sporadically
throughout the 1680s and 1690s.

Naval history was far from being the only learned subject on which Evelyn
expounded. The epic letter of 26 August 1689 (**C47**) was clearly a synthesis of
some of the material he was accumulating for his projected book on medals
(*Numismata*, 1697). The 10 July 1682 (**C14**) letter concerned with the military
prowess of dogs, must surely be one of the most abstruse of the series yet it
had clearly grown out of a conversation between the two. Collectively the
letters are useful records of the minds of virtuosi, their anxiety to collect
knowledge and their attempts to organise it.

By 1680 Evelyn was sixty years old. His public duties were largely over,
apart from a spell as a commissioner of the Privy Seal under James II; even
though he had once been a prolific author he published nothing at all from
1676–90 (in the previous fifteen years he had produced more than sixteen
different works). Much of his reading seems to have been directed towards
Pepys's projected book. Pepys never wrote it despite Evelyn's repeated

encouragements. In the short term this may have been due to Pepys's gradual restoration to his former prestige. He not only participated in the Duke of York's expedition to Scotland in May 1682 but was also despatched to Tangier in August 1683 to supervise the demolition of the harbour mole there.

These episodes are represented in the correspondence, providing a compelling sense of immediacy to contemporary events, especially Evelyn's palpable relief on learning that Pepys had sailed in a different ship to the Duke of York in 1682, thereby escaping shipwreck. Pepys's re-appointment to Secretaryship of the Admiralty in 1684, followed by his election to the Presidency of the Royal Society, not only restored his fortunes but also consolidated his personal status. In the past, particularly in the 1660s, Pepys had looked up to Evelyn; now there was something of a role reversal as Evelyn came to Pepys for favours of influence, provoking another series of letters. There was Frederick Collier, Evelyn's waterman, who wished to avoid naval service and thereby 'enjoy the wife of his youth' as Evelyn so aptly put it on 31 July 1688 (**C41**). The longest sequence of these letters, beginning in late 1685, concerned the promotion of an Edmund Dummer. This should have been relatively straightforward but for the complication that Dummer's wife was engaged in a much-gossiped-about liaison (of the kind Pepys had himself been so frequently a party to in the 1660s) and which Evelyn evidently found amusing.

None of these, however, had the drama of the late summer of 1685. At the end of July Evelyn's second daughter, Elizabeth, eloped with a relative of a navy commissioner in the dockyard next to Sayes Court. Fortunately, in addition to the diary reference, the episode is recorded in three of the most powerful letters he ever wrote (29 and 31 July, and 3 August 1685, **C21–23**). The passion with which Evelyn expressed his feelings is exceptional, marking a relatively unknown side of his personality and one which is certainly barely evident in the diary. His shame and anger exceeded his feelings about Margaret Godolphin's clandestine marriage a decade before (above, p.77). He solicited Pepys's help to apprehend and punish his daughter's accomplices. Elizabeth's death shortly afterwards, also from smallpox, turned a family humiliation into a catastrophe. The letters not only give an indication of Evelyn's temper but also suggest that he was regarded with hostility and disdain by some of his neighbours, who celebrated his humiliation with ill-disguised triumphalism. It is particularly unfortunate that Pepys's replies on the subject are amongst those lost.

Evelyn repaid Pepys with genuinely touching gestures of loyalty (for example, 8 September 1685, **C30**, and 12 December 1688, **C45**). Pepys's imprisonment which followed in 1689 marked the end of his career. Thereafter neither man retained a prominent public role. In the 1690s they increasingly withdrew to their homes, families, and intellectual pursuits, only to be distracted by ill-health and the need to make provision for their descendants.

C1. JOHN EVELYN TO SAMUEL PEPYS[1]

Evelyn encourages Pepys to write

For my honor'd Friend
Samuell Pepys Esqr etc
in Yorke Buildings

Whitehall
30 January after Supper [1680][2]

Sir,

It has ben greatily my hopes, and continualy my Wishes, (from some little hints that I have observ'd sometimes to fall from you) that upon this Recesse especialy, and calme from publique buisinesse; furnish'd as you are with a noble Library; and instructed by the greatest experience, joyn'd to an Industrie and Capacity (beyond any Mortal man that I know) of undertaking so use-full and desir'd a Work; That from *You* the Learned and curious World, might one-day receive that hitherto conceil'd *Arcano del Mar*,[3] with the most consummate perfection and advantage: Sure I am, there is no Subject more worthy your choice, more illustrious for dignitie, and more capacious for the exercising all the parts of Historical, Mathematical, Mechanical; yea, the Critical and politer Learning, than what Lies fairely within the Circle of that Mysterie, and within your ample Sphære – *Macte ergo vir Cl[arissimum]:*[4] and give your Prince, your Country and your Friends a Treasure, which 'tis certaine you have improv'd, and owe, if not to the whole ungratefull World, yet to in-numerable in it, who love and honor you; and by a generosity becoming a better nature, diffuse that good amongst us.

As to Books, and Multitude of Authors, subsidiary to this Attempt; They may possibly serve others (as me they have, and some few smatterers for incouragement and diversion,) whilst You have at once but to Recollect your owne Experiences, and Methodize those rich Materials which I am confident

---

[1] Source: Huntington Library, HM25797 (Davey Catalogue Item 2863). Endorsed by P, 'Janry 30th 1679/80 Mr Evelyn to Mr Pepys, towards the Gen[eral] History of Navigation expected from him, and pressed upon him by Mr Evelyn, with mention alsoe of some relation to the Business of the Navy now discoursed of for himself'.

[2] MS: 'White-hall 30:Jan: after Supper' at foot of letter. Date confirmed by endorsement. E dined with Sir Stephen Fox, recently appointed a Commissioner of the Treasury (diary). He lived in Whitehall near Scotland Yard (de Beer, IV, 179, n. 3). E evidently stayed the night there or nearby for he was present at a service held at Fox's (?) 'house' on the day after next (1 February).

[3] 'The Mystery of the Sea.' Also the title of Robert Dudley's naval compendium.

[4] 'So set to it, eminent fellow!'

you have prepar'd in aboundance, and dispos'd for such a structure: You were lately pleas'd to enquire of me, what Authors I knew, that had treated on this Subject *Data operâ*:[1] It were but to cast a Mite into your opulent stock, should I undertake to enumerate any you have not consulted: In a trifling *Essay* I cursorily made use of some notes, that in my Course of reading, I had transcrib'd into my *Adversaria*;[2] but I cannot call to mind any of importance (antient or modern) after I have nam'd Duke Dudly, Furniere, Marisotus,[3] the late *Architecture Navale* publish'd in French, and that Worke of de Witesen in the Belgic tongue; which I conceive to be the most perfect extant as to the purely Mechanic part:[4] The Historical and Ornamental, which should give grace to the whole, are to be fetch'd from the Philologians, Athenæus, Plinie, Vegetius, Frontinus: and you are not unacquainted with Lazius Baijfius, Czesentias, Meibonius, our Selden, Grotius;[5] nor the Fragments in the *Notitia Imperii*, the Learn'd Bochartus, Simeon Admirandus,[6] his Laws and Ord'nances of the Admiralty, *gli Navigatione di Nearcho*,[7] and the various Tracts *de dominio Maris* to be found all together (as I remember) among the MSS of Mr Selden in the publique Library at Oxford: All the Greeke and Latine Historians contribute to this noble work; especially Herodotus, Thycidides, Polybius, Diodorus, Livy, Justine, Pomponius, Mela, Plutarch, Strabo, the French, Dutch and Spanish Navigations, above all, the English for such Adventures and Exploits as any way concerne the Sea etc: But the greate, and usefull part will be the Mathematical and Mechanical, both for the structure and Government of these stupendious and goodly Machines, together with a Rationale of every particular that concernes a Royal Navy, ships of War, and Onerary[8] Vessels for Trading; Harbour, Moles, Docks, and Magazines, The Admiralty, and other Oficers, with the universal Œconomic belonging in any sort to this Mysterie; of all which you can certainly give the most usefull and distinct Accounts, with what improvements have ben made from all ages, downe to the present, and what are the desideratos wanting to its perfection.

---

[1] 'By producing works'. If the request was in letter form it has not survived.

[2] E's volumes of notes taken from his extensive readings. Now mostly in the British Library (but one also at Houghton, Harvard, MS Eng 992.7).

[3] Sir Robert Dudley, Duke of Northumberland, his *Dell'Arcano del Mare*; Georges Fournière, his *Fortifications, ou Architecture Militaire*, Paris, 1650; and, Claude Barthelemy Morisot (see p.108, note 3).

[4] Possibly Johann de Wit, his textbook on the mathematics of curves.

[5] Lazarus Baif, his *De Re Navali*; Czesentias not identified (including in E's Library Catalogue, BL Eve MS.20a); Meibonius is probably Marcus Maybaum and his edition of Greek authors; Selden's *Mare Clausum* 'The Closed Sea' (1635) was an answer to Grotius' *Mare Liberum* 'The Open Sea' (see also p.110, note 7).

[6] Samuel Bochart, his *Geographia Sacra*(?); Admirandus as Czesentias, note 5.

[7] Flavius Arrianus, 1588. For Nearchus, see p.106, note 3.

[8] Designed to carry loads.

Sir, I wish with all my heart, I could be any ways capable of subserviency in this, or any thing else;[1] I confesse, in reguard that providence has cast my Lot so neere to Zabulon[2] and a Naval Station, I have often wish'd I had ben worthy some inferiour Employment, that might (by this time) have render'd me more fit to Serve you; but it has not ben my good fortune hitherto; and howev[er][3] you may have heard, that I am now a Candidate for some such thing in this Shuffling of the Cards; yet my prospect reaches (I assure you) no farther, than the good wishes of some Friends, who I have heard have mention'd me; but truely, with very slender concerne or importunity of my owne; though I can see no reason why I should reject any honorable Employ, which I might fairely obtaine, without Envy, or reproch; since as to the discharge of such a Trust, as every one had a beginning once; so 'tis possible, an extraordinary application and religious integrity, might perhaps supply the defects of profounder Science; And he that has given Hostages to Fortune, as I have don,[4] cannot, I perswade my selfe be reprov'd by so worthy a Friend, as I esteeme You to be; without whose Counsel and Assistance, I should never hope to Emerge in any Sort: This just Apologie I make to Encounter the Reports which Mr Hewers told me Yesterday went about, as if I aym'd at high matters, and things that I understand not:[5] But of all this, with the frankest Offer of my humble Service in any Capacity within my narrow reach; I shall declare my Thoughts further to you, when I may not importune you, and that you are at any Leisure to Sacrifice so much time to the Impertinences of

Sir, Your most humble and
faithful servant

JEvelyn:

---

[1] Copy-letter (CLBII.409) begins with this sentence and then continues with the opening passage of the letter-sent. Some internal restructuring occurs later to accommodate the change but the text is otherwise broadly similar.

[2] *Matthew* IV.13.15. An area by the sea beyond Jordan. E means that it has been has his lot to have to deal with naval and coastal matters.

[3] MS torn.

[4] Bacon, *Essays* ('Of Marriage and the Single Life'), 'He that hath wife and children hath given hostages to fortune; for they are impediments to great enterprises...'

[5] P (who resigned from the Secretaryship of the Admiralty in May 1679, and was living with Hewer) had long believed that E would make a suitable member of the Navy Board (P's diary, 28 January 1666). In 1680 he may have renewed his attempts to have E appointed. However, this had invoked hostility from unknown quarters that E was seeking status. E's diary gives no clue to the goings-on apart from a cryptic reference to 'special buisinesse' on 18 January. Proceedings against P were still active which may have compromised E by association. E never became a member of the Board, a matter of some regret to him (see below, p.124, 6 December 1681, **C9**). The wording of the suppression of E's book, *Navigation and Commerce*, in 1674, gives a flavour of how E was sometimes regarded (below, p.130, note 3).

C2. SAMUEL PEPYS TO JOHN EVELYN[1]

Pepys to be at full leisure after 4 o'clock

[No place]
31 January 1680[2]

Sir,

Much I ought, and much I would say to you, in answer to your kind transport in yours of last night, and the point more particularly relateing to your selfe in the Close;[3] Wherein I would to God any Service or advice of mine may bee usefull. But an attendance I am now bound upon into London, will not give leave presently to doe it. I shall nevertheless bee at full leisure after 4 a Clocke to wayte on you, and will doe it where-ever you will appoint mee by a word directed to mee at my Lord Privy Seale's in Drury-Lane,[4] where I am under an obligation of dineing to day in company with Mr Povey.[5] I am

Your most affectionate and obedient Servant
SP

To Mr Evelyn

---

[1] Source: Bod MS Rawl. A194, f.135. Copy in P's hand in the bound copy-letter book for 1679–80.
[2] MS: 'Janry 31th 1679/80'. The MS originally read '21' and has been altered by P.
[3] I.e. at the end of the letter.
[4] This is Arthur Annesley, first Earl of Angelsey, 'a grave, serious man' (P's diary, 3 December 1664). In 1667 he had been made Treasurer of the Navy followed by his elevation to Lord Privy Seal in 1672. He was dismissed for his criticism of the government in 1682 (DNB). From 1673–9 he was Admiralty Commissioner (Latham and Matthews, X, 9). He lived in Drury Lane from 1669 until his death in 1686 (Weinreb and Hibbert, 239).
[5] Thomas Povey. He lived at the north-west corner of Lincoln's Inn Fields, not far from Drury Lane. He had held various offices including the treasureship of Tangier and was a close friend of P's. If E and P met that day or shortly afterwards it is not recorded.

C3. JOHN EVELYN TO SAMUEL PEPYS[1]

On behalf of the disconsolate Mr Turner

[No place]
27 February 1680[2]

Sir,

I have to my uttmost endeavour'd to Vindicate, our disconsolate Neighbour Mr Turner[3] befor the Admiraltie, who I find have ben prepossessd to his prejudice by the subdolus[4] undermining of one, who promis'd me with many assiverations[?], that he would never so much as attempt any thing in that nature, and protested he had no other ambition than to serve his Majestie in some more inferiour office, and attend advancement; if I would but do him the kindnesse to recommend him to some friends of mine in the Admiralty, and thinke himselfe the most obliged to me in the world:[5] Since he is taken into place (and by their favour and for my sake), relieved from the very ill circumstances he was in: forgetfull of his promise, he now ungratefully seekes to supplant the good old man: Of this I have loudly complaind, and perhaps displeasd some of them for appearing so zealous, when I plainly told them I should be very sorry any body whom I recommend to them, should tread on my back to get into that Saddle: They Confess'd they had nothing to accuse Mr Turner of, But that of being Superannuated, and are sensible that he is sufficiently capable to sustaine the Charge; and yet are meditating to put this Sycophant over his head; which as I take very hainously from Hosier: so I looke upon as unjust and rigorous in the Commissioners (therefore you ought to interpret in this concerne for the good man, who has ben Master to those who now abandon him, and is yet able to teach the proudest of them: You see I am in some passion upon this account, and cannot forbeare this complaint, and I hope you will joine with me in it, even to his highness the Duke himselfe, who certainely will never suffer so injurious and ungratefull an example, without due resentment: which is all I have to desire of you in his behalfe who am   Yours etc

---

[1] Source: BL CLBI.397. Endorsed by E, 'To Samuell Pepys Esqr' with marginal note 'Late Secretary of the Admiralty'. See note 5 below.

[2] MS: '27 Feb 79'. This copy-letter misdated and misplaced by E; see note 5 below.

[3] Thomas Turner, storekeeper at Deptford dockyard.

[4] Cunning.

[5] Francis Hosier, Clerk of Control at Deptford. A copy-letter from E on his behalf (BL CLBI.396; '16 Feb 79'), addressed to 'Sir Henry Capel... one of the Lords Commissioners of the Admiralty', and Pepys's resignation of his Secretaryship in May 1679 proves that both letters belong to February 1679/80: Capel was not appointed commissioner until April 1679 (diary, 14 July 1679; de Beer, IV, 171, n.2).

C4. JOHN EVELYN TO SAMUEL PEPYS[1]

An offer of help from Evelyn

Sayes Court
15 June 1680[2]

Sir,

It was not 'till Sunday last[3] (for I had been almost an intire weeke before from home) that Mr Holden[4] acquainted me you would be willing to know, where one might finde that *History of the Navy*, which in my Booke of Commerce I speake of as sett forth by Edward 3d:[5] I have as near I could in soe cursorie a Trifle, obtruded nothing upon the Reader, but what I have Authority for, and therefore not to send you to the Reports of suspected writters you may please at your Leasure to Consult the Roll it selfe, as it was lately extant (and doubtless yett is) in the Accompt of his Majesties Great Wardrobe, whereof one William Nowells was the Keeper: The Accompt is from 21th [sic] Aprill in that Princes 18 yeare[6] to the 29th of November of his 21th, and for all those 700 ships 14151 Mariners the whole expense amounted not to above £337000: 9*s*: 4*d*: which is worthy observation; as alsoe that Yarmouth sett forth as many more ships as any Port of England. There is not yett by 400 Vessells, soe Vast a Navy as you will finde this noble Prince to have equipp'd for another expedition, which consisted of *Undecies centum Naves, et cum hoc apparatu, ad humiliandum Francorum factum*[7] (to use my Authors owne words) Thomas Walsingham in his *History*; but the other was for the Seige of Callais, Sir I have noe more to add, but that if I were soe happy as to know wherein I might contribute to any thing which might be of use to your more curious researches, you have ever at your Service

Sir Your most devoted and humble Servant
J Evelyn.

---

[1] Source: PL.2873.53–4, copy in P's hand. Endorsed, 'A Letter from Mr Evelyn to Mr Pepys, in general relation to Navall Matters'. The lost letter-sent (Davey Catalogue Item 2865, and Langham Catalogue Item 568) was endorsed by P, 'resolveing his (the writer's) doubts touching the number of King Edward and his Fleet' (as recorded by the Langham Catalogue entry).

[2] MS: 'Says Court Deptford 15 June 1680'.

[3] Sunday, 13 June. In the diary E states that he had returned home on 8 June.

[4] Richard Holden, vicar of Deptford.

[5] *Navigation and Commerce*, 1674 (paras 31, and 47 – but no mention of a *History*).

[6] In the 18th year of Edward III's reign.

[7] MS: marginal note: '*Anno* 1359'. The Latin means, '[In the year 1359] eleven hundred ships, and thus well-prepared, to the humbling of the French'. Referred to in *Navigation and Commerce*, para 32. From Walsingham's *Historia Anglicana*.

C5. SAMUEL PEPYS TO JOHN EVELYN[1]

Queries for Evelyn

[no place]
25 June 1680[2]

Mr Pepys's Enquiries to Mr Evelyn, and His Answers[3]

Enquiries.

Instances of any Nationall Mistakes, either new or old, whether at home or abroad, in the over-valueing their owne knowledge or Force, or under-valueing those of other Countryes; and may not the ill-success of the Spaniards in 88 bee in some measure chargd upon a Mistake of this Kind in reference to Us, as ours seems to bee at this day in that against the Moores in Barbary?

Instances of any considerable Inventions or particular peeces of Knowledge, whether in Trade, Sciences, or otherwise, wherein We may rightly value ourselves before our Neighbours?

Books of Stratagem and particularly Navall?

Why should other Nations more ancient in their Navall Actions then Wee, bee thought less Inventive and improv'd then Us in the Art of Navigation, While they are found soe much to outdoe us in all other Arts, Viz., Architecture, Painting, etc., and most other parts of Humane Knowledge, whether for use or Pleasure?

Instances of any Defeats anciently given us at Sea, or Invasions made upon our Land by Forreiners from the Roman Conquest upwards to this day; and more especially from the French.

---

[1] Source: Pforzheimer MS 105B. Two copies of these enquiries exist. One copy was retained in the Pepysian Library (PL 2873.61–2) and was the text used by Marburg. This one, in P's hand, seems to have been attached to E's reply in Pepys's library as it bears the title page 'Mr Pepys's Enquiries to Mr Evelyn and His Answers'. The queries, and the protracted reply (7 July 1680, C7), were sold together in the Davey Catalogue (Item 2867). They were purchased then, or later, by Alfred Morrison and disposed of in his sale at Sothebys 1919, Lot 2820. They were acquired by Carl Pforzheimer and are now separately catalogued in that collection as MS 105B and MS 35D.

[2] Marburg supplied the date of 7 July 1680 but overlooked that E's letter of 25 June 1680 (C5; which she transcribed, M30), makes it clear that E has received the 'Enquiries' and will respond to them at length later. This manuscript, the one actually received by E, is dated 25 June 1680.

[3] The manuscript is in a clerk's hand, not P's. This heading appears on the MS.

Who was Genebelli that built the Block-Houses in 88 at Gravesend, and first used the Stratagem about three years before, of Fire-Boats at the Siege of Antwerp?[1]

Who was Henry the 8th's Engeneer in the Castles hee built, and have wee ever had any Considerable Engeneers of our owne Country?[2]

Queen Elizabeths forbidding King Henry the 4th of France to build any new Ships:[3] May not actions of his implying the contrary be instanced in,

Q[uery]: the Records in the Great Wardrobe and Walsingham's words.

The Date and Author of the old Prologue[4]

The History of D[uke] Dudley[5]

And of Gabot[6]

And the Fight at Lepanto[7]

Notable Ignorances of a Nation; Such as the burning of a Bishop[8] for asserting the Antipodes.

---

[1] See p.112, note 2.

[2] See p.112, note 4.

[3] See p.108.

[4] Hakluyt, see p.114, note 3, where Walsingham's words are to be found.

[5] Sir Robert Dudley. See p.95, note 3.

[6] Gabot, or Cabot. See p.113–4, note 7.

[7] See pp.114, and 117.

[8] MS: 'Bpp'.

C6. JOHN EVELYN TO SAMUEL PEPYS[1]

Pepys summoned to a Royal Society meeting

Hon Samuell Pepys Esqr
at Mr Ewer's in York Buildings

Whitehall,
25 June 1680[2]

Sir

I did not intend to have given you this interruption this morning, and therefore did not write any answer to your kind-forbidding me to trouble you this day, when you had so much better Company: but when your Servant was gon, reflecting on the Excuse you injoyne me to make to Sir Joseph Williamson this Evening, I could not forbeare to wish, that (if it were possible) you would give one half-houre of your presence and assistance toward (as I think) the most material Concerne of a Society, which ought not to be dissolv'd for want of a redresse, which is yet certainly in its power;[3] and I would not have it thought, that you therefore absent your-selfe, because in giving a free Suffrage, it may possibly displease Some-one in the Company, that will be brought to no tollerable termes: I do assure-you we shall want some of your Courage and addresse to encourage and carry-on this affaire: You know we do not usually fall on buisinesse 'til pretty Late, in expectation of a fuller Company; and therefore if you decently could fall-in amongst us by 6 or 7, it would (I am sure) infinitely oblige not onely those who meete, but the whole Society.

As to your Quæries, they are of that Substance, as I were immodest to pretend I should at any time (much lesse at present) be able to give you full Satisfaction; But, so soone as I get home (which I hope to do after I have kissd your hands to morrow) and have a little time to rummage my slender Collections; I will endeavor to let you see how exceedingly I am dispos'd to promote any Commands which come from Mr Pepys, to
　　　　　Sir, his most humble Servant
　　　　　JEvelyn:

---

[1] Source: Pierpont Morgan Library MS, no number: 'G[abriel] Wells – March 1919 $185' (formerly Davey Catalogue Item 2866, where erroneously dated the 23rd, and marked in pencil 'Pepys find – 1889). Endorsed by JJ, 'June the 25th 1680. Mr Evelyn to Mr Pepys – about being present at a Committee of the Royal Society, and his answering SP's Quæries to him about the Navigation of England.'

[2] MS: 'White-hall 25 June –80'. They dined the following day (E's diary).

[3] Robert Hooke had proposed that the Royal Society publish a 'philosophical gazette', a kind of fortnightly newsletter for members only, to replace the more substantial *Philosophical Transactions* which had been aimed at a wider audience before it was abandoned in 1679 (see M. Hunter 1989, pp. 197–8).

C7. JOHN EVELYN TO SAMUEL PEPYS[1]

Mr Evelyn to Mr Pepys, in answer to the preceding Queries[2]

Wednesday-night after the Musique
7 July 1680[3]

I will begin this Night (late as it is) to pay Mr Pepys some Tribute, for the losse of his time, in diverting me this afternoone, and when ever I waite upon him, and interrup his more serious affaires:–

To the first Enquiry, a Volume might be compil'd to discover the Mistakes both in under and over-valueing our owne, and others knowledge, force, and Exploits beyond that of other Nations, as far almost as we can deduce the Sea-adventures of former ages from authentique testimonies; and much more might we have knowne, had we the writings of Philo-Romanus the Rhodian (as Suidas makes him) which are perish'd and supplied to us out of the fragments in Cælius Rodoginus and some few others: And as to undertakings upon the opinion of our owne dexteritie and vertue above our neighbours, I do not see that we have much to boast of, at the foote of the reckoning, when we shall have discounted for the mischiefe we have receiv'd, from the first Invasion of the Romans, 'til our shamefull disgrace at Chatham — I neede not tell you what the Saxons, Danes and Normans did but you shall find that none of them ever landed on us with any considerable force, but they carried the whole Iland (if they persisted) unlesse some un-foreseene disaster befell them, which was not in humane power to prevent, such as the storme that dissipated the Spanish Armada more than the so celebrated Fire-ships of Sir Francis Drake; the number otherwise, of Men and Vessels being certainely sufficient for that expedition and design'd attempt; so as we may justly Sing — *Non nobis domine, non nobis*[4] Pray what have we gotten by our late War with the Hollanders, whom Albemarle did so despise; and yet, 'tis certaine, we have

---

[1] Source: Pforzheimer MS 35D (Davey Catalogue Item 2867). Endorsed by JJ, 'July the 7th 1680. Mr Evelyn's Answers to severall Quæries given him by Mr Pepys touching Navigation.' P made a copy (PL.2873.65–89) which differs only in spelling and punctuation. Much was repeated by E in the letter of 19 September 1682 (C15). The wording, anecdotes (for example that about Edgar), and historical facts sometimes so similar, that E clearly wrote both either from the same set of notes or had retained a copy of this letter (not extant) to which he referred. However, it should be noted that the letter of 19 September 1682 exists only as a retained copy-letter and there is a possibility it was never sent to P in the form retained.

[2] This appears at the beginning of P's own copy (see note 1). The letter-sent MS bears '1325', corresponding to the page number (since revised) of P's copy.

[3] MS: 'Wednesday-night after the Musique: July.7.1680'.

[4] 'Not unto us, Lord, not unto us' (Bible: Vulgate, *Psalm* 113.9; Auth. Ver. 115.1).

infinite advantages of Ports and havens, to go-in and refitt: Let us remember, how not onely Carthage, but some little Commonwealths, and Citties in Greece, contested ages[1] the power of almost Universal Monarches; and those who over-ran all the world besides; and that we have not ben Subject to those frequent Invasions of former times, is onely due to the care of those Princes who succeeded the Conqueror,[2] and yet the strength did then consist more in hired Ships, than such as we had built at home, 'til of later ages: Indeede Egbert, and his successors began to furnish them selves with numbers hardly to be credited: Edgar,[3] 'tis said, had a Navy of neere 4000; but after all the Danes began their Expedition but with 35 ships, and after with 84 with which they infested our Coasts neere 200 yeares, 'til Egelred ord[e]red that every 300 hide of Land should set-forth a ship, which amounted indeede to a numerous but unsuccessful Fleete:[4] Since the Conquest the French in King Johns time came into England with neere 700 ships, but were indeed invited by the Barons: In Edward the 3ds we were worsted by them, when they burnt Southampton; but their greatest Navy was in the Reigne of our 2d Richard, which is said (even by our owne Writers) to consist of 1000 saile mannd by 600000 souldiers, though it came to nothing: yet not long after, they did us infinite mischiefe all the South Coast over: And such another Fleete for Men though but of 200 Vessells, invaded the Ile of White in Henry the 8[th's] time, from which it may be computed of how much greater burden and capacity they were compared to those superior in numbers; though I think it were not hard to demonstrate, how former ages, did much exceede the later even in that particular; how could they else beare from 2 to 15 banks of Oares on a side? and when one of their biremes computed to be neere of 600 tun; perhaps those might rather be for pomp than use; But how so many bancs could be contriv'd, you will see in that excellent Critic Palmerius upon the antient Greek Authors Philopaters Vessell had 4000 men at Oares, and what numbers of those Xerxes carrid will be found in Herodotus,[5] Thycidides, and I think in Pliny.

Now as to Inventions, (which is your 2d Quærie) remitting you to Polydore Virgil, Pancirella, Britannia Baconica, Dr Plot, where he speakes of what any Englishman has produc'd, that ever was of Oxford Universitie (most worthy your perusal) you may please to consult Sir Richard Bakers collections, especialy for the Learned men, and benefactors, and for those trancendencies, you desir'd to know, wherein we exceeded other Nations, (if I mistake not) Peter Hylin has spoken some-thing: You will in the meanetime, reckon our Women, Horses, Dogs, Cocks, Rabits, Artichock, Tin, Lead, Wool, Black-

---

[1] 'over' is perhaps missing from before 'ages'.

[2] 'Egbert' appears after 'succeeded', then struck out and replaced by 'the Conqueror'.

[3] Eadgar, King of Mercia and Northumbria 957–9, King of all England 959–75.

[4] The king, correctly, was Æthelred II. The order was given in 1008 (*The Anglo-Saxon Chronicle*, trans. N. Garmonsway 1972, p.138). They were ready in 1009.

[5] Herodotus VII.184 gives a figure of 241,000 men in 1207 ships.

Lead, red-Marking-stone, Oaker, Oakes, Herrings, Painters in Miniature, Musitians on the Viol de Gamba and now of late, Joyners, Carver, Lock-Smiths; Engin for Weaving Stockings etc: Ribbon, Fullers Earth, Sea- and pet-Coale, Bowling-greenes, Taverns, Inns, Rings-of bells, Mony, Pinns, and variety of Religions —— I Name them all promiscuously for I have not time to range them in order, and therefore proceede to Shipping, in which all Nations that have any ports, seeme to be piqu'd with the ambition of being the Inventors, and of having Sovraignty on the Seas. It were losse of time to repeate what I have published[1] concerning Minos of Creete, the Syrians, Egyptians, Cypriots, Rhodians, Phoenitians, Assyrians who succeeded the Egyptians: The Persians, vanquishd by the Greekes and Macedonians, Then the Romans, Jews, Mores, Arabs renoun'd over Asia and Africa: I come therefore to the Later; among whom the Italians and Portugezes do not agree who were first in this Art, whilst the Spaniard pretend themselves equall to them all, and the English, Normans, Danes superior: and this leads me to your 3d Enquirie, and truely 'tis hardly imaginable how Nations so much celebrated for their Navall Actions and Exploits, should be lesse inventive in the Art of Navigation, who so far outdid us both in the liberal, and politer illiberal arts: As to Actions and Exploits at Sea, Those of Corinth doubtlesse were the first of any we reade of, who fought upon the Waters, if Thycidides may be credited, as I think he may:[2] we have after them those vast Fleetes of the Assyrians, then of the Persians, which Darius and successor Xerzes equippd to the number of 5600 Vessels, covering the Helespont: though I fancy, they could not be of any great bulke, their Antagonists (the Athenians) being open, and without any deck (see Diadorus Siculus) such were likewise those of the great Alexander, built on the river Indus, to put to sea in the greate Ocean, in all 1000; but of which 800 very slight: Indeede those of Athens, (before Darius alarm'd them) had not 60 Gallies, and they ill mann'd, nor had they any harbours considerable: 'til Themistocles that brave Captaine, made those three commodious ports (mentioned by Pausanius) built them stouter ships, and encourag'd them to use the Seas, t'were worth your time to read in Diodorus, by what addresse he perswaded them, and obtaind that glory from the Læcedemonians: There we shall heare what Aristides accomplish'd: What Pericles did with good pay to the Sea-men warring against the Persians: How the Athenians became Sovraignes on the Seas, braving it with 300 Galies, and bravly succouring those of Sicily: Licurgus equippd neere 500, and it was in those 3 Harbours where they had their ἐπινειον ναυσ[τ]άθμον, ὁπλοθήκην or σκευοθήκην[3] Stations, Yards, docks, Arsenals and Stores, which certainely are markes of the greatnesse of a people; and power at Sea; such as formerly

---

[1] In *Navigation and Commerce*, 1674.

[2] Indeed he may: Thucydides I.13.

[3] 'Sea-port, harbour, armoury, or arms-store. Marburg 'corrected' the Greek from P's transcription but supplied erroneous spellings herself.

were the Venetians, whose Arsenal is at this day, the most glorious thing of that kind in the world;[1] though 'tis reported, the French Kings comes very neere it: Over these had the Athenians their Magistrates, Store-keepers, Masters of Attendants, etc: here Herodotus, Thycidides, Plutarch etc: are to be consulted, and I think Budæus or Pandects, gives you the Commissioners and other officers, who delivered the new-built Vessel at the place of Rendizvous, to the Prætor, or General; and there you'l see who were made τριηράρχοι, στρατήγοι and πολέμαρχοι[2] Captaines, and Military officers with the number of their souldiers, as the occasion requir'd for such were Nicias, Demosthenes, Alcibiades, Pericles Cimon etc: and sometimes one alone, for so was Euribiades, General at the Salaminian and decretal[3] bataile against Xerxey's Fleete of 500,000 men: It was doubtlesse a noble and brave designe that Alexander undertooke, when after his last Victory over Darius, he would have discover'd the Asiatic and Indian Sea, and so have circl'd the whole globe of Earth, under the direction of Nearchus, Onesicritus, Diognetes, Belon[4] etc: and had it in his vast thoughts: to have set forth a fleete of 1000 ships, upon the report of the Carthaginian power at Sea; but death put a period to this, though not to the attempts of some of his Successors, Nicanor Seleucus etc when Patroclus went to discover farther into the Indies: but above all renown'd were the Ptolomys, particularly Philadelphus, by the discoveries of which, Megastines and Dionysius made into those parts, and there is yet mention of the Commission which was given to Dicearchus to measure the Mediterranean: But, Sir, I grow tedious to you, and will therefore now contract my Sailes, and come neerer home, How this Iland was first peopl'd, I had rather you should reade out of that excellent little booke written by our Country-man Twyne,[5] where, waving the figments of King Lud and his Trojans, you will see his conjecture about the rupture of an Istmus that in all probabilitie might formerly have united this Land to the Continent, and as to what concernes our being visited by the ships of other nations; how the Phoenicians and Tyrians were the most famous planters of Colonies wherever they came, how they crept to Gades[6] thence to our Country, for Gold, Silver, Tin and plunder: and though that booke were written in Henry the 8th time, Dialogue wise, it is yet in so pure and chast a style, and with that judgment, that you will be exceedingly delighted with it; and track Mr Cambden, who has not ben a little obliged to the Author: I also mention it the rather, that you may see, what learnd persons some of our Countrymen were at that time: You will also take notice how handsome a Character he gives our Henry the 7th:

---

[1] E had visited it himself in July 1645 (diary).

[2] Commanders of triremes, generals, and war-leaders.

[3] As the result of a decree.

[4] Generals of Alexander the Great.

[5] Probably John Twyne, his *De rebus Albionicis, Britannicis atque Anglicis, commentarorium, libri duo at Thomam Twinium filium.*

[6] Cadiz.

but to proceede: The Phoenicians came first as far as Utica, Hippo, Leptes etc in Africa, also Thebes in Greece, then into Spaine, not forgetting Carthage, which I should first have namd, as there deriving their dominion, and from whence they made most ample discoveries even as far even as far as the Æquinoxial,[1] and some (you know) tell us that Hanno came about even to Arabia: There was a journal of this renound Captains written in the Punic-tongue, and afterward translatd into the Latine by injunction of the Roman Senat, which is now lost, ah, what pitty![2] They also dispatchd Himilo[3] with a like commission and Fleete to discover the rest of Europ, and they were these Carthaginians or Phoenicians (for 'tis all one) who planted the Coasts of Spaine, built another Carthage there for security of their Fleetes, and had for ought appears, held that whole country to this day, but for the Romans, who were themselves beaten out, by the Vandals, Goths, and Saracens: But, not onely greedinesse of Riches, caused these and other people to wander thus, and undertake adventure of danger, but the more frequent and tirrible deluges, Earthquakes, Conflagrations, Plagues and Warrs; with which God-Almighty chastizd the vicious Heathen world in those early daies; for else hardly would they have ben perswaded, to change those warmer Climats, for these more northern and uncultivated places of France and Britaine – But of this enough, and perhaps, too much —— I returne therfor to Inventions againe, and to shew what incredible things they did by their dilligence and Expedition; we read of the whole Fleete in which Duillius was General in the first Punic-war, that it was built and set out in five and fifty dayes, and against Hiero 220 saile in 45 daies, and within the space of two-moneths, Scipio's Fleete in the 2d punic-War was built, the wood and timber growing within that space: but of this, I have spoken more at large in my *Sylva*,[4] Thus for their curious forme and naval Architecture, There were two, the *Salaminia* and *Paralus*, which were cald the Sacred, the first consisted of 30 Oares, these are reported to conduct[5] Theseus to Crete, and this was that reverent Vessell, which we reade was so often re-built as it decayd (you know the storie) and preserv'd to the time, of Demetrius Phalerius;[6] how gloriously she was carvd, and adorn'd, how she sai[l]d to Delos to a solemn sacrifice, and that from the day of her seting-out to her returne, 'twas not Lawfull to put any malefactor to death in Athens, Diodorus and other Authors informe us: *Paralus*, the other ship, had likewise, her privileges apart which concernd the Mariners and officers too long to reherse: and I should not have mention'd these things, but to comply with your

---

[1] I.e. as far south as the Tropic of Cancer.
[2] He had circumnavigated Africa, reaching Arabia. His account was translated into Greek and is extant.
[3] Correctly Himilco.
[4] The information is from Pliny, *NH* XVI.192; see *Sylva* (1664), ch. xxix, para 29 or *Writings* 1995, 301.
[5] Sic, though presumably should be 'to have conducted'.
[6] Demetrius Phalereus, late fourth century BC. His works are lost.

Enquiries, and because they will be Instances of Ornament, to such a Work, as I hope you have your thoughts on: and to which (among other good Authors) Pausanias will contribute more: And though this last vessell had nine benches of Oares on a side, and 9 upon each bench, I do not think it is comparable to the Venetian *Bucentoro*, in which the Duke and Senate espouse the Adriatic on Ascension day, at which Ceremonie I have ben present:[1] What Vessels we have built of this nature you better know than I ten-thousand times: and what our Neighbours have set out for pomp, as the Sweden *Megalesia*, the Spanish *Stanto-Spir[i]to*. The French kings, that when built, could not be launch'd; the *greate Henry* in Henry the 8th time was of 1000 tuns: I had quite forgot the Ship of Hiero which had Gardens and Ortchards etc in it, so gloriously defended by Athenæus, and I say nothing of those reportd to be in China, fearing them fables:——

Now I should come to Authors, Engineeres, Stratigematists and other shorter quæries in your paper, amongst which I find that common Tradition of Henry 4th of France, being prohibited to build any ships of War by Queene Elizabeth: It dos not occurr at present, where I have read it, onely this I know, in contradiction of it, That he did not neglect his Interest at Sea, as appeares, by his many projects for Trade, and performances at Marseilles, all that Richelieu and his Successor[2] pursued being projectd by this greate prince, as you may see in Morisotus's præface:[3] And having said this, I will honestly declare to you, what, after all my Enquiries, (betweene you and I) seemes to be the case as to our pretence to the dominion of the Sea and Fishery; and this I will the rather adventure to enlarge a little on, because it is a point, you cannot leave untouch'd, and perhaps, may gather something use-full to you, though the doctrine be so heterodox to what I my selfe have publishd,[4] and why I am not asham'd to make this retraction, I shall signifie in the Close: I accknowledge in my Booke, I sought industriously to assert our Title, and as *pro hic et nunc* it became me, the Circumstances of that time, and his Majestys expresse Command to me, consider'd: But betweene friends, when such-like topics are us'd (as sometimes even in Parliaments they were) 'tis plaine they were passd over upon important reasons – (But 'tis now neere Three in the morning, I will sleepe a little, and finish what I have more to say, before I waite on you to the Philosophers this day,[5] for with day it is)

---

[1] In June 1645 (see de Beer, II, 432).

[2] Cardinal Mazarin.

[3] Claude Barthelemy Morisot, his *Orbis Maritimi Sive Rerum in Mare et Littoribus Gestarum Generalis Historia*, Dijon, 1643. E's copy had originally been presented to Sir Richard Browne.

[4] In *Navigation and Commerce*.

[5] A Royal Society meeting 'on the first Exp: of my L: Bacon' (diary, 8 July).

ThursDay
8: July. To begin where I left now I am up againe—

Supposing the old Britaines did prohibit Forreiners to come into their Country
it inferrs not any claime of dominion in the narrow, but a jealosy rather over
their proper Coast nor read we that they ever practis'd it over the Gaules: The
Chineses (as I suggested to you yesterday) forbad all to come into their
country for political reasons; are they therefore lords of the Oriental Seas, or
ever did we heare they pretended so to be? As to king Arthur (abating what is
fabulous) that is, his legendary Dominion, the *Comes litoris Saxoniis*[1] and the
like, either it inferrs too-much, or nothing at all: His dominion stretched to
Denmark, Sweden, Norway and Iseland; have we therefore any right of claime
to those realmes at present? Why then to the Seas? Againe, admit the most;
Cannot Dominion be lost, or extinguish'd? was not his rather a momentary
conquest or excursion rather than any establish'd dominion! was it not lost to
the Danes? Had they not all the characters of dominion imaginable? (reade our
Histories) Lords of our Seas, of our Shores; and the tribute of Dane-gelt from
England and Ireland; so as if ever there were a real Dominion of the Seas in
the World, we must yeild these people to have had it, and if their Title cannot
be extinguish'd by subsequent revolutions, I much question whither ours will
ever be evinced: The story of King Edgar is certainly horribly fabulous, and
the pretended deede I feare as spurious;[2] truely, if forraine C[h]ronicles had
ben as much stuff'd with his renowne, as with King Arthurs, more credit were
to be given to it: In the meane time what is said of Athelred is against us: Since
'tis evident, he paid the Danegelt as a Tribute to them, and settled it to that
end. 'Tis a quærie, whither the Scots-seas, and Scotland too, be not a fee to
England, since with as good reason we might challenge it, if the producing of
rolls, records, and Acts of Parliament, and of statutes to that purpose were of
any importance; because we can shew many more to that sense, than in the
other case; but how would then the Scots take it; and what become of their
Laws about fishing? 'Tis declared in our Laws that we are Lords of the 4 Seas;
and 'tis so adjudged in our Courts, as to those born upon these Seas, and yet
the Parliament of Scotland can lay a Tax on our Fishermen, (as I am assurd)
which is a considerable argument against us: I never read that our Kings ever
prohibited any to fish on the Coasts of Scotland, or charg'd them with
Usurpation, for taking Toll and Custome for the Herring-fishing, though the
papers which were given me to contract, and insert in my booke, faine would
have it so: The truth is, the Licences, (which I mention as from Scarbrough)
were onely to fish on the Dogger-bank, such English as were to fish on the
Scotch-Seas about Orkney, Shetland, Iseland and Fero etc: did all take licence

---

[1] Count of the Saxon Shore – a late Roman military post covering the coastline of
Gaul, Germany, and Britain. Referred to in *Navigation and Commerce*, 87, para 43.
[2] See p.104, note 4, and Latham and Matthews VI, 81, on his 17th century reputation.

from the Kings of Norrway[1] at Bergen or North-barum and this Jurisdiction, and sovrignty undoubted of the Norwegian-kings, is recogniz'd by our Parliament in a Statute of 8 Henry 6th, and by innumerable Treaties betweene the two Crownes, even within a centurie of yeares, and if so, consider how fraile a proofe is the famous roll *pro hominibus Hollandiæ*,[2] and ho[w] it is to be limited in it selfe (by the History and occasion that caus'd it) to the narrow, or Chanell onely: 'Tis also to be considerd, that the Danes pretended at Breda, that the Cession of the Scots-fishry about Orkney and Shetland, was never made to King James, on the Marriage of Queene Anne (as the vulgar story gos) nor any time before to any Scotch-king, and supposing there were any such authentique deeds, it were better to fix the fishry (we contend for) even in the Dutch, than either to suffer it to be regulated by the decrees of a Scotch Parliament, or transfer it to that Nation, whom I take to be an hardier, and more industrious people; and you may remember, what old George Cock[3] was wont to say, that it was incompatible with our English ease and luxury, to set up that Trade to the prejudice of our Neighbours who were better husbands, and fared harder: As to the vast Trade, and multitude of English Ships, by the Histories of the Hanse-Townes, their priveledges and strength in England, one shall find (as before, I noted) that for the bulk, most of our navies were hired Ships of the Venetians, Genoezes and Ansiatics[4] 'til Queen Elizabeth, whose Number I think exceed[e]d not much above 24 good Vessells. Then the right of Passes and Petitions was founded on another part of the *Ius Gentium* rather than on our pretended Dominion of the Seas, which (to speake ingenuously) is hard to find expressly accknowledg'd in any Treaty with forrainers: And as to the fishing of the Dutch without Licence, the *Intercursus magnus* so boasted was a perpetual Treaty, and was made with the people as well as the Princes of Burgundy, and so as to be obligatory, though they rejected their Princes, as we see most of them did, and as they might, according to the *Lætus Introitus*,[5] which I mention: And that the Dutch are still (and by Queen Elizabeth, were so declard to be) a *Pars Contrahens*,[6] after their revolt and defection (yea, abjuration of Spaine) dos much invalidate the proceedings of King James and Charles I who both sign'd the *Intercursus*, and were in truth, included thereby, though they had not don it. The nature of præscription too would be look'd into, as well when it makes against us, as for us; and therefore it should be inquir'd whither Queen Elizabeth did not first affect the *Mare Liberum*[7] in opposition to the Danes, and whither his present Majestie has not don it at

---

[1] MS: 'Denmark' struck out.

[2] See *Navigation and Commerce*, 102, para 56.

[3] This is the Captain George Cocke featured so frequently in P's diary.

[4] Towns of the Hanseatic League.

[5] Happy beginning.

[6] A lesser or diminished area, or an area of smaller parts drawn together.

[7] An allusion to Grotius' work of the same title in which he firmly denounced the English claim that they had title over the sea between England and Holland.

Jamaica against the Spaniard;[1] pray consider the Seale of that Admiralty. To say truth, when I writ my book (which was but for præface to the Piece I told you of, and a Philological exercise to bespeake the Reader, and gratifie the present persons and Circumstances) I could not clearely satisfie my selfe in sundry of those particulars, nor find realy, that ever the Dutch paid Toll, or tooke License to fish in Scotland, after the Contest: Indeede (as I relate) they tooke Browne[2] who came to exact it, and detain'd him in Holland severall moneths: but I find not they ever paid peny for it though the papers Sir Joseph Williamson put into my hands speake of Assise-hering; Nor find I that any Rent (whereof I calculate the arreares)[3] for permission to fish was ever fix't by both parties, and so cannot be properly cald a settld rent; this would therefore be exquisitiley searchd into and perhaps both for these and divers other particulars, a thorough search in the Paper-Office may give better light, if there have ben any due care taken to collect and digest such important matters, which I much feare, seing it lie in such dissorder, when I had permission to make use of what I thought fit upon that occasion: As to the yeare 1636 and –37[4] you cannot but see through the intrigue, the equipping that formidable Fleete, that they were more to awe France, than terrifie Holland: And that any Licenses were taken in those yeares, I cannot be convinc'd of, that of –36 being but a single act of force, on particular men, the States never owning them in it; and you know the Admiral Dorp, was Chashier'd, for not quarreling it with Northumberland, and our Conducts and Licenses flatly refus'd in 37, when Captain Feild came: finaly (for I grow very tedious to one so far more inlightnd than I am) when King James did fix his Chambers, did he not either renounce the English Sovrainty of the Seas, or violate therein his League with Spaine (as that Nation urg'd it, pleading that the British-Seas were *territorium domini regis*) but he did not the latter, nor am I single in this deduction: In a word the whole Argument of the Fishry is too controvertable to be too peremptorily decided by the pen, and on many other accounts, and as I said, a project uselesse: and therfor might with much more ease and facility be supplied by encouraging our Fishery at New-found-Land:

Sir, Lastly, as to our Commerce in general, by all that I could observe, during the short time of my being at the Council,[5] where I a little look'd into these matters, (now utterly laid aside) I concluded it a very vaine thing to make any probable, certaine, or necessary proposal about Trade; not but that it might be infinitely improv'd, if Princes and people, did steadily, unanimously,

---

[1] Jamaica was seized from Spain in May 1655 by William Penn and Robert Venables.
[2] I cannot locate such a reference in *Navigation and Commerce*. This passage is repeated in 19 September 1682 (**C15**), see p.139, where he is called 'Braun'.
[3] Coming 'to more than half a Million of pounds' (*N and C*, 108, para 58).
[4] MS: '1637 and –37', clearly an error. See reference to 1636 four lines below.
[5] E was a member of the Council of Trade and Plantations from 1672–4.

and with a publique spirit, (and as our advantages, of situation etc prompts) set themselves honestly, and with Industry about it; but for that as things go, and are hitherto maneg'd (since Queen Elizabeths time) the whole advantage this Nation receives thereby, is evidently carryed on more by antient Methods, and the sedulitie of private persons than by any real publique encouragement: and as to the present (whatever we boast) it certainly languishes under insupportable difficulties, and does not stand upon a solid base, so long as we are in this uncertaine condition among our selves at home:

Thus Sir, I choose to convey you my 2d and more serious reflections upon a subject, which in your excellent Work, cannot escape your discussion speaking of the importance of shipping; and I do it with all manner of selfe-denyall imaginable, after what I have publish'd to the Contrary: by which you may conclude how suspicious wise-men ought to be of other Histories, how specious soever, unlesse where there is demonstration, that the Authors had no interest of their owne to serve, and were not influenc'd by their Superiors, or the publique cry; Nor whilst I make this Confession to you, dos it raise any blush, which certainly it would have don, had I publishd any thing on this subject, but what I receiv'd out of Authors before me, or from the papers which were sent me to peruse, and reduce into the method you see, which was in truth, to usher in the pretence we would have had to justifie an unsuccessfull (I would I could say a righteous) quarrell; but that, I was not to be judge of: And now though I should not be prudent to destroy and pull downe what I have built, if it may serve the present turne; yet, were I to begin that work againe, (as now inform'd) I would temper the cement after another manner, and write less magisterialy; that is, more ingenuously: But you will still consider the time and Circumstance. In all events, I have this for my excuse (as to you) that one of the most pious and usefull-bookes of that learn'd and excellent Father St Augustine, was his *Retractions:*[1] you have mine in this part of my Letter, and for that, the best part of it, next to the profession of my being, your very humble Servant — And to this I would subscribe my name, and make an End: But that something remaines to be said upon your other Enquiries: First

Who Ganebelli was I have told you;[2] Now as to Henry 8th Fortifications, tis evident he made severall Bullwarks on the Sea-Coasts *Anno* 1539 (if I mistake not the yeare) upon apprehension of Invasions, when he fell-out with the Pope[3] but who were his Engineers I do not know;[4] unlesse Santa Cicilia

---

[1] I.e. his *Confessions*.

[2] Presumably in person. There is no prior reference in the extant correspondence. The reference to Ramelli (below, p.115) indicates that they had conversed the previous day (the 7th July) at a booksellers.

[3] On 17 December 1538 Paul III (1534–49) issued the Bull of Excommunication against Henry VIII creating a fear that Charles V of Spain and Francis I of France would organize a combined invasion of England.

[4] The overseer of Henry's fortications was the comptroller of fortifications at Calais,

whom I also mention'd to you: As to the exploit don on the bridge at Antwerp, Famianus Strada will give you more particulars,[1] and the *Mercurius Gallo-belgicus* of that yeare,[2] which I think I have by me, though I am not certaine: Except Dr Dee,[3] I learne not who Queen Elizabeth made use of, but there was a Neapolitan sent from Spaine privately by Sir Nicholas Throckmorton who 'tis probable might serve her; in the meane time, though King John built divers castles on the coast and midland places, during the Barons-warrs, I read of very few or none built after Henry 7th came to the Crowne and had suppress'd the Barons; but in former times, there was very good reason to defend our selves, the French continualy molesting our Coasts from the reigne of William the Conquerur, even as far as Gravesend, which they tooke, and burnt, and therefore I suppose that Fort to be antienter then Henry the 8th: They also invaded the Ile of Wight, burnt Rye, nay Ports-mouth, Dartmouth and Plymouth: But whilst I speake of Engineers, I cannot forbeare to provoke your curiosity (if you have not considered it already) to reade the description our Hollingshead[4] has made of the building or repaire of Dover-peere, it being the first Mole-worke, I reade of in this nation: because you will find it so particular, as if you were now spectator of the work; and in truth I was much affected with it, it is describd so warmely, and gives us an idea of the worthy Industry of that age *viz:* Queen Elizabeth you'l finde it in his folio 2d Volume[5] and in it divers observable things: The first Engineer seemes to have ben one Thomson a priest, (cal'd Sir John Thomson, as then the manner was, and yet is in our Universities to style Batchelors of Art) who first undertooke it in Henry 8th's time: There you shall reade of one Joseph Young, who invented the way of transporting huge Stones etc: and how (like Americus Vespatianus) he began with an Eg-shell: There youl find another Engineer, cald John Trew, who intended a Mole of Stone, like that of Tangier instead of wood:[6] Ferdinand Pains Succeeded him, (a Jersey Man I Fancy) and there also of a Cofir dam – and mention made of a Peter Pet, and one Baker shipwrites, who were for the Timber Wall:

Sebastian Gabot, or Cabot was borne at Bristol, his Parents of Genoa, and was sent out by Henry 7th and left a Chart of his Passage to Cathaia;[7] which

---

Sir Stephen Ryngley, assisted by the Bohemian engineer Stephan von Haschenperg.

[1] In his *De Bello Belgio Decas Prima* (Library Sale Lot 1427).

[2] Probably *Mercurius Gallobelgicus*, Cologne 1596–1630.

[3] Presumably the mathematician, Dr John Dee; he was much favoured by Elizabeth.

[4] Raphael Holinshed.

[5] Of his *Chronicles*, issued from 1575 on. The Evelyn Library copy came from Sir Richard Browne (Sale Lot 766).

[6] The Tangier stone mole contract was signed by P amongst others on 30 March 1663 (diary). P witnessed its demolition in 1683 ('Second Diary', Howarth 1932, 411).

[7] Cathay (i.e. China). E seems to have conflated the activities of John Cabot and his son Sebastian. Cabot the elder was born in Genoa but was in Bristol by 1490. He was despatched by Henry VII in 1497 to explore to the west. He landed in Newfoundland

hung-up in the Privy Gallery at White-hall long time after, what became of it I cannot tell; Enquire if Chiffings[1] has it:

The fight at Lepanto, I charge my Selfe to shew you, with other things of that nature, when you have an idle afternoone to spend in the Country; the booke of that Collection being too unwieldy to remove:[2]

Walsingams words are to be found in Hackluit[3] as I remember when I Speake of the Prologue; or from the fountain in his History:

I mentioned Sir Walter Raleighs confidence with the charge of £200,000 for but two yeares, to subdue the greatest power in the world[4] (which then was Spaine and the Turk) and you will finde it, with divers other worthy remarks, in Sir Walter Raleigh's *History* if you search the Tables:[5]

As to Trade, it were a noble Collection, could we procure all that has ben printed (which would make a very usefull and considerable volume, because for most part publish'd by wise and knowing men) since Henry the 8th's time to this they are comonly in the bulk but of pamphlets, but in my opinion of much esteeme: out of them it would be enquir'd, when the English Staple was remov'd into Brabant being 100 years and more, since fixed at Dort; And this leads me to your last quærie what Bookes are to be consultd for these particulars: First, Boxhornius has written an history of the Anseatic Townes,[6] where you'l find in what condition and credit Holland was for Trafique, and so in the Danish Annales:

Concerning Shiping and Sea matters, twere good to read Pausanius in *Atticis*. Issodori *Originali de Navigatione*,[7] Lilius Gyraldus *de re Navali*;[8] Rosinus *Antiquities*,[9] Ferrier (whome yesterday you enquired for) *de re Navali*[10] also; though some of those I fancy scarce ever saw the Sea, but for as much as there are many worthy Antiquities, and other passages fit to

---

or nearby but believed he was in China. This led to the mistaken belief that a short route lay to China. He was lost on a follow-up voyage in 1498. His son, Sebastian, became map-maker to Henry VIII.

[1] Possibly a reference to Charles II's closet-keeper William Chiffinch.

[2] See letter of 6 September 1680 (C8), p.117.

[3] Richard Hakluyt, *The Principal Navigations, Voyages, Traffiques and Discoveries of the English Nation*. A second edition (1599–1600) was in the Evelyn Library.

[4] MS: 'in the world' inserted.

[5] *The Historie of the World*. E possessed his father-in-law's 1628 edition. It was extensively annotated by E and is now in the British Library (shelf-mark Eve.b.36.).

[6] Marcus Zuerius Boxhorn. E means either *Theatrum sive Hollandiae Comitatus et Urbium*, 1632, *Nederlantsche historie...*, 1649, or *Commentariolus de Statu Confœderatarum Provinciarum Belgii*, 1649.

[7] Perhaps Isidore of Seville's *Etymologiarum l.x, cap.* 1, entitled *De Navibus*.

[8] Lilius Gregorius Giraldus. Probably *de Nautici libellus*, 1540. A copy of his *Opera Omnia*, 1696, was in the Library Sale (Lot 633; probably a later addition).

[9] Joannes Rosinus, *Romanarum Antiquitatem libri decem, ex variis ...*, 1583

[10] Julius Ferretus, *de iure et re navali et de ipsius et belli aquatici præceptis...*, 1579.

and adorne a consummate piece these are not to be neglected; I cannot here but note, that the French pretend to have had Admirals from the very foundation of their Monarchy, even at the time of the antient Gaules, but in earnest, who ever can name us any before Euguerrant de Caucy, aboute the time of Phillip[1] Sonn of S. Louis, must violate all good History: This by the way onely, Bessonius has his *Theatrum Machinarum*, (which I have in Spanish)[2] with Beroaldus's notes and addition, since publish'd with Paschalis's suppliment in which some Enginers for the construction of Moles, weighing up sunk-ships, and other inventions of that sort:

Ramelli, you had yesterday,[3] in your hands at Mr Scots,[4] in which are few that signifie to Ships: What those of Causes are I will Show you, it is a noble booke, but not for your turne I think, unless it be Curiositie: I need not mind you of Vegetius and Frontinus, where you will find what was invented for old Fire-workes; but not so accurately and usefully as in Monsieur Malletts 3d Volume, *de les Travaux de Mars*, publish'd aboute 8 years since,[5] and highly worth your having; though I doe not much preferr it to our Country-man Cyprian Lucars[6] his Appendix to Nicholao Tartaglia an Italian, whom I should have conjectur'd to have ben one of Henry 8th's Engineers (of which you so enquire) and to whom he dedicates his booke; but for some passages in his Epistle: Has not our late Sir Jonas Moore left something of this subject, I meane concerning Fireworks and Artillery:[7] for my part, I do not finde much has ben added, since Lucar though neere an hundred-yeares since; unlesse in the Magnitude of Bombs —— Of this Subject also has written Girolamo Catanea aboute the same time,[8] and it were good to compare them, and what has been improv'd:

For lifting Engines, have you the Invention of Domenico Fontana, who in the reigne of Sixtus Quintus Pope,[9] erected the Gulias[10] or Obelisks, that had been prostrate neere 1000 yeares for want of an Engineer?[11]

---

[1] Philip III, the Bold (1270–85), son of Louis IX, St Louis of France.

[2] Jacques Besson, *Teatro de los Instrumentos y Figuras Matemiaticas y Mecanicas....* E's copy (ex-Mazarin's library) is now in the British Library (shelf-mark Eve.c.21).

[3] Agostino Ramelli, *Le Diverse et Artificiose Machine...* Paris 1588. E's copy (Library Sale Lot 1237) was bought by him in Paris in 1650.

[4] The bookseller Robert Scott of Little Britain, London.

[5] Alain Manesson Mallet, *Les Travaux de Mars, ou l'Art de Guerre*, various editions.

[6] *Three bookes of colloquies concerning the arte of shooting in greate, and small peeces of artillerie... in Italian... translated into English by Cyprian Lucar*, 1588.

[7] Sir Jonas Moore, his *General Treatise of Artillery*.

[8] His *Dell'arte militare libri tre...*, 1571.

[9] Sixtus V (1585–90).

[10] This extremely archaic and obscure term is a variant of 'gule', itself derived from the Latin *gula* meaning the neck (OED). The word was occasionally used to describe the neck of a column, the resemblance being that they were both long and thin.

[11] The obelisks concerned are: the so-called 'Obelisk of St Peter', transported to

The French Edition of *Recreations Mathematical* with the English Bates may be perused also Baptiste Porta;[1] but above all Galileo of the most subtiler parts of the *Mechanics*,[2] and there is extant of old, Archimedes his Treatise *de ijs quæ vehuntur in acquis* published by Commandinus with a comment.[3]

Explicatio des Termes de Marine was printed at Paris above 40 yeares since.

Dr Gilber, our Ridly and Ward[4] of the Load-stone not forgetting Kircher.[5]

And I am sure you have Sir Walter Raleighs select *Essaies* upon the first Invention of Shipping a little octavo booke: and now the other day has not our Minister Mr Holden[6] presented you with his Trinity Monday Sermon, a learned piece:

One Baillot, sett forth a small volume in French about artificial fire-works,[7] and so did Monsieur Bourel:[8] I name them all promiscuously, as they come to my memory, for I protest I write all these two sheetes without booke, and should I think do so till night if by it I might do you any service: and now I am going to speake with Sir Dennis Gauden, who has made me stay within all this morning: pardon this confusd scribble; this desultorie and immethodicall trifles, and lore

    Sir   Your most humble Servant
                    J Evelyn

I have no time to read what I have written and I am sure 'tis swarming with faults, for I am very giddy-headed; But if it do not serve to stay your stomach til I come, and that within one quarter more, stay not for me longer:

Rome by Augustus, erected by Caligula in his stadium in AD 37 where the Vatican now lies, and raised by the architect Fontana in the Piazza San Pietro in 1586; and, an obelisk bearing the names of the pharaoh Tuthmosis III which, after being brought from Egypt, was placed in the Circus Maximus. Fontana re-erected it in the Piazza San Giovanni in Laterano in 1587. E saw them on 19 and 20 November 1644 (diary).

[1] Giovanni Battista della Porta.

[2] Galileo Galilei, *Dialogo...sopra I Due Massimi Sistemi del Mondo Tolomaico, e Copernicano*, 1632 (Library Sale Lot 607, Sir Richard Browne's copy passed to E).

[3] E had a copy of Archimedes *De Insidentibus Aquæ liber primus*, published by Curtius Troianus at Venice in 1570 (Library Sale Lot 43).

[4] Dr William Gilbert, his *De Magnete, Magneticisque Corporibus* (1600); Mark Ridley, his treatise on magnetism was published in 1613; Seth Ward, bishop of Salisbury, who published a number of mathematical works.

[5] Athanasius Kircher, his *Magnes Sive de Arte Magnetica Opus Tripartitum*, Rome 1641. E purchased his copy at Rome in 1645 (Library Sale Lot 854; now in the British Library shelf-mark Eve.a.161).

[6] Richard Holden; in 1680 he was vicar of Deptford.

[7] Presumably Joseph Boillot, *Modelles Artifices de Feu et Divers Instrumens de Guerre*, 1598 (Library Sale Lot 191).

[8] Giovanni Alfonso Borelli.

C8. JOHN EVELYN TO SAMUEL PEPYS[1]

On early vessels

Whitehall
6 September 1680[2]

Sir

Since this Paradisian Weather has not all this while incited you downe the River, and that being soe very well in health as I could waite on my friends in London untill now, you will easily excuse my not giving you a more accurate Account of the Battell of Lepanto, which you will finde in severall Histories of that time especially in the Life of Pius Quintus,[3] written by Girolumo Catena, where, at the end you'l finde, an exact List of all that Armada on both Sides, with the Comanders and Orders of Squadrons. The Booke is printed at Mantua, 1587.[4] Something of it is said alsoe in the History of the Knights of Malta, as farr as concernes that particular Order, in a large Volume, but not soe fully as in the other. And now I will give you what has occurr'd to me, in some scattering Notes, by me written downe in my *Adversaria*,[5] at several times without any Method.

The first mony I finde said to be stampt was that of Janus's head, and, on the Reverse a Ship.[6] The History you have in Macrobius Satur:*l*:i:[7] for when Sailing with Saturne he in recompence taught that Hero Husbandry and how to meliorate Fruites, he was received as partner in the Empire which occasion'd this Medaile to be Stamp'd. It was with this farthing, that the little Boyes were wont to play at *Capita* and *Navia*, which we now, call Cross and Pile (Pile is an

---

[1] Source: PL 2873.56–9. Copy of E's letter endorsed, 'A Letter from Mr Evelyn to Mr Pepys concerning the Battle of Lepanto and the Antiquity of Shipping'. The letter-sent was featured in the Davey Catalogue (Item 2868) but has now disappeared.

[2] MS: 'Whitehall 6th 7br 1680'. E's diary entry for 6 September 1680 is entirely devoted to a meeting with Sir Stephen Fox, and a character portrait. There is no mention of Pepys in any of the entries at around this time.

[3] Pope Pius V (1566–72). His naval force, in alliance with Venice and Spain, defeated the Turkish fleet at Lepanto in the Gulf of Corinth on 7 October 1571.

[4] Giovanni Girolamo Catena, his *Vita gloriosissimo Papa Pio Quinto...Con una raccolta di lettere di Pio v. à diversi principi, et le riposte, con altre particolari. Et i horni delle galee e de' capitani, cosi Christiani, come Turcki, che si trouarono alla battaglia navale*, Mantua, 1587.

[5] Now in the British Library, various Evelyn MSS (e.g. 36, 44, 54, 65, and 173).

[6] This is the base-metal *as* of the Roman Republic, cast in bronze around the middle of the third century BC. In the second century BC they were struck. They were not the first coins. E makes the same reference in *Numismata* (1697), 38.

[7] Aurelius Macrobius Ambrosius, his *Convivia Saturna*, I.7.

obsolate French word for a Ship, and thence Pilott).[1] See the Antiquity of that Childish Play, the oldest I read of butt the Coine it selfe was called *Restitus Nummus*.[2]

Amongst Cups and Gobletts to drink in[,] some were of old made like Boates, and the Beakes of Ships, The Greekes had their *Carchesia*[3] or *Cymbia* (a diminutive of *Cymba*)[4] as the Romans – Cape Macony Carchesia Bacchi and *Hic duo rite mero, libans Carchesia Baccho* and of Boates *In ferimus tepido Spumantia Cymbia Lacte*, The Carchesians Soe call'd a *navali re*. See it describ'd by Asclepiades, quoted by the same Author *Li* 5 and it seemes there were diverse other Cupps, amongst the merry Greekes of this sort but the Cyssymbium[5] was a wooden Vessell, comonly of Ivy and such a Cupp was sometimes used by the Greek Poets – figuratively for a Ship see Menander in *Nanclero*, they feign'd that Hercules was transported in one of those as far as Gades:[6] Pherecydes is made the Reporter, but rather in truth in a Ship *cui Syphonomen* for all these were *Navigiorum Vocabula*.

You have Hiero's great Vessell (for enough of small Craft) describ'd in Athenæus and Casaubons[7] notes to the full, he had Gardens and Fruite trees Floating, Tenis Courts and what not: But if it be true, what I finde of the Spanish Carracas, or (as they call them) *Na[v]es des Indias*, they were not much Inferior for Largeness, some of them being built with six Decks or stories, and all of halfe pike height to the Roofe. Some of these Vessells were 180 paces in Length, and forty in breadth, and have been knowne to carry from Spaine to the Indies 500 Families, their Children, Servants, and Household Stuffs, with provision for a 6 months Voyage the Passengers Living in as a Citty, yett unknowne to one another, as if many miles distant.

I forgott to adde (as to the small but very curious Craft) that amongst the Reliques of the Cathedrall at Tolledo, there is shew'd a Ship wrought all out of Rock Chrystall, with the very Cordage of the same, such of Ivory I have seen in other places which is not soe Curious.[8]

The *Navigatione* and exploits of the Portugueses are at Large in Hieron Osorius,[9] both in Latine and French from Emanuel the first 1496, to Sebastian

---

[1] The closest modern equivalent is probably 'heads or tails' as opposed to 'heads or ships'. This and other ancient games are discussed by W. Ramsey, *A Manual of Roman Antiquities* (17th edition, revised by R. Lanciani), London 1901, 498.

[2] 'Restored coin'.

[3] Καρχησιον. A drinking cup whose waist was narrower than the top or base.

[4] A boat or skiff.

[5] Κισσυβιον. The ivy wreath would probably have been carved on it.

[6] Cadiz, Spain.

[7] Isaac Casaubon; E had a 1657 copy of his edition of *Athenæus*.

[8] As E had never visited Toledo he was not in a position to make the comparison.

[9] Jeronimo Osorio, his *Histoire de Portugal, contenant les Enterprises, Navigations, and Gestes Memorables ... en la Conqueste des Indes Orientales*. E owned a 1581 copy of the first French edition (Library Sale Lot 1107).

the first, wherein are all their Navigations and Conquests of the East Indies at Large worth the perusall, I think you asked me about this.[1]

Pray Consult the Comentators on 27 *Ezek*: from the 4th to the 9th where you'll finde mention'd Plancks of Firr, Masts of Cedar, Oake for Timber Speaking of the Tyrians, There's alsoe mention of Pilotts, Caulkers, Mariners and Vessells, some soe rich, as to have the Benches and Hatches (See in Margines) inlaid with Ivory, and in that Chapter a wonderfull Account of their early Traficque,[2] the Critica at large will satisfy you in this, But I tire you and therefore for this time (and till you open my mouth againe) conclude with what I lately found reading over Dr Burnetts excellent history of our Reformation,[3] that one of Henry the Eighth's excuses for the demolition of the Monasteries etc was the building and fortifying of Ports in the Channell and other Places: See his 3d booke pp 269: 284 etc

> *haec Raptim*[4] from
> Sir
> Your most humble Servant
> JEvelyn

[1] Emmanuel I, or Manuel I 'the Great' or 'the Fortunate', King of Portugal 1495–1521; Sebastian, King of Portugal 1557–78.

[2] *Ezekiel* xxvii.12.

[3] Dr Gilbert Burnet. His *History of the Reformation of the Church of England* was first (part one) published in 1679 (E's copy, second edition, 2 volumes printed 1681–3, is now at the British Library, shelf-mark Eve.b.34, but clearly post-dates this letter). He may have had a first edition which he replaced.

[4] An allusion to *haec scripsi raptim*, 'I write this in haste', for example Cicero, *Epistulæ ad Atticum* ii.9.1.

C9. JOHN EVELYN TO SAMUEL PEPYS[1]

On sermons and extraordinary ships

For Samuell Pepys Esqr
at Bouckingam buildings[2]
Mr Hewers

Sayes Court
31 October 1681[3]

Sir,

I do at last send you the Letter which I have ben so long recovering,[4] and what else I have of that nature which afford you diversion are at your service; nor should I forget the prophetic passages I promisd to send you, if I could come at that Volume of Dr Jacksons[5] where I have noted it, but which at present I have not by me: In the meane time 'tis observable what I above 30 yeares since marked in the Margin of Bishop Andrews's Sermons:—[6]

What say some other? You shall change for a fine new Church-Government. A Presbyterie would do much better for you then an Hierarchie, and (perhaps) not long after a Government of States than a Monarchy: Meddle not with these changers:[7]

Bishop Andrews 6: Sermons: on 5: November 1614 at White-hall *Coram Rege*, the Text 24: *Pro*: 21, 22, 23.

---

[1] Source: Collections of Maine Historical Society (Fogg Collection; formerly Davey Catalogue Item 2869). Endorsed by P?, 'October 31 1689 Mr Evelyn to Mr Pepys'.

[2] Probably an error for 'York Buildings, Buckingham Street', Hewer's home.

[3] MS: 'Sayes Court 31:Oct:81'. The date was the occasion of E's 61st birthday.

[4] Not attached and not identified.

[5] Dr Thomas Jackson, dean of Peterborough. This is possibly his *Comentarii super 1 Cap. Amos*, 1615. It did not survive to the Library Sale.

[6] Bishop Lancelot Andrewes, *XCVI Sermons*, 1641. E's annotated copy survived to the Library Sale (Lot 30) and is now at the British Library (shelf-mark Eve.b.50). The passage following appears on p.951 and is marked by E's pencil and the comment, 'whether this not a true prophecy.' On the end-leaf of the book, in pen, is E's note, 'prophecy –p:951', written in the spidery handwriting more characteristic of E's old age suggesting he added the note when writing this letter. The book bears little sign of use apart from the marking of this passage.

[7] The transcription by E accords with the original book.

But I mentiond also some thing concerning the more accurate gust and distinction, which those who are Masters perceive in the severall straines of Art, above others, and which the lesse exercis'd and skillfull take no notice of: It is Ciceros in *Academica Quæstiones Lib:* 2:6:21.[1]

Quam multa vident pictores in umbris, et in eminentia, quæ nos non videmus! quam multa, quæ nos fugiunt in Cantu, exaudiunt in eo genere exercitati! qui primo inflatu tibicinis Antiopam esse æiunt aut Andromacham, cum id nos ne suspicemur quidem.[2]

And now we speake of Music, have you taken notice of that Criticisme of Mr Seldens, of the Νομος[3] in that antient art? it is a very curious and learned discourse publishd (amongst other things) by Humphry Prideaux in the late *Marmora Oxoniensia*,[4] amongst his *Notæ Historicæ ad Chronicon Marmoreum*, p:168 *ad* 181,[5] with that most ingenious persons Mr Aldriches[6] additions *ad Veteres Græcorum Gnochas* which will be worthy your perusal: It is some time since that I read the passage and now have also turning to it, met with some sprinklings that may happly more gratifie your Curiosity of another kind:

There is in the famous Epoche of the antient Grecians, mention made of the wonderfull ship cal'd the Πεντηκοντρος,[7] or fifty-oard Gally rather, which saild out of Ægypt to Greece fifteene hundred-yeares before Christ, which being almost 800 yeares before Rome was built and 300 before the destruction of Troy, will be worth your looking over the annotations of our Country-man Thomas Lydiate, for the Chronologie part,[8] in which you are worthily so

---

[1] In fact II.vii.20.

[2] 'How many things, which we do not see, painters perceive in the shadows and the foreground! How many things we miss that are heard by trained musicians, who when the flautist blows his first note say, "That's *Antiope*", or "*Andromache*", when we have not even an idea!'

[3] 'Musical mode, song, or war-tune'.

[4] Published at Oxford, 1676. E had participated in negotiating the transfer of the Arundel marbles to the University. His copy survived to the Library Sale (Lot 1215). The Sale Catalogue (Volume III, M–S), notes that E's copy contained copies in his hand of various thanks. E records the gift of the book in the diary (28 April 1676) from the then Bishop of Oxford, John Fell. It had many typographical errors which earned Prideaux opprobrium in the eyes of Henry Aldrich (see next note) for being an 'unaccurate, muddy-headed man' (DNB).

[5] Selden's views on the Νομος were referred to in the *Notæ Historicæ* (by Thomas Lydiat, see note 8 below) rather than being presented as a self-contained discourse, and in fact between pp. 170–81.

[6] Henry Aldrich, dean of Oxford, and musician.

[7] Sic, correctly: Πεντηκοντερος ('Pentekonteros'). From, for example, Pindar, *Pythian* 4.245; however, in view of E's misspelling it is interesting that this is not how the vessel is described in the *Marmora Oxoniensia*. See next note.

[8] This is the second part of Prideaux's *Marmora Oxoniensia*, entitled *Thomas Lydiati Oxoniensis Annotationes ad Chronicon Marmoreum*. The reference to the galley

curious: Nor may it be omitted what Jacobus Palmerius (whom I named to you) has written upon the antient building of Ships and Gallies to containe so many banks of Oares and stupendious numbers of people, in an ample paragraph upon a fragment of *Memnon* in *Phoc*: 717,[1] but of this more when I have the honour to waite on you, which I thinke to do before this weeke expire:[2] In the meane time to fill up this impertinent scribble: I find that

Amongst Roman *Vexilla*[3] the *Caeruleum*[4] or blewish representing the Sea, was usualy the *Præmium* given onely to the Captaine in Naval Fight, as we find it (in Suetonius *Augustus*) bestowd by Octavianus on Marcus Agrippa in Cilicia after that Sea Victory there mentioned,[5] and so Sir,

> I remaine
> Your most obedient Servant
>
> JEvelyn:

Pardon my shamefull hast, for I did not think of sending you this to day, but one going nearer your person, I would not omitt to salute you, as I am able.

---

appears on p.22, and in Selden's supplementary *Apparatus Chronologicus et Canon Chronicus*, p.242. In neither case are Greek letters used for the name which is, instead, spelled 'Pentecontoros'. E's Greek spellings were frequently wrong.

[1] In Palmerius' *Exercitationes in optimos fere auctores græcos ... ut et in antiquos poetas*, Leiden, 1668. E's copy survived to the Library Sale (Lot 1127), but was not acquired by the British Library.

[2] If he met P that week it is not recorded though on 3 November E went to London spending the next few days there (diary).

[3] 'Standards'.

[4] 'Dark blue/green' (sea-coloured).

[5] *Augustus* xvi.3. E repeated the same anecdote in his letter to P of 22 September 1685 (**C25**).

C10. JOHN EVELYN TO SAMUEL PEPYS[1]

More answers for Pepys's queries

Sayes Court
6 December 1681[2]

Sir,

In complyance with your commands, etc, I have sent you already two large sea-charts, and now with a third I transmit the sheetes I have long since blotted about the late Dutch-War, for which I should yet make another apology (besides its præface) were it not that you well understand the prejudices I lay under at that time, by the inspection of my Lord Treasurer Clifford, who would not indure I should moderate my style when the difference with Holland was to be the subject;[3] nor with much patience suffer that France should be suspected, though, in justice to truth (evident as the day), I neither would, nor honestly could, conceile (what all the world might see) how subdolusly[4] they dealt, and made us their property all along: The interception of de Lyonne's[5] letter alone to his Master, p.260, is abundantly pregnant of this, and ought to open our eyes, unlesse it be that we designe to truckle under that power, and seeke our ruine with industrie. Sir, you will pardon this severe reflection, since I cannot thinke of it without emotion. Now as to the compiler's province; 'tis not easily to be imagined the sea and ocean of papers, treaties, declarations, relations, letters, and other pieces, that I have ben faine to saile through, reade over, note, and digest, before I set pen to paper; I confesse to you the fatigue was unsufferable, and for the more part did rather oppresse and confound me than inlighten, so much trash there was to sieft and lay by, and I was obliged to peruse all that came to hand, and a better judgement than mine had ben requisite to elect and dispose the materials that were apt for use. And this, Sir, I dare pronounce you will find, before you have

---

[1] Source: Tanner 1926, i, no. 12 (PC MS.i.29). Endorsed, 'accompanying diverse books, papers etc., in answer to several Quæries of his contained in a memoire given Mr E. by Mr P. to that purpose'. The draft at BL.1533 has many minor differences.

[2] E's copy-letter book has an incomplete version of this letter (BL CLBII.436), dated 5 December 1681. The loose draft was also retained, dated 6 December 1681. E was responding to queries sent by P which were subjoined to the copy used by Bray (see his footnote in various editions) and Tanner (1926, i, no. 12, p.14, n. 4). It is clear from E's reply that he omitted to answer some of P's queries (for example regarding Walter Raleigh) and others he could not find the books for (Drake). A letter in the Davey Catalogue (Item 2870) appears to be a follow-up reply (see C11).

[3] See diary, 28 August 1670: E describes how he was encouraged to be anti-Dutch.

[4] Cunningly.

[5] Hugues de Lionne, Louis XIV's foreign minister.

prepared all your *materiam substratum*[1] for the noble and usefull worke you are meditating. Nor did I desist here, but had likewise made provision for that which was to follow to the Treaty at Breda, though I honestly restored every scrip that had ben furnished me from the cabinets of the Secretaries and other persons which were originals, yet blame myself for returning those letters and pieces I received from my Lord Treasurer, because I think I might have retained them with better confidence than he to carry them quite away with him into Devonshire, *unde nullis retrorsum*.[2] That I did not proceede with the rest is accountable to his successor, who cutting me short of some honest pretensions I had to his kindnesse more than ordinary (if you knew all), I cared not to oblige an ungratefull age; and perhaps the world is delivered by it from a fardle of impertinences. Clifford, his prædecessor, was (abating his other imperfections) a generous man, friendly to me, and I verily believe of cleane hands. I am sure I was obliged to him; the other had ben so to me and mine. A hautie spirit is seldome accompanied with generosity. But that's all past.

I know it has been wondered upon what pretence I should have sought to sit at the Navy-board,[3] and I have ben as much astonished why some honoraries (who sate long there) were no more industrious or usefull than haply I should have ben, whilst to commute for my ignorance of weare and teare I might yet perhaps have ben subservient to such a genius as Mr Pepys, and by his direction and converse not altogether an unprofitable member. Something (you see) I should have ben digging for my wages, and serve the master builders, though I were my selfe no architect. But let that go also.

Now to your quæries, which I will take in the series you put them downe;[4] and first,

I have nothing relating to the Prize-Office; and for that discourse wherein I did attempt to shew how far a gentleman might become very knowing, and to good purpose, by the onely assistance of the modern languages (writen at request of Sir Samuel Tuke for the now Duke of Norfolk), to my greate regrett I feare 'tis lost, for lending it to Sir James Shaen some time since, he tells me he cannot finde it. There is in it a usefull rescention of good authors, and a method of reading them to advantage; besides some thing in the discourse (after my way) which perhaps would not have displeased you; nor was it without purpose of one day publishing it, not for ostentation, but because 'twas written with a virtuous designe of provoking the Court fopps, and for incouragement of illustrious persons who have leasure and inclynations to cultivate their minds beyond the farce, 'A whore and a dog',[5] which (with

---

[1] Foundation work.

[2] 'From where nothing returns.' Clifford retired to Ugbrooke near Exeter in 1673 following his refusal to undertake the requirements of the Test Act.

[3] This had been the cause of some ill-feeling, see above, p.96.

[4] E's answers do not correspond to the order of the queries appended to the letter.

[5] The draft at BL.1533 gives 'A horse, a whore, and a dog'. Not identified.

very little besides) are the confines of their greate understandings. I will yet desire Sir James to make (if possible) a more accurate search to recover it when I have an opportunity.

The print of the battail of Lepanto[1] you will find thus indorsed ⚓, and a description of the naval preparation in Eighty-Eight,[2] written in Spanish about that time, which I believe very authentique, marked 8 ⚓ 8.

The sculptures of the Trajan's pillar, ingraven by Villamena, with the notes of Alphonso Ciaconius,[3] referring to the severall bass'-relievos by figures. You will find some hints about the forme of their ships and gallies, as in 57, 243, 260, 153, 24, 235, 236, 239, 152, 155, and especially 303, where he speakes of the preference of brasse instead of yron worke in ships, and the best season for felling tymber, etc., with other curious notices; but they are but touched, and there is subject of a world of erudition, beyond what Ciaconius has don, that would deserve a larger volume.

Sir Francis Drake's *Drake's Journal* (lying amongst a rude and monstrous heape of other books and papers) I have not as yet ben able to find-out, but being now about new ranging and making another catalogue of my poore library, I shall not forget to send it you so soone as I lite upon it; In the meane time, I substitute a journal of Sir Martine Fourbisher's to the North West,[4] and of Captain Fenton's (both famous sea-men) towards the South as far as Magellan, etc., marked ┿.

A volume in folio of Sir Richard Browne's *Dispatches* during his ministerie in the French Court.[5] They containe onely his correspondencies, not his negotiations, which are not bound up. When you have don with this (if the entertainement affect you) you may command the rest. This begins at 1644.

A packet of original letters to the greate Earle of Lycester[6] (14 in number) together with a declaration of William Prince of Orange, and the last Will and Testament of the said Earle; which, together with those you have already, are all I can find, redeemed from the fire, and, *spurcis utroque*,[7] marked

---

[1] E saw Vasari's painting of this event when in Rome, on 18 January 1645 (de Beer, II, 297), and Andrea Vicento's version in Venice in June 1645 (ibid, 444).

[2] The Armada, 1588; PL.2503, p.445 in the Pepysian Library, dated 9 May 1588.

[3] Alfonso Ciaccono, *Historia utriusque Belli Dacici in Columna Expressi, cum figuris æneis*, 1616 (Library Sale, Lot 363). See also the letters below, 28 March (**D13**), and 12 April 1692 (**D14**).

[4] Frobisher made his first voyage to find the north-west passage in 1576.

[5] In the British Library (see *The Book Collector*, Summer 1995, 196–8).

[6] See *The Book Collector* (op. cit., 191–3).

[7] 'With filth on either side', Tanner points out that the manuscript indicates that E

A packet of 33 original letters to and from greate persons during the late Rebellion in England, surprized at the battaile of Worcester, etc.[1] ◎.

Another pacquet of letters, and papers of State, in number (80) marked ☿.

A bundle containing about 38 papers and fardles, being for the most part instructions and matters of State, etc. ♃.

To these, *ex abundanti*, I have cast in a rude copy of what I delivered next to my Lord Arlington concerning the Fishery and duty of the Flag, marked ♃ (1) (2).

And an old draught of a sea fight ⚔.

A paper written in French touching the severitie of the Marine Lawes in France. ⛵.

A booke containing the pay and wages due to the Deputy, army, and government of Ireland. ♉.

The map of a certaine harbour.] ✦ E

A scheme of the action of the Dutch at Chatham, 1667, marked ♄ (3).[2]

Lastly, A Relation of His Majesty's Action and Escape at the fight at Worcester when he came into France; which Sir Richard Browne tells me he copied out of the then Queene Mother's letters. This was it which I believed he had taken from his Majesty's owne mouth, for 'tis long since I cast my eye upon it. But (as I told you) there was one realy which Sir Richard did write, his Majesty dictating; and now he calls to mind that he sent the original to Monsr Renodaut to digest and publish in the French *Extraordinaries* of the yeare 1651. I have them bound up with the *Gazetts* of that yeare in French; but I heartily wish we had preserved the originals.

There accompanies this an Order of Council at State (as then called) for the apprehension of Charles Stuarte.

Your Memoire speakes of Cromwell's Letters (which is, I suppose, mistaken) for I find none amongst all my papers; but of other matters, letters, petitions, bonds, and obligations to be true to the new State, perfidious men betraying divers loyall persons, copies of letters from his Majesty, and other letters and transactions, there are yet by me many thousands; but I suppose I send you enough to wearie you for a time. You also desire Monsr Monconys

---

originally wrote *spurcos* and then changed it to the ablative.

[1] These may be the Nicholas papers, now with the Evelyn manuscripts at the British Library (see *The Book Collector*, op. cit. 198–200).

[2] In the Pforzheimer Collection (MS 35B); see pp.335 and 337, Figure 4. See also 20 January 1668 (**A26**), note 5.

Travells.[1] I think I informed you that what I read was borrowed of Mr Oldenburg some years since and returned; but is to be found amongst the French bookesellers.

Thus, Sir, you see how ambitious I am to serve you. If in any thing else I may signify to your designe or curiosity, freely command.[2]

Your most obedient servant,

J Evelyn

These pieces[3] and particulars when you have don with, you may please to take your owne time in returning them.

Memoire of enquiries given Mr Evelyn by SP[4]

To begg the perusall of what he has writt upon the subject of our last Navall Warr.

Ditto, his papers relating to the Prize-Office.

Ditto, the sea-platts he shewed me at Deptford.

Ditto, the residue of his original letters of State.

Ditto, Sir Francis Drake's Journall, which he tells me has somewhere by him.

Ditto, his account of Trajan's Pillar.

To looke out for what he seems to recollect of Sir Walter Raleigh's having somewhere noted touching the difficult defence of England.

To recover his Discourse to Mr Howard touching the best furniture for a library to be collected out of moderne authors.[5]

Monsr Moncomy's account of his travells.

The Battle of Lepanto.[6]

King's Escape.

Two volumes which, as I remember, Mr Evelyn tells me has bound up together of letters to Sir Richard Browne dureing his Ministry in France.

Ditto, Sir Richard Browne's share of the letters of State found among the Council-papers at the King's coming-in.

Memorandum that the papers sent me by Mr Brisbane[7] did fully answer Mr E's seedule,[8] saveing that there was none of those mentioned in the postscript relating to Dr Burnet.

---

[1] Balthazar Moncony, *Journal de ses Voyages*, Lyons 1666.

[2] A list of books lent to P is in the British Library at Add.MSS 15948, f.156.

[3] Marginal note reported by Bray: 'Which I afterwards never asked of him'.

[4] Not in E's or P's hand.

[5] Henry Howard, afterwards 6th duke of Norfolk.

[6] This had previously been dealt with (above, pp.114, and 117).

[7] Possibly John Brisbane, judge-advocate of the fleet.

[8] Sic = schedule.

C11. JOHN EVELYN TO SAMUEL PEPYS

LOST   *post* 6 December 1681

The Davey Catalogue entry is:

John Evelyn *to* **Samuel Pepys**

2870   A.L.S. 1 p.4to. December, 1681, and complete with autograph
              address and with notes by Pepys at the back, as follows:–"Mr.
              Evelyn to Mr. Pepys, referring him to a quotation in Sir Walter
              Raleigh's history touching ye difficult defence of England
              against a foreign enemy." *Very interesting and unpublished*,
              £15.

It was implicitly considered by Marburg in 1935 that this letter was the same as the previous one, dated 6 December 1681 (**C10**). However, that letter does not contain a reference to Walter Raleigh's history, though Pepys had included a specific query in the list appended to that letter (see previous page). He knew that E had Raleigh's *History* for it had been mentioned in the epic letter of 7 July 1680 (**C7**). The letter of 6 December is also approximately three times longer than the '1 p. 4to.' length assigned to this letter. It seems that E had continued to work on the queries and sent P a further letter, now lost, carrying further answers.

This the first of four letters included in the Davey Catalogue which are now completely lost (no copies or drafts surviving to make good). Two reappeared in the Langham Catalogue of 1900 but from that date to this none has apparently reappeared on the open market. All the known letters from the Davey Catalogue, apart from those acquired by the Evelyn family, made intermittent appearances in sales until they entered institutional libraries. The disappearance of this letter and three others can only be explained either by their being incorporated into private family collections where they either remain, or have since been destroyed, or otherwise lost.

C12. JOHN EVELYN TO SAMUEL PEPYS[1]

How men of status depend on vulgar imagination

Samuell Pepys Esqr
at Mr Ewer's in
Yorke-buildings

[Sayes Court]
28 April 1682[2]

Sir,

Considering how far your laudable zeale still extends to all things that do any-
wayes concerne the Actions of this Nation at Sea, and that you despise not the
least things that may possibly be of use; I make no Scrupul of sending you all
my blotted fragments, which yet with no small paines you will find I had
collected in order to a farther progresse in the History of the late Dutch-War: I
should be perfectly ashamed of the *farrago* when I reflect upon the more
preceous materials you have amassed, but you know where Virgil found
Gold,[3] and you will consider that these were onely minutes and tumultuary
hints relating to ampler pieces, informe and unfit to be put into the building,
but prepar'd to work on: It is not imaginable to such as have not tried, what
labour an Historian (that would be exact) is condemn'd to: He must reade all,
good, and bad, and remove a world of rubbish before he can lay the
foundation: So far I had gon, and it was well for me I went no farther, and
better for the Reader on many accounts, as I am sure you find by what I have
already ben so weake as to shew you, and yet I cannot forbeare. You will find
among the rest in a little Essay, how what I have written in English would
shew in Latine; asham'd as I was to see the Historie of that Warr publish'd in
that universal and learned Language, and that in just and specious Volumes,
whilst we onely told our tale to our-selves, and suffered the indignities of
those who prepossess'd the world to our prejudice; and you know how
difficult a thing it is to play an after game, when mens minds are perverted and
their judgements prepossessd: our sloth and silence in this diffusive age,
greedy of Intelligence and publique affairs, is a greate fault and I wonder our
polititians that are at helme, take no more care of it, since we see what
advantages Reputation alone carries with it in Holland, Genoa, Venice, and
even our East-India Company's action, whereas all wise men know, they are
neither so rich, wise, or powerfull as they would be thought intrinsecaly, and

---

[1] Source: PC MS.i.31. Endorsed, '28 Aprl.1682. Mr Evelyn to Mr Pepys.'
[2] MS: '28 Apll–82'. 'I stirr'd not forth this Weeke... the season unusualy wet, with
such stormes of Raine and Thunder, as did greate damage:' (E's diary, 23 April 1682).
[3] Possibly in the sea (*Aeneid* VIII.672).

that it is the Credite and estimation the Vulgar has of them, which renders them Considerable. It was on this account I chose the Action at Bergin;[1] not that I thought it to be the most glorious and discreete (for in truth I thinke much otherwise) but for that the Exploit was intire, and because I had seene what the Dane had publish'd in Latine so much to our dishonor: How close I have kept to my Text, you will find by Collation, and whither nervous and sound none can better judge, and that I did not proceede, needes not be told you: The peace was concluded; my patron resign'd his staff; his successor was unkind and unjust to me.[2] The Dutch Ambassador complaind of my *Treatise of Commerce and Navigation*, which was intended but for a prolusion,[3] and published by his Majesties encouragement before the peace was quite ratified, though not publiquely told til afterwards: In summ, I had no thankes for what I had don, and have ben accounted since (I suppose) a useless Fop, and fit onely to plant Coleworts, and I can't bussle,[4] nor yet bend to meane submissions, and this, Sir, is the Historie of your Historian. I confesse to you I had once the Vanity to hope (had my patron continud in his station) for some (at least) honorary Title that might have animated my progresse, as seeing then some amongst them whose talents I did not envy; but it was not my fortune to succeed: If I were a young-man, and had the Vanity to believe any industry of mine, might recommend me to the Friendship and Esteeme of Mr Pepys; as I take him to be of a more inlarg'd and generous Soule, so I should not doubt but he would promote this Ambition of mine, and not thinke one that would labour for the honour of his Country in my Way, unworthy some reguard: This almost prompts me say the same to him that Joseph did to Pharaoh's exauctorated[5] Butler (whos restauration to grace he predicted)

Tantum memento mei, cum bene tibi fuerit

Thinke on me when it shall be well with thee;[6] and so

Farewell, Deare Sir,

Raptim[7]   JE:

---

[1] The action took place in August 1665 when a unit of the Royal Navy under the command of Sir Thomas Teddeman attempted unsuccessfully to intercept the homeward-bound Dutch East-India fleet off Bergen. Clifford handed E the relevant official records on 15 October 1670 (diary).

[2] Clifford resigned on 19 July 1673 (E's diary); succeeded by Sir Thomas Osborne.

[3] It was composed as a preface to the projected History of the Dutch War which was never published. E had some reason to feel insulted; the order for the suppression stated that he 'uses several expressions derogatory to the amity and understanding between us and some of our allies, and wherein he intermeddles with certain matters of state beyond what becomes him or belongs to him' (Charles II to the Stationers' Company, 12 August 1674, State Papers Domestic. Precedent, 1.f.16).

[4] Coleworts = cabbages; bussle = be noisily active.

[5] 'Removed from office' i.e. dismissed.

[6] *Genesis* xl.14.

[7] In haste.

C13. JOHN EVELYN TO SAMUEL PEPYS[1]

Fears that Mr Pepys was nearly drowned

Sayes Court
5 June 1682[2]

Sir,

I have ben both very Long, and very-much concern'd for you, since your Northern Voyage, as knowing nothing of it 'til you were Embarq'd and gon, (though I saw you few daies before)[3] and that the dismal Accident[4] was past, which gave me apprehensions for you, and a mixture of Passions, not realy to be Express'd, 'til I was assur'd of your Safty; and I now give[5] God Thankes for it with as much Sincerity, as any Friend you have alive: —

'Tis sadly true, these[6] were a greate many poore-Creatures lost;[7] but there are some worth hundreds Sav'd: Mr Pepys was to me the *Second* of those some, and if I could say a greater thing to expresse my joy for it, You should have it under the Hand, and from the Heart of,

Sir,
Your most humble servant,
JEvelyn:

---

[1] Source: Houghton Library, Harvard, Amy Lowell Collection, 1925. Endorsed by JJ, 'June the 5th 1682. Mr Evelyn's Congratulatory Letter to Mr Pepys for his safe returne from Sea after the losse of the *Gloucester*.' There are several differences from the copy transcribed by Upcott for Bray's diary editions (now at BL CLBII.430).

[2] MS: 'Says-Court 5 June –82'. When making the copy E mistook the year and incorrectly dated this letter to 5 June 1681. The mistake was repeated in Bray editions of the diary and correspondence, despite the reference to the Duke of York's shipwreck which took place on 6 May 1682.

[3] Since 1679 the Duke and Duchess of York had been in exile in Scotland. In 1682 James's request to return was granted and he sailed on 3 May in the *Gloucester* with a flotilla of vessels to collect the Duchess. Due to the 'obstinate, over-winning of the pilot' (Bod MS Rawl. A194; Howarth no. 123) the *Gloucester* was wrecked off the Yorkshire coast on 6 May with the loss of almost every one on board except for the duke, his dog, his footman, John Churchill, and a handful of others. The episode was described by Pepys in a letter to Hewer (ibid) from Edinburgh on 8 May. There is no recorded meeting between P and E in the days before though P may have been at the philosophical supper held at the Royal Society on 12 April (diary).

[4] Copy-letter adds 'and astonishing' before 'Accident'.

[5] Copy-letter supplies 'gave' for 'now give' suggesting its retrospective compilation.

[6] Sic, presumably a mistake for 'there'.

[7] Copy-letter adds here, 'and some Gallant persons with them'.

C14. JOHN EVELYN TO SAMUEL PEPYS[1]

The Martial performances of Dogs

For Samuel Pepys Esqr
at Mr Ewers house
Yorke buildings

[no place]
Moneday, 10 July 1682[2]

Sir,

It was upon the Bantam Ambassadors extravagant negotiation (worthy doubtlesse of a journey from the Indies) that you were asking of the other day,[3] whither Dogs was usefull to make War with, that I transcribe you this Note of their Militarie Virtues for the present, out of an Ampler Discourse upon another Subject which you have given me leave to revise a litle before it be worthy the rank you have advanc'd it to in your Elegant and accomplish'd Blbliotheque: The tediousnesse of writing, and much-more, of your Reading it, makes me passe-by innumerable Instances of the War-like Exploits of Dogs amongst the Magnates, the Caspii, those of Colophon: Cimbrians, Gaules, and other fierce people, as they are recorded by Valerius Flaccus, Julius Pollux, Strabo, Plinie, Valerius Maximus, Appion, and severall more of unspotted credite. Everybody knows how faithfully they guard the Town of St Malos in Bretagne, to this day, as many ages since they did a certaine Citty belonging to the Romans neere Coös. Nicetas Comiates[4] tells us how after a cruel Batail fought by the Latines against the Greekes, near Thessalonica, the Citty Dogs, that came out to the prey, would not touch the Carcasse of a Greeke, but feasted themselves upon their enemies with so strange a rabidnesse and

---

[1] Source: BL.1537 (ex-Davey Catalogue Item 2871, and Langham Catalogue Item 572). Endorsed, 'Monday the 10 July 1682. Mr Evelyn to Mr Pepys giveing an Historicall Account of the Martiall performances of Dogs.' This is the letter-sent, bearing a seal, but with a modern forged signature (p.135, note 4). Marburg supplies a partial transcription without giving her source, particularly curious as the BL manuscript is the only version known and, at the time she wrote, it was probably in the Evelyn archive, then inaccessible. However, the forged signature may indicate that a third party owned the letter after 1900, but prior to the Evelyn family's acquisition of it, perhaps making the manuscript available to Marburg on condition of anonymity.

[2] MS: 'Moneday 10 July'. Year given by endorsement and diary (see p.135, note 3).

[3] Described at length in the diary (20 June 1682).

[4] Presumably this is Nicetas Acominatos, the Byzantine scholar and historian.

appetite, that they scraped them out of their graves after they had ben buried: The like almost is related by Sabellicus,[1] of their distinguishing a Christian from a Turk, however disguisd, and that they did notable service in the War against those Miscreants: Of what considerable advantage they were to Massinissa[2] by giving intelligence of the Enemys approches by the sagacity of their noses, Historie tells us; and therefore those of Colophon[3] train'd them-up for War, and form'd them into Companies under Militarie Discipline, as finding them of excellent use upon Camisades and nocturnal exploits:[4] Nay we reade of a mighty Prince, driven by his rebellious subjects out of his Countrie, to have ben restor'd by the bravery of his 200 hunting Dogs, as Pliny *Naturalis Historiæ L.*8 *c.*40:[5] and tis out Joachimus Camerarius (whenever that excellent author had it)[6] that our Henry VIII should send Charles the Vth a Foote-Company of 400 men, who had attending on them as many stout Mastives, arm'd with Yron-Collers, set about with Sharp Spikes to defend their throats, but upon what stratagem I find it not mention'd: nor, it seemes was this the first time that British-Dogs were of use upon such occasions; since we find in Strabo that they assail'd the Gaules with them, and had an expresse Officer over them, appointed by Imperial Order;[7] perhaps these might be of the Agæsean race mentiond by Oppian and our learned Cambden; This more is remarkable, that two greate Armies of the French and Swisse being on the point of joyning Battell, all the Dogs of the French Camp leaving at once their Masters, ran-over to the Enemy, Fawning and crouching to them, upon which presage, the Swisse giving a fierce Charge, the French gave ground, and were utterly defeated as Paulus Jovius[8] relates the passage; Marcus Pomponius the Praetor was the first we reade of, who in the Sardinian War made use of dogs to find out the sculking fugitives among the Rocks and fastnesses,[9] and hence 'tis probable the Spaniards might put into practise their late barbarities in the Western Indies: Oviedo[10] recounts how Diego Salazare's Bezerillo (for so was his Dog call'd) being set on a poore Salvage-Woman, and spoken to in a submissive tone by the title of Don Pirro (Sir dog) to spare her; the disdainefull Cur, having thrown the feeble Creature downe,

---

[1] Marcus Antonius Coccius Sabellicus.
[2] Masinissa, King of Numidia.
[3] A town in Ionia.
[4] A camisade is a 'nocturnal exploit' or nocturnal attack.
[5] In fact VIII.142. The 'prince' was the King of the Garamantes.
[6] A marginal note 'Histor Milit' indicates this is the German classical scholar Joachimus Camerarius the Elder, and not his botanist son of the same name.
[7] Not strictly accurate. Strabo died c. AD 25, before any such imperial order might have had weight in Britain. At IV.v.2 Strabo describes the British dogs bred specially for hunting and which were exported to the continent.
[8] Paolo Giovio, the Italian historian.
[9] I have not been able to trace the source of this tale.
[10] Francisco de Oviedo.

onely piss'd on her,[1] and generously return'd to his more brutish Master, who had barely accustom'd him to that cruel[2] and inhumane Chace, and Le Pois[3] tells us of a Souldier there, who receiv'd double-pay for himselfe and a truculent Mastive of his, which made prodigious slaughter in that War, if so that feritie[4] were worthy he be nam'd, which was waged against naked and defencelesse people as Bartholomew de las Casas (a Bishop of their owne and an eye-witnesse) has set it forth in the most sanguine Character:[5] But I should quite tire you in a Letter with what I have reserv'd upon another Argument to entertaine you with, wherein I shall also give you my conjectures how an Automate may possibly be Mechanicaly contriv'd to utter articulate Words as well as sounds which was another question the other day: In the meane time, all we have produc'd as to what real service Dogs may be said to have perform'd in the Wars, 'tis certaine they sometimes mistake their Masters and Leaders, when contending with their Enemies, Lions, Beares, Bulls, and other Brutes (being train'd up on the same account) I finde they were soon left-off againe; because they could not possibly discipline them to distinguish their Keepers and Commanders from their Enemies.

—————— *in munere belli*
Tentarunt etiam tauros etc

Lucret. *L*.5[6]

When Bulls for feats of wars they did array,
Turning Wild-Boares against their Enemie;
And Parthian Lions their Vaunt Guard supplie,
Under arm'd Leaders, and fierce keepers, who
Could chaine and govern them: Yet vainly though;
For chas'd in Fight, promiscuously they slue
Without distinction, and over-threw

---

[1] The Davey Catalogue compiler expressed the view (1889, 2871, p.9) that this letter 'with a slight omission would form an entertaining article'. It may be assumed that this is the passage earmarked for excision. Marburg (1935, 152) followed his advice.

[2] Reading uncertain. Perhaps alternatively (but less likely) 'orbel', for 'ordel' (a variant of 'ordeal'), which would also fit the context.

[3] Antoine le Pois. E possessed his *Discours sur les Medalles et Graveures Antiques*, Paris, 1579 (Library Sale Lot 898).

[4] Someone or something with the quality of being barbarous and savage.

[5] In his 'History of the Indies' which includes graphic accounts of Spanish atrocities. He was made Bishop of Chiapa in 1544.

[6] This varies from the modern text of Lucretius, *De Rerum Natura* V.1308, which reads: *Temptarunt etiam tauros in mœnere belli*, 'They also tried bulls in acts of war.' It was not unusual for E to paraphrase his Latin quotations but it is not always obvious whether this was deliberate or due to an unreliable memory. The following English verse is E's translation of this and successive lines from Lucretius.

Whole Legions, shaking their horrid Crist[s];[1]
Nor could indeede the Cavalrie resist,
Nor rule their Horse with bitts, or qualifie
Their Beasts, [affright'd][2] with the rabid Crie;
On each side the inraged Lionesse
Teares-out the throats of such as forward presse,
And at their back surprizes e're aware,
When sitting loose, they pull'd them down and tare
Them with their fangs and paws: The Bull, the Bore,
O're-turned, tramples, and with his hornes did gore
The Horses in the Belly, and their side:
Boares with their Tuskes their fellows slue, and dy'd
The scatter'd darts ith' blood o'th slaine, which put
In strange confusion both horse and foote.

So as it seems they were faine to give over this barbarous way of fighting.

My Apologies for this impertinence I intend you shall have to morrow, when I waite on you to the Morocco Audience[3]

[Yours

JEvelyn][4]

---

[1] Variant form of 'crest' (the meaning here is probably the lions' manes); perhaps E had in mind Lucretius' *cristas* here (plural, but made singular in English to scan).

[2] Reading uncertain, perhaps 'affrit'd'; however, this is the meaning of the Latin *perterrita* which Lucretius uses here.

[3] This reference helps confirm the date of the letter. E tried to see the Moroccan Ambassador on 11 July (diary), having seen him before on 24 January 1682 (ibid), but Albemarle's invitation to the ambassador to visit his house at New Hall near Chelmsford meant that E missed him.

[4] The words 'Yours JEvelyn' are modern forgeries. This much is clear from the wording (which would normally be 'Your most humble faithfull and obedient servant'), the formation of the letters, and the different pen and ink used for them. E had closed the letter before the ink had dried, leaving a reverse impression of the text of the final leaf on the opposite blank, but no mirror image of the signature appears. Neither the Davey Catalogue nor Langham Catalogue, in which this letter appeared, describe the manuscript as being 'A.L.S.' (autograph letter, signed). Instead they distinguish it from the others as an 'Autograph MS', indicating the forged signature was added after 1900 (this is not the only victim of modern additions to the letters – see p.165, note 9). E did not sign the letter because, as was clear from his postscriptum, he planned to hand it to P in person.

C15. JOHN EVELYN TO SAMUEL PEPYS[1]

Evelyn recants his views on England's dominion of the seas

To Samuell Pepys Esqr
Late Secretary of the Admiralty

Sayes Court
19 September 1682[2]

Sir,

In Answer to your quæries,[3] I will most ingenuously declare my thoughts, upon second meditation, since I publish'd my *Treatise of Commerce*,[4] and what I have ben taught; but was not there to speake in publique without offence: I will therefore reply in the method you seeme to hint; and after say what I have concerning our pretence to Dominion on the Seas: To the first—

Buxhornius has written an historie of the Ansiatic Townes, where you'l find in what Condition and Credit Holland was for Trafique and Commerce, and in the Danish Annales: It would be enquir'd when the English staple was remov'd into Brabant, being 100 yeares since, and more, fixed at Dort: How far forth Charles the fift[h] pursued, or minded his Interest at Sea? As to Henry the 4th, of France, 'tis evident he was not negligent of his Interest there, by his many Projects for Trade, and performances at Marseilles: all that Richlieue and his successors in that Ministrie produc'd, was projected by their Greate Henry, as is plaine out of Morisotus[5] his præface. And now

To our Title of Dominion and the Fishry (which has made such a noise in this part of the World) I confesse, I did lately seeke to magnifie and assert it, as

---

[1] Source: BL CLBII.445. Much of this letter is verbatim repetition of 7 July 1680 (**C7**, see above). E's lengthy letters of 7 July 1680, 26 August 1689 (**C47**), and 4 October 1689 (**C49**) all survive as letters-sent, with variously two also in copies by P, and two in copies by E; the replies by P to two of them survive as well. In view of this, the repetition, and the fact that the only known version is a bound copy there is a possibility it was never sent, at least in this form (see also below, note 2, and p.140, note 3). A note by E in the margin at the beginning of the letter has been heavily deleted by him and is not legible; however it begins with 'I' and may be a comment on the fate of the letter.
[2] MS: 'Says Court 19 Sept 82'. According to the diary E was in London on this date.
[3] Not extant but perhaps a retrospective reference to those of 1680 (**C5**) or 1681 (**C10**, p.127).
[4] *Navigation and Commerce*, 1674.
[5] Claude Barthelemy Morisot, his *Orbis Maritimi Sive Rerum in Mare et Littoribus Gestarum Generalis Historia*, Dijon, 1643.

became me *pro hic et nunc*[1] (to speake with logicians), and as the Circumstances then requir'd you know;[2] But betweene friends, (and under the Rose as they say),[3] to tell you realy my thoughts, when such like Topics were us'd (sometimes in Parliament) 'tis plaine they were pass'd-over there upon important reasons. To begin with the very first, supposing the old Britains did prohibite forainers to come into their Country, what inferrs that to any Claime of dominion in the Narrow, but a jealosie rather over their proper Coasts: Nor reade we that they ever practis'd it over the Gaules: The Chinezes (we find) forbad all to enter their Countrie: are they therefore Lords of the Oriental Seas? As for King Arthyr (abating what is fabulous, viz, his Legendarie Dominion), the *Comes Litoris Saxonici*,[4] etc, stretch'd to Denmark, Sweden, Norway, and Iseland, infers either too much or nothing. Have we, therefore, any right of Clayme to those Realmes at present? Why then to the Seas? Againe, admitt the most, May not Dominion be lost? or Extinguish'd? Was not this rather a Momentarie Conquest or Excursion, rather than an establish'd dominion? Was it not lost to the Danes? Had they not all the characters of domination imaginable? Lords of our seas; Lords of our shores too, and the Tribute of *Dane-Gelt* from England and Ireland both? If ever there were a real dominion in the World, the Danes must be yeildid to have had it: and if their Title cannot be extinguish'd by subsequent Revolutions: I greately question whether ours will ever be evinced. In short, the story of King Edgar[5] is monstrously romantic, and the pretended deede I doubt will appear but spurious:[6] Truely, if forraine Chronicles had ben as much stuff'd with the renowne of this Prince, as with King Arthyrs, I should give more credit to it: In the meane time, what they report of Athelred is totaly against us, since 'tis plaine, he payd the *Danegelt* as a tribute to them, and settled it to that end. One may querie whether the Scots Seas, and Scotland (too boote) be not a fee[7] to England; for with as much reason we might challenge it, if the producing Rolls, Records, and Acts of Parliament, and of Statutes to that purpose were of any importance; because we can shew more to the purpose, than in the other Case: but how would then that Nation take it, and what become of their Laws about Fishing? 'Tis declar'd in our Laws, that we are Lords of the *foure Seas*, and so adjudged in our Courts, as to those Born upon those Seas; and yet the

---

[1] For here and now.

[2] The circumstances of the Third Dutch War.

[3] In secret.

[4] Count of the Saxon Shore. See p.109, note 1.

[5] See pp. 104, note 4, and 109, note 2.

[6] E reported the tale in *Navigation and Commerce*, 1674, 94, para 50: 'We have but mention'd King Edgar, whose survey is so famous in story, when with more than four thousand vessels he destin'd a quarternion to every sea, which annually circl'd this Isle and, as a monument of their submission, was sometimes row'd in his royal galley by the hands of eight kings.'

[7] A feudal estate held on condition of payment and homage to a superior.

Parliament of Scotland can impose a Tax on our fishermen, which is a shrew'd argument against us: Who ever read that the Kings of England prohibited any to fish on the Coasts of Scotland? Or charg'd them with Usurpation for taking Toll and Custome for the Herring-fishing? The truth is, the Licences (which I speake of in my Book, from Scarbrough)[1] were onely to fish on the dogger-bank: Such English as were to fish in the Scotish Seas, about Orkney, and Shetland, Iseland, and Fero, etc, did take Licences to fish from the Kings of Norway at Bergen and Northbarum, and this jurisdiction and sovrainty undoubted of the Norwegian-Kings, is recogniz'd by our owne Parliament in a statute of Henry the 8th, 6, *c.*, 2, and by innumerable Treaties betwixt the two Crownes, even within a Century of Yeares; and if so, consider how feeble a proofe is that famous Roll *pro hominibus Hollandiæ*,[2] and how it is to be limited in itselfe (by the Historie and occasion that caus'd it) to the Narrow or Chanell only: 'Tis also to be Consider'd that the Danes protested at Breda, that the Cession of the Scots fishrie about Orkney and Shetland was never made to our King James upon his Marriage of Queen Ann (as our Tradition is), nor any time before to any Scotish King; And, supposing that there were any such authentique Deede, it were better to fix the Fishrie (we contend about) even in the Dutch, than either permit it to be regulated by the decrees of a Scotish parliament, or transferr it to that Nation. Now As to the great trade, and multitude of English Vessels, by the Historie of the Haunse Townes, their priveleges and power in England, one shall find, that for the bulk our Navies consisted most of hired-ships of the Venetian, Genoezes, and Ansiatics, 'til Queene Elizabeth, though her father Henry the Eighth had a flourishing fleete. The Right of Passes, and Petitions thereupon, were form'd upon another part of the *Jus Gentium*,[3] then our pretended Dominion of the Seas; which (to speak ingenuously) I could never find Recognizd expressly in any Treaty with forrainers. As to returne to the Fishery, that of the Dutch fishing without License, the *Intercursus magnus*[4] (so boaste'd) was a perpetual Treaty, and made as well with all the people, as the princes of Burgundy; and so, as to be Obligatorie, though they rejected their Governors, as we see most of them did, and as (perhaps) they might, according to the *Lætus Introitus*.[5] And that the Dutch are still (and by Queen Elizabeth were so declar'd to be) a *pars Contrahens*,[6] after their Revolt and abjuration of Spaine, dos as much invalidate that proceeding of King James, and Charles the first, who both

---

[1] *Navigation and Commerce*, 105, para 57.

[2] 'That famous Record *Pro Hominibus Hollanidiæ* (so the Title runs) points us to as far as our first Edward, not only how obsequious then they were in Acknowledging the King's Dominion on the Sea, but his Protection and permission to Fish on the environs of it...' *Navigation and Commerce*, 102, para 56.

[3] International law.

[4] Great intervention.

[5] Happy beginning.

[6] A lesser or diminished area, or an area of smaller parts drawn together.

sign'd that *Intercursus*, and were in truth included thereby, though they had not sign'd it. But besides all this,

The nature of Prescription would be enquir'd into, as well when it makes against us, as for us; and therefore it should be demanded whether Queene Elizabeth did not first assert the *Mare Liberum* in opposition to the Danes? and whether his present Majestie has not don it at Jamaica against the Spaniard: Pray Consider the Seale of that Admiralty: To speake plaine truth, when I writ that Treatise, rather as a philological Exercise, and to gratifie the present Circumstances, I could not clearely satisfie my selfe in sundry of those particulars; nor find realy, that ever the Dutch did pay Toll, or Tooke License to fish in Scotland after the Contest, from any solid proofes: Indeede (as there, I relate), they surpriz'd Braun[1] who came to exact it, and detain'd him in Holland severall Moneths; but I think they nere' pay'd peny for it; though the papers I have perus'd, speake of an *Assize Herring*: Nor did I find, that any Rent (whereoff in my (108 page) I calculate the Arreres)[2] for permission to Fish, was ever fixed by both parties; and so cannot properly be call'd a settl'd Rent. This would, therefore, be exquisitely inquir'd into, and perhaps both for these and many other particulars, a thorough search in his Majesties Paper Office may afford clearer light, if there have any due care taken to Collect and digest such Important Matters.

As for the Yeares 1635 and 37, you cannot but espie an Intrigue in the Equipping those formidable Fleets, and that they were more to awe the French than Terrifie Holland (See how the Times and Interests Change! but no more than that, 'tis now a tender point!) I fancy were no difficult matter to prove: And that any Licenses were taken in those Yeares, I could never be assur'd of: That of −36 being but a single Act of force on some particular men, the States never owning them in it; and you know the Admiral Dorp[3] was casheer'd for not quarrelling it with our Northumberland, and our Conduct and Licenses flatly rejected in 1637, when Captain Field came. Lastly,

When King James fixed his Chamber, did he not either Renounce the English Sovragnety of the Seas, or Violate therein his League with Spaine? (as that nation urged, pleading that the British Seas were *Territorium Domini Regis*) but he did not the latter; wherefore I am not single in this declaration. In a word, the intire Argument of the Fish'ry, is too Controvertable to be too peremptorily decided by the penn, and upon many other Accounts (of which the plenty and wantones of our full-fed, and un-frugal people, which deterrs them from hard Labour, is not the least) a project wholly Uselesse as Circumstances be, and therefore might with much more benefit, ease and facility, be supplied by increasing our Fishery at New-found-land: Finaly

---

[1] See p.111, note 2.
[2] To 'more than half a Million of pounds', see p.111, note 3.
[3] Not identified.

As to Commerce in generall, of this Nation, from all that I could observe during my short being of that noble and honorable Council,[1] and informing my-selfe as I was able by books and discourses of experienc'd persons; I say, after all this, I concluded it a very vaine thing to make any (the most probable, certaine, or necessarie) proposal about Trade, etc: Not that it might not be infinitely improv'd, if princes, and people did Unanimously, and with a true publique Spirit, and as our natural Advantages prompt us; apply them selves honestly and industriously about it; But, for that as things now are, and have hitherto ben maneg'd (since the renown'd Queene Elizabeth, for that *encomium*[2] I must give her), the whole advantage this Nation receives thereby, is evidently carried on more by antient Methods, and the sedulitie of Private Men, than by any publique Encouragement; And as to the present, it certainely languishes under insupportable difficulties: And thus, Sir, I choose to convey you my second more digested thoughts, of a point which in your Excellent designe and Work cannot escape the ample handling, as one of the most considerable, when you come to speake of the importance of our shipping, and trade, or pretence of dominions etc. And I do it, you see, with all Selfe-denyal imaginable (and not without some reproch) after what I have publish'd to the Contrary; by which you may conclude, how suspicious wise men should be of other Histories and Historians too, how confident and specious soever, unlesse it were almost demonstration, that the Authors had no Interest of their owne to serve, and were not influenc'd by their superiors, or the publique Cry: Let this ingenuous Confession commute for my faults in that Treatise, and be put amongst the Recantations of Sir[3]

Yours, etc

---

[1] E sat on the Council of Trade and Plantations from 1672–4.

[2] Panegyric-like praise.

[3] In view of the possibility that this letter was not sent (above, p.136, note 1) this closing statement should be considered in association with E's diary entry for 30 [sic, for 31] October 1682 where he describes his 'serious Recollection of the yeares past'. A letter to P may thus have represented a convenient formula in which he could examine his conscience for his own benefit to recant his views rather than actually having ever had an intention to express it to P in this way. There is no extant evidence to verify that P ever received it.

C16. SAMUEL PEPYS TO JOHN EVELYN[1]

Mr Pepys about the voyage to Tangier

Portsmouth
7 August 1683

Sir,

Your kinde Summons of the 2d instant[2] has overtaken mee here, where it cannot be more surprising to you to finde mee, than it is to mee to finde myselfe; the King's Command (without any account of the reason of it) requiring my repayre hither at lesse then eight and forty hours warning. Not but that I now,[3] not only know, but am well pleased with the errand; it being to accompany my Lord of Dartmouth (and therewith) to have some service assigned mee for his Majesty) in his præsent Expedition, with a very fayre Squadron of Shipps to Tangier.

What our Worke nevertheless is, I am not sollicitous to learne, not forward to make guesses[4] at, it being handled by our Maisters as a Secret.[5] This only I am sure of, that over and above the satisfaction of being thought fitt for some use or other ('tis noe matter what,) I shall goe in a good shipp, with a good fleete under a very worthy leader, in a Conversation as delightfull as companions of the first forme in Divinity, Law, Physick, and the usefullest parts of Mathematics can render it, namely, Dr Ken, Dr Trumbull, Dr Lawrence, and Mr Shere; with additionall pleasure of concerts (much above the ordinary) of Voices, Flutes, and Violins; and to fillings[6] (if any thing can do't where Mr Evelyn is wanting) good humour, good Cheere, good books, the company of my neerest friend Mr Hewer, and a reasonable prospect of being home againe in lesse than two months.[7] But, after all, Mr Evelyn is not here, who alone would have beene all this, and without whom all this would bee much lesse then it is, were it not that leaving him behinde, I have something in reserve (and safe) to returne to, wherewith to make-up whatever my best Enquirys and Gatherings from abroad, without his guidance shall, (as I am

---

[1] Source: BL Upcott Antiquaries II. Endorsed by E, 'Mr Pepys. Portsmouth 7:Aug:1683 about the Voyage to Tangier'.

[2] Unknown.

[3] MS: 'new'?

[4] Braybrooke supplied 'griefes' here, repeated by Howarth who did not have access to the manuscript; 'guesses' is, however, quite clear.

[5] Pepys was told by Dartmouth on 13 August following (Howarth, 380).

[6] Not certain. Braybrooke supplied 'fill up all'.

[7] He did not return until March 1684.

sure they must) prove defective in. With which, committing my selfe to your good wishes, as I doe you and your excellent family to God-All-mighty's protection, I rest,

> Dear Sir,
> Your most faythfull and most obedient Servant,
> S Pepys

If you have not allready done it at my last request, pray let me repete the necessity I am under of using your authority with my Lady Tuke,[1] in getting my not wayting on her excused; her favors to mee (for your sake) haveing long since challenged those thanks from mee which now must bee respited till my returne, unless you'l give me credit, and pay them in my absence.

---

[1] Mary, née Sheldon, Lady Tuke. She was second wife of Sir Samuel Tuke.

C17. JOHN EVELYN TO SAMUEL PEPYS[1]

To Samuel Pepys going to Tangier etc in Answer to his from Portsmouth

For Samuell Pepys Esqr at
Ports-mouth in the Fleete
with my Lord of Dartmouth: Portsmouth

Sayes Court
10 August 1683[2]

Sir,
I find my-selfe surpriz'd and over-joy'd together; The One, by so unexpected
an occasion of your absence from us; The other, for aboundance of reasons;
and that you are come into the Publique againe, and do not who[lly] resigne
your-selfe to Speculation, nor withdraw your industrious and steady hand
from the helme of that greate Vessel in which we are all Imbarked with you:
Mithinke I respire againe, and (tir'd as I am) hope to see the good effects of
God-Almighties Late providences: 'Tis a faire Omen, Sir, and an illustrious
marke of his Majesties discernement, that he recalls, and makes choice of such
worthy Instruments, and no small blessing, that he has faculty (at last) to
govern and dispose as he dos, after all the hardships and contradictions of a
wanton and giddy people, through which he struggles. For the rest, I dive not
into Seacrets, but infinitely congratulate your felicitie, and the greate
satisfaction you must needes derive from such a union as you describe:
Mithinke when you recount to me all the Circumstances of your Voyage, your
noble and choyce Companie: Such usefull, as well as delightfull Conversation;
You leave us so naked at home, that 'til your returne from Barbarie, we are in
danger of becoming Barbarians: The Heros are all Embark'd with my Lord
Dartmouth and Mr Pepys; nay they seeme to carry along with them not a
Colonie onely, but a Colledge, nay a[n?] whole Universitie, all the Sciences,
all the Arts, and all the Professors of 'em too: What shall [I] say! You seeme to
be in the ship that Athenæus[3] speakes of, was so furnish'd with all that the
land afforded, as it more resembl'd an imperial Citty, than the floating, and
artificial fabric of a Carpenter:– May you be bless'd Sir with as prosperous a
Voyage and Expedition as the possessors of so much real Virtue, and an
Assembly of so many excellent and worthy persons highly merite; and may I
allwayes be number'd amongst the many who greately honour you, and who
remaines, Sir
          Your most humble, and faithfull Servant,
                    JEvelyn: [*letter continues overleaf*]

---

[1] Source: Bod MS Rawl. A190, f.10. Endorsed by P, 'Aug.10.1683, Mr Evelin to SP'.
[2] MS: 'Sayes-Court 10 August'. Year from endorsement.
[3] See p.118, note 7.

Sir, Amongst so many worthy persons particular obligations, call for the presentment of my most humble Services to my Lord Dartmouth, Dr Trumbal, Mr Ewers,[1] and Mr Sheeres,[2] etc.

I have not forgotten to make your Complement to my Lady Tuke, some time since, and I shall let her know how worthily you have her in your thoughts:

The inconvenient circumstances Captain Fowler has ben forc'd to leave his Wife in here, makes me beg he may partake of your favour upon occasion: I thinke him an honest, loyal and sturdy sea man.[3]

I am sure you cannot but be curious (among other things) to enquire of Medails and Inscriptions, especialy what may be found about old Tangier, etc: Mr Sheeres will remember also the poore Gardener, if he happen on any kirnels or seedes of such Trees, and plants (especialy, ever-Greenes) as grow about those precincts: Were it not possible to discover whither any of these Citrine-trees are yet to be found, that of old grew about the foote of Mount Atlas not far from Tingis?[4] and were here-tofore *in deliciis* for their politure[5] and natural maculations[6] to that degree, as to be sold for their weight in Gold: Cicero had a Table that cost him ten-thousand sesterces,[7] and another, which I have read of, that was valu'd at 140000 sesterces which at 3d [per] sesterce amounted to a pretty summ, and one of the Ptolomies had yet another of far greater price,[8] inso-much as when they us'd to reproch their Wives for their Lux and excesse in pearle and paint they would retort, and turne the Tables on their husbands: Now for that some Copies in Pliny reade *Cedria*, others *Citria*,[9] 'twould be enquir'd what sort of Cedar (if any) grows about that Mountaine! But Sir, you see I am growing very impertinent, and humbly beg your pardon for this hasty scribble, fearing, or rather hoping, you are in a propitious Gale.

---

[1] William Hewer, at the time of writing Treasurer of Tangier.

[2] Henry, later Sir, Sheeres. He had been Engineer at Tangier since 1669.

[3] See Mary Evelyn's letter of 7 September 1687 to P (Bod MS Rawl. A189, f.5; Howarth no. 170) on Mrs Fowler's behalf, and E's letter to P, 1 March 1688 (**C40**).

[4] Tangier. The reference is probably to Pliny, *NH* V.14 or XIII.91.

[5] 'In favour/fashion' for their smooth, polished finish.

[6] Stains or marks. Pliny describes the marks as having formed veins or spirals and that this was considered the wood's principal and most attractive feature (*NH* XIII.96).

[7] Pliny in fact reports that Cicero's citrus-wood table cost half-a-million sesterces (*NH* XIII.92). Sesterce = sestertius, the main unit of Roman pricing.

[8] E's estimate equals £1,750 in his day. Pliny gives 'Ptolemy of Mauretania' (*NH* XIII.93) as the owner of the largest citrus-wood table known to him, but supplies no price. He does describe another which was once sold for 1.3 million sesterces.

[9] *Cedria* = 'Cedar-resin'; *Citria* or *citrea* = 'that of the citrus-tree'.

C18. JOHN EVELYN TO SAMUEL PEPYS[1]

On Thomas Burnet, the Universe, and news of an eclipse

For Samuell Pepys Esqr at his
lodging in Yorke-streete

Sayes Court
8 June 1684[2]

Sir,

With your excellent book,[3] I returne you likewise my most humble thanks for your inducement of me to reade it over againe; finding in it severall things (as you told me) omitted in the Latine (which I had formerly read with greate delight) still new, still surprizing, and the whole hypothesis so ingenious and so rational, that I both admire and believe it at once. I am infinitely pleased with his thoughts concerning the Universe (intellectual and material) in relation to this despicable mole-hill on which we mortals crawle, and keepe such a stirr about as if the τὸ πᾶν (this All) were created for us little vermine. 'Twas ever my thoughts, since I had the use almost of reason. I know nothing of the author's person or circumstances, but he has a genius greate, and bravely inlarges the empire of our narrow speculations and repent[4] spirits, whose contemplations extend no farther than their sense. In the meane time, I cannot but wonder any man should imagine that this theorie does in the least derogate from the Holy Scriptures, as some peevish and odd men (I have met with) pretend. Was ever any thing better sayd to convince the atheist than what he has written concerning matter and motion and the Universal Providence, to the reproch of chance and our contingent fops?[5] There needes no more than his 10th and 11 chapters, *lib.* 2, utterly to confound those unthinking wretches. In a word, Sir, the gentleman has doubtlesse a noble, and large soule,

---

[1] Source: Tanner 1926, no. 14 (PC MS.i.32), and BL CLBII.479. Endorsed, '[Mr Evelyn to Mr Pepys] giving his opinion to the advantage of Mr Burnett's new Theory of the Earth'. The book is Thomas Burnet's *Telluris Theoria Sacra*, 1681. The Evelyn Library copy was a 1689 edition purchased by E's grandson in 1724 (Lot 274).

[2] E's copy is dated 30 May 1684. See p.146, note 2, for why it should have been obvious to him that the copy was misdated.

[3] See note 1 above.

[4] The term is a botanical and zoological one used here in an analogous sense to mean creeping under the surface and unable to rise to higher thoughts.

[5] I.e. the fools who come about as a result of chance.

and one would wish to be acquainted with him; for one that is so bright, and happy in his owne thoughts, cannot but influence and illuminate all that converse with him, with that generous and becoming candor which is due to so much reason, and to greate delight. I am, Sir, for this and innumerable civilities, Sir,

Your most humble and faithfull servant
JEvelyn:[1]

Mr Flamsted has lately advertized me of an eclipse of the moone which will happen the 17th of this moneth about 3 in the morning,[2] and wished I would give you notice of it, that if your leasure permitted he might have the honor of your company;[3] and I should readily waite upon you.[4]

---

[1] The copy-letter adds the following postscriptum, absent from the letter-sent: 'Somethins I have yet to object, concerning the Torrid Zone, the Whales, and the Sea, to reconcile[?] 1.*Gen*:21.26'. It is crammed in, in smaller handwriting, and seems to be an afterthought, added when the copy-letter was written up.

[2] The moon passed through the periphery of the Earth's shadow (a penumbral eclipse of the moon) between the hours of, approximately, midnight and 0400 Greenwich Mean Time on the morning of 17 June 1684, Old Style (27 June 1684, New Style). (I am grateful to Ian Ridpath, I.O.U., for this information). In using the words 'this moneth', which also appear in the copy (dated 30 May instead of 8 June) E shows that he should have realised the copy was misdated. It incidentally also indicates that any draft was also written in June, and that when writing up the copy E was guessing its date.

[3] Copy adds here, 'at his Observatorie'.

[4] Although E does not mention observing this lunar eclipse, he did attend the solar eclipse which took place a fortnight later: 'I went to the Observatorie at Greenewich, where Mr Flamstead tooke his observations of the Ecclipse of the sunn, now hapning to be almost 3 parts obscur'd' (E's diary, 2 July 1684). This solar eclipse occurred on 2 July 1684, Old Style (12 July, New Style), between 1415 and 1630 (Greenwich Mean Time) obscuring marginally more than fifty per cent of the solar disk. (ibid, Ian Ridpath).

C19. JOHN EVELYN TO SAMUEL PEPYS[1]

Evelyn is obliged to proclaim James II in Bromley

To Samuell Pepys
Secretary of the Admiralty

Sayes Court
9 February 1685[2]

Sir,

I doubt not but our Præsident and Council[3] will think it our Duty to make our humble Submissions and Congratulatorie Addresses to his Majestie and Crave his protection of a Society founded by his Royal Predecessor:[4] If that should happen to be the Business of the day among you, it will be my misfortune to be detain'd at home, upon an inevitable Occasion:[5] And on Thursday I am oblig'd to attend on the Sherif of this County (at Bromely) for the Proclayming the King there:[6] I am not so vaine to expect this Addresse should be deferr'd on my account, but if it should be appointed any day the next Week (which time every body will be in their mourning Weekes) I should be very ready to waite upon the Ceremonie; and I believe our Præsident will think fit, that in the meane time, we bespeake the Countenance of Assistance of the Duke of Norfolck, Earle of Clarendon, Lord Vaughan and other noble persons of our Society to accompanie and introduce[?] me. Sir, You will do me the favour to acquaint me by this bearer, What is resolv'd in this matter, who am

Sir Your etc

---

[1] Source: BL CLBII.492.

[2] MS: '9:Feb:1684/5'.

[3] Of the Royal Society. P had been its president since 1 December 1684.

[4] Charles II had died on 6 February 1685. He had granted the Royal Society a charter of incorporation in 1662 (see E's diary for 13 August 1662).

[5] There is no indication from the diary what this might have been.

[6] E describes his participation in the proclamation of James II at Bromley in his diary entry for 11 February 1685 which was a Wednesday. He also says that the Sheriff's summons to him came on 10 February. In view of the dating problems with E's copy-letters it is probable that the letter is wrong and the diary right.

C20. SAMUEL PEPYS TO [JOHN EVELYN][1]

Pepys will help but apologises for being remiss

[no place]
Saturday 4 July 1685[2]

Sir

I have received your Commands (from the Ladys)[3] and if the person they and you are pleas'd to recommend to mee, will give mee opportunity of informing my selfe from him, under what Character (as to his former Service and præsent Qualifications) I may best propose him for favour to his Majesty; you may depend upon't, hee shall loose nothing that I can adde to it to his just advantage.[4]

If I thought I could need any excuses with you, who know the Condition I now serve under here,[5] for my not doeing what the rest of your Civill Friends doe in wayteing on my Lady and your Selfe upon the same Melancholly errand;[6] I should thinke it a great fault not to doe it. But I know, you can, and I am sure of your Justice, that you doe distinguish of Friends in this Matter; and therefore will say noe more, then that if ever the Fullest Cause of Affliction mett at once with the best of Preparatives of Philosophy and Duty for supporting it, it is in my Lady's case and yours. I am

Your most faythfull and most
humble and affectionate Servant
SPepys

---

[1] Source: BL Add. MSS 29300, f.25. Labelled, 'Purchased at Messrs Puttick 6 June 1874' (perhaps once in Upcott's collection?). Published by Howarth (Hw 46) under an incorrect date (1675; see note 2). No endorsements. The corrected date, the content, and the letter of 8 September 1685 (**C24**) make E the likely addressee.

[2] MS: 'Saturd July 4 1685', using '∞' for '8'. In view of Howarth's misdating it may be noted that 4 July 1685 <u>was</u> a Saturday, and 4 July 1675 was a Sunday.

[3] Probably Mrs Evelyn and Ann, Lady de Sylvius (see next note). E last saw the latter on 4 June (diary); however he dined with several other female friends on 2 July (ibid).

[4] In the letter of 8 September 1685 (**C24**) E states he is repeating a request on behalf of Ann, Lady de Sylvius, that P assist the promotion of an unnamed individual; he appears to confirm the content of the present letter, which therefore seems to be P's response to the initial request.

[5] P had found enormous problems in the Navy, following his reappointment as Secretary of the Admiralty in June 1684. Early in 1685 he had produced a major report on the state of the navy (Ollard 1991, 312–3).

[6] Assuming E is the addressee this is a reference to the death of E's daughter Mary from smallpox on 14 March 1685. E states many of his friends condoled with him (diary). P is not among them, and is here apologising for not attending.

C21. JOHN EVELYN TO SAMUEL PEPYS[1]

The shame of a clandestine intrigue

For Samuell Pepys Esqr:
Secretary to the Admiralty
at his house
in Yorke-buildings

Sayes Court
29 July 1685[2]

Sir,

The Common Cryer has by this prevented my sad storie, and it would but renew the trouble it has already caus'd you, to repeate what I presume, my Son has told you of our reproch: So strange, and altogether surprising is this clandestine Intrigue, that I protest, I do not so much as know the unworthy fellow, should I meete him in the streetes:[3] And though I should not despise the Circumstances of his Condition, I cannot but think it a meane, and tretcherous part in any, to enveagle a Child in so infamous a manner: I have heard you are meditating Laws this Parliament[4] to render Capital these irreparable Injuries to Families: I wish it for the peace of others,[5] whilst 'tis my hard fate to suffer an irremedilesse affront: The exceeding Care we have ever had of instilling pious, and honorable principles into all our Children, and their Susception of them to all appearance ('til this unhappy moment) banish'd

---

[1] Source: Pforzheimer MS 35E. Endorsed by P, 'July 29th 1685, Mr Evelyn to SP upon his late Misfortune in the Clandestine Marriage of his Daughter'. This letter and the next two (**C22**, and **C23**) were listed in the Davey Catalogue of 1889 collectively as Item 2872, where it was added that they were not for sale on account of their 'family matters' content. Despite this Victorian sensibility to the Evelyn family's feelings 204 years after the events described the letters unaccountably (but fortunately) appeared in the Morrison Sale at Sotheby's in 1919 as Lot 2822. From there they went to the Pforzheimer Collection.

[2] MS: 'Says-Cot: 29 July:–85' at foot of letter.

[3] E's daughter Elizabeth had eloped with the nephew of Sir John Tippet, Surveyor of the Navy on the night of the 27 July 1685, marrying him the following day. The nephew is otherwise unknown and E never supplies his name in other correspondence or in the diary; but see Appendix 2 under Sir John Tippets for possible candidates.

[4] P had been elected MP for Harwich in April 1685.

[5] The sentence beginning 'I have heard...' to this point occurs in the copy-letter for 3 August but is absent from the letter-sent of that date (see p.153, note 5, **C23**).

from us all suspicions; and this being now become my Elder daughter,[1] she had certaine assurances of our decent provision for her: There is no Creature in the family we can (upon the severest scrutine) so much as suspect of Complice, which redoubles our astonishment: What shall I say? I would support this disgrace with the best remedies to allay the passion and Indignation of an injur'd parent and a Man; but confesse it harder to me, than had ben her Death, which we should have lesse regretted: and you will by this imagine (and with some pitty) the overwhelming sorrows under which my poore Wife is labouring afresh, for the losse of One Dutifull, and becomming her affection, and of another so unworthy of her family, and the kindnesse we had for her:

But Sir, this gos no farther in interrupting you, then is necessary to introduce our humble Accknowledgements for the generous Concerne I heare you were pleasd to shew, and the Trouble you put your-selfe to, had it ben possible to Retrive the Fugitive and miserable Creature:[2] What's to be don I know not! but I am highly sensible that for This and all your Favours, I must ever be

Sir,
Your
most humble,
and most Obliged servant:
JEvelyn:

---

[1] E's previous eldest, and most beloved, daughter Mary had died of smallpox on 14 March 1685 at the age of 19. Her monument is still in St Nicholas, Deptford. See above also, p.148, note 6.

[2] P had evidently instigated some sort of official investigation with the intention of apprehending E's unwanted son-in-law; however, apart from E's letters on the subject no other documentation connected with the incident appears to have survived.

C22. JOHN EVELYN TO SAMUEL PEPYS[1]

The wretched folly of an abused girl

For Samuell Pepys Esqr:
Secretary to the Admiralty
at the Admiralty in Yorke-buildings

Sayes Court
31 July 1685[2]

Sir,

You have rightly judg'd, and I concurr with you, that the Indignity [which][3] has ben don me, and the Losse sustain'd, is not to be put in Balance,[4] with that incomparable Child you are pleas'd to mention, as (some time or other) I may to your admiration shew you:[5] But these two disasters falling so upon the neck of each other, *Cicatricem obductam refricāt,*[6] and afresh exasperate the almost obduced wound: I greately despize the unworthy Action; but there is an appendant dishonor in it, hard to digest, as it exposes to the contempt and prate of Gosships, and is a reproch to an unspotted family of worthy Relations, and the pitty of some, among whom I have had the honor to be esteem'd: I blame the wretchd folly of an abused Girle; a child of so many precepts, and (though I say it) examples of a virtuous and orderly family, and who had so little reason to cast her-selfe away in this manner: But I no lesse abhorr the meane stratagem, of the betrayers and unworthy Abettors: In my Life was I never addicted to Revenge, (especialy on meane persons);[7] nor am I conscious to my-selfe of ever having merited the least un-neighbourly Office from any Creature in his Majesties Yard, every one of which I have ben allways disposd to serve, and oblige upon all occasions to my power; though Indeede I do not ordinarylie Club with them, nor have ben us'd to the Conversation: This onely

---

[1] Source: Pforzheimer MS 35F (ex-Davey Catalogue 2872; see note in previous letter, **C21**). No endorsement visible.

[2] MS: 'Says-Cot: 31 July–85' at foot of letter.

[3] Not in the MS but required by the sense.

[4] MS: appears to read 'Bilance'.

[5] A number of Mary Evelyn's manuscripts are amongst the Evelyn archive at the British Library. E may here have had in mind her *Book of several designs and thoughts of mine for regulating my Life upon many occasions, 1683* (Eve MS.92).

[6] 'It opens the wound afresh'. The phrase is commonly used in Latin. Note that the Pforzheimer Catalogue erroneously supplies the meaningless *voluctam* for *obductam*.

[7] I.e. on people of lower social standing.

Sir, I promise my-selfe, that those Welsh-Gent[1] here, who I am told boast of their assistance, and seacresy in this wondrous Exploit shall not often Feast upon the Entertainements this greate purchase is likely to procure them:[2] Mr Tippet has but to Consult the Will of his greate Heyress's Grandfather[3] (which he may peruse at the probate-Office for a groate)[4] to find the thousands he gives out she has title to: I had almost five-yeares since, given her £2000 (and did now intend to have improv'd it) which I have struck out of my Will, this very afternoone:[5] In the meane time Sir, Your handsome, and noble Resent'ments for me are still so honorable and Obliging, as can proceede from none but a breast truely Generous and worthy a brave mind, and for which I shall ever cherish, publish, and owne your Friendship as becomes

Sir
Your ever most obliged,
and most humble servant
JEvelyn:

---

[1] Presumably a regiment or troop of soldiers from Wales, stationed in the Yard.

[2] The assistance which Elizabeth had evidently enjoyed during her escapade is perhaps indicative of how E was perceived by some, at least, of his neighbours.

[3] Sir Richard Browne.

[4] Four pence, or one-third of a shilling.

[5] 'This Accident caus'd me to alter my Will; as was reasonable; for though there may be a reconciliation upon her repentance, and that she has suffer'd for her folly; yet I must let her see what her undutifullnesse in this action, deprives her of; as to the provision she else might have expected; solicitous as she knew I now was of bestowing her very worthily...' (diary, 2 August 1685).

If E felt it was appropriate to introduce financial sanctions on his wayward daughter it seems the rest of his family did not necessarily share his views. His son John's account book for this period survives (Evelyn archive, British Library). On the 2 August 1685 he records a payment of £5 7s 6d 'To my Sister Tippets', who can only be Elizabeth. The sum, not an inconsiderable one, is for such a specific amount it suggests that rather than making a general gift he was paying a debt of hers incurred during the elopement.

C23. JOHN EVELYN TO SAMUEL PEPYS[1]

Mr Evelyn betrayed by his neighbours

For Samuell Pepys Esqr:
Secretary of the Admiralty
at the Admiralty

Deptford
3 August 1685[2]

Sir

By what you were pleas'd to Communicate to me Yesterday, that you had written to Sir John Tippet:[3] I find I am every moment oblig'd for the Zeale you still expresse in my Concerne; He were a very malevolent Caytif,[4] that knowing of an intention to rob his neighbours house, should not give notice of it: yet such kind Neighbours I have found: I think our Laws would find them Accessories, and punish them too:[5] As for the little Clearks, who think they have assisted in a goodly Exploit, and merited of their Hero: I passe not for them: nor looke for other from giddy fellows who have no notion or sense [of] honor or good manners: But why I should find so little humanity for Sir Edisbury[6] (whom in all my life, I never injurd so much as in a thought and who values himselfe to have seene the world); dos extreamely abate the opinion I had of his better manners to say no more: There is one Prestman,[7] (if I mistake not his name) a perfect stranger to me, who has had the impudence to glory in the menagement of this seacret, to one of my family that casualy met him: I am not willing to name the other, out of the greate respect I have to

---

[1] Source: Pforzheimer MS 35G (ex-Davey Catalogue 2872, see p.149, note 1), and BL CLBII.502. No endorsement.

[2] MS: 'Dept:– 3:Aug:–85'.

[3] Both letters are unknown.

[4] Worthless, useless fellow.

[5] The copy-letter of 3 August has here a sentence which, although absent in the letter-sent, does appear in the letter-sent of 29 July (above **C21**), itself unrepresented in the copy-letter book (see p.149, note 5). This is further evidence that E used his copy-letter book as a device or *aide-memoire* rather than as a true record of correspondence.

[6] Presumably related to the Navy Surveyor variously known as Sir Kenrick/Kendrick Edisbury/Edgbury (from 1632 until his death in 1638). He had at least one descendant in naval administration in 1702 (Latham and Matthews, X, 120). However, the name does not recur elsewhere in E's diary or correspondence with P.

[7] Or 'Priestman' (copy-letter). The name does not appear elsewhere in E's diary or correspondence but a 'Preestman' does feature in P's so-called 'Second Diary' concerning the 1683 voyage to Tangier (15 October 1683, Howarth 1932, p.415).

Mr Shish (our Master Builder) whose Relation and Assistant I understand he is: his Brother in Law (my kind and worthy neighbour) would, I am Confident, have detested the thought of so base an action: These, for being house-keepers and men of Yeares, I might have hoped better from, though both so meerely strangers to me: that I know neither of their faces, nor, 'til now, their names; so little indeede has my Conversation ben in the Yard of late yeares, and since the old knot of more friendly people there was dissolv'd: Sir, All the Revenge I shall ever take, will be to despize, and pitty their Malice and Insults; and all I shall desire of you, is that you will give them such a Reprimand, as may make the proudest of 'em sensible, they have ben privy to an Action you resent in my behalfe, and don an irreparable injurie to one [who] deserv'd it not from them upon any account: This coming from you, will mortifie their Confidence; and let them know 'tis the pure Indulgence of the Family they so unworthily have affronted, that you resent it not in the highest measure it will beare; and that Officers who are plac'd here to mind his Majesties Service should be combining in so vile an Outrage:

This Sir, is what I am assur'd your pitty and generosit[y] will prompt you to, and 'tis all the Revenge I shall ever seeke or meditate: 'Tis enough, you take my Cause to heart, and owne my Complaints: The Reproof, I think is reasonable, and perhaps lesse Rigorous than your Justice, and the sense you are pleas'd to expresse for what I suffer, would make you use; should I take Advantage of the reiterated, and generous permission you allow me to discover, and expose them to your Animadversion:

Sir, I am for this infinite Civilitie and all your honorable procedure on this Occasion

Your most obliged and
most humble servant
J Evelyn:

My poore Wife (having ben these two days ill of a feavor, the affliction has cast her into) most humbly kisses your hands, etc.[1]

There is also one Mrs Beckford[2] I understand has ben assistant to this Connivance: I am sorry that I trouble you with this so long; but am not displeasd to find that though the Yard have ben so injurious;[3] the rest of the Towne had no. hand in it:

---

[1] See Appendix 1, no. 7, for E's letter to his wife concerning Elizabeth Evelyn's subsequent illness from smallpox. Elizabeth died on Saturday 29 August 1685. She was not mentioned again by her father.

[2] Otherwise unknown but see Appendix 2.

[3] The plan (see below, p.338) shows how the Sayes Court house lay only a matter of yards from the dockyard wall, making close personal contact inevitable between E's family and naval staff.

C24. JOHN EVELYN TO SAMUEL PEPYS[1]

A request on behalf of Lady Sylvius and a declaration of friendship

For Samuell Pepys Esqr
Secretary of the Admiralty etc:
at The Admiralty

[Chiswick?]
Tuesday morning [8 September 1685][2]

Sir,

I am at this moment importun'd againe by my Lady Sylvius,[3] to recommend this Bearer[4] and his Supplication to your favour: I assur'd my Lady I had formerly shew'd you her Request in his behalfe, and that you promis'd to Enquire of his Merite and see what might be don for his promotion: She will not yet be pacified without I give you this second Trouble, and send him to you with is[5] Certificate and pretences.———

Sir, After the little glaunce I had of you on Sonday at Windsore[6] Sir Henry Sheeres is wittnesse how earnestly I sought you: I have had greate kindnesses and honour don me by many Friends; but none I assure you, to whom I think my-selfe more Oblig'd than to Mr Pepys, in all respects, and upon all Occasions, in my Afflictions[7] as well as prosperitie, which are the onely Trials of a generous and Valuable Friend, and for which, I am all my life to acknowledge my Selfe

Sir, Your most humble
and most Obliged Servant
JEvelyn.

I will endeavor to kisse your hands some time this day, and were I assur'd you din'd at home, it should be this Morning.[8]

---

[1] Source: Guildhall Library (Corporation of London) MS 22425/8 (ex-Davey Catalogue Item 2873; Sotheby's 9 April 1968, Lot 481). Endorsed by P, '8th Septr 1685 Mr Evelyn's Acknowledgement Letter to Mr Pepys'. The content is closely associated with that of 4 July 1685 (C20), now identified as being to E from P.
[2] MS: 'Tuesday mor:'. Date from endorsement. For Chiswick see note 6 below.
[3] Ann, Lady de Sylvius, née Howard.
[4] Not identifiable but perhaps Edmund Dummer (see C28–30).
[5] Sic, probably for 'with this'.
[6] E went to Windsor with Clarendon on 5 September (diary), but does not mention P. E left on 7 September, staying with Clarendon at Chiswick on the 8th (diary), writing also to his wife from 'Sir C[yril] Foxes at Chiswick' on the 8th (BL.1546).
[7] E's profligate daughter Elizabeth (see C21–23) was buried on 2 September (diary).
[8] On 15 September E and P went to Portsmouth with James II's party (diary).

C25. JOHN EVELYN TO SAMUEL PEPYS[1]

An account of Colours

For Samuell Pepys Esqr etc
Secretary of the Admiralty at his
house in Yorke-streete

Sayes Court
22 September 1685[2]

Sir,

I were very unworthy of your Late and former Favours, should I not returne you some Assurances, that I often meditate on them,[3] and that I shall ever (according to my little force and Capacity) endeavour to Obey your Commands:– Without more Ceremonie then, I am in the first place, to give you an account of Colours: But you'l be better pleas'd to receive it from the Learned Gilbertus Cuperus's *Apotheosis Homeri*,[4] and his Conjectures upon an Antique Sculpture: Where, speaking of the Rhapsodists that were us'd to sing the Ballads of Ulysses's Errors, and Maritime Voyages; he tells us, they were wont to be clad in Blew Coates; when his Iliad and fighting Poëms, in Red; and were therein so superstitious, as allways to wrap, and cover those Books or Rolls in parchment of these two Colours: He pretends that one Oenomanus[5] first invented Distinction of Colours in the *Ludi Circenses* (or Combatants), where Greene was the Ensigne of Fighters at Land, and Blew at Sea: so as when those who were clad in Greene gain'd the prize, they Look't on it as præsage of a fruitfull harvest that yeare; If the Blew-Coates, successfull Voyages and Exploits by Sea: The first, it seemes, concern'd the Husband-man, the other the Mariner: He farther observes, that when there was any Commotion or Rebellion in the parts of Italy, or Gaule, the General of Horse carried a Blew Cornet; for as much as that generous creature was first rais'd by Neptune's Trident (as you know the Poets tell us) and then maneg'd by that Sea-God; and therefore he who signaliz'd himselfe on that Element,

---

[1] Source: BL.1547 (ex-Davey Catalogue Item 2874, and Langham Catalogue Item 569). This is the letter-sent. Endorsed, 'Sepr 22.1685. Mr Evelyn to Mr Pepys, touching the different signification of Colour among the Antients, and other learned matters.' Also represented by CLBII.507, with many mostly minor differences.

[2] MS: 'Sa-Cot: 22 Septr:–85'. Copy-letter is dated 23 September.

[3] E had taken his leave of P at Portsmouth on 19 September.

[4] *Apotheosis, vel consecratio Homeri*, Amsterdam, 1683.

[5] Sic, in error for Oenomaos (Οἰνόμαος), mythical charioteer-son of Mars. Told he would be killed by his son-in-law. He therefore said he would only allow his daughter to marry a man who had defeated him in the circus. He died after being tricked into using a faulty chariot.

was honor'd with a flag of the same Colour; of which Suetonius gives a remarkable Instance in Octavius Augustus: *M. Agrippam in Sicilia, post navalem victoriam, Cæruleo Vexillo Donavit;*[1] this was in his expedition against young Pompey: It were but ostentation to cite[2] for these particulars Statius, Diodorus Siculus, Plutarch in *Vita Themistocles* and other Authors: This being onely in discharge of my promise that I had something (though no greate matter) to say upon these Colours, and that when there dos (in my desultory course of reading) occurr anything, relating to the sea, I esteeme my-selfe oblig'd to give you testimonie that you are ever in my thoughts: Nor neede I add any more to give you an impatient desire of the excellent Entertainement that Author will aford you, not on this subject alone; but in a world of choice Erudition:

I do not remember you charg'd me with any other particular of this sort: but, as I am both dispos'd, and esteeme my-selfe highly honor'd in serving you, though but as a pioner, to dig Materials, for a more skillfull hand to square and polish, and set in Work; so, if among my Rubbish, I lite on anything that may Contribute to it: You have in me (permit me againe the repetition) a ready and faithful Servant, acquir'd by many Obligations; but by none (I assure you) more, than that singular Love of Virtue, and things worthy in an excellent person, which I discover and honour in you.

In the Notes of Isaack Vossius upon Catullus, *Sive utrumque Juppiter simul secundus incidisset in pedem,* etc.[3] he has many learned Observations about Navigation: particularly, the Sailing to several opposite ports by the same Wind: *ijsdem ventis in Contrarium navigatur prolatis pedibus* (as Pliny expresses it);[4] it was (you may remember) on this hint, that I inform'd you Vossius had by him a treatise Περὶ Ταχυπλοὶα:[5] I Enquir'd of him (when last I was at Windsore)[6] whether he would publish it; to which he gave me but an uncertain replie: In the meane time, you'l not be displeas'd at what he tells us of a certaine harmony, produc'd by the flapping of Carters' Whipps, at the

---

[1] Suetonius, *Augustus* xvi.3. This repeats 31 October 1681 (**C9**, p.122, note 5).
[2] 'Cole' (a variant of 'cull', meaning 'select') is a possible reading here. However, 'cite' is certainly used in the copy-letter. E's ambiguous letter formation would allow 'cite' to resemble 'cole' where the dot over the 'i' is not visible. Either is possible.
[3] Vossius' edition of Catullus appeared in 1684. The only copy of Catullus' works in the Evelyn Library sale was Joseph Scaliger's, Antwerp, 1582 (Lot 316). The quotation is from Catullus iv.19, 'or Jupiter came down astern on both sails at once.'
[4] Vossius produced an edition of Pliny's *Naturalis Historiæ* in 1669. 'The sailor is driven in the opposite direction to each side by the wind-maximising sheets' (*NH*. II.47, 48, and 128).
[5] 'All about fast ships.'
[6] A reference presumably to his visit there on the preceding 5–6 September (see diary, and letter of 8 September, **C24**). However, E makes no reference to seeing Vossius during the visit and indeed his last-ever reference to Vossius in the diary is nearly a decade before (28 March 1676; see also 31 October 1675.)

feasts of Cybele and Bacchus; and that the Tartars use, to this day, no other Trumpets, and are so adroite, as at once, to make the Whippe give three distinct Sounds (or Snapps), so loude, as to be heard a greate distance off; and on this occasion speakes of a Coach-man at Maestricht, who plays severall Tunes with his Whip:– To a lover of Harmonie and Musique I could not omitt this passage, though you will laugh at me for the extravagance, and pay me with tongues and Grid-yron,[1] but I recurr – *Omnis historia est bona*[2] – I am sure you have perus'd what he says (in his late *Opusculum*)[3] touching the Reformation of Longitudes and Eclipses; and his Asserting the Mediterranean and other places to be much larger than our Geographers report: He has something also of the North Passage towards the Indies, and of the fabrique of Gallies, of which you are able best to judge and have doubtlesse made your remarke on; which minds me to tell you that I have (this very morning) had a Visite from Mr Dummer, and am so exceedingly pleas'd with his Acquaintance, that I look on it, as a new obligation to you; and that I cultivate it for my owne sake; you will let him understand (by all that I am to speake to you of him upon this little tast) how much I wish him the improvement of your special favour,[4] who am

Sir Your most humble,
and most faithfull obedient servant
JEvelyn:

Sir,
I am sensible that what I have written to you, is errant Rhappidoe, and can contribute nothing of Solid to your maturer and more usefull Thoughts; but I serve you in what I can, and you will accept of my best Inclinations.

---

[1] An instrument for torture by fire. It may be therefore that the preceding 'tongue' should be for 'tong' but E may simply mean that P would make verbal fun of him.

[2] 'Good history is for everyone.'

[3] 'Little work.' Presumably *Variarum Observationum liber*, 1685 (Library Sale Lot 1546).

[4] Identifiable as the Edmund Dummer who subsequently became a surveyor of the navy. From 20 July 1682 to 30 March 1684 he was on a voyage of the Mediterranean aboard HMS *Woolwich*. On his return he produced a lavishly illustrated log of the voyage, containing a series of pen-and-wash vistas of harbours and ports such as Genoa and Marseilles, as well as 'pop-up' models of '24 Sorts of Vessells, of common Use in those Seas' (British Library, King's 40). The work is of outstanding quality. In late 1685 E began assisting him with his career (**C28–30**, but see also **C24**, above), complicated by a scandal involving Dummer's wife. In 1698 Dummer uncovered corruption at Portsmouth dockyard but was falsely accused of receiving bribes by the guilty party. Dummer was suspended and it took about 18 months for him to clear his name (PRO S.P. 44/204, 238). Curiously, despite E's high opinion of him he never features in the diary. Once vindicated in June 1700 Dummer embarked on developing a postal scheme for maintaining contact with the colonies. He may or may not be the Edmund Dummer recorded as a ship-builder at Blackwall between 1704–9 (P. Banbury 1971, *Ship-builders of the Thames and Medway*, London).

C26. SAMUEL PEPYS TO JOHN EVELYN[1]

I have something to shew you

Thursday night
2 October 1685[2]

Sir,

mighty sorry I am that I was not in the way to enjoy you to day, being gone (the only time I have beene able to doe it this Summer)[3] to make a visit to good Mrs Ewer at Clapham. But I have[4] 2 reasons to desire you will give mee your company to morrow noone, first because wee will be alone, and next I have something to shew you, that I may not have another[5] time,[6]

Your most obedient Servant,
SPepys

That[7] which was shew'd me was two papers
attested by his present Majesties hand, to be
true Copies of the Originals, which some
day before he had showed Mr Pepys privately:
That his late Brother Charles the first,[8] was   *second.*
of Long time since a Roman Catholique:
The papers contained severall points of
Religion, labouring to cast Heresy, Schisms,
etc. on the Church of England: but on
my judgement without any force or reason,
and a thousand times confuted.

---

[1] Source: BL Upcott Antiquaries II. Endorsed by E, 'Mr Pepys 2d:Octr:–85: Concerning the Religion of his Maj K: Charles the 2d'. The letter is illustrated in *The Book Collector*, vol. 44, no. 2, Summer 1995, p.154.

[2] MS: 'Thursd: night. 2.Oct:1685'.

[3] In July 1685 P had been made Master of Trinity House (see Latham and Matthews, X, 457) at Deptford, and this may have kept him busy.

[4] 'I have' inserted.

[5] Replaces 'againe', deleted.

[6] In the diary for 2 October 1685 E records the receipt of this letter and the meeting with P to be told of Charles II's death-bed conversion to Catholicism.

[7] Footnote in E's hand, but see note 8.

[8] Sic, E's error for Charles II. P has added 'second' to the side by way of correction.

C27. JOHN EVELYN TO SAMUEL PEPYS[1]

Instructions on running a household

For Samuell Pepys Esqr:
Secretary to the Admiralty
at the Admiralty Office
in Yorke-buildings:

Sayes Court
3 October 1685

Sir,

To speake in the style of Selvedge[2] etc were too Low for my worther
Conceptions of you, who would make-use of the Sublimest Expressions,
consistent with the greate sincerity of my heart, to assure you, that I should
esteeme my-selfe very happy, were I capable of doing you those services,
which the Excesse, and continuance of your Civilitie is pleas'd to Accept: In
Confidence of that, I readily Obey your Commands in the Bills of Fare etc:
which you require: I assure you I was very long in finding the mislaied Paper,
though I remember'd when Mr Godolphin (now my Lord) after his Ladys
decease,[3] put all her letters, and Collections into my hands, to sort, and take-
out, what I would, for the designe I had of (some-time or other) saying
something extraordinary, of that concealed Saint, and incomparable Creature,
so well known to me, and my Wife in particular:[4] I send it therefore to you as
it is; and though it be little worth;[5] Yet, for the Method, and that I cannot

---

[1] Source: Pforzheimer MS 35H (ex-Davey Catalogue Item 2875). No endorsement
relating to E's letter but instead the enclosures, 'Aprill 13th: 1675. A Copies of Mrs
Evelyn's Instructions to Mrs Blague [=Blagge] for setting up and keeping house,
upon her Marriage with my Lord Godolphin. With my Lady Rolles's Qualifications
of a good Housekeeper.' See note 4 below.

[2] Literally an ornamental boundary or edging to a piece of cloth, i.e. it would not be
good enough to make vapid complimentary remarks.

[3] Sidney Godolphin, cr. Baron Godolphin in 1684. His wife, Margaret, née Blagge,
was the Mrs Godolphin of E's great friendship and subject of his spiritual biography
The Life of Mrs Godolphin, first published in 1847. She had died in 1678.

[4] E was always anxious to emphasise how Margaret Blagge had first and foremost
been his wife's friend and that it was she who had encouraged his relationship with
the young woman (Hiscock 1951, 21).

[5] The letter survives with the manuscript of the present letter in Texas. It is a
discourse addressed to Margaret Blagge (afterwards Mrs Godolphin) of prices and
costs of running a household, dated 13 April 1675. Its length has precluded its

readily tell, where I have met with any thing of this (in my fancy) usefull kind, and that it may be directive to my remaining young Girle (if God give her Grace to make a fitter choice than her unhappy sister)[1] I should not be unwilling to receive it againe, if you think it worth your Clearks Exscribing; for I scarse believe you will care to keep a [th]in[g so][2] negligently written, as I find this is, according to the familiarity I us'd in all [thi]ng[s][3] I sent to that deare Creature: In the meane time, this is by no meanes Calculated for the Meridian of Mr Pepys, nor therefore have I dared to utter one word of it to my Wife,[4] so many Circumstances distinguishing your Familys and Occasions, from those of this Ladys, who never was House-keeper before, had lost her Mother long since, and being from a Child, bred in Courts, may be thought (without reproch) not much to have buisied her head about Oeconomique matters: Nor is it possible this should signifie to any purpose of Instruction to you, who have your-selfe ben so long the Master of a Familie, the Husband of so excellent a Lady,[5] and whose Circumstances exact other Measures, and neede not be Confin'd: But you will have me obey you, and I do it as you see.——

And now Sir, *Dum animus in patinis*,[6] Though I pretend not to Regale you with Ortolani[7] (as you did me yesterday)[8] Yet I presume to send you an Houre-glasse.[9] You smile at the Coherence, and wonder what relation an

---

inclusion in Appendix 1 of this volume. However, it includes such information as an estimate of £197 for silver for the household made up variously of £7 for 12 spoons, £6 for 12 forks and a covered porringer for £7. The total food bill for the week is estimated at £4 and 12 shillings (£4.60). Annual living expenses in London are computed at £480 and 4 shillings comprised partly of a £244 housekeeping bill, a clothing bill for the wife of £66 and the husband's of £40. A fuller passage is quoted by H.B. Wheatley in his supplementary volume to his edition of Pepys's Diary, called *Pepysiana*, 1918, pp.95–7, using the transcription in the Davey Catalogue.

[1] This is Susanna Evelyn, afterwards Mrs William Draper, E's youngest daughter.

[2] MS badly smudged.

[3] As note 2.

[4] He did subsequently. Mrs E wrote to P on 29 November 1685 at E's behest to recommend a 'neat' and 'excellent housewife', whom she knew, to be P's housekeeper (Davey Catalogue Item 2889, now at HL Harvard, MS Eng 992.6).

[5] It is not clear whether E means P's real wife Elizabeth who had died in 1669 or his 'housekeeper' and presumed common-law wife Mary Skinner.

[6] 'While my mind is on my saucepans'. An allusion to *Jam dudum animus est in patinis* (Terence, *Eunuchus* IV.vii.46).

[7] Jacobus Colius Ortelanius.

[8] This was the meeting with P to which E was summoned in the previous letter, C26.

[9] Amongst the items sold in the 1889 Davey Catalogue (which included this letter) was a manuscript (now lost) describing an hour-glass (Item 2882) described thus:

'Holograph Manuscript, 1p. folio, and endorsed by Pepys "Mr. Evelyn's Description of a ncw Sea Hour-Glass." This manuscript is illustrated by a pen-and-ink sketch, by John Evelyn, of a new timepiece for use on board ships. He gives minute details

Houre-glasse has to Birds: why in good earnest, I can't imagine, except it be, that we often paint it with Wings, to represent how Swiftly Time passes and fleet's-away; But whilst that little time lasts with me, I shall cherefully Employ it in your service, who am

Sir,

Your most humble

and most Obedient Servant

JEvelyn:

Sir, Let me obtaine of you (on my recommendation) to have by you that booke of Monsieur Jouriens, *Préjugez Legitimes contre Le papisme*[1] etc for an *Armamentarium* and Magazin upon (almost) all possible Occasions and Encounters, without toile: Though it [would][2] cost you two Volumes in quarto you will not repent it, for the choice furniture which you will find in it of all sorts, and in defence and solid Replies of such as oppose that Greate Fable of the Church of Rome, as now its Doctrine would impose upon all the world besides: You will there find Reason, Antiquity, Truth without secular Interest, and that all people are not fooles and phænaticks who are not of her Communion; They are little, poore decasted[3] Arguments that unhappy greate person had inculcated into him, ten thousand times evicted by the Church of England divines, but they never reade, nor search nor care to [let continue etc].[4]

---

of its construction, and the diagram is marked with figures, to which he appends explanations. Says that this sandglass should be applied to a board, after the manner of a thermometer, and gives directions as to the best methods of doing this. A very curious and interesting MS, *unpublished*, £12 10s.'

[1] Pierre Jurieu, *Préjugés légitimes contre le papisme*, Amsterdam, 1685.

[2] Not in the MS but required by the sense.

[3] Reading seems certain; perhaps a variant of 'decass', meaning 'break down', i.e. 'broken-down arguments'.

[4] Reading uncertain.

C28. JOHN EVELYN TO SAMUEL PEPYS

In favour of Mr Dummer

LOST   6 December 1685

The Davey Catalogue (1889) entry is:

John Evelyn *to* **Samuel Pepys**

2876   A.L.S., 1 p., 4to. Dec., 1685, and complete with autograph
             address. A neat and desirable specimen, asking him to assist a
             friend into a place in the Navy Yard, etc. *Unpublished*. £12 10s.

The Langham Catalogue (1900) entry is:

570   EVELYN (John). To Samuel Pepys
             A.L.S. 1p., 4to. Dec. 6, 1685. Complete with autograph address
             and seal, and endorsed by Pepys. "In favour of Mr. Dummer."[1]
             Very neat and desirable specimen asking him to assist a friend
             into a place in the Navy Yard. UNPUBLISHED.   £15 15s.

It is certain that the two items are one and the same. The date supplied by the
Langham Catalogue makes it possible to distinguish this letter from the next two
(**C29**, and **30**) which are concerned with the same subject. The endorsement on that of
2 January 1686 (**C29**) also states that it is the '2d' on the subject, indicating a
previous letter which must be this one dated 6 December. It is worth noting that,
sadly, a page corresponding approximately to the date of this letter has been torn out
of Evelyn's copy-letter book (BL CLBII); as the next two in the series are represented
on later pages in that volume it seems probable that this letter too was included by E
amongst those letters chosen for copying. The index to the copy-letter book in E's
hand indicates a letter to Pepys of approximately this date is missing. See also above,
p.128.

---

[1] Edmund Dummer – see letter of 22 September 1685 (**C25**), p.158, note 4.

C29. JOHN EVELYN TO SAMUEL PEPYS[1]

A favour for Mr Dummer, and a dockyard Intrigue

For Samuell Pepys Esqr:
Secretary of the Admiralty at
his house in
in Yorke buildings[2]

[no place]
2 January 1686[3]

Sir,

Though I am sufficiently assur'd the favour you have shew'd Mr Dummer [4] (and of which he is so gratefuly sensible) proceedes merely from your owne discernment of his merits; yet (seing he will needes perswad me that you were the kinder to him upon my Intercession) mithinks there lies an Obligation on me to give you thanks for it; at least he thereby fancies his owne Accknowledgement will come with the more enforcement: I therefore most humbly thank you in his behalfe, and that with the greater alacrity, as I verily believe his Majestie will receive the fruites, and you the satisfaction of having advanc'd so diligent and Ingenious a young man. I am indeede Sir (as I ought to be) much pleas'd with what you have don for him; but if I might have beg'd a favour for my-selfe without prejudice, it should have ben for his continuing in that station here, and not at Chatham: That had been indeede doubly to have oblig'd me, and I am perswaded, not have displeas'd Mr Pepys, when he should have come to know, the reasons of the others refusall[5] of Chatham, (contrary to his first resolution) but on which depends a seacret, which might moove[6] you to suspend your yet consenting to his Choice, 'til you are

---

[1] Source: Houghton Library, Harvard University bMS Eng 9991 (118), and used by permission (formerly Davey Catalogue Item 2877). Endorsed by P, 'Jan 2. 1685/6. Mr Evelin to SP. a 2d in favour to Mr Dummer.' This letter is matched by BL CLBII.612, dated 31 December 1685. The textual differences are minor and of little significance. This letter is second in a series of three (**C28–30**) concerning Mr Dummer's career progression (see note 4 below) and E's intercession on his behalf. The first letter's whereabouts and text are unknown beyond sale catalogue references (see p.163).

[2] MS: 'in' is repeated.

[3] MS: '2: Jan 85/6'. Note that the 'a' is not fully closed and this letter seems in the past to have also appeared as '2 June 85' – see Phantom Letters in the Catalogue.

[4] Edmund Dummer. See p.158, note 4.

[5] Replaces 'choice', deleted.

[6] Reading uncertain; perhaps 'mouve'.

inform'd of the Intrigue: Now should I whisper, what is the talke o'th'Towne, (and no seacret at all,) That there is a certaine proper gentleman very sweete with his wife,[1] who has prevail'd with him by all meanes to stay at Deptford; you would pronounce me an errant Goship, and should I name Mr Ed. ——[2] that there remain'd something – *alta mente repostum*.[3] I acknowledge I can have no mighty fondesse for either; but, at the same time, Conjure you to believe, that I am much superior to that poore revenge: There's not the least Ingredient of it in me: And this, I confesse, that if by removing a Scandal,[4] or idle habitude,[5] Mr Dummer were fixed here, and the other remov'd to Chatham, I should not be sorry. Thus you see Sir, how far selfe Interest extends, nor will you reprove it, if I rather wish, that (by Mr Pepys addresse) I might have the Neighbourhood of an ingenious man (whom I could sometimes converse with)[6] than of Persons I have so little reason to Esteeme either for their Neighbourhood[7] or their Morals: But all this in perfect submission to those better Reasons, by which you allways govern[8]

> Sir, Your
>
>> most-humble
>> faithfull servant
>>
>>> JE[velyn][9]

---

[1] Copy-letter: 'his wife' omitted and indicated '——'. If Mr Dummer's wife was indeed engaged in a scandalous liaison it may be noted that Dummer himself seems to have been away from home between 1682–4 on a voyage to the Mediterranean (see above, p.158, note 4) and thereafter engaged on writing it up, perhaps explaining his wife's dalliance.

[2] Name left blank. Evidently the individual was known to P but sadly he is now entirely unknown. The allusion 'Mr Ed.' is omitted from the copy-letter.

[3] Perhaps an allusion to *manet alta mente repostum iudicium Paris*, 'The Judgement of Paris lies stored deep in her [Juno's] heart' (Virgil, *Aeneid* I.26).

[4] MS: 'Scadal'.

[5] 'Familiar intimacy' (OED).

[6] It seems that 'Mr Ed.——' had been offered a post at Chatham, which he had turned down in order to carry on his affair with Mrs Dummer. When Dummer was then offered the post, at E's behest, 'Mr Ed.——' was horrified and tried to persuade him to stay. E's new suggestion seems to be that the indiscreet 'Mr Ed.——' be transferred to Chatham to get him out of the way, and thus allow E the pleasure of Dummer's company for the forseeable future, even if that serves to restrain Dummer's promotion.

[7] A retrospective reference to the involvement of dockyard staff in E's daughter Elizabeth's elopement in July 1685.

[8] Copy-letter: 'by which you are always govern'd'.

[9] The Davey Catalogue entry notes that the letter is signed with E's monogram only. The letter now bears a full signature and it can be seen from the MS that 'velyn' has been crudely added in a pitiful imitation of E's hand. This had been done, presumably to elevate its value, by 1934 when it was illustrated in the *Catalogue of Union Art Galleries*, New York, 27 February 1934.

C30. JOHN EVELYN TO SAMUEL PEPYS[1]

An inconsiderate cavalier

[no visible address]   Sayes Court
                                                        8 January 1686[2]

Sir,

I am sure that what you excogitate[3] to bring about, cannot but obtaine its
desired Effect; therefore as to Mr Dummers Concerne, I leave that to you with
intire acquiescence: Indeede I think him worthy of your favour, for never in
my Life have I observ'd a Young man (qualified as he is in his way, and
susceptible of what can be wanting) lesse pragmatical, and of greater modesty;
beside his so submissive, and cherefull dedication of himselfe to his patron
alone, which is a mark of his discretion, as well as of his duty.

Now Sir to the other part of your Letter I cannot but think it a very venial
fault (in the Cavaliere you speake of) to Consigne a Wife to her owne
Husband, whose Charmes (as I am told) are not at all extraordinary, before
they be quite vanish'd and effeete: Mithinks he ought to give *You* thanks for
making it so easie to him, and so decent: But (whatever the good man may
faile in this particular) I am sure I am to pay you my most humble thanks for
the honour you have don me, in making me the proxy on so weighty a
Negotiation, as in the Commands you mention: Be assur'd I shall take care to
performe your trust with all fidelitie; but whether the Lady you speake of
accept of your Substitute, because I represent Mr Pepys, I much doubt whether
the whole Sex would be as kind (or rather I am sure they[4] would not) to Sixty,
as to fourty; were there no other Consideration (as there is a greate deale to the
advantage of Mr Pepys) betweene the principle and the proxie:– But

Sir, to leave this part of Gallantrie 'til we meete, and have opportunitie of
proposing it to the Ladye: Receive from both your Proxies our reiterated
Acknowledgements, (with the Augure of many happy new-years) for all your
greate Civilities, and in particular for this last to
                    Sir
                        Your most obliged
                        humble Servant   JEvelyn:

---

[1] Source: Historical Society of Pennsylvania MS (British Authors Case 10, Box 29;
formerly Davey Catalogue Item 2887 – which states the MS had a visible address
which is no longer present). Endorsed by P, 'Mr Evelin to SP about Mr Dummer'.
The letter is also represented by BL CLBII.614, dated 1 January 1686.
[2] MS: S–Ct: 8–Jan–85/6
[3] Contrive.
[4] MS: 'the'; CLBII.614 has '(Or rather do not doubt but they would not)' here.

C31. JOHN EVELYN TO SAMUEL PEPYS[1]

The Royal Society's building plans

For Samuell Pepys Esqr:
Secretary of the Admiralty
at his house in
Yorke-buildings

[No place]
Monday morning, [1 March 1686][2]

Sir,

Some Gentlemen of the Society (who Deipnosophize[3] this night at Sir Joseph Williamsons) have lay'd their Commands upon me to entreate their President would give them a Meeting in St James's Park aboute five-a-clocke this Evening; to View a Spot of Ground, which they believe his Majestie might be induc'd to grante the Society to build on:[4]

I did thinke to have waited on you yesterday at my Spouses[5] in Lincolns-Inn-fields, being so unfortunate as not to find you at your house, (where I was Saturday-Evening to kisse your hands, and discharge my selfe of an Injunction lay'd[6] on me Wednesday last) but have ben Diverted, not halfe so well as I should have ben in doing my Duty to our President[7] whose

Most humble Servant is
JEvelyn:

---

[1] Source: BL.1549 (ex-Davey Catalogue Item 2878). The letter bears a seal. Endorsed by P, '1 March 85/6 Mr Evelyn to Mr Pepys.'

[2] MS: 'Moneday morning'. Date from endorsement (1 March 1686 <u>was</u> a Monday).

[3] Best rendered in English as 'who partake of a philosophical supper'.

[4] The question of permanent premises for the Society, which met at Gresham College, had been ongoing since its foundation. A scheme in 1667–8 had fizzled out thanks to inadequate subscriptions. The present scheme also came to nothing and it was not until 1710 that the Society gained permanent premises at Crane Court, Fleet Street (see Hunter 1989, 156–84 for an account of the saga).

[5] E's meaning is not entirely clear – there is no relevant entry in the diary for Sunday, 28 February; however, the entry for 1 March is entirely concerned with the 'obnoxious' Sir Gilbert Gerrard who had plans that his son might marry E's daughter Susanna. The arrangements foundered on the inadequate provision to be made on any children, and Gerrard's poor standing with the king.

[6] MS uncertain here. The 'Injunction' is presumably the subject of the letter. On Wednesday 24 February E noted that he had attended the Royal Society but gives no details (diary).

[7] P had been elected President of the Royal Society on 1 December 1684.

C32. JOHN EVELYN TO SAMUEL PEPYS[1]

A complaint about mud from the dockyard at Sayes Court[2]

To Samuell Pepys
Secretary of the Admiralty[3]

Sayes Court
29 June 1686[4]

Sir,

You were pleas'd not long-since, to say you would Continue to us the favour of Ordering that the Watch-man (whose station is at the Dore of his Majestys Yard, very neere my Stayers)[5] should – as formerly he did, take Care of Clensing them, and the Causey,[6] which, Since this Late, though Short, Interruption, are allmost quite cover'd with mud, and made use-lesse by it: I come with the more assurance that I shall obtaine this kindnesse of you (without prejudice to his Majesties Service) Inasmuch as by our Articles, those stayers, and Ca[u]sey are to be maintaind and repaird by his Majesty during the terme of the Lease; and that in case they be neglected, they will soone require it: One thing more I make bold to mention, that in regard of the Passage (wholy reserv'd by me out of Sir Dennis Gaudens Lease) through which I consent that Workemen etc may at all times have recourse to the Mast-docks;[7] it was mutualy agreed, that the Watchman who kept that doore, should

---

[1] Source: Marburg M35 (Rosenbach; ex-Davey Catalogue Item 2880), and BL CLBII.534. The letter is no longer in the collection of the Rosenbach Museum in Philadelphia and its present location is unknown. Apart from the postscriptum the text published by Marburg differs from the copy-letter only in occasional adjustments of word order and syntax; it may be assumed therefore that her text is generally reliable.
[2] The saga was long-standing (see E's letter to Brouncker of 2 September 1672 PRO S.P. 29/328, f.140), continued in a further letter to P of 3 October 1687 (C39), and can be found as the subject of a letter of 9 May 1690 to Edmund Dummer (BL.1559i).
[3] From the copy-letter as the MS of the letter-sent is not available.
[4] From the copy-letter (MS: 'Says-Court 29 June: 86'). Marburg states the MS of the letter-sent had no date; but the Davey Catalogue's description of its date as 'June, 1686' (probably from an endorsement) and quotation from the text makes its identification with the copy certain. As most copy-letters differ in precise date from the letter-sent it is probable that the latter was not dated exactly the same day.
[5] These stairs were at the end of a track leading from E's estate around the naval dockyard wall, and were where he, his family, and their visitors, embarked and disembarked from river-boats (see plan, p.338).
[6] Archaic form of 'causeway'.
[7] This was presumably connected with Gauden's construction of a house and

also have a key to the stayers for the use of the Commissioners onely; so that there was to be no other intercourse through it, but to them and my family, for the more security of the Dock: In order to this, Such a Lock was promis'd should be put on, and will be so, and all the rest perform'd, when you shall be pleas'd to signifie so much to your commissioner here, who, I am Sure, will be a kind Neighbour to us: As for the Watch-man, (who has Little to do a greate parte of the day, but to walk about), it will be but a short exercise to him, when a foule tyde requires it, and I do not use at the yeares end to forget the poore man. Sir, You will also think at some convenient time, to call for the Book, and give Order that the Lease be impress'd and seald, which as yet it is not, through the unaccountable neglect of our late famous Admiralty, or Officers: This, I mention to prevent accidents,[1] and I will tell you what I meane when I have the honor to see you, and how I merit for this Advertisement: But, I would derive all my greate Obligations from your kindnesse alone, who am

Sir, Your most faithful
humble Servant   JEvelyn:

Sir, I should be glad to know when I might wait on you to my Lord Dartmouth, confident of giving all Satisfaction to his Lordship[2] on that other affaire:[3] Be so kind to me as to let me know when you will also accumulate this favour on me.[4]

---

victualler's yard in the dockyard at Deptford in 1671 (Latham and Matthews, X, 154). A plan of Sayes Court made in 1692 by Joel Gascoyne (British Library K18.7.2) is extant and shows that access to the mast-docks was through part of the Evelyn estate (see plan, p.338). A plan of the dockyard in 1753 by Thomas Milton (reproduced in Barker and Jackson 1990, 74–5) shows the 'Mast Pond' in the northern part of the yard. A few metres north are the ruins of what are described as 'Victualling Storehouse ruins' – presumably that built by Gauden.

[1] Copy-letter adds here: 'in this mutable world'.

[2] MS (according to Marburg): 'Ld'. Normally E would supply 'Lp'.

[3] Alluded to in the next letter (C33) below. The great issue of the moment, with which Dartmouth (and P) was mostly involved, was the restoration of the navy. It is not certain if this is what concerned E. He had also written to Dartmouth on 3 June 1686 (BL.1551, draft; the letter-sent is published at HMCR XV, 1896, App. 1, Dartmouth III, 132–3) about the illegal building activities of a Mr Laurence who had 'turn'd over an Arch in order to a Bridge, for the making a Drift-way, and common Roade through his Ground; which in truth, he cannot do, without illegal Trespasse; the abuttment of it resting on my Sons land, and passing over a Ditch within his sole Repaire', and it may be this which is being referred to.

[4] The postscriptum is completely absent from the copy-letter.

C33. JOHN EVELYN TO SAMUEL PEPYS[1]

A Privy Seal and a promise of a poem

[no place]
21 July 1686[2]

[Sir,]

... It is say'd that my Lord Dartmouth will be at Redriff [3] tomorrow in the afternoone, where I should be glad you did accompany him if your occasions permitt[4] ... We have this morning pass'd a privy Seale of £27,000 for Sir Dennis Gauden and partner.[5] I wish it may operate to his owne advantage as well as to my concernes. If you dine at home and are free from Company I will deign to share a few minutes with you, and present you a poeme before I embarke homeward.[6] Deale like a philosopher and friend with me if you be empedit...[7]

[Your most faithfull
humble servant   JEvelyn:]

---

[1] Source: Davey Catalogue Item 2884, and Langham Catalogue Item 571. The letter could not be located. However, both catalogues include excerpts from the letter making it possible to restore some of the text (the Langham entry retains the original spelling and appears to be more accurate apart from giving evidently the wrong date). The catalogue descriptions of the letter being '1 p. 4to' in length indicates that it was fairly short. The letter was not represented in the copy-letter book.

[2] The date is as given by the Davey Catalogue. The Langham Catalogue provides a demonstrably incorrect date ('21 July 1697'; see Phantom Letters in the Catalogue of Letters, below, p.306) explicable as that catalogue's typesetter simply picking up the next numeral in sequence, i.e. '9' for '8' and '7' for '6'.

[3] Rotherhithe.

[4] The Davey Catalogue does not include the text up to this point which is taken from the Langham Catalogue. Both include the next section.

[5] Probably connected with the substantial sums owed by the government to Gauden from the Dutch Wars for his victualling services. However, see previous letter, 29 June 1686 (C32). E records that he went to London for a seal on 19 or 20 July but does not specify the purpose.

[6] If he did, the visit and the poem are not recorded.

[7] Davey Catalogue supplies *impedit* here, for 'hindered' or even 'embarrassed'. The incomplete transcription makes the meaning unclear.

C34. JOHN EVELYN TO SAMUEL PEPYS

A request for samples from Virginia

LOST   September 1686

The Davey Catalogue entry is:

> **John Evelyn** *to* **Samuel Pepys**
>
> 2885   A.L.S. 1 p., 4to, Sept., 1686, and complete with autograph
> address and Seal. Mentions a Captain whom he had the pleasure
> of meeting when he last dined with Mr. Pepys,[1] and suggests
> that, as this gentleman is about to take command of some forces
> in New England, he would do him a favour if he would collect
> for him some of the vegetables and natural productions
> growing in that country. He encloses a list (1 p., 4to, also
> Signed) of the names of the plants he requires, and also those
> growing in Virginia, and of which he is anxious Captain
> Nicholson[2] should obtain some seeds. At the bottom of the list
> is a memorandum that a copy of this letter be placed in Captain
> Nicholson's hands. Very interesting and *unpublished*. £20.

No relevant reference to Virginia or New England could be traced amongst Pepys's
papers apart from a note on the 'produce of Virginia' at Bodleian MS Rawl. A271,
f.47. This, however, carries no endorsement by P and is not in E's hand. Evelyn
possessed a 1671 edition of John Ogilby's *America: being the latest, and most
Accurate Description of the New World* (Library Sale lot 1093). Of 19 maps two were
missing in 1977, one of which was the map of Virginia.

This is probably the most significant missing letter, considering its association
with E's interests reflected in his *Sylva* and *Kalendarium Hortense*. An undated MS in
E's hand, 'A Catalogue for Tryals', now at the Clark Library in Los Angeles
(*fPR3433 E5Z7), lists garden experiments which include number '11 See what ships
balast from the Indies will produce'. This shows that the letter is not the only
evidence for Evelyn's interest in the flora of distant lands. He wrote that 'Gentlemen
who have concerns in our American Plantations' be encouraged 'to promote the
Culture of such Plants and Trees... as may yet add to those we find already agreeable
to our Climat in England' (*Silva* [sic, for that edition], 1706, p.134). But otherwise, if
the letter yielded any useful information or plants, this was not mentioned in post-
1686 editions of Evelyn's published works.

---

[1] The last record of dining together is 15 December 1685.

[2] Probably Francis Nicholson, made lieutenant-governor of Virginia in 1690, and its
governor in 1699. It may also be Nicholson who is referred to in the letter of 22 May
1694 (**D20**), p.241, note 5 (also 14 August 1694, **D23**, p.247); if so, it suggests that
this correspondence had continued.

C35. JOHN EVELYN TO SAMUEL PEPYS[1]

Naval history and Royal Society finances

To Samuel Pepys
Secretary of the Admiralty
and President of the Royal Society

London
28 November 1686[2]

Sir,

I was with my Son to waite on you with Dr Reeves, it is an excellent and Learned piese; but, it seemes, the *Infima*[3] is not easily to be met with:[4] If you had ben then at home, I should have acquainted you, that your Neighbour Mr Bridgeman,[5] takes it somewhat ill, that he never receiv'd any Summons to meete upon our Anniversarie, he having now ben of our Society, many yeares, and I apprehend will resent it more, not so much as to find his name in the printed List of Fellowes: You may please to order a printed note, to be left at his house before our day of meeting, and to excuse other omissions as you see occasion.

He gave an hint, as if Gresham foundation would be inquired into by the Ecclesiastical Commission (to which, you know he is Secretary) and that it might possibly be in his power to oblige[6] our Society; supposing that the Salaries of some of the present Professors (Such as Law, Rhetoric, etc) might be transferr'd to the benefit of our Society, without invæsion of the Gresham founders intentions:[7] How far this is practicable, I cannot tell, however you will not omit the compliment to Mr Bridgeman[8] I am etc

---

[1] Source: BL CLBII.552.

[2] MS: 'Lond: 28:Nor–86'.

[3] 'The last one', i.e. the final volume.

[4] Sir Thomas Ryves's *Historia Navalis* (incompletely published: 'lib. i', 1629, *'H.N. Antiqua* lib. iv' 1633, and *H.N. Media* lib. iii' 1640 – DNB). P returned Sir William Trumbull's copy noting in a letter to him (9 May 1683, Bod MS Rawl. A194, f.286; see Howarth, no. 134, p.150) that he had added the *'Pars Media'* and would have added the *Infima* but it was apparently unobtainable. P certainly acquired his own copies of *lib*. iv and *lib*. iii, now at PL.760 (1) and (2), not before 1683.

[5] William Bridgeman, at this time Clerk of the Council.

[6] I.e. assist.

[7] The arrangement was that the Royal Society was allowed to use Gresham College for meetings. In return the College earned prestige by association and its professors were allowed free membership (Hunter 1989, 156). Bridgeman seems to have conceived a way of improving the Society's advantage.

[8] MS: 'Mr B:'

C36. JOHN EVELYN TO SAMUEL PEPYS[1]

On an historical periodical

[no place]
15 March 1687[2]

Sir,

I was yesterday to kisse your hands, with your Historical, and Political Mercurie[3] if you had din'd at home, and being making a step downe the River for two or three-daies,[4] I will not detaine your Books any longer: I had read the last (viz‡: January) before the former two, (my Son having gotten the whole Set about a fortnight since) but I went not back to the two-former moneths, 'til your Letter[5] injoyn'd me to give you my thoughts upon them: But do you in earnest take me for such a Polititian? or rather for *one*, that being lately dismiss'd of so greate an Office (as you know I have had the honour to be employ'd in)[6] must needes have acquired an Universal Talent? I had rather Mr Pepys should call me *Planteur des Choux*,[7] *herba parietariam*,[8] *Sir Roger* – any thing, than *Sir Politick*: Never-the-lesse, upon Condition you will hereafter put me upon some serious Subject; Such as entertain'd us th'-other day,[9] when we miss'd of hearing the Wooden-head Speake:[10] though I shall not adventure to hyper-criticize; I make this Reflection on the Reflecter,

---

[1] Source: Davey Catalogue (frontispiece facsimile, Item 2879) and BL CLBII.561.

[2] MS: '15 Mar: –86/7'. BL CLBII.561 is dated 19 January 1687 and contains some textual differences, principally the political comment at the end which appears in the copy-letter only; but see note 6 which shows that the text cannot have been written before 10 March. Marburg misread the date of the letter-sent as 14 March.

[3] *Mercure historique et politique contenant l'état present de l'Europe*, Parme, chez Juan Batanar 1686–8 (and La Haye chez Henri Bulderen 1688–1703). P's copies now at PL.258–92 (35 vols).

[4] To Deptford. He left for there on 16 March (diary).

[5] Unknown.

[6] E was nominated a Commissioner of the Privy Seale in September 1685. On 10 March 1687 he and the other commissioners were dismissed (diary). The copy-letter also contains this reference to the dismissal and thus demonstrates that it is misdated.

[7] Literally 'planter of cabbages' but an idiomatic term for retiring to the country.

[8] This is the wall-climbing herb Pellitory, with various medicinal purposes. Also used as a Latin sobriquet for one who had been responsible for numerous wall inscriptions; perhaps E is referring to his arrangements for transferring the Arundel classical marble inscriptions to Oxford University (diary, 19 September 1667).

[9] There is no reference to P in E's diary at this point, unless E had indeed seen P at Christ's Hospital on 13 March (diary; P was a governor of the school). But it is implicit from the opening of this letter that E had not seen P on that occasion.

[10] Not identified.

that he is now and then mistaken in his Politics; though for the most part, I belive, more than a very shrewd Guesser: Pag 101 December: *On croit que la retraite de la Cour de plusieurs grands Seigneurs d' Angleterre* etc to the end of that Paragraph, is a Super-refin'd notion upon those who have parted with their White-Staves,[1] but are not yet gon into the Country, as he seemes to think: Pag 187 *Si le Roy Jaques*[2] etc I should rather suppose he meant Charles II, for certainely, the Martyr his Father, did not balance so truly[3] the two Religions (as he pretends) *Sans pouvoir decider quelle étoit la meilleure*; Since I take him to have ben (though a very unfortunate prince) yet well assur'd, and firme in his perswasion, and that it was his stiffenesse (if I so may call his perseverance) which cost him his head: Is not our states-man mistaken p.52: line 1 November where he makes mention of the Duke of Ormond etc:[4] as well as in the next Leafe p:54 *Le fils naturel du Roy* etc whose mother is not at Court:[5] though you guesse at the Lady he meanes? but neither is she there, nor the Mother of the young Heroe he speakes of: What Lapses (at this distance) there may be in his Reflections upon the other states, I pretend not to give account of; but could not passe by these without notice; and perhaps, 'twere not amisse the Author were advertiz'd of them: For the rest, he seemes to be a person of extraordinary penetration, and Intelligence: The *Mysteries* and *Arcana* of state are in good-earnest generously communicated, and *Nouvelles* to us indeede, if what he suggests in the following-page 55 be the plan projected, and which I leave you to exercise your thoughts upon by your Selfe: The intire discourse is very hardy, as well as that 19th December: In all events We see *Louis le Grand* is to have the Glory of all that our wise and Valiant prince has in designe: He it is has shew'd the Way to the Sûblime. see: January pp: 288: and 290: The whole Reflection requires your attention; add to it pp: 277. 278: But Sir, I will no longer detaine you from these curious pieces: Mithinks I am my selfe in the Cabinet, and bidding faire for a Privy Counselor, Secretary of State, Ambassador What not? Without raillery: I am extreamely delighted, and edified, and for my owne Satisfaction cannot but encourage the prosecution of a Worke, which affords so universal an Entertainment, this Inquisitive Age: We have doubtlesse here all that is on the Carpet of Considerable in the Conjectures of the ablest Observers, and the publique may learn to take their measures accordingly: In the meane while, the poore Hugenots are (I perceive) in an ill case, though the *Fistula* should (at last) make way for the Successor:[6] se[e]: p: 112. The Summ is, that the Emperors

---

[1] A symbol of office.

[2] 'Jacques' means someone who seeks to be amusing and fun.

[3] Reading uncertain, perhaps 'throly' for 'throughly'.

[4] James Butler succeeded as twelfth Earl of Ormond in 1633 but was not created first Duke until 1661 in the Irish peerage and 1682 in the English peerage.

[5] Monmouth? and his mother, Mrs Lucy Barlow, née Walter. She died in 1658.

[6] In early January 1687 news circulated that Louis XIV was 'sayd to be healed or rather patch'd up of the fistula in *Ano* [a rectal ulcer], for which he had been severall

progresse gives jealosie to the German Princes: That the Augsburge Combination is a trifle: that the Swede is to be crush'd betweene the King of Denmark, and Poland by a separate peace with the Turk: that Mantüa is selling to the French, the Swisse Corrupted, and consequently Italy open'd to the Conqueror; that We with France and the King of Siam are to ruine the Hollander in the Indies and in fine, poore Spaine utterly forlorne and undon. *Car tel est notre bonne plaisiere*: The Universal Monarch, and Le Marquis de Louvois[1] has determin'd it: I am come to the end of my paper, which by my Sonne being gon with the Key of his study, and the boates staying for me and tide neere spent, makes writing on this course paper, irkesome: But you will pardon all undecencys of this nature, and ever account of me for Sir[2]

Your most faithfull and
most humble Servant   JEvelyn

Before yet I quite leave the poli[ti]cks, I would indeede recommend to your reading a shorter treatise entitld *Le Vrai Interet des Princes Chretiens* etc: pretended to be printd at *Strasbourg*:[3] which I think worth your reflection.

---

times cutt' (E's diary, 5 January 1687).

[1] François Michel le Tellier, Marquis de Louvois.

[2] The copy-letter omits the text from 'The Universal...', replacing it with: 'Le Marquis de Louvois has determin'd it, and Louis *le grand* is to be the Universal Monarch: But the Greater God is above all, and in my Conscience we shall see another Revolution that will shew it: Pardon the Rhapsody of Your etc *Si vis capere vocem Caperis ad Capiendum Vul[gis?] Cantantis, Cape* [sic, for *capite?*] *Itur* [sic, for *iter?*] *ad Capellam Divi Jacobi: Est ibi Statio sancti Fr; de Salis, quondam Genebensis Episcopi: Interim Cave ne sis in Babyloniâ Captus: M[..] Sinon Capi[t?]us, Capiat qui capere potest iterum Vale*'. The reading of the Latin is uncertain and appears to contain some mistakes. It could not be traced but presumably originated in a tract circulating during the turbulence leading up to the Glorious Revolution: 'If you want to seize a voice you are tied to the seizure by the howling rabble, [so] capture the road to the chapel of the holy James: there is the meeting-place of the holy Francis de Sales, sometime Bishop of Geneva: in the meantime watch out you should not be a captive in Babylon: [Mount Sinai having been taken?], he who is able to seize, may seize the way. Farewell.' The chapel referred to is: either, the Catholic Queen's Chapel at St James's Palace, begun in 1623 in anticipation of Prince Charles's marriage to the Spanish Infanta, but completed in 1627 for Henrietta Maria; or, a chapel built at Whitehall for James II in 1685–6 (see Beard 1982, 36; described by E, with some horror in the diary, 5 January 1687 – destroyed 1698 by the Whitehall fire. N.B. Bray editions of the diary give 29 December 1686 for this entry in error).

[3] *Le Vrai interêt des princes chretiêns, opposé aux faux interets, qui ont été depuis pue mis en lumiére*, P. Marteau, Cologne, 1686. The British Library catalogue states that the imprimatur is fictitious.

C37. SAMUEL PEPYS TO JOHN EVELYN[1]

An invitation to hear Cifacca sing

[no place]
Tuesday morning [19] April 1687[2]

Sir

Though my Lady bee out of towne[3] (for which I am sorry) and that my Lady
Tuke (to whom I owe the favour) is not in præsent condition by the death of
her Father to take any share her selfe of it,[4] Yet I did not know but you might
thinke it worth your while to make a stepp hither about 8 this evening to hear
Cefache;[5] where you will bee most wellcome to

Your most humble Servant
SPepys

---

[1] Source: Historical Society of Pennsylvania MS (Dreer Collection; English Prose
Writers). Endorsed by E, 'Mr Pepys Inviting me to heare the Eunuch Cifacia Sing:
Aprill: 1687'. How this letter entered the private market is unknown. It was not in
Upcott's album of letters from P to E, but was probably extracted by him from the
Evelyn archive. It was at the HSP by 1934 when Marburg saw it. It bears a price tag
of '$15', suggesting a sale around the year 1900 or before.
[2] The 19th April was a Tuesday; exact date indicated by E's diary. See note 5.
[3] On 9 April the Evelyn family had left their winter lodgings in London and returned
to Sayes Court.
[4] Mary, Lady Tuke, had told P of the prospect of the celebrated eunuch Giovanni
Francesco Grossi, 'Cifacca', visiting his house in a letter a few weeks before (2 March
1687, Bod MS Rawl. A189, f.296, published by Howarth, no. 163, p.178), 'I having
told him you have the best ['Harpsicall'] in England and are a great Lover of
Musick... you may have the pleasure to heare him sing without putting your self to
charge in other places... I only design'd it as an divertion for your self and your frinds,
of which nomber I hope to make up one'. Her father's death prevented her attendance
(Edward Sheldon of Stratton, see de Beer, III, 512, n. 2).
[5] E described the occasion at Pepys's house on Tuesday 19 April 1687 (diary) thereby
dating the letter, 'I heard the famous Singer the Eunuch Cifacca, esteemed the best in
Europe and indeede his holding out and delicatenesse in extending and loosing a note
with that incomparable softnesse, and sweetenesse was admirable: For the rest, I
found him a meere wanton, effeminate child; very Coy, and prowdly conceited to my
apprehension: He touch'd the Harpsichord to his Voice rarely well, and this was
before a select number of some particular persons whom Mr. Pepys (Secretary of the
Admiralty and a greate lover of Musick) invited to his house, where the meeting was,
and this obtained by peculiar favour and much difficulty of the Singer, who much
disdained to shew his talent to any but Princes.'

C38. JOHN EVELYN TO SAMUEL PEPYS[1]

Praise for Mr Pepys

To Samuell Pepys Esq etc
Secretary of the Navy   Deptford
                                                   20 June 1687[2]

Sir,

It has often come into my mind, that observation of Velleius Paterculus (speaking of the greate Scipio) as often as you have come into my thoughts (which is I assure very often) that never any body did more worthily Imploy the Intervale of Buisinesse: *Recquisquam elegantius Intervalla Negotiorum otium dispunxit* (the whole passage is this) *Semperque aut Belli aut Pacis servyt certibus: semper inter arma ae studia versatus, aut corpus periculis, aut animum disciplinis exercuit:*[3] That you, either to the affaires of the Navy, or to the Culture of the mind, by reading, and studying and encouraging all that is greate, and becoming a generous Soule: No person that I know of has more fortunatly pass'd the Adventures of an unquiet and tumultuary Age, and in so buisy a station, if that may so be calld, which is so full of motion, as that which is upon the floods and waters: This is, and has ben your province, and speakes a universal spirit and extraordinary Abillity: But that which adds to all this, and indeare you more than all this to me, is your Sincerity, and the experience I have had of your Vertue, and of your obliging nature, which must be ever acknowledgd by

Sir Your etc

---

[1] Source: BL CLBII.565. Apparently an unsolicited eulogy on P's character. There is no reference to a meeting or a favour done which might have merited the letter. E's diary and Bryant's detailed account of the period (*Saviour of the Navy*, 1938, 215–8) give no indication that P's official business might have stimulated E to write the letter. As with several others, extant only as E's copies, there is no means of verifying that P ever received it; indeed its tone sits oddly beside that written on 3 October 1687 (**C39**), thus it seems improbable it was sent, at least on the date recorded.

[2] MS: 'Deptford. 20 June –87'.

[3] Paterculus' text has been subject to much revision since the 1600s, accounting for the modern state of this passage: *Neque enim quisquam hoc Scipione elegantias dispunxit semperque aut belli aut pacis serviit artibus: semper inter arma ac studia versatus aut corpis periculis aut animum disciplinis exercuit*, 'No man more than Scipio ever relieved the impositions of an active life by a more elevated use of his leisure time, or was more constant in his devotion either to the arts of war or peace. Always involved in the pursuit of arms or his studies, he was either training his body by exposure to danger or his mind with learning' (*Historiæ Romanæ*, I.xiii.3).

C39. JOHN EVELYN TO SAMUEL PEPYS[1]

Mud at Sayes Court and the death of Lady Mordaunt

For Mr Secretary Pepys etc
at the Admiralty
in York-buildings

Sayes Court
3 October 1687[2]

Sir,

I have (as became me) ben twise to kisse your hands since I came out of my long Surry-ramble; but was not so fortunate as to find you: and now I would not at my first Addresse, have Importund you with my Complaints; but at a second,[3] I should have beg'd the favour of you (from your promis'd Order) that some reguard might at last be had to our Stayers, being of dailie, and mutual use:[4] Some of the steps etc are faulty, but the greatest inconvenience is, the choking up of the Causy,[5] by the mud, which makes it altogether unservicable:[6] One line from you to our Commissioner, would without any expense considerable, oblige a family; though I do not relinquish the Covenants of our Lease, for the maintaining of it:[7] You were pleas'd to say, the next Watchman to the pale,[8] should receive your Commands to take some care of it, and clense it of the slubb;[9] as for some yeares one of them did, whilst his station was nerer it; not onely for inspection of the staye[r]s, but repelling such, as (to his Majesties dammage as well as mine) leaping the ditches, and landing on any part of the Wharfe, trespase upon both by daily

---

[1] Source: Hyde Collection, New Jersey MS (ex-Davey Catalogue Item 2886) from microfilm in Adam extra-illustrated volume of Johnson's Volume III, p.155, at the Firestone Library, Princeton University Libraries. Endorsed (and with a seal), 'Deptford October 3rd 1687. Mr Evelyn to Mr Pepys, complaining of some publick hardshipps about his house there.' The letter also exists as a scrawled and undated draft at BL.1559ii with a variety of minor differences, not affecting the meaning.

[2] MS: 'S Court: 3d 8br–87' at foot of letter.

[3] On 19 July 1687 E and his family left for Wotton where they stayed for five weeks. E made a number of trips around Surrey during that period, returning to Deptford on 22 August. E then made trips to London on 27 August, and 20 September (diary).

[4] These are the river stairs down which E walked to take boats to London.

[5] Correctly 'causey', an archaic form of 'causeway'.

[6] Replaces 'impassable', struck out.

[7] For this lease and its provisions see the letter of 29 June 1686 (C32).

[8] To the zone, or enclosure.

[9] Thick mire.

running from their Worke, and back to the *Calle* againe,[1] for want of some body to stand Centinel where the former watch-man did: There is also a greate Elme, subverted by the Wind, neere Mr Grandsdens stables,[2] which has ruin'd a pen-stock[3] of mine, that of necessitie must be repair'd, that I may retaine water for my family, when they divert, and take it off, upon divers occasions of the Yard: I forbeare to mention my other griefs of this nature through the damage I suffer by the leaking of the Mast-dock;[4] because I was still in hope, I might some time or other have opportunity, of shewing you all my sorrows upon the place, which I am sure would affect you. But since I may not promise my selfe that happy moment, necessity makes me petition for your redresse of the rest, with all modesty and submission.

And[5] now, even now, whilst I am writing this, comes my Wife from London with the lugubrous[6] tidings of my Lady Mordants[7] being dead;[8] for which as I most heartily Condole with you, so, I am confident we have all who knew that excellent Creature, sympathizing with us: We have sent to Condole the surviving Lady her sister;[9] and I assure you Sir, I am in particular sensibly, and extreamely concern'd for our mutual losse, for so permit me to call it, because I had the honour of her Esteeme, through your meanes, who are allways Obliging

Sir,

Your most humble, and

most obedient Servant

JEvelyn:

---

[1] Probably the summons, perhaps by bell, to return to work.

[2] Draft omits the reference to Grandsden's stables. For their probable location see the plan on p.338, no. 7. 'Mr Grandsen' may be the Robert Gransden (sic) who donated land for a nearby charitable foundation in the late 1600s (Dews, 1881, 171).

[3] Water-regulating sluice or pump.

[4] For the mast dock see the plan on p.338.

[5] Replaces 'But', overwritten.

[6] Archaic form of 'lugubrious', meaning 'sorrowful' or 'dismal'.

[7] MS: 'L: Mordants' That this is 'Lady' is self-evident from the phrase 'the surviving Lady, *her* sister', below. The Davey Catalogue ignored that and stated this was 'Lord Mordaunt'. In fact, it is P's friend, and cousin by marriage, Elizabeth, Lady Mordaunt (c. 1645–87), widow of Sir Charles Mordaunt, bart., (see notes 8 and 9).

[8] At the beginning of his 1687 Surrey trip E dined with a Lady Mordant (sic) at 'Ashsted' (de Beer, IV, 557, n. 1), probably the same lady referred to here. The only other titled Mordaunts of E's acquaintance to die during his lifetime were John, first Viscount Mordaunt, and his wife, also Elizabeth (died 1675 and 1679 respectively).

[9] This is Lady Mordaunt's sister, known only as Mrs Steward (see 10 September 1688, **C42**, p.183, note 3), another member of P's close family circle.

C40. JOHN EVELYN TO SAMUEL PEPYS[1]

Mr Pepys's charitable concern for Mrs Fowler

For Samuell Pepys Esqr Secretary of
the Admiralty at the Admiralty etc.

Deptford
1 March 1688[2]

Sir,

It being my Intention to kisse your hands and in Person give you thanks for
your Letter without Writing; The surprizes and Continuance of this rude
season, has diverted me from either waiting on, or ('til now) of writing to you.

I shew'd Mrs Fowler your Charitable Concerne for her,[3] at which she was
not a little troubl'd, apprehending that you might think her coming to waite
upon you the last weeke, was to put you in mind of Mony etc, which, she
assures me, was not so much as in her thought: But the occasion of her
coming, was to have intreated the favour of you, to quicken Mr Gibson (who
seem'd to make some difficultie)[4] to let her have a Bed, and some small
conveniences (according to his promise and agreement she allowing the full of
the Appraisement) for the furnishing a little humble building[?] which she has
found-out in Greenewich; being now hourely cal'd-upon by Sir William
Hooker[5] (her Land-Lord) in whose house she still is at present: This being the
sole inducement of her application to you at that time, she humbly begs, that
for the rest (namely his Majesties Bounty and your greate kindnesse) you will
take your owne time, full and best convenience, without pressing in the least.

---

[1] Source: Bod MS Rawl. A179, f.8. Endorsed by P, 'March 1 1687/8 Mr Evelyn to
Mr Pepys. Touching the businesse of Widdow Fowler and Mr Cowes and
accompanying an Originall Book of Rules of the Navy 1588'. The latter may be
identified probably as that bound at MS Rawl. A171, f.308, entitled 'The booke of
rates for her Majesties Shipps 1588' and addressed to P in E's hand.
[2] MS: 'Deptf: 1.Mar:– 87/8' at foot of letter.
[3] Pepys had responded to letters from E's wife. Mrs Evelyn had written to P on 16
July 1686 (Davey Catalogue Item 2890 – lost) and 7 September 1687 (Howarth 170;
Bod Rawl. MS A189, f.5) about Mrs Fowler's predicament following her husband's
death and requesting that P intercede on Mrs Fowler's behalf with the King. Captain
Thomas Fowler had died in debt but was owed arrears from the Crown. See also E's
letter to P 10 August 1683 (above, **C17**). E seems to have discussed the matter with P
over dinner on 10 December 1687 (diary).
[4] Probably Richard Gibson, at this time chief clerk of the Victualling Accounts.
[5] The Alderman Sir William Hooker.

The like Mr Cows (her Brother) humbly desires you will do as to his Concerne, who dos so intirely resigne himselfe;[1] that as to Conditions, he is not at all solicitous: Whatever may be thought a Competency for a diligent, and faithfull servant in that station, he is most gratefully ready to accept, without giving you the trouble of seeking precedent; and for his Industry, sobriety and greate honesty, I am still his Voucher, and shall for these, and all other your great Civilitie ever remaine[2]

> Sir
>> Your most humble, and
>>> most faithfull servant
>>>> JEvelyn:

I send you another rag of paper,[3] as the Country-man offerd an handfull of Water to the Persian Monarch; and your Acceptance of such trifles shall be to me a Kingdome.

Mr Gibson and Mrs Fowler are since agreed, so as you shall not neede give your selfe any more trouble:

---

[1] See letters 10 and 11 September 1688, **C42** and **C43**, below.

[2] The affair of Mrs Fowler had, shortly afterwards, a happy outcome. Her letter of thanks to P is bound at MS Rawl. A179, f.88 dated 14 April 1688 and endorsed by P, 'Mrs Fowler, Widdow of Captain Fowler her letter of thanks to Mr Pepys for one hundred pounds obtained by him for her of the King as his Charity to her and her child'. She wrote:

'Honoured Sir. The Kings most gracious Bounty and Charity I have received and because I am very sensible I have found the effect of his Majesty's favor by no other meanes but through your mediation I presume to render you my most humble thankes praying for his Majesties health and happiness and continuall prosperity to your worthy selfe. I remaine, Your most obedient and most humble Servant Anne Fowler. Greenwich Aprill the 14th 1688'.

[3] See P's endorsement, p.180, note 1.

C41. JOHN EVELYN TO SAMUEL PEPYS[1]

That Frederick Collier enjoy the wife of his youth

To Samuell Pepys
Secretary of the Admiralty

Deptford
31 July 1688[2]

Sir,

In Antient Times there was (you know) a Law, That the new Married Man in time of Warr, should for the first yeare of his Espousale, be indulged and stay at home and Enjoy the Wife of his Youth: Whether this be Moral, and still Obliging (as I know no reason why it should not) I do not dispute: Sure I am it was Divine, and very Reasonable: That when so many went abroad, and loose their Lives for their Country, some should be excus'd, stay at home and get Children to repaire the common losse: Sir, you will naturaly gather from this, that poore Frederick Collier (who is our Constant Water-man here at Deptford) dos most humbly beg your Protection; It is my Wifes (whose health is I thank God much improv'd)[3] as well as the Request of Sir Your

I send you herewith the old smoky Pamphlet you desir'd, which had it taken Effect, might have sav'd the burning of a Greate Citty:[4] I Acknowledge my Mistake of the Statute you were enquiring after: But certaine I yet was such a Law there was, as you will find p:18:[5] and I am perswaded there is also something like it in Holingshed: But my Son has the *Hist: et Lond:*[6]

---

[1] Source: BL CLBII.581. See note 4 for some evidence that this letter was never sent. E had watched fireworks for the Queen, following the birth of her son James Stuart on 10 June, from P's house (diary, 17 July 1688), but this is not mentioned in the letter.
[2] MS: 'Deptford last July 88'.
[3] She had suffered a fainting fit two days previously. In accordance with custom she was let blood, which E was confident had brought about her recovery (diary, 29 July). It did not last and she became rapidly more seriously ill (see **C42** and **43**).
[4] E's tract *Fumifugium: or the Inconvenience of the Aer and Smoak of London dissipated*, 1661. It contained his hopes and plans such as, 'That this Glorious and Antient City, which from Wood might be rendred Brick, and (like another *Rome*) from Brick made Stone and Marble'. *No copy* has ever been catalogued in the Pepysian Library suggesting that this letter was never sent, at least in this form.
[5] Here in *Fumifugium* E quotes an act of 1610 concerning the burning of 'Ling, and Heath, and other Moor-burning' in various northern counties.
[6] Ralph Holinshed, his *Chronicles* (1587; Library Sale Lot 766), and John Stow's *Survey of London* (1598).

C42. SAMUEL PEPYS TO JOHN EVELYN[1]

Mrs Evelyn's health and Mr Cowes' job

Windsor
10 September 1688[2]

Sir,

It has beene my misfortune not to bee in the way of knowing any thing concerning you till Saturday last, when wayteing on Mrs Steward[3] (which I had not been able to doe, I thinke, in 6 weekes before) I mett the newes (that much grieves mee) of Mrs Evelyn's ill state of health[4] when Mrs Stewart was lately with you. Pray favour mee with letting mee know by the bearer how my Lady now is: for I am with all my heart concerned for her doeing well, both for her sake and yours, and a great many more besides my selfe. I hope to bee in London to morrow, and have appointed my messenger to meete mee there with the Newes hee shall have to bring mee from you, which I hope will bee of her amendment.

To this lett mee adde, that I have been lately called upon afresh by him who gave me formerly occasion of remembring Mr Cowes,[5] and if Mr Cowes bee still under the same circumstances hee was, lett him (if you please) adventure the trouble of letting me see him once more as soone as hee pleases. But I being now mostly here, it may be easiest for him to come to mee when I am in towne, which probably be[6] to morrow about Noone, and Wednesday all the morning; the character you have heretofore given mee of his Modest Dilligence and Sobriety, as well as his other Capacitys, greatly disposing mee to serve him, especially where I may serve a friend allsoe, with whom those virtues will bee valued. I am, with all faythfullnesse,

Your most humble Servant,
SPepys

---

[1] Source: BL Upcott Antiquaries II. No endorsement but bears E's drafted reply (see [11] September 1688, **C43**).

[2] MS: 'Windsor, September 10th 1688'.

[3] Sic. Only known as Mrs Stewart, she makes a single appearance in E's diary as godmother to one of E's grand-daughters (diary, 12 January 1692). Sister of Elizabeth, Lady Mordaunt (see above, p.179) – the pair were close friends of P's.

[4] See next letter (**C43**).

[5] Brother of a Mrs Fowler (see 1 March 1688, **C40**) who had earlier sought E's and his wife's assistance in interceding with P. The same letter had also raised the question of a position for Cowes.

[6] Braybrooke erroneously here adds 'may' before 'be'.

C43. JOHN EVELYN TO SAMUEL PEPYS[1]

An urgent reply on Mrs Evelyn's health

[Sayes Court]
[11 September 1688][2]

If the state of Sicknesse be capable of any Satisfaction one would almost contentedly be a clinike for the many kind friends and numbers that are concern'd for us: We are infinitely obligd to the Lady you mention for her greate Civilitie, and to you for youre kind Inquiry after us: My poore Wife has indeede been very ill, and so afrited us with frequent fits and faints; that I feard my days of mourning[3] now neare at hand: But a critical[?] and spontaneous and often bleeding at nose about the beginning of last weeke, has so disposd her and recovered her,[4] having never had any paroxysme since, that she rises, and is about the Chamber and gathers strength, and I hope may live to give you and all her worthy friends her humble accknowledgements for all their kindnesse; and til she is able to do it in person I will endeavour to kisse your hands on Wednesday next[5] my selfe, for I long to see you and receive your Commands having never ben in London since my returne from Althorp, now almost 3 weekes since:[6] I shall in the meantime acquaint Mr Fowler[7] of his greate obligations to you, and am assurd that he will most thankfully[?] and gratefully[?] embrace whatever[8] Condition your kindnesse still resumd him to; I shall persist in all I have ever sayd of good in his behalfe: and I looke upon this favor of yours as a fresh[?] obligation continud to

Sir Your

---

[1] Source: BL Upcott Antiquaries II. Scrawled on the bottom of P's letter of 10 September 1688 (**C42**). It is highly abbreviated and scratchy and in consequence unusually difficult to read. Some details of the text must be regarded as unconfirmed.

[2] The draft bears no date or place. E's diary implies he was at Sayes Court at this time. The letter is clearly a 'by return' reply, as P requested, and was either composed on 11 September or very shortly after (see note 6).

[3] MS: 'mourng'.

[4] ? MS: 'rec..d'.

[5] Probably 19 September (see next note). There is no reference to a visit in the diary.

[6] E returned from Althorp on 24 August 1688 when he heard news of his wife's sickness (diary). Three weeks forward would be 14 September showing that this letter was written between 11 and 13 September.

[7] Presumably E's slip for Cowes, the brother of Anne Fowler (see p.181, note 2) whose welfare was an Evelyn family concern. E had also sought a position for Cowes (see **C40** and **42**) which is being referred to here.

[8] MS: 'wtvr'.

C44. JOHN EVELYN TO SAMUEL PEPYS[1]

In favour of Dr Gale

To Samuell Pepys Esqr
Secretary of the Admiralty

London
2 November 1688[2]

Sir,

Being lately to Visite Dr Godolphin,[3] who is one of the Residentiarie Præbends of St Paule's, and gathering by Discourse on the impendent Revolution (which cannot but produce greate Alterations and changes amongst us) it fell naturaly into my thoughts, whether, if his Majestie should think of promoting any of those Eminent Divines, Dr Stillingfleete, Tillotson[4] etc to be Bishops; it might not be a seasonable Instant, in which to Bespeake his Majesties Favour for one, whom I am sure, you have as greate a value and just veneration, as you have daily, and yet happy Opportunities. You will Infallibly Conclude, I meane that Worthy, and Learned Person Dr Gale,[5] Scholemaster of St Paules,[6] and that, without the least Intimation from one whose Modestie would, I feare, not give me leave to mention him on this Account: I yesterday attempted to have kiss'd your hands, but was not so happy as to find you within: Considering how Slippery Time, and Occasion are, especialy in this Crisis, I Adventure on my owne-head onely to suggest this to you, before it be too Late: If you Conspire with me herein, I will Aske no Pardon of the Doctor for my presumption, nor of Mr Pepys for shewing my profound Respects, and sincere good-wishes for one whom he also honors, and all that know him:

Your [etc]

---

[1] Source: BL CLBII.592.

[2] MS: 'Lond: 2:Nor–88'.

[3] Dr Henry Godolphin. E had visited Sir William Godolphin (on 27 October, diary) recently but does not record a meeting with his brother Henry until 8 November (ibid). Of course there may have been an earlier, unrecorded meeting but it is equally possible (and likely) that the copy-letter is misdated by a matter of days or weeks.

[4] James II did not. The crisis had arisen out of the refusal by the 'Seven bishops' (Bath and Wells, Bristol, Canterbury, Chichester, Ely, Peterborough, and St Asaph) to sign his Declaration of Independence. William III made Stillingfleet bishop of Worcester in 1689, and Tillotson archbishop of Canterbury in 1691.

[5] Thomas Gale's highest ecclesiastical position was as dean of York which he did not reach until 1697.

[6] Marginal note by E.

C45. JOHN EVELYN TO SAMUEL PEPYS[1]

An offer of support for Mr Pepys

For Samuell Pepys Esqr,
Secretary of the Admiralty
in York-buildings

Sayes Court
12 December 1688[2]

Sir

I left you Indispos'd and send on purpose to learne how it is with you, and to know if in any sort, I may serve you in this prodigious Revolution:[3] You have many Friends, but no man living who is more sincerely your servant, or that has a greater value for you: We are here as yet (I thank God) unmolested; but this shaking menaces every Corner, and the most philosophic breast cannot but be sensible of the motion: I am assurd you neede no precepts, nor I Example so long as I have yours before me, and I would governe my selfe by your Commands to Sir[4]

Your
most humble
faithfull servant
JEvelyn:

---

[1] Source: Bod MS Rawl. A179, f.84. Endorsed, 'Deptford.12 Decr.88. Mr Evelyn to Mr Pepys upon the great Convulsion of the State upon the King's with-drawing'.

[2] MS: 'Says Cot 12.10br–88'.

[3] The crisis was at its height: James II had fled early in the morning of 11 December, two days after the Queen and the baby prince. P's proximity to the centre stage is exemplified (*inter alia*, see for example Hewer to P, 19 December 1688 – Howarth no. 188) by an unpublished document in his hand of 4 December 1688 in the name of, and signed by, James II: 'To Captain William Sanderson, Commander of Our Yacht the *Isabella*. James R. Our Will and Pleasure is, That, upon sight hereof, you receive on board our Yacht the *Isabella*, whereof you are Comander, the Comte de Lauzun, with his Company Baggage and Servants, and him and them haveing so taken on board you, You are to transport them, with the first opportunity of Wind and Weather, to such Port of Flanders or France as shall desire. Where haveing landed them, you are to returne with all Expedition to Margatt, there to attend Our further Order. Given at Our Court of Whitehall this fourth day of December 1688. By his Majesty's Command. SPepys' (Maine Historical Society, Fogg Collection). De Lauzun subsequently commanded James II's French forces in Ireland. E noted (diary, 2 December 1688), 'The Greate favorits at Court... flie or abscond'.

[4] P resigned his post as Secretary of the Admiralty on 20 February 1689 and was imprisoned between May and July.

C46. JOHN EVELYN TO SAMUEL PEPYS[1]

Preventing physick has not staved off an indisposition

For Samuell Pepys Esqr etc
at his house in
Yorke-Buildings

[Sayes Court]
10 May 1689[2]

Sir,

'Tis to me an Age since I saw you,[3] having almost ever since ben afflicted with my taking Cold upon entring a familiar[4] Course of preventing Physick:[5] My Indisposition still hangs upon me, which confines me to my little family: I could not else have deny'd my selfe the satisfaction of kissing your hands: I have nothing here to aleviate[6] that unhappinesse, but the Confidence I have, of your believing me (in all Revolutions and Vicissitudes whatsoever)

Sir,
Your
most faithfully, steady,
humble, and Affectionate Servant
(*Sans Reserve*)
JEvelyn:

---

[1] Source: Bod MS Rawl. A170, f.64. Endorsed, 'May 10th 1689. Deptford. Mr Evelyn to Mr Pepys. A Letter of Respect, with reguard to the present publique State of Things.' The handwriting of the MS is more scrawled than usual even for E. Some of the letter strokes are uncharacteristically thick and blotted. It suggests he was writing in haste and with some physical discomfort.

[2] MS: '10:May:89.' No place but the diary indicates he was at Sayes Court.

[3] P had been arrested on 4 May 1689 (Ollard 1991, 348) on a charge of Jacobitism. E, however, dined with him on 8 June 1689 (diary).

[4] An archaic meaning of this word is 'of, or pertaining to, the family'. This is possible here though it may equally mean that it was something E was becoming used to taking.

[5] See E's diary 19 May 1689: he was too ill to go to church until Whitsunday (the 19th) when 'though very weake, I got thither'.

[6] MS: replaces 'supply[?]' struck out.

C47. JOHN EVELYN TO SAMUEL PEPYS[1]

An epic letter on medals and other curiosities

To Samuell Pepys Esqr:
at his house in Yorke-buildings

Deptford
26 August 1689[2]

Sir,

I was on Wednesday last (after-noone) to kisse your hands But finding you abroad and my selfe oblig'd to Returne that Evening (that I might receive my Lady Sunderland who sent me word she would call at my house the next morning early, before her Embarkment for Holland)[3] I do now write, what I should have said to you, if Time had permitted: And that is, To let you know, that upon your Late Communicating to me your Designe of Adorning your Choice Library with the pictures of Men Illustrious for their parts and Erudition, I did not in the least suspect your Intention of placing my shallow-head amongst those Heros, who, knowing my Unworthynes of that honour will in spight of your good Opinion of Mr Kneller for his skill of Drawing to the Life, either condemn his Colouring, that he made me not Blush, or me for Impudent that I did not:[4] But this is not all – For men will question your Judgement, or suspect you of flattery, if you take me not down, for in good earnest, when seriously I Consider, how unfit I am to appeare in the Rank of those learned Gentlemen: I am perfectly asham'd, and must say, with much more reason than Maxullus (after his Recension of the famous Poets)

---

[1] Source: Pforzheimer MS 35I (and BL CLBII.616), ex-Davey Catalogue Item 2881. No endorsement. The MS of the letter-sent is extremely badly damaged. The text has been restored here from E's copy, and P's scribal copy at MS Rawl. A171, f.316ff (marked 'Rec^d.Aug.30.1689'). The omission of some passages (present in the copy only), occasionally clearly accidental, indicates there was originally a draft. Restored passages are marked [] here, and these include passages only present in the copy.
[2] BL CLBII.616 is dated 12 August 1689.
[3] E visited her on Wednesday, 21 August, to take her leave. There is no mention of an attempted visit to P (diary).
[4] E was sitting for a portrait by Kneller, commissioned by P (diary, 9 July 1689). This portrait survives, having been bought by E's grandson from Ann Jackson, widow of Pepys's nephew and heir John Jackson in 1724. A copy was presented to the Royal Society in 1707 by Mary Evelyn. E seems also to have sat to Kneller in 1685 (diary, 8 October 1685) but this painting is lost. On P and E's interest in prints and portraits see below, p.223, note 4.

Nos, si quis inter cæteros locat vates
Onerat, quam honorat verius.[1]

'Tis pitty and a diminution, so elegant a place and precious Collection should have anything in it of Vulgar; but such as Paulus Jovius[2] has Celebrated, and such as (you told me) you were procuring; the Boiles, the Gales, and the Newtons of our Nation: What in Gods name, should a planter of Cole-worts[3] do amongst such Worthies: setting him aside, I Confesse to You, I was not displeas'd with the fancy of the late Lord Chancellor Hyde, when to adorne his stately Palace,[4] he Collected the Pictures of as many of our owne famous Country-men as he could purchase or procure, instead of the Heads and Busts of forrainers, whose names, through the un-pardonable mistake or pride of painters, they scorn to put to their pieces; imagining it a dishonor to their Art, should they transmitt any-thing to Posterity, besides Faces, which signifie nothing to the Possessors; so as one cannot tell whether they were drawne from any of their Relations or Ancestors, or the Picture of some Porter, or squalid Tinker, whose prolix beard, and wrinkl'd forehead, may passe him for a Philosopher: I am in perfect Indignation at this folly, as often as I consider what extravagant summs are given for a dry scalp of some (forsooth) Italian painters hand let it be of Raphael or Titian himselfe, infinitely more estimable, were one assur'd it was the Picture of the Learned Count of Mirandula, Politian, Quicciardini, Machiavel, Petrarch, Ariosto or Tasso; some famous Pope, Prince, Poet, Historian or Hero of those times: Give me a Carolus Magnus, a Tamberlan, a Scanderbeg, Soloman the Magnificent, Matthew Corvinus, Lorenzo, or Cosmo Medices: Andre D'Oria, Fernando Cortez, Columbus, Vesputianus, Castrucci Castracano, a Sforza, Galiazi; The effigies of Cardan, and both Scaligers, Tico Brahe or Copernicus etc: Give me, I say, the Portraits of an Isabella Aragonia, or Castile, (and her four learned Daughters) Lucretia d'Este (to whom our Queene's related)[5] Vittoria Colonna, Hippolita Strozzi, Petrarch's Laura etc (not forgetting the Illustrious of our owne Country of both sexes) and a world more, renouned for Armes and Arts, rather than the most beautifull Courtezana or Prostitute of them all, who has nothing to commend in her but her Impudence, and that she was a painted

---

[1] 'If anyone should place us amongst poets, he burdens, rather than truly honours us.'
[2] Paulo Giovio, the sixteenth-century Italian historian.
[3] Cabbages.
[4] This was Clarendon House in Piccadilly. It was demolished in 1683 (see E's diary, 19 June 1683). In his copy-letter E added 'since demolished' to the text here, presumably for the benefit of his descendants who might read the letter. P could hardly have been unaware of the mansion's unhappy fate.
[5] This is a slightly curious reference as the date of the letter is August 1689 by which time William III and Mary II were on the throne. E seems, however, to be referring to James II's queen, now in exile, the former Mary Beatrix Eleonora D'Este; unless that is, E is correctly regarding Mary of Modena as Mary II's stepmother.

strumpet:[1] Did it ever prejudice the glory of in-imitable Holben, for his putting the Names of our greate Duke of Norfolck, Charles Brandon, Althea Talbot, Henry the Eighth (when very young and lesse Corpulent) his Chancellor Cromewell, Sir Thomas Moore, and learned Daughters, Dr Nowell, Sir Brian Tuke; Erasmus, Melanchthon, and even honest Froben, amongst innumerable more Illustrious of that Age, for Learning and other Vertues? I Aske if this were the least diminution to the fame of One, who realy Painted to the Life beyond any man of this day Living? But, in good earnest, they seeme from the very beginning jealous of their owne honor, and afraid of being forgotten, which they'l be sure to prevent, by Leaving some Character of their owne name whilst they remember not the other: We see ΓΛΥΚΩΝ ΑΘΗΝΑΙΟC ΕΠΟΙΕΙ[2] insculp't on the Farnesian Hercules.[3] And *Michael Angelo fecit, P.P.P. Peter Paule Rubens Pinxit, Marc Antonio sculpsit, R: Nanteiule faciebat* etc nay Tom Crosse and William Marshal nor is there that wretched Print or Rhipograph,[4] but weares the Name of the (no) Artist, whilst our Painters (I say) take no care to transmit to posterity, the names of the Person whom they present; Through which negligence, so many excellent pieces, come after a while, to be dispers'd among the Upholsterers and Brokers in every dusty corner: 'Tis amongst their Lumber we find Queen Elizabeth, Mary Queen of Scotts, The Countesse of Penbrock, The Earles of Licester, Dudly, Essex, Buckhurst, Burleigh, Sir Walter Raleigh, Sir Philip Sidney, Cecil, Walsingham, Sir Francis Bacon, King James's favourit Buckingham, and others who then made the greate figure in this Nation: There 'tis we sometimes meete with Charles the Fift, Philip the Second, Francis the first, the Dukes of Anjou, Alva Parma, Count Gondomar, William and Morice of Nassau: of John Husse, Zisca, Luther, Calvine, Beza, Socinus, Authors of Sects, Great Captaines and Polititians, famous in other Countries, and our Historie, flung oftentimes behind the doore, cover'd with dust and cobwebs – Upon this Account it is, men curious of Books and Antiquitie have ever had Medalls in such estimation, and rendered them a most necessary furniture to their Libraries;[5] because by them, we are not onely inform'd whose Image and

---

[1] Probably Nell Gwynne whom E called an 'impudent Comedian' (diary, 1 March 1671). He had strong feelings about over made-up women which he expressed when he encountered the 'Countess of Monte Feltre, whose husband I had formerly known... accompanied with her Sister, exceedingly skild in painting; nor indeede did they seeme to spare for Colour on their owne faces:' (ibid, 3 September 1683).

[2] 'Glycon of Athens made this.'

[3] E had seen it in 1644 at the Palazzo Farnese but the statue was an ancient copy with a new head. It no longer exists (de Beer, II, 216, n. 4).

[4] Pornographic print. P was not unfamiliar with them (diary, 9 February 1668).

[5] E had long had an interest in coin and medal collecting (as had P). See, for example, de Beer, II, 343, and 368, while E was in Italy in 1645. The whole of the following section served E as a rehearsal for his Chapter III of *Numismata* (1697). Certain passages, such as the list of ancient building types recorded on coins, so resemble the

Superscription they beare, but have discover'd in the Reverses, what heroic Exploits they perform'd,[1] what famous Temples, Thermæ, Amphitheaters, Triumphal Arches, Bridges, Aquæducts, Circus's, *Naumachiæ*,[2] and other pompous structures were erected by them, which have ben greately Assistant to the Recovery of the Antient and magnificent Architecture, whose real Monuments had ben so barbarously defac'd by the Goths etc, that without this light, and some few Ruines yet extant, that so usefull Order and Ornament of Columns and their decent members, were hardly to be knowne by the Text of Vitruvius, and all his Commentators: Daniel Barbaro, Philander, Leon Alberti, Michel Angelo, Raphael and others rais'd up out of the Dust and Rubbish, and restor'd that noble Art by their owne, and other mens consulting the Reverses of Medals and Medalions; besides what they farther Contribute to the Elucidation of many passages of Historie and Chronologie etc: so as I do not see how Mr Pepys [library] can be long without this necessary Adjunct: It is amongst the Medals he shall meet Legislators, Solon, Lycurgus, Numa etc. There we find [Orpheus, Linus, and the old bards; and there is mention of *nummus Homericus* by Strabo, and (if I well remember) by Aristotle himself too]; as there is still extant of the brave Hector and Achilles: so as tis among them we may see [what kind of persons were] Aristides, Themistocles, Epaminondas, Miltiades, Alexander, and Cyrus, [Darius, etc. The grave] philosophers Socrates, Pythagoras, Plato, Aristotle, Epicurus, Zeno and Demosthenes, shew now to this day their reverend Faces in Medals: The Hebrew represent to us the Rod of Aaron and pot of Manna, and shew disconsolate *Iudæa capta*:[3] We come by Medals to understand the ancient Weights, and value of Monies: you shall see ther, when Princes tooke the radiant Crowne, and what the Diademe was: I might proceede to the Punique [Hannibal, Juba, etc], The Consulars, Imperial of the Romane, from Romulus [the Scipios, Catos,] downe to this Age of ours, if after Pertinax and Decline of that Empire, Sculpture and all good Arts had not fall'n with it: You will therefore be curious of haveing the first Cæsars, the great Julius after his Pharsalian Victorie[4] being the first honour'd with having his Effigies (old, leane and bald as he was) in Medals, which are very rare to procure in Gold or

---

printed sentences in *Numismata* that it seems likely E wrote the letter and the book from the same notes. Indeed he may have composed the two at around the same time, revising the book text later as time wore on.

[1] 'The very sight of their Effigies call'd to their minds the glorious Actions they had perform'd, and even inflam'd them with an Emulation of their virtues,' *Numismata*, 66. On the same page E also cites a passage from Cicero's oration for Archias, 'How many portraits of noble men traced for us, not only to look at, but to emulate, have Greek and Latin authors bequeathed us!' (*Archias*, vi; *trans*. Palmer Bovie).

[2] Mock sea-battle (see for example, Pliny, *NH*, XVI.200).

[3] This type, depicting a personification of the province of Judaea in mourning, was issued during the reign of Vespasian (69–79) on a number of denominations.

[4] In 48 BC.

small Coper especialy.[1] There are of these, and the other Emperors, with Greeke Inscriptions also:[2] Who is not delighted to behold the true Effigies of the famous Augustus, Cruel Nero and his master Seneca? Vespasian, Titus, Nerva, Trajan, Antoninus, Severus etc. The greate Constantine and his [devout] mother Helena? For we have in our Medals, the beautiful [Cleopatra and her paramour;[3] Drusilla,] Livia, Julia, Agrippina, Antonia, Valeria Messalina,[4] Octavia, Sabina Poppæ (all of them Augustæ) and divers more of the faire Sex, who rul'd the World, or those who did: I have seene an intire Series of the Popes from St Peter, and among the reputed Heresiarks, that medallion of John Husse[5] and (his companion in suffering) Hierome of Prague['s martyrdom], with the memorable Inscription *Post centum Annos omnes vas cito*, which fell out at the appearing of Martin Luther exactly [at that period]:

But, Sir, I am sensible I have quite tired you [by this time] with Medals and therefore will say nothing concerning those Observations on the filing, sharpnesse, and due extancy,[6] Politure, Vernish and other markes, criticaly necessary to be skill'd in, to prevent the being [cheated and] impos'd on by Copies [and counterfeits] for Originals and Antique: Though all copies, if well [dissembled,] stamp'd, or Cast, are not to be rejected, whose originals are hard to come by (as are Cæsonia Augusta, Diva Domitilla, daughter of Vespasian, Annius verus, Antonius Gordianus Africanus, Heliogabalus, and especially most of the Roman Ladys etc) Because you will both for this and all the rest, consult Fulvius Ursinus, Goltzius, Dupois, Monsieur St. Amant, [Otto,] Dr Spon, Vaillant, [Dr Patin,] and above all,[7] the most learned Spanhenius [in that treatise *De præstantia et usu Numismatum Antiquorum*[8]]: You will

---

[1] Although Cæsar's portrait does appear on a limited series of posthumous bronze coins, it featured much more commonly on various silver *denarius* issues.

[2] Known now as 'Greek Imperial issues' these coins were struck in the major cities of the eastern Roman Empire during the imperial period. The denominations were modelled on traditional Greek units. Conversely, in the Latin west, coins were mainly struck only in Rome, and occasionally Lyons, and bore Latin legends. The situation altered by the late third century; from then on coins were issued at most major cities. The exception was gold which was struck only at Rome to begin with.

[3] A reference to a *denarius* bearing Mark Antony's portrait on one side and Cleopatra's on the other (Sear, 1981, *Roman Coins and their values*, no. 363).

[4] Some printed versions of this letter add a comma after Valeria – but this was the full name of Claudius I's third wife, depicted on a *didrachm* of Cæsarea.

[5] E saw this medal in the collection of the late Ralph Sheldon on 3 December 1684 (diary; also de Beer, IV, 396, n. 4).

[6] Copy-letter 'extanic varnish.'

[7] Copy letter: *instar omnium*.

[8] *Dissertationes de Præstantia et Usu Numismatum Antiquorum*, Amsterdam 1664. E's own, annotated, copy of the second edition (1671) is now in the British Library (Eve.a.121). E met the author on 31 October 1675 (his own 55th birthday) while dining with Arlington, and refers to the book on medals.

likewise make use of Friends upon whose [skill and] Judgement you may depend; Though even the best skill'd may (now and then) be mistaken; But you shall be sure not be paied with Trash, such as I do not (as I said) call the *Antico modern* if well dissembl'd. Our common friends Dr Gale, Mr Henshaw, Hill, and Justell will be ambitious to assist in this Laudable Curiositie: And, if they can be purchas'd at once (as some-times accidentaly they may be) it will save you a greate deale of paines, and Inrich you on the suddain, but otherwise, they are likliest met with all, amongst the Gold-Smiths, and casualy, as one walkes in the Streetes on foot, and passes by their stalls; for the Country people do not bring them to the Virtuosi, and inquisitive strangers, as they do at Rome, where they are greedy of them: Mr Ashmole [our common friend] had collected all the Ancient and Modern Coines of this Kingdome,[1] which was very rare, together with severall Medals of our [British, Saxon, and other] Kings upon Occasion of Births, Coronations, Marriages, and other Solemnities: I know not whether they escaped the burning of his study in the Midle Temple;[2] But for the [most] accurate Ordering and disposal of Medals, so as one may more commodiously, take them out of their repositories, Mr Charleton[3] (a gent of that Inne of Court) has a peculiar Method, and Addresse, as he is indeede the most Elegant [and rarely furnished] in all his other Collections. In the meantime, the Curious in this sort of Erudition (I meane of Medals) were formerly, and (I believe at present) but very few in England. For besides Sir Robert Cotten, Mr Selden, Sir Simon D'Ewes, Sir Thomas Hanmer of Hanmer, the late Mr Hervey and Sir William Paston I find hardly any: Thomas (that greate lover of Antiquity) Earle of Arundel, had a very rich Collection as well of Medals, as of other Intaglios, belonging to the Cabinet he purchas'd of Daniel Nice at the rate of ten thousand pounds sterling: which, with innumerable other Rarities, have been scatter'd and squander'd away, by his Countesse when she got over that Treasure to Amsterdam and Antwerp, whilst her husband was in Italy, where he died:[4] Aboundance of them she bestowed on the Late unhappy Viscount Stafford,[5] her beloved son and such as remaind: Lely, Wright, and the rest of the Painters, Foxes, Panders, and Misses, cheated the late Duke of Norfolck of:[6] The same fate befell a noble Collection of Medals belonging to the then

---

[1] E saw his collection of curiosities on 23 July 1678, but makes no mention of the medals.

[2] The fire occurred in 1688 (Weinreb and Hibbert, 515).

[3] E took the Countess of Sunderland to see his 'rarities'. E thought the collection, which included medals, drawings, and preserved animals more remarkable than any private collection he had seen anywhere to date (diary, 16 December 1686).

[4] Arundel had been a friend to E during the latter's travels in Italy in the 1640s and had shown him around Padua where he died in 1646.

[5] William Howard, executed in 1680. E saw his trial (diary, 2 December 1680ff).

[6] The reference is perhaps to the debts incurred by the sixth duke's grandfather, Thomas Howard, Earl of Arundel, 'This Gent: had now compounded a debt of neere

curious Sir Simon Fanshaw of Weare-parke,[1] which after his decease were thrown about the house [as that worthy gentleman his son, Sir Richard, Lord Ambassador in Spain, from whom I had the relation, has told me] for children to play at Counters with; as was those accurate Greeke Types at Eaton, which the learned Sir Henry Savell procured [with great cost] for his Edition of St Chrysostome; the Schoole boys had their pockets full of them soone after that famous Impression, as it commonly fares with most Curiosities, where the next Heire is not a consummat Virtuoso; so vaine a thing it is to set one's heart on any thing of this nature with the passion and Mania, that unsatiable Earle (I mentiond) did, to the prejudice and detriment of his [estate and] noble and Illustrious family; *mediocria firma*[2] – The Medals in our Universitie Librarye are not [yet] at all Considerable, though Obadiah Walker were an Industrious promoter of it, and not unskillfull in them: Mr Ralph Sheldon of Weston [in Warwickshire], left a Very handsom Collection, both Gold, Silver, and Coper, antient and modern, part of which were bequeath'd to a sister of my Lady Tuke's, who not long-since offer'd to sell them: I brought Monsieur Justell to see them,[3] but they were much over-valued, and whither she have since dispos'd of them I never enquir'd: At present, I know of none, who is able to shew a better Collection and chosen set of Medals than the Earle of Clarendon, to whose late father (after all this tedious Parenthesis) I Returne, and have a mind to Entertaine you a while longer with what I had begun, where I spake of his purpose of furnishing all his Roomes of State and other Appart'ments with the pictures of the most Illustrious of our Nation, especially of his Life time and Acquaintance, and of divers others befor it. There was at full length[4] (and as I doubt not but you may remember some of them your selfe) The Greate Duke of Buckingham, and Hamilton, Lord Montrose, Lord Treasurers Weston and Cottington, the Earl of Holland, Carlile, Derby, Lindsey, Carnarvon, Kingston, Northumberland, Bristol, Falkland, Capel, Southampton, Sandwich, Manchester, St Albans, Mr John and William Ashburnham, Secretary Nicholas: Duke of Albemarle, Duke of New-Castle and his brother Sir Charles Cavendish etc: of the Cony robe and Coife, Arch Bishops Laud, Sheldon, Juxton; Duppa and Morley of Winchester, Mr Chillingworth, Dr Sanderson: Judge Cooke, Barkeley, Bramston, Sir Orlando Bridgeman, Jeoffrey Palmer, Mr Dugdale, etc, which were plac'd in his Library: And which was most of all agreeable to his Lordships genial humor (in the place where he us'd to dine publiqly) the heads of Chaucer, Shakespeare, old Ben, Beaumont and Fletcher

---

200000 pounds, contracted by his Grandfather' (diary, 19 June 1662).

[1] In fact Sir Henry Fanshawe, father of Sir Richard (see below).

[2] E used also this phrase, 'With constant mediocrity', in his 1673 commemoration of inviolable friendship with Margaret Godolphin.

[3] E thought they were over-priced by a factor of five (diary, 3 December 1684).

[4] Differences (apart from descriptive comments) in the copy-letter are not indicated in the following list which E proceeds to supply. The names mentioned are broadly similar but with considerable though unimportant differences in the order.

(both in the same piece) Spencer, Daniel Waler Cowley, Hudibras, etc: I had forgotten Sir Robert Cotton, who had in his hand (I well remember) a Medal; he had likewise Mr Seldens, and Sir Henry Savells, most of which, if not all, are at the present at Cornebery in Oxford-shire;[1] with the Library, which the present Earle, has wonderfully improv'd; besides what bookes he has at Swallow-field[2] (not contemptible) and the Manuscript Copies of what Concernes the Parliament Records, and Journals [and Transcriptions], which I have heard both him, and the late [unfortunate] Lord of Essex (who had the same [curiosity]) affirme cost them £500 transcribing and binding, and they furnish two sides of a pretty large roome: But, to returne to Portraits and encourage his Fathers [noble and singular] Collection of renouned persons, I sent his Lordship in a letter[3] which I writ him [a list of the Names] upon this Topic: He had already procur'd (you see) besides those of the Royal Family ... from Queen Elizabeths to his time: But still there wanted: Bishop Usher, Mr [Hooker], John Berkeley, Mr Hake of Eaton, Sir Henry Wotton, Dr Harvey, Mr Oughtred, Mr Ascham, Sir Thomas Bodley, Fulk Grevill, Sir Francis Bacon, Scholars and men of letters: To these I added the greate Ea[rls of Leice]ster Essex, Treasurer Buckhurst and Burleigh: Walsingham, Cecil, Sir Philip Sidny, Sir Hor and Francis Vere [Bishop] Fisher, and Fox Bishop of Winchester, Cromwell, Chancellor and Sir Thomas Moore, Sir Thomas Smith, Cardinal W[olse]y and Poole, Mr Spelman, Cambden, Charles Brandon, Owen the Epigrammist, Dr Nowel, Deane [of P]aules, Sir Robert Twisden and Sir John Marchan, Sir Norton Knatchbull, Dr Grave severall others I do not at present call to mind, nor have I rang'd them here like an Herald or Historian: but I well remember, I would have provok'd his Lordship to enquire, if it had ben possible, to have found any old portraits of Alexander *ab* Hales, Tutor to Charlemagne; Venerable Bede Scotus, Ocham, Riply, Roger Bacon, (a Catalogue where off we find in Pitse, Baleus etc) nor did I forget Sir Francis Drake, Sir Richard Hawkins, Cavendish, Frobisher, Hawkins those brave discoverers – And some of them his Lordship procur'd, but was as (you know) Interrupted, and after all this Apparatus and Grandure [died an exile, and in the displeasure of his Majesty and others who envied his rise and fortune] – *tam breves Populi Romani amores*:[4] I shall say nothing more of his Ministrie, and what was the pretence of his fall, than that we have liv'd to see greater Revolutions; The Pimps, Concubines and Bouffoons who supplanted him at Court came to nothing in a while after, and were as little pitied: 'Tis somewhat yet too early, to publish the Names of his Delators [for fear of one's teeth]; but

---

[1] Clarendon's seat.
[2] An estate six miles south-east of Reading, which came to Clarendon from his wife, Flower, widow of Sir William Backhouse, bart.
[3] The letter was dated 18 March 1667 and appears in various printings of the Bray edition of E's diary as a footnote to the diary entry for 20 December 1669.
[4] 'How shallow the love of the Roman People is.'

Time will speake Truth, and sure I am, and the Event has made [it good]. Things were infinitely worse menag'd since his disgrace, and both their late majesties [fell into as] pernicious Counsels, as ever Princes did, whilst (whatever my Lord Chancellor's skills were in [Law or] Politics) The Offices of state and Justice were furnish'd with men of old English hon[our] sobriety [probity, less open bribery] and ostentation: There was at least, something of more gravity and forme [kept up (things, however railed at, necssary in Courts)] of magnificence and antient Hospitalitie in his Majesty's Houses, more agreable to the Genius of this Kingdom [than] the open and avowed Luxurie [and profaneness] which succeeded, *à la Mode de France*, and to which this [favourite] was a declar'd Enemy upon my certaine knowledge: There were indeed heinous [matters and] Miscarriages laid to his charge, which I could never yet see prov'd; and you and I [can tell] of many that have fall'n, and yet suffer under that Calamity: – But, what's all this [you'll say] to our Subject: Yes, He was a great lover (at least) of Books, furnish'd a very ample Library, Writ himselfe an Elegant style, favour'd and promoted the Designe of the Royal Society; Built a magnificent Palace, and it was for this, and in particular, for his being very kind to me both abroad and at home, that I sent *Naudæus*[1] to him in a dedicatory Addresse, of which I am not so much ashamed as the Translation: There be some who (not displeas'd with the Force and style of that Epistle) are angrie at the Application: But, they do consider, that greate Persons, and such as are in place to do greate, and noble things (what ever their other defects may be) are to be panegyris'd into the Culture of those Vertues, without which, 'tis to be presum'd they had never ariv'd to a power of being able to encourage them.

>   *Cui monet ut facias quod iam facis, ipse monendo*
>   *Laudat, et hortatu, comprobat acta[?] suo.*[2]

And 'tis a justifiable Figure nor is it properly Adulation, but a Civilitie due to their Character: As for the Translation it has been so unseasonably abus'd by the Presse, that the shame any uncorrected Copy, should come abroad has made me suppresse as many as I could light on, not without purpose of Publishing a New edition which now perhaps might be the more seasonable,

---

[1] *Instructions Concerning Erecting of a Library: Presented to My Lord The President de Mesme*, By Gabriel Naudeus, P. and now Interpreted by Jo. Evelyn, Esquire, 1661. It had been prepared around 1658 on Thomas Barlow's suggestion (see next page, note 2) but the manuscript was lost (M. Hunter, 1995, 'John Evelyn in the 1650s' in *Science and the Shape of Orthodoxy*, 93).

[2] 'He who points out that you may do what you are already doing, in the pointing out he praises himself, and by encouragement, he was sanctioning by his action.' (*acta* in the MS should perhaps be *actu*). In the copy-letter E supplies only these first four words together with 'you remember the sequel'.

since the Humor of Exposing Libraries *sub hasta*[1] is become so Epidemical, and that it may possibly afford some direction to Gentlemen who are making their Collection out of them: Besides, the Impression is, I heare, pretty well worn-out: and I should be strangely unfortunate it should twice miscarry, or meete with such another Accident as happen'd [it seems] to the [blotted] Manuscript, I sent Dr Barlow [at Oxford], the Circumstances whereof, I shall not now trouble you withall.[2] – And so I have done with my Lord Chancellor. But not so soone with my worthy Friend Mr Pepys, to whose learned, and laudable Curiositie, of still Improving his choice Collection, I should not Advise a solicitous Expense of having the Pictures of so many greate Persons, painted in Oyle (which were a vast, and unnecessary charge (though not so extraordinary a one to my Lord Chancellor as one may imagine; because, when once his Designe was once made-known, Every body (who either had them of their owne, or could purchase them) [at any price] strove to make their Court by such Presents, by which meanes he got many excellent pieces of Vandykes, and other Originals of Lelys, Johnson, Daniel Myttens and other and the best of our Modern Masters hands: – But if, instead of these you think fit to add to your Volume of Title-Pages, the Heads [and effigies] of All I have enumerated and of as many other as either in this, or any other Age have ben renoun'd for Armes and Arts etc. In *Taille Douce*, and (with very tollerable expense) to be procur'd amongst the Print sellers; I should not reprove it: I am confident you would be exceedingly delighted with the Assembly; and some are so very well don and to the Life, that they may stand in Competition with the best paintings: This were I say, a Cheape, and so much a Usefuller Curiositie, as they seldome are without the Names Ages, and Elogies of the Persons whom they are made to represent: I say, you will be infinitely pleas'd to Contemplate the Effigies and Icons of those who have made such a noise and bussle in the World, either by their Madnesse and folly, as well as greater Figures by their Wit and Learning: Nor should I confine you to stop here; but to be continually gathering as you happen to meete with other Instructive Types: For in this Classe come in Batailes, Sieges, Triumphs, Justs and Turnaments, Huntings, Coronations, Cavalcades, and Entries of Ambassadors, processions, Funebral and other Pomps, Tombs, Tryals, Executions, Exotic Animals, Monsters: stately Edifices, Machines, Antique Vases, Reliques,

---

[1] 'Under the spear.' The spear was a symbol of an auction sale, so 'exposing books to auction.' (Livy, xxiii.38.7). Book auctions in England were running by 1676.

[2] Thomas Barlow was the Bodleian librarian from 1652–60. E had sent him a copy of the manuscript of his translation of Naudæus some time before the eventual date of publication in 1661. Barlow, it seems, lost the manuscript. E eventually had to have it printed in London but the typographical errors (not an uncommon problem for him, though he always felt the fault was someone else's, perhaps with justification) caused him shame and embarrassment. He was still planning a second edition in 1698 (letter to Dr Henry Godolphin at Eton, 8 February 1698 – a copy of this letter closed BL CLBII and was unfinished).

[Spoils, Basso-relievos,] Intaglios, and Camæos (taken from Achats, Onyxes, Cornelians, and other precious stones) Ruines and Landscapes etc from real Subjects, not fancies (which are innumerable and unnecessary) but such as relate [to history], and for the Reasons specified more at Large in my Treatise of *Chalcographie*.[1]

Your library through this Accession, suitable to your generous mind, and steady Vertue; I know [of no] man Living Master of more happinesse; since besides the possession of so many Curiosities, you under[stand] how to Use and Improve them likewise, and have declar'd, That you'l endeavor to secure what (with [so much] Cost and Industrie) you have Collected, from the sad dispersions, many noble Libraries [and Cabinets] have [suffered] in these late times: One Auction [I may call it diminution] of a day or two, having scatter'd what has ben gathering many [years]. Hence proceedes it, that we are in England so defective of good Libraries among the Nobilitie[2] and [in our] greatest Townes: Paris alone, I am perswaded, being able to shew [more than all the three nations of] Greate Britain: [those of Mem'ius, Puteanus,] Thuanis, [Cordesius,] Sequire, Colebert, Con[dé, and others] innumerable more of Bishops, Abbats, [advocates, antiquaries,] and a world of learned persons [of the long robe; besides the] public [libraries] at St Victoire, Sorbonne, and, above all, that of Mazarinis [now], with the Richelieu [and sundry others] swallow'd up in the present Kings[3] – far exceeding any thing we can shew at home, though we have as much, if not greater, plenty and variety of the best Books as any country in the learned World: But, as I said, they are in private Cabinets, and seldom well Chosen, and unlesse in the Universities, where (if one may Judge by the production of so many Learned Men there at Leasure) they signify so very [little][4] to the Learned World: This greate and August Citty [of London], abounding in so many Witts and Leter'd Persons, has scarse one Library furnish'd and endow'd for the Publique: Sir John Cottons (Collected by his learned Unkle) is without dispute, the most Valuable in Manuscripts, Especially of British [and Saxon] Antiquities; But he refuses to give us the Catalogue of this Treasure, for feare (he tells me) of being disturb'd:[5] That of Westminster is little considerable, Lesse that of Sion College: But there is hope his Majesty's at St James's may yet emerge, and be be in some measure restor'd againe,[6] now that 'tis coming under the Inspection of the learned Monsieur Justel, who you know, was owner of a very Considerable one at Paris: [There are in it a great many noble manuscripts yet remaining, besides the Tecla; and more would be, did some royal or generous

---

[1] *Sculptura: or the History, and Art of Chalcography and Engraving in Copper*, 1662.
[2] Copy-letter: gentlemen.
[3] Louis XIV.
[4] In the Pforzheimer Catalogue transcription 'much' is restored here; the copy-letter however shows what E meant at this point.
[5] Robbed?
[6] See letter of 7 July 1694 (**D22**), p.246, note 9.

hand cause those to be brought back to it, which still are lying in mercenary hands for want of two or three hundred pounds to pay for their binding; many of which being of the Oriental tongues, will soon else find Jews and chapmen that will purchase and transport them, from whence we shall never retrieve them again. For thus has a cabinet of ten thousand Medals, not inferior to most abroad, and far superior to any at home, which were collected by that hopeful cherisher of great and noble things, Prince Henry, been embezzled and carried away during our late barbarous rebellion, by whom and whither none can or is like to discover. What that collection was, not only of books and Medals, but of statues and other elegant furniture, let the learned library-keeper, Patritius Junius, tell you in his notes ad Epist. S^{ti} Clementis ad Corinthos: '*Quem locum*,' (speaking of St James's) '*si vicinam pinacothecam bibliothecæ celeberrimæ conjunctam, si numismata antiqua Græca ac Romana, si statuas et signa ex ære et marmore consideres, non immerito thesaurum antiquitatis et* ταμιειον *instructissimum nominare potes*,' etc.[1]

Were not this loss enough to break a lover's heart?']² The Royal Societys is a mixture, (though little proper to the Institution and Designe of that worthy Assembly, yet) of many excellent books, given (at my Instance) by the late Duke of Norfolck, and is but a part of that rare Collection of good authors and valuable Manuscripts, which by the Industrie of Father Iunius Mr Seldon and the purchase of Pinellis Library etc was nobly furnish'd, but out of which, the best were cull'd, and Conveid away, through the negligence of those his Grand-father had committed the care of them to, whilst that magnificent Earle and Mecænas, was in Italy, where he died: And now I mention Mr Selden, there is a fragment of that learned Antiquaries Library at the Midle Temple; but [his] Manuscripts and best Collection were bequeath'd to the Bodlean at Oxford, to which both he and especially Arch Bishop Lauds were the most Munificent Benefactors, though with all these, so poore in Manuscripts [that] they thought not convenient (not to say asham'd) to publish them, with the *Impressi* [but which might yet have been equally enriched with any perhaps in Europe, had they purchased what was lately offered them by the executors of Isaac Vossius,³ though indeed at a great price, who have since carried them back into Holland, where they expect a quicker market. I wished with all my heart some brave and noble Mæcenas⁴ would have made a present of them to Trinity College in Cambridge, where that sumptuous structure (designed for a

---

[1] Of St James's Palace, 'which place, if you were to take into account the neighbouring art gallery joined to a very famous library, the ancient Greek and Roman coins, the statues and marble busts, you could not undeservedly call it a treasury and the best-arranged collection of antiquity'. Patritius Junius' real name was Patrick Young. He was librarian to Prince Henry and the early Stuart monarchs.

[2] This entire section is in the copy-letter only.

[3] Isaac Vossius. See p.157, note 2. E first met him on 16 March 1673 (diary).

[4] A Roman knight, renowned for his patronage of learning. Virgil dedicated the *Georgics* to him (e.g. *Georg.* II.41).

library) would have been the fittest repository for such a treasure. Where are our Suissets, Bodleys, Lauds, Sheldons, bishops and opulent chancellors? Will the *Nepotismo* never be satisfied. – *Sed præstat motus componere*[1]]: Next to it are the Libraries of Magdalen, University College, Christ Church, Merton, and for Manuscripts, (and lately through the bounty of Sir Thomas Wendies legacy of a greate number of many Curious Books) Balliol Colledge is inferior to none: I neede not acquaint you, how glorious a structure [at Trinity College] Sir Christopher Wren has prepar'd for Cambridge; but perhaps, we know not, how 'tis like to be furnish'd, since [the dec]ease of the uncomparable Doctor [Isaac] Barrow, whom we may name the Founder of it, by the generous, [and in]defatigable paines he tooke to promote it: To returne then neere this Citty, That of Lambeth ([re]plenish'd at present with excellent Books) Ebbs and flows like the Tide,[2] at every Arch-prælat's succession or Translation: [there is at present a good assembly of manuscripts in a room by themselves:] The Bishop of Ely[3] has a very faire[4] library; but the very best is that of the Deane of Paules Dr Stillingfleete at Twicknam, ten miles out of Towne, so as onely that good, and learned Man of St Martines (Dr Tenison) your neighbour, has begun a Charity (for so I reckon it, as well as that of his [two] Schooles) worthy his piety, publique [and generous] spirit and the Esteeme of all who know him. Our greate Lawyer Sir Edward Cooke[5] bought a very Choice Collection of Greek Manuscripts and other Books, which, I think, were sold [him] by Dr Meric Casaubon, son of the learned Isaac, and these (together with his delicious villa of Durdens) came to the possession of the present Earle of Berkely from his Uncle Sir Robert Cook: He has often[6] told me he would build a convenient Repository for them, which should be publique for [the use of] the Cleargy of Surry; but what progresse is made in it, I cannot learne.[7] [Why is not such provision made by a public law and contribution in every county of England? But this genius does not always preside in our representatives. I have heard that] Sir Henry Savil was Master of divers precious Manuscripts and he is frequently Celebrated for it by the Learned Valesius almost in every page of his Annotations on Eusebius and the Ecclesiastical Historians [published by him]: [The late] Mr Hales of Eaton [whom I mentioned,] had likewise a very noble Library, but that of the Coledges there (with what Sir Henry Wotton left) very despicable: John Cosin

---

[1] 'But the act serves to make a comparison.'

[2] Copy-letter: 'Thames running by it' replaces 'Tide'.

[3] Francis Turner. The Pforzheimer Catalogue restores 'John Moore' to the text here but this is incorrect. Moore did not become the incumbent at Ely until 1707. Turner was there from 1684–91.

[4] Copy-letter: 'well-stored'. Apparently the library was purchased by George I for the University at Cambridge.

[5] Coke.

[6] Copy-letter: 'sometimes' replaces 'often'.

[7] Copy-letter: 'but what he has done or thinks to do herein, I know not.'

Bishop of Durham, was a greate Collector of good Books, which I heare he has plac'd in that Cathedral:[1] But the learned primate Usher's, which was inferior to none for [rare] Manuscripts: etc (being saved out of Ireland, and given to his son in Law, Sir Timothy Tyrrill) was dispos'd of to give bread to that incomparable Prælate, during our late Phanaticismes: There remaines yet one of the noblest Collections of Manuscripts, this Nation ever had brought to her from abroad at once, in danger of being devour'd by Mr Scott and other of our Auction-men, if neither of our Universities or some Munificent and noble Benefactor do not rescue them: I meane, the library of the late Isaac Vossius neere Windsore, a greate part of which, were his learned Fathers, and many of them[2] which Isaac himselfe brought from Queen Christinas out of Sweden, in Recompense of his honorary sallarie, whilst he was invited thither with De Cartes, Salmasius, Blundel, etc by that Heroine and Royal Errant. [But those birds, as I said, have taken their flight, and are gone.] I forbeare to name the late Earle of Bristols,[3] and his kinds-man Sir Kenhelme Digby's, Libraries of more pomp, than intrinsique value, as greately consisting of Astrological books, Modern poets, Romances, and Chymical treatises: I had the Catalogue of them long 'ere they were sold [put into my hands by my Lord Danby, then treasurer,[4] who desired me to give my opinion of them, which I faithfully did. As for those of Sir Kenhelmes, the Catalogue was printed, and most of them sold in Paris, as many better have lately been in London]: The Duke of Lauderdalls[5] is yet intire, choicely bound; and to be sold by a friend of mine [to whom they are pawned]; but comes far short of his Kindsmans, the Lord Mateland's,[6] which was certainely the noblest, and most substantial [and accomplished] Library, that ever pass'd under the speare, and it griev'd me heartily to see its limbs (like those of the Chast Hippolytus) [separated and] torne from that well [chosen and] compacted body: The late Earles of

---

[1] The copy-letter differs at this point with the sentence preceding being replaced by: 'and so had John Cosin [late] Bishop of Durham, a considerable part of which I had agreed with him for myself during his exile abroad, as I can show under his own hand, but his late daughter since my Lady Garret, thought I had not offered enough, and made difficulty in delivering them to me 'till near the time of his Majesty's restoration, and after that, the Dean, her father, becoming Bishop of that opulent see, bestowed them on the library there.' Cosin's letter of 18 July 1651 is quoted in some Bray editions of E's diary in a footnote to this letter. The library's price was £105.

[2] Copy-letter differs from 'There remaines yet' to this point: such as remained yet at Dublin were preserved, and by a public purse restored and placed in the college library of that city. I have already mentioned Isaac Vossius brought over, that had been his learned father's, and many other manuscripts which...'

[3] George Digby, second Earl of Bristol.

[4] Sir Thomas Osborne; he was Lord High Treasurer between 1673–9.

[5] This is John Maitland, second Earl and first Duke of Lauderdale. He had died in 1682, and was succeeded by his brother Charles Maitland as third Earl.

[6] Probably Lauderdale's grandfather, John Maitland, first Baron Maitland.

Angleseas and several others since [by I know not what invidious fate], have pass'd the same fortune, by whatever [influence and] invidious Constellation at present reigning, Malevolent to [books and] Libraries, which can portend no good to the future Age: – And so I have don with Libraries too, but yet not quite with Mr Pepys. For I mention none of these, as if I thought it convenient, or reasonable every private gentleman's study should be made Common: But, wish we had some more publique [communicative and] better furnish'd Libraries, in one of the greatest citties in the World[1] (London), and for that end a stately Portico were to be contriv'd at the West End of St Paules, as might support a Palatina, capable of worthy a designe: and that every Company [and Corporation] of the Citty, Greate Officer, and even every Apprentice at his taking Freedome, assisted [at first] by a General Collection through out the Nation, did cast in their Symbols,[2] for a present stock of Bookes and a future ample Funds: But this we are to expect when Kings become Philosophers, or Philosophers Kings – which I think may happen about Platos Revolution[3] – All that I shall add, concerning Gentlemen, furnish'd with competent Libraries, and for most part Residing in Towne, is, how Obliging a thing it were, and of glorious[4] Effect for promoting a noble, usefull (less Mechanique) Conversation, of Learned persons, If, as there is already a Society for the Improvement of Natural knowledge (and which 'twas fit, should be first, since Things were before Words) so there were an Academie for that of Art and the Improving of Speaking, and Writing well: Of which sort, there are (you know) some in Paris, and almost every Considerable Citty in Italy which go under the devises of *La Crusca, Humoristi, Insensati*, etc, as that of the *Beaux Esprits* in France, set up by the late great Cardinal Richlieu, for the polishing and inriching of the Language publishing those many accurate pieces, which it has ever since[5] produced: It is in these Academies where a select number of learned persons of the greatest rank and qualitie, not onely come to heare, but esteeme it an honour to have their Ingenious Exercises passe the Test and Censure of so many Civil and polish'd Witts: And all the Apparatus for this, is onely the Use of one Competent Roome in the Gentleman's house, where there are Chairs and a Table and Where the Person, who Declaimes, being seated with a little more Eminence, like the Roman *Rostra*, (and choosing his Subject, prose or Verse) Recites [or reads] his composures before the Companie: This, for being but one halfe day [or afternoon] in the Weeke, and [retiring] in due houre, is of very little Inconveniency to the Master of the Famely. Here it is (I say) Gentlemen and Scholars bring their Composures, Translations, Poems, and other oratorious

---

[1] Copy-letter: 'Universe'.
[2] Contributions.
[3] Discussed in *The Republic* 487b ff.
[4] Copy-letter: 'infinite'.
[5] Copy-letter: 'from time to time'.

Essays upon a thousand curious subjects; and here they give Laws to [words and ph]rases, and the *Norma loquendi*:[1] These pass censure and bring Authors to the Touch, Reject [or enter]taine and Indenizon Exotics: I need not enlarge to Mr Pepys the use and nobleness of such [assemblies] who has himselfe seene what Illustrious persons us'd to honour Monsieur Justell and how [many great dukes and blue ribbons, ambassadors as well as bishops, abbots, presidents, and other learned men and travellers, this brought together into conversation the most humane and obliging in the world; and how][2] exceedingly it were to be wish'd some [noble and] worthy Gentleman would give the diversion so becoming and [usefully entertain]ing as it would be. We should not then have so many crude [and fulsome] Rhapsodies impos'd upon the English World for genuine Wit, Language and the stage, as [well as the] Auditors and spectators which would be purged from things Intollerable: It would [Inflame], Inspire, and kindle another Genius and tone of Writing, with a nervous, natural strength and beauty, [genuine and of our own growth, without] allways borrowing, or stealing from our Neighbours: And indeede such was once design'd since the Restauration of King Charles II,[3] and in order to it, Three, or foure Meetings were begun at Gray's Inn, by Mr Cowley, Dr Sprat, Matthew Clifford, Sir Cyrill Wych, Duke of Buckingam, Mr Dryden,[4] and other promoters of it; But then by the Death of [the incomparable] Mr Cowley, the [distance and] Inconvenience of the Place, [the contagion,] and other Circumstances [intervening], it crumbld away and came to nothing: What straw I gatherd for the Brick, towards that Intended Pyramid (having the honor to be admitted an Inferior Labourer) you may Command, and dispose of, if you can suffer my Impertinencies, and that already, I have not shew'd you the Plan I drew, relating to that designe; which was (I said) the Polishing of the English Language, and to be one of the first Intentions and Chiefest subjects of the Academicians: – And now for shame give over – me thinks I hear you Crie-out, what a ramble has Mr Evelyn made, what a deale of Ground, for so little Game![5] You see then what the setting up an Empty Noddle has brought upon you; Another Sheete begun! Ô the deale of Inke that's run to wast! And in good earnest I had ben Criminaly answerable of Detriment to the Publique (as well as to your own Repose) should I have dar'd to Debauch you with so tedious, and Intemperate a scribble, whilst you were

---

[1] 'The rule of language.'

[2] This passage is in the copy-letter only. The use of the words 'and how' prior to, and at the end of the omitted section, suggests that the omission was accidental and E's eyes jumped a few lines while copying from the draft.

[3] Margin note: '1665'.

[4] E thought little of 'Dryden, the famous play-poet and his two sonns...' who 'were said to go to Masse; and such purchases were no greate losse to the Church' (diary, 6 January 1686).

[5] = Gain?

not [(*tuo jure*)¹] your Owne-Man – But if notwithstanding all this, it prove an Affliction to you (as I have reason to apprehend it may) The onely Expedient to be rid of such Impertinents will be to Assume your Late buisy and honorable Charge againe, When no Man can [be] so Impudently Uncivil as to Expect you should Reade his Long Letters, when he Considers how many you will then be Oblig'd to write.

Aug. 30th²

Sir, I do not forget your Commands to Mr Boile upon my first coming to Towne and opportunity.³

[JE]⁴

Another Lucretia Daughter of that Illustrious familie of Cornaso, the father now living and *procuratore di San Marco*) who had the honour of his Doctorate, at Padoa upon the importunity of that Learned University, and dying foure yeares since, was celebrated with funebral Orations of a pompous Celvemanie by the *Academici Infecundi* at Rome: such as has not ben any more remarkable since the Inauguration of Petrarche.⁵

---

¹ 'By your authority.' P was imprisoned in the gatehouse at the Tower between May and July 1689.
² E evidently took four days to write the letter, as P's reply suggests (see p.205). The date is in E's hand, not P's as the Pforzheimer Catalogue (1940, 1226) states.
³ At this point on the original P subjoined the draft of his shorthand reply, dated 30 August 1689 (below, **C48**). A facsimile of the shorthand draft was included in the Davey Catalogue.
⁴ Uncertain squiggle, partly obscured by P's shorthand draft.
⁵ This paragraph sits in isolation on the verso of the last leaf of the letter. Though in E's hand (and not P's, as the Pforzheimer Catalogue states) it is much more neatly written than the rest. It is perhaps an afterthought, or an earlier note on a sheet which E reused. But, as E had modified P's copy of his letter of 21 August 1669 (see p.72, note 3) he may well have added it long after P received the letter; this is the most likely explanation because the addition is absent from the end of P's copy of the letter at Bod MS Rawl. A171, f.325.

C48. SAMUEL PEPYS TO JOHN EVELYN[1]

Pepys humbled by Evelyn's learning

[no place]
30 August 1689

Honoured Sir,

I shall never bee anxious about Pardon for not doeing what I ought, where what I ought is what I can't. And such is the giveing a due Answer to the inestimable Honour and Favour of your Letter of this Day, and soe much the less estimable, by that alone for which you would censure it, its Length; as containeing, in lesse than 5 pages, what would cost me 5 volumes reading from any other Hand but Mr Evelin's. And yet some answer you shall in time have to it, and the best I can give you, namely, by endeavouring to leave noe one syllable of it unpracticed, of what[2] you have had the goodnesse to teach mee in it, and lyes within the reach of my Pate and Purse to execute.

Lett this (I begg of you) suffice to bee sayd upon't at the first view. For though I could hardly finde time to take breath till I had gone through it, yet I won't promise to have done readeing it this month. One word only I would now say to you upon your first words, about the Place I have beene bold in doomeing your picture to, namely, that besides 40 other Reasons that I had (founded upon Gratitude, Affection and Esteeme) to covet that in Effigie which I most truly value in the Originall, I have this one more, that I take it for the onely Head liveing I can hope to invite most by after it, of those few whose Memorys, when Dead, I finde myself wishing I could doe ought to perpetuate. Among which fills a principall place, the most Excellent Mr Boyle, concerning whom I lately bespoke your favour, and dare now bee the bolder in doing it againe, from my haveing heard that he has newly beene prevayl'd with by Dr King,[3] to have his head taken by one of much lesse Name than Kneller's, and a stranger, one Causabon.[4]

I am ever,
Your most obedient Servant and Honorer,
SPepys

---

[1] Source: BL Upcott Antiquaries II. Endorsed by E, 'Mr Pepys 2d[?] 30 Aug 89'. Unusually for P this letter also appears as a shorthand draft (on the MS of 26 August 1689), and longhand copy in another hand (Hewer's?) (Bod MS Rawl A171, f.326–7). Except in spelling and two insertions the draft, copy, and letter-sent all correspond.
[2] MS: 'of what' absent from shorthand draft but inserted in the copy.
[3] Dr, Sir Edmund King, Robert Boyle's, and Charles II's, physician.
[4] Sic. This is Frederick Kerseboom (DNB; but also *see* Maddison, 'The Portraiture of Robert Boyle', in *Annals of Science*, 15, 1959, p.159. Information: Michael Hunter).

C49. JOHN EVELYN TO SAMUEL PEPYS[1]

On conversation and language

Deptford
4 October 1689[2]

Sir,

I had newly ben reading Aristotle's Book Περὶ της μαντικης, etc or *Divination by Dreames* (which follows his other Treatises, *De Anima, Memoria* and *Reminiscentia*)[3] when the very Night after, me-thought Mr Pepys and I were (amongst other things) discoursing in his Library, about the Ceremonious Part of Conversation, and Visites of Forme, betweene well-bred-Persons: and I distinctly Remember, that I told him (what is true, and no Dreame) that the Late Earle of St Albans[4] (I meane unkle to Henry Germine, the present Earle of Dover) tooke extraordinary care at Paris, that his Young Nephew should Learne by heart, all the Formes of Encounter, and Court Addresses; such as the Latines would expresse by *Verba honestatis*,[5] and the French, if I mistake not (who are Masters in these Civilities to excesse) *l'Entre-gens*:[6] As upon occasion of giving, or taking the Walle; Sitting-downe; Entring-in at or going-out of the doore; Taking Leave at parting; *l'Entretiene de la Ruelle*,[7] and other Encounters *à la Cavaliere* among the Ladys, etc – In all which, never was Person more adroit, than my Late Neighbour, the Marquis de Ruvignie:[8] And indeede the Italians and Spaniards

---

[1] Source: BL.1557 (ex-Davey Catalogue Item 2888), and BL CLBII.619 (E's copy, published in Bray's editions of E's diary). Endorsed, 'Deptford Octobr 4 1689 Mr Evelin to Mr Pepys in prosecution (in all respects) of his former of the 26th August.' No address as it is evident from the last section of the letter that E delivered it by hand. There are some differences from the copy-letter. The letter includes a passage from an earlier letter to Sir Peter Wyche (20 June 1665; published in Bray editions of E's diary with correspondence). The copy-letter version contains E's own cross-reference for the remainder in the Wyche letter at CLBI.245.

[2] MS: 'Dept: 4 Octob:–89'.

[3] E's copy was *Aristoteles: Opera Omnia, Græce et Latine* ... Guillelmus Du-Vallius. Paris, 1654. Now in the British Library (Eve.c.15).

[4] Henry Jermyn, first Earl of St Albans.

[5] 'Noble words'.

[6] 'Discretion.'

[7] 'The conversation of a social clique.'

[8] See E's diary 24 April 1687, and 2 October 1689. The copy-letter adds at this point, 'even to foure score (nor lesse, that truely *honnete homme* his son, whom I love with all my heart)'. This oblique reference to the Marquis's facility, at past the age of eighty, with women was excised in earlier publications of the copy-letter text.

exceede us infinitely in this point of good-breeding; Nay, I observe generaly, that our Women of Quality often put us to – *O Lord, Madame!* when we have nothing to fill up and reply:[1]– But *quorsum hæc?* (a little patience) – I was never in my Life subject to Night-Visions 'til of late, that I seldome passe without some Reverie; which verifies that of St Peter (cited from the Prophet) That your Old-men shall dreame dreames[2] – and so you will shortly give me over for a Dotard, should I continue to Interrupt you thus with my Impertinences:[3] I will onely tell you, that my Wife (who is of a much sedater Temper, and yet often Dreaming) has now and then, diverted me with Stories, that hung as orderly together, as if they had ben studied Narratives, some of which[4] I had formerly made her write downe for the prettynesse of them; Very Seldome broken, or Inconsistent (such as commonly are mine, but) such as the Peripatetic[5] meanes, where he says, *quieto sanguine fiunt pura somnia;*[6] comparing those other Extravagant and Confus'd Dreames to the Resemblances which the Circles of disturbed and agitated Waters reflect that blend, and confound the Species, and present us with Centaures and tirrible Specters; whilst the Calmer Fountaine gives the intire Image (as it did Narcissus in the Fable) and entertaine us with our waking thoughts: What could be more Explicit of the Cause of this Variety of Dreames? which He, as well as Hippocrates, and others from them, attribute to the *Crasis*[7] and Constitution of the Body, and Complexions domineering, with other Perturbations affecting the phancy: But leaving these to the *Oneirocritics*;[8] I shall make use of it no farther, than to let you see, how often you are in my best and serenest Thoughts:[9] *Amici de Amicis certa sæpe somniant:* ἔρωτηκὸς εν ἑρωτι:[10] And if the Subject of my Wild Phantasme (which was a Dialogue with you about Formes of speaking upon Ceremonious Occasions) naturaly leading me to something which I lately mention'd (where I spake of Academies and the Refining of our Language) have not already quite worne-

---

[1] Copy-letter adds here (omitted by Bray), 'this literaly true, that I have seene two Ramuneus [sic, for *Ramoneuse* = 'sweeps'] de Chiminée, Chimny-Sweepers, dirty Boys of the Black-Guard, meete and Acost each other in perfect forme'.

[2] *Acts* ii.17 (from *Joel* ii.28).

[3] The interest in language was, at the time, more than merely social. Locke, in his *Essay concerning Human Understanding* (1690), explored the importance of clarity in words and terms, thereby avoiding the misunderstandings and conflict that arise from ambiguity and confusion. Although E's earlier letter to Wyche that follows is more pedantic than profound it shows that he had anticipated some of this idea.

[4] Copy-letter adds here '(for their extraordinary prittinesse)'.

[5] Aristotle.

[6] 'Undisturbed sleep is made by calm blood.'

[7] Κρασις, or combination of bodily humours.

[8] From the Greek: 'interpreters of dreams'.

[9] Copy-letter adds here, 'and when I am far from dreaming'.

[10] 'Firm friends often dream about friends: a state of eagerness for a cherished one'.

out your Patience; I would Entertaine you here with a Copy of what I sent our Chayre-man, some yeares since, as an Appendix to my former Letter, and as you Injoyn'd me.[1]

I Conceive the Reason both of Additions to and Corruptions of the English Language (as of most other Tongues) has proceeded from the same causes; Namely, from Victories, Plantations and Colonies, Frontiers, Staples of Commerce, Pedantry of Scholes, Affectation of Travellers; Fancy; Style of Court, Vernilitie and Mincing of Citizens; Pulpets, the Barr, Politicians, Remonstrations, Theaters, Shops, etc.

The Parts Affected with it may be found to proceede from the Accent, Analogie, direct Interpretation, Tropes, Phrases, and the Like:

I did therefore humbly propose, that there might first be compil'd a Grammar for the Præcepts; which (as it did the Romans)

1. When Crates transfferr'd the Art to that City,[2] follow'd by Diomedes, Priscian,[3] and others who understood it might onely insist on the Rules, the sole Meanes of rendering it a Learned and Learnable Tongue.

2. That with this, a more certaine Orthographie were introduced, as by leaving out superfluous Letters, etc: such as (o) in Weoman, People; (u) in honour; (a) in Reproach; (ugh) in Though, and the like –

3. That there were invented some new periods and accentuations, besides such as our Grammarians and Critics use, which might assist, in spirit and modifie the Pronunciation of Words and whole Sentences, and to stand as Marks and warnings before them, how the Voice and Tone of the Reader is to be govern'd; as in Reciting of Plays, reading over Verses, etc, for the key, and varying the tone of the Voice and Affection; not without some Directions for the hand, and gesture of the body:

4. To this might follow a Lexicon, comprehending all the pure and genuine English Words by themselves: then such as are Derivatives from others; with their prime, certaine, and natural Significations: Then, the Symbolical, so as no Innovation might be admitted or favour'd, 'til there should arise (at least) some necessity of providing a New Edition, and of amplifying the Old, upon mature consideration.

5. That, in Order to this, some were appointed to Collect all the Technical Words and Termes; especialy those of the more liberal Imployments, as the Author of the *Essaies de Merveilles de la Nature et des plus nobles Artifices*[4] has done for the French; Monsieur Felibien, the Mechanical; Mr Moxon, for some of the English; and Francis Junius, John Laët, and others endeavourd for the Latine: But these must be glean'd from Shops, not from Books.

---

[1] In CLBII.619 here is a marginal note that the rest of the letter is a copy of an earlier letter to Sir Peter Wicke (sic, correctly Wyche) with a reference to BL CLBI.245.

[2] Suetonius in *De Grammaticis* II. Crates of Mallos arrived in Rome *c.* 169 BC.

[3] Both grammarians. Priscianus was a contemporary of Justinian.

[4] René François. Various editions, e.g. Rouen 1622.

6. That things difficult to be translated or express'd, and such as are, as it were, incommensurable one to another: *verbi gratia* determinations of Weights and Measures, Coines, Honors, National habits, Armes, Dishes, Drinks, Municipal Constitutions of Courts, Old and abrogated Customes, etc were better interpreted than, as yet, we find them, in Dictionaries, Glossaries, and noted in the Lexicon:

7. That a full Catalogue of Exotic words and Phrases; such as are daily minted by our *Logo-dædali*,[1] were exhibited; and, it were Resolved on, that what should be sufficient to render them Current *ut Civitate donata*;[2] since without some restraining that same *Indomitam novandi Verborum Licentiam*,[3] it must in time quite disguise the Language: There are some elegant Words introduc'd by Physitians chiefly, and Philosophers, etc, worthy to be entertain'd; others, perhaps fitter to be discarded seing there ought to be a Law, as well as a Libertie in this particular: – And in this Choyce, some regard would be had to the well-sounding and more harmonious Words, and such as are numerous and apt to fall gracefully into their Cadences and Periods, and so recommend themselves at the very first sight, as it were: Others there are which (like false stones) will never shine, or be set to any advantage in whatever light they are plac'd, but embase the rest: And here may be noted, that such as continue long in Universities greately affect Words and expressions, Nowhere in use besides, as may be observ'd, in Cleaveland's *Poemes for Cambridge*,[4] – and there are some Oxford words usd by Others, as I might instance in severall –

8. Previous to this Inquirie would be made what particular Dialects, Idiomes, and Proverbs are in use in severall-Parts and Countries of England; for the Words of the present Age being properly the Vernacula (or Classic rather) special regard is to be had of them; and this Consideration alone admits of vast Improvements.

9. And happly it were not amisse, that there were a Collection of the most quaint and Courtly Expressions, by way of *Florilegium*,[5] distinct from the Province, etc: For we are exceedingly defective in our Civil Addresses, Excuses, Apologies, and Formes, upon sudden and unpremeditated (though daily) encounters, in which the French, Italian, and Spaniard have a kind of natural Grace and Talent, which furnishes the Conversation and renders it very agreable: Here might come-in Synomyma's, Homonymia, etc —

10. And since there is likewise a manifest Rotation and Circling of Words and Phrases, which go out and in, like the Mode and Fashion: Books would be consulted for the Reduction of some of the Old layd-a-side Words and

---

[1] Those who devise new words.
[2] 'Naturalized'.
[3] 'Uncontrollable lawlessness of coining [new] words.'
[4] This is the royalist poet John Cleveland. His poems appeared in 1655.
[5] Anthology.

Expressions, had formerly *in Deliciis*; for our Language is in some places sterile and barren by reason of this depopulation (as I may call it) and therefore such wasts and desarts should be cultivated and enrich'd, either with the former (if Significant) or some other: For example, we hardly have any words that so fully expresse the French *Clinquant, Naïveté, ennuy, bizarre, Concert, Façonnier, Chicaneries, Consommé, Emotion, Defer, Effort, Chocq, Toure, detaché*: Ital: *Vaghezza, Garbato, Svelto, Cruppo*, etc – We should therefore (as the Romans did the Greeke) make as many of these do Homage as are like to prove good Citizens.

11. Some thing might be well Translated out of Cicero, Demosthenes, etc, the Greeke and Latine poets, and even of the Modern Languages, that so some judgement might be made concerning the Elegancy of the Style and Colours, and so a laudable, and un-affected Imitation of the best and Choicest recommended; nor should there be wanting *Copia* of Epithetes, and Varietie of expressing the same thing severall wayes, such as the *Poetiche Dicher[i]e* of Tomaso Caraffa,[1] for the helpe of Poets, Preachers, Orators, etc

12. Finaly, there must be a Stock of Reputation gain'd by some publique writings and Compositions of the Members of the Assembly, that so (as I intimated in my Letter to you) others may not thinke it dishonor to come under the Test and accept them for Judges and Approbators, etc. And were the Designe thus far advanc'd, I conceive a very small matter would dispatch the Art of Rhetoric, which the French propos'd as the next to be recommended to their Academitians.

Ταῦτα μὲν οὖν τοῦτον ἔκατον τρόπον[2]

So much for this, and I feare too much now I see how I have blurr'd, but 'tis not worth the writing fairer.

Sir,

I staied at Lambeth with his Grace[3] 'til past 4: being to Returne with the Bishops, and go home (as I was engag'd) that evening; I call'd at your House, but you were gone forth, they told me, in your Coach, which made me Conclude it was not to Lambeth, wher I should have ben sorry not to have waited on you.

I have now gotten me a paire of new horses; but they are very young, and hardly broken to the Coach as yet; so soone as I may trust them, and that the weather be a little settled, I shall not faile of waiting on you to Mr Charletons[4] and those other Virtuosos.[5]

---

[1] *Dicerie Poetiche; overo vaghissime descrittioni e discorsi accademici*, Venice, 1655.
[2] 'So much for this a hundredfold'.
[3] Dr William Sancroft, archbishop of Canterbury 1678–91. E had visited him on 21 September 1689 (diary).
[4] Probably William Courten/Charleton, but possibly Dr Walter Charleton.
[5] The closing passage was written after the main body of the letter (see p.206, note 1).

4 The 1690s

By the 1690s Pepys was firmly marginalised from centre stage by his age, health, and loyalty to James II. Evelyn was not so politically compromised but he suffered from increasingly frequent bouts of ill-health. Both became preoccupied with family prospects. Pepys had no children and by way of substitute came to focus his hopes for the future on his nephews Samuel and John Jackson, sons of his sister Paulina, Mrs John Jackson. Samuel was initially named his heir but due to a marriage of which Pepys disapproved he was supplanted by 1703 in favour of his younger brother who had, it seems, already appeared a better prospect. In 1699 he was sent on a grand tour in the interests of education and in order to buy prints for his uncle's collection.

Evelyn's family expectations were more complicated. His son John, the only one to survive childhood, was a gifted linguist but suffered from depression and ill-health. In 1692 he became a commissioner for the Revenue in Ireland. In consequence the upbringing of his own son, also called John, became the responsibility of the diarist. Evelyn became dedicated to the boy not least because it was becoming obvious that his elder brother George would have to leave the Wotton estate to him. George's dissolute son died in 1691. In 1694 Evelyn and his wife left Sayes Court to live at Wotton and, despite wrangles with George's daughters over division of the estate, it passed to the diarist on George's death in October 1699. Evelyn's own son John had died in March that year leaving his grandson the sole prospect for the future. In an age of premature mortality such a turn of events was hardly unusual but this was no consolation to Evelyn.

Pepys did choose to publish his *Memoires relating to the Royal Navy* in 1690. This was a defence of his position and Evelyn was anxious to be seen to be supporting him. Thereafter their letters turned to social occasions, shared interests in prints, tracts, and books, and the activities of their heirs. Once installed at Wotton Evelyn became frustrated by his remoteness from the social and professional contacts he had enjoyed in London. He took to wintering there but it seems he and Pepys did not meet particularly frequently. Ill-health begins to feature more regularly in the correspondence as the two virtuosi confronted the inevitable end. Evelyn produced his last original works in 1697 and 1699. *Numismata*, a rambling disourse on coins and medals, and *Acetaria, a Discourse of Sallets* [salads], were not major monuments to his life and work. Nevertheless they show that he retained some of his indefatigable energy and application.

D1. JOHN EVELYN TO SAMUEL PEPYS[1]

New Year's Greetings and a broken-down vehicle

For Samuell Pepys Esqr
at his house
York-building

[no place]
11 January 1690

> *Exacto feliciter veteri, novus Annus*
> *ingreditur, eius opto D: P et Cl D: Gale*
> *felix auspicium, ut et præsentem, et plurimos*
> *futuros prosperrime decurrat.*[2]

'Tis a Yeare since I saw my worthy friende. My Vehicle has ben out of Order, and I my Selfe not in so perfect health:[3] I could not else have ben so long from giving you the *buenas entradice de Anno nuevo*:[4] If you are within this Afternoone, I will endeavour to see you, who am[5]

Your

en tout et par tout
JE:

---

[1] Source: BL.1558 (ex-Davey Catalogue Item 2864). Endorsed by P, 'Jan. 11 1689/90 Mr Evelin to Mr Pepys his New-Yeare's salutation and wishe[s]'.

[2] 'The old year is happily ended and a new one comes in. May it be an auspicious one for "Dr" Pepys and the celebrated Dr Gale, and may he prosper both this year and for many years to come' (trans. R.C.A. Carey, 1996). The wording alludes to P's unpleasant year in 1689 when he had confronted the coming of William and Mary and been imprisoned.

[3] It is, perhaps, slightly strange that E omits any mention of his grandson's (just short of his seventh birthday) attack of scarlet fever on 11 December 1689. This caused several days of family concern (diary, 11 and 16 December). He makes no reference in the diary to his own state of health in the last quarter of 1689.

[4] 'Best greetings for the New Year.'

[5] E does not record meeting P on 11 January; this may have been due to there being 'this night, so extraordinary a storme of win'd accompanied with snow and sharp weather, as had not ben known the like, in almost the memory of any man now living' (diary, 11 January 1690).

D2. JOHN EVELYN TO SAMUEL PEPYS[1]

On John Locke's writings

To Samuell Pepys Esqr
at his house in Yorke-Buildings
with a Book:

Soho Square
26 February 1690[2]

Sir,

I have many Ingredients towards a Lawfull Excuse, and to justify my not waiting upon you all this while: But that I had indeede no sooner return'd you the Doctor's[3] Booke, let the Author be accountable, who had Baited,[4] and Entertain'd me with so rare and excellent a piece, that 'twas not possible for me to dismisse him at once Reading: And if I be not thoroughly[5] convinc'd, that there has nothing appear'd (to me at least) written with so much force, upon the Subject which he handles, I am content you deliver me up to a forlorn condition as to Sense and Reason: I must yet ingenuously confesse, my apprehensions, least some Advantage might be taken by the Admirers of our Man of Malmesbery,[6] and some perverters of Des-Cartes, to the prejudice of Religion, (notwithstanding all that Gassendus has produc'd)[.] But I soon, and with no small satisfaction, found my selfe convinc'd to the Contrary; nor know I of any (even amongst our most learnd Theologu[e]s,) who has Vindicated, and Asserted the Existence of God Almighty in all his Attributes, with more solid, and incontestable Argument. In the meane time, I was not much in paine; That supposing, nay Assenting (with that no lesse pious, than Learned Prælate whom I mention'd to you) that the Knowledge of a Deity, was not

---

[1] Source: PL.2421, MS bound into P's copy of Locke's *Essay concerning Human Under-standing*. No endorsement but the letter bears a seal. There are many minor differences from the copy at BL CLBII.625 (inexplicably dated 7 April 1690).

[2] MS: 'So-hoo Square: 26:Feb:89/90'.

[3] Copy-letter only supplies a marginal note 'Dr Luck'. This is John Locke the philosopher (see note 1, and also the letter of 7 July 1694, **D22**). E had dined with P and Sir Anthony Deane on 7 March preceding (diary) where the conversation had concentrated on the state of the navy. The book, evidently returned with this letter, according to the address (above), may have been loaned then.

[4] Reading uncertain; copy-letter is clearer but evidently the same word.

[5] MS: 'thrôly'.

[6] Thomas Hobbes. He was born near Malmesbury and brought up there. E knew him in Paris (E's diary 7 September 1651).

Connatural to our Soules (præexistence not admitted) through any In-bred-notion *ab Initio*;[1] but that she came into the World *Rasa Tabula*,[2] without the least print or Character on her; for which Reason (whatsoever Crimes contracted, God might please to connive for a time, 'til the use of Reason, Complex Ideas[3] and Deduction, should render men without Excuse) we no where find Men charg'd with their Ignorance of God on that account; se[e]ing they cannot rationaly ground their Knowledge of his Existence upon Selfe Evidence: For who shall convince a person that either denys or doubts it, by telling him *he must Believe it*, because it is Selfe-Evident; when he himselfe knows, that he onely (and *eo nomine*)[4] Doubts, or dos not believe it, because 'tis not Selfe-Evident? I say, supposing so, (and as firmely I believe) yet, that God *is*, will aboundantly appeare by connextion, and the Apostles every-days-phænomena; Their dependence on Inferior Beings, leading us irresistibly, to the Supreme Independent Being, or Nature of Infinite Perfection, the powerfull Cause of all other Beings whatsoever: And to this sense of our Doctor, the Doctor Angelical — *Deus* (says Aquinas) *est suum Esse, sed quia nos non scimus de Deo, quid est, Non est nobis per se notus; sed indiget demonstrari per ea quæ sunt magis nota, quoad nos, et minus nota quoad Naturam, scilicet per Effectus* — [5]

There are other Incomparable Notions sprinkl'd throughout this learnd Treatise, concerning the nature of the Soule, Thought, Spirits; Chaine of Creatures, (happily induc'd with qualities, senses and glorious Receptacles, totaly unknowne to us) Of Time, Duration and Eternity; Of Space, Extension, Matter, Bodys, Substance, and Substantial formes: The Use of Words in relation to Ideas; of Rhetoric, and Scholastic Science, which he worthily explod's, as of no manner Advantage to use-full Learning; yet so fruitlessly retain'd in Universities: Celebrates the stupendious operations of Algebra, Mechanical Arts, and Experimental Philosophy; and that all we know, or are capable of knowing is the pure result of the Species and Objects which we receive and take into us by the ministrie of our senses; simple Ideas so derived from sensation, Reflexion, though the Boundaries of all we know; yet such, as is able to produce infinite variety of Complex ones; and all this, without the least prejudice to what we ought to conceive of God, and other Immaterial Beings: He treates of Virtue and Vice; the *Summum Bonum*,[6] Of Truth and moral Demonstration: describes the measures of probability; Of the Bodys

---

[1] 'From the beginning'.

[2] 'With a blank slate.'

[3] MS (here and elsewhere in this letter) apparently: 'Idïas'.

[4] 'By his name'.

[5] 'God is his own essence. But because we do not know what God is he is not known to us in himself but needs to be known through the things which are known with respect to ourselves, and to a lesser degree in nature, that is to say, through his works.' (Trans. R.C.A. Carey).

[6] 'The highest good.'

Resurrection, Divine Revelation, and where Faith takes place of Reason: Of Indulging, amplifying and Inlarging the Empire of Conscience and Christian Communion; freeing it from the narrow and slavish Circumstances under which it universaly suffers: In a Word, The Work speakes the Author to be of a Cleare, and subacted[1] Judgement, free, and manly Thoughts, conducted with greate modesty: The style is natural, and as perspicuous as so sublime, and noble a Subject is capable of: Explaines Metaphysical Notions, strip't of the Jargon and Gibbrish of the Cloister: In short, I looke upon it, as what may serve for Institution, as well as Instruction, in the most necessarie, and least understood part of Real Φhilosophy[2] (the Knowledge of our selves) as far as our Attainements can pretend in this umbratile[3] State:[4]

And now (deare Sir) though I should not have presum'd to say halfe of this to Mr Pepys, had he not oblig'd me to Returne his Book with my Thoughts upon it: I am perswaded the Worke will live, and obtaine, and deserve so to do; and that when you shall have perus'd it, you will concurre in your Suffrage with[5]

                    Sir, Your most humble
                        faithfull servant   JEvelyn:

---

[1] Worked-up, as in well-cultivated.

[2] Sic.

[3] Shadowy, obscure, secluded.

[4] Although it is hardly appropriate to attempt to summarise Locke's thinking in the space of a footnote, it is worth briefly outlining some of the views he expressed as reflected in this letter. The essence of the *Humane Understanding* was that individual belief should be founded on individual intellectual exploration, using reason as the basis of judgement. Locke was interested in exploring how the human mind was quite capable of understanding by using knowledge and rational thought, but how this was not always very successful in reality. The latter part was related to the problem of free will and its relationship to the limits of God's responsibilities for human actions. From E's point of view this interest in the philosophy of rational thought illustrates the manner in which he represents to us a bridge between the medieval and modern mind. On one hand his own intellectual curiosity, which P shared, unfailingly drew him towards the pursuit of knowledge while on the other he was imprisoned by his unassailable belief in God's involvement in his, and everyone else's affairs as witnessed in his fatalistic acceptance of his daughter Elizabeth's death (see **C21–23**).

[5] The last two lines and closing are crammed into the margin of the letter. It is perhaps worth commenting that although P paid E the compliment of binding the letter with the actual book, he did not endorse the letter in any way.

D3. JOHN EVELYN TO SAMUEL PEPYS[1]

Pepys's book is perfectly consummate

For Samuell Pepys Esqr
at his house in
York-Buildings.

[no place]
11 June [1690][2]

My deare and worthy Friend,

For under that Compellation, permit me sometimes to value my-selfe in a period so rare to find him ——

When I Reflect (as who can but Reflect) upon what you were pleas'd to communicate to me Yesterday;[3] so many, and so different passions crowd on my thoughts, that I know not which first to give vent to: Indignation, pitty, Sorrow, Contempt and Anger: Love, Esteeme, Admiration, and all that can express the most generous Resent'ments of One, who cannot but take part in the cause of an Injur'd and worthy Person! With what Indignation for the Malevolence of these men, pitty of their Ignorance and Folly, Sorrow and Contempt of their Malice and Ingratitude, do I looke upon and despise them! On the other side, In what bonds and obligations of Love, Esteeme, and just admiration, ought we to Reguard him who dares Expose himselfe to all this suffering with so intrepid a Resolution; because his Innocence and Merite will not onely justifie him to all the World, but to it, and to his Country, if sensible of their Obligations, and the Injuries some base and Envious men have labourd to do him, they become worthy of him. I speake not this to flatter my Friend, nor needes he my Comfort or Counsel: He has within him, and of his Owne bravely to support him; It would go very ill with me else, who have the same

---

[1] Source: PC MS.i.36. Endorsed by P, 'June 11.1690. Mr Evelin to Mr Pepys upon occasion of Mr Pepys's communicateing to him his Memoires of the Navy.'

[2] MS: '11 June.' Date indicated by endorsement and E's diary. See note 3.

[3] 'Mr. Pepys read to me his Remonstrance, shewed with what malice and injustice he was suspected, with Sir Anthony Deane, about the Timber of which the 30 ships were built by a late Act of Parliament: with the exceeding danger the present Fleet would be shortly in by reason of the Ignorance and incompetency of those who now manag'd the Admiralty and affaires of the Navy ...' (E's diary, 10 June 1690). The reference is to *Memoires relating to the State of the Royal Navy of England, For Ten Years, Determin'd December 1688*, published December 1690 (see Howarth, 219, n. 2), P's account of his second Secretaryship to the Admiralty. E expanded his views on the book later, below 17 June 1690 (**D4**).

thoughts and principles, and set my heart upon the Person, that every day accumulates to the greate Esteeme I have for greate Merites and no lesse Vertue, in an Age so degenerate and voide of both: I protest (in the meane time) and that sincerely, that I am so far from being concern'd that these angrie Men (whose folly I pitty) so unjustly provoke you; That I thinke, they could not have contributed more to your honour, and their owne deserv'd Reproche. So Reasonable, so every way Ingenuous; in so just, modest, and generous a style; in a Word, so perfectly consummate is your excellent Remonstrance, and so incontestably Vouch'd![1] This Sir, is my Sense of it, and I value my selfe upon my Judgement of it, that it will stand like a Rock, and dash in pieces all the effects and efforts of spitefull and implacable men, who because they cannot bravely emulate, Envie your worth, and would thus seacretly undermine it: But you are safe, and I will boldly say, That whoever shall honestly compile the Historie of these prodigious and wonderfull Revolutions, (as far as concernes this miserable and unhappy Kingdome) has already the most shining and Illustrious part drest to his hand, if there be any of that profession, who dare do right to Truth in so vitious an Age, be the Event what it will; And that unlesse we pluck-out our owne Eyes; we must see in spite of 'em, That You, and your Collegues, have stood in the breach, when the safety of a Nation was in uttmost danger, and by whose prudence, Experience and Industrie, it can onely be yet Rescu'd from perishing now:—— Do not think I speake a big word, or am so vaine to believe you are to be taken with magnificent sounds (though a Lover of Music) I have no such designe, and you know me better: But I have deeply, and sadly consider'd the state; and Circumstances into which we are unhappily fall'n; and that no personal Resent'ments, or reflections on the useage from ungratefull, and Wicked Men whatsoever, ought to cancel our Endeavors to support ones native Country, what ever Sacrifice we make with Honour, and a good Conscience: Wherefore, as I cannot but approve of what you have so maturely digested, so nor can I but wish to see it publish'd; the just, and proper timing of which is (as with yourselfe) with me the onely remaining difficulty, which may perhaps require Consideration, and that for the Objections occuring to you, should it be look'd-on as if you fear'd it should have seene the lights, 'til the King's back was turn'd; and the late Parliament scatter'd by this Adjournment[2] etc that you steale it now out before their next Session, to conciliate Friends, and make a party etc whilst these, or the like suggestions may perhaps (though of no real force) cause your suspence, why might you not resolve to communicate your

---

[1] The title page of P's *Memoires* carried an entirely appropriate quotation from Cicero's *Tusculanæ Disputationes* (V.36.105): *Quantis molestiis vacant, qui nihil omnino cum Populo contrahunt? Quid Dulcius Otio Litterato?* 'What troubles are avoided when one has nothing to do with the rabble? What is sweeter than scholarly lesiure?' It symbolises not just P's retrospective views on his past but also his own and E's approach to their final years.

[2] Parliament had been adjourned on 23 May 1690, until 7 July (Salmon, 1723, 200).

thoughts to my Lord Godolphin?[1] whom you will allow and find to be a person of a cleare discernment, and greate probitie, and has (to my certaine knowledge) the same honorable sentiments with your selfe, and upon whose integrity you may relie, and determine according as you see cause? Thus Sir, I take the boldnesse to give you my calmest Thoughts upon this Article; since you are pleas'd so far to honour me, as to give me so greate a share in your Confidence, who am, and (with very greate Respect) shall ever remaine,

                    Sir,
                         Your most faithfull
                         and intirely devoted Friend and servant,
                                        JEvelyn:

                                                         verte

                                        12 June [1690][2]

Sir,
I had begun this Letter very late the last night, when company was gon, when on a suddaine so very painefull a fit of the Colic surpriz'd my poore wife, that put me into greate dissorder; but, I thank God, (after a night of much torment) having ben let bloud, with other applications, she is now at much ease: she had else appointed this very day (and by long designement) to have gon to Clapham to visite that good person Mrs Ewers: as she still intends to do, so soone as she is a little better compos'd:

The Addresse I gave a poore modest Creature last night, has I believe 'ere this, fully answer'd the Character I gave you of his out-side, and what I left in your hands of his, that the noblest Accomplishments lie often hid *Sub Lacera Tunica*:[3]

---

[1] 'Carried my Lord Godolphin (now resuming the Commission of the Treasury againe to all his friends wonder) Mr. Pepys *Memoires*' (E's diary, 23 November 1690).
[2] MS: '12 June'. Overleaf from the preceding text, hence *verte*.
[3] 'Under a ragged tunic.'

D4. JOHN EVELYN TO SAMUEL PEPYS[1]

In Rei Memoriam [2]

[no place]
17 June 1690[3]

I have seene and perus'd certaine *Memoires relating to the Royal Navy of England for Ten yeares*,[4] etc, And am so thoroughly Convinc'd of the Truth of every period, both as to what has ben don towards the extricating of it out of the Ruinous Circumstances under which it then labourd, and the greate Improvements it has since received, by the Integrity, Prudence, Courage, and Industrie of the Person who has Written it etc, That, as I Judge no Man on Earth so fit to Restore the Navy againe (now, in all appearance, hastning to as deplorable, if not to a Worse state and Condition), so should he, and his Collegues Decline to set their hands to its Restauration and Recovery againe (the Fate and Preservation of their Countrie, (than which nothing ought to be more deare) so depending) being thereto Requir'd: He the Writer, and They, whom he may think fit to call to his Assistance, ought to be Animadverted on as Enemies and Betrayers of it:[5]

Ita Testor [6]

JEvelyn:

---

[1] Source: PC MS.i.37 (and BL CLBII.621). Endorsed, 'Mr Evelin's censure of S.P.'s Memoires about the Navy and its author'. Illustrated in the Sotheby and Co. 'Relics of Samuel Pepys' sale catalogue for 1 April 1931, opposite p.13. Note that the letter-sent to P is presented in the form of an open statement rather than a letter and lacks the opening 'Sir,' while the copy-letter is presented in conventional letter form.

[2] E's heading: 'In recollection of the work'.

[3] MS: '17:June:1690' at foot of the letter. Oddly the retained copy-letter of this text is dated clearly 20 January 1689/90. This discrepancy is one of the most substantial between the date of one of E's letters-sent and its corresponding copy. The original letter (now in the Pepys-Cockerell papers) was kindly made available to settle the question and there is no doubt that 17 June 1690 is the correct date. Moreover, P did not show E the text until 10 June 1690 (diary). It is probable that E misread his own 'Jun' for 'Jan' when making the copy though it seems remarkable that his own memory did not alert to him to the mistake.

[4] See above p.216, note 3.

[5] Copy-letter adds here, 'I forbeare to say who it is I meane, *Ita Testor*, but do you guesse'.

[6] 'Thus I testify.'

D5. JOHN EVELYN TO SAMUEL PEPYS[1]

The Bishop of St Asaph will discuss the Apocalypse

For Samuell Pepys Esqr etc

[no place]
[14 August 1690][2]

Sir,

This hasty Script is, to acquaint you, that my Lord Bishop of St Asaph[3] will take it for an honour to be thought able to give Mr Pepys any light in those Mysteries, you and I have discoursd of:[4] He would himselfe waite upon you, but I did not think it convenient to receive that Compliment for you at first: Tomorrow (friday) his Lordship says, he eating no dinner, shall be alone, and ready to receive your Commands, if it be as seasonable for you: I suppose about 3 a clock in the afternoone may be a convenient time for me to waite upon you to his Lordship or at what other sooner houre you appoint:

JE.

The Lords in the Tower, and other prisoners against whom there is no special matter chargeable are to be freed upon baile. My Lord Clarendon[5] is also within that qualification, as the Bishop tells me.

---

[1] Source: PC MS.i.39. Endorsed, 'August 90. Mr Evelyn to Mr Pepys, signifying to him the Bishop of St Asaph's readinesse to receive and discourse to him the Business of the Apocalypse and his Conceptions thereon. Also the Resolution of a general Bailing of the Tower-prisoners, and particularly Lord Clarendon'.

[2] MS: No date. See note 1 for endorsement, and note 3 for diary entry.

[3] Dr William Lloyd, bishop of St Asaph, 1680–92. He met P and E on 15 August 1690 (E's diary, thereby indicating the date of this letter).

[4] See endorsement.

[5] Henry Hyde, second Earl of Clarendon, imprisoned in the Tower in 1690 for his opposition to the accession of William and Mary. He was released on 15 August. E states in the diary (15 August) he was to be one of those standing bail for him but according to de Beer (V, 32, n.2) he was not.

D6. JOHN EVELYN TO SAMUEL PEPYS[1]

Pepys is obliged to publish, and a trip to Wotton

Deptford
25 September 1690[2]

Sir,

'Tis now (mithinks) so very long since I saw, or heard from my Excellent Friend, that I cannot but enquire after his Health: If he Aske what I am doing all this while? *Sarcinam compono*,[3] I am making-up my fardle that I may March the free'r: In the mean time ———

Do you expect a more proper Conjuncture, than this approching Session, to do your selfe Right, by Publishing that which all Good men, (who love and honor you) cannot but rejoice to see? You owe it to God, to your Country, and to your-selfe, and therefore I hope you seriously think of, and Resolve upon it.[4]

I am just now making a step to Wotton, to Visite my good Brother there, Importunately desiring to see me; himselfe succumbing apace to Age and its Accidents: I think not of staying above a weeke or ten-daies, and within a little after my Returne be almost ready to remove our small Family neerer you for the Winter, In which I promise my-selfe the Hapynesse of a Conversation the most Gratefull to Sir,

Your most humble,
faithfull Servant,

JEvelyn:

Give my most humble Service to Dr Gale:
I rent this page from the other before I was aware, and now 'tis to Late to begin againe for good manners:

---

[1] Source: Houghton Library, Harvard *64M–118. No endorsement. The copy (CLBII.633), dated 2 October, has a completely different second half (see note 4).

[2] MS: 'Depfd 25–7br:–90:' (copy-letter '2d Ocbr 1690'). No destination address.

[3] 'I make up a burden'.

[4] The copy, has no reference to a prospective journey to Wotton (see p.222, note 5), and continues from this point with: 'I dream'd last night (for you know I have little else to entertaine you with for the most part, besides Dreames) that you sent me word you would dine with me to day: which according to the Oneiocritics (or as Homer his, ὀνειροπώλης [sic]) are to be Interpreted by the Contrary, and by that Rule, I should Dine with Mr Pepys: But since the times of Joseph and Daniel, I have found them oft mistaken, and the Truth is, I am Ingag'd to Dine at White hall to day, though I assure you, I had rather eate a Sallad on a joynt-stoole with you, and Dr Gale, than with all the pompe of Courts: This is no Complement upon the honest word of Sir...'

D7. SAMUEL PEPYS TO JOHN EVELYN[1]

Pepys wants prints for his collection

[no place]
Thursday night, 25 September 1690[2]

Sir,

'Tis an hour and more since I had your kinde Remembrance; but it found mee
with Company that I have not beene delivered of till just now, that Mr
Strickland[3] is (at my desire) return'd for an Answer, and its growne too
darkeish to keepe him therefore for a long one.

Sir, I have thought it, and soe have many more besides my selfe, long since
wee saw you. I have sent and gone divers times to Mr Evelin's[4] to listen after
you. I will not doubt your being well employ'd, if well at all. But of that I was
covetous to heare, and had my satisfaction in it; though I had rather much have
beene able to have told my selfe I had seene you well.

You that can bee soe good a friend, can't bee an ill Brother, and soe I dare
not complaine of the Journey you speake of,[5] though I can't but wish it over,
and you in your Winter-Quarters, since they are likely to bee soe neare mine.

You speake too kindely (as you ever doe) of what I have calculated for
publique view. But bee assured, I won't take that last stepp of publishing it,
before I have consulted my Oracle (your selfe) once more touching[6] the
timeing it.

But one word I must now say to you before your journey, namely, that I
want Mr Evelin's head,[7] as in a thousand senses more, soe particularly for the

---

[1] Source: PL Pepys Ancillary MSS, file 25. Endorsed by E, 'Mr Pepys Lond 25 Sepr:
–90: Concerning his Apologies etc'.

[2] MS: 'Thursd. night. 25 Septr 1690.'

[3] John Strickland, E's servant at Sayes Court in Deptford.

[4] Pepys means E's son, John Evelyn the younger who lived in Dover Street in
London. E also used the house from time to time.

[5] This was E's trip to Wotton to see his brother George, mentioned in the letter
written earlier in the same day (above, p.221). It confirms the text to be that which P
had received, and not that of E's copy at CLBII.633 enigmatically dated 2 October
(ibid, note 4). E cancelled the trip on the 26th and wrote to his brother (letter at
BL.1563) making his excuses. That E's copy of the letter of the 25th is dated
2 October, and lacks a reference to the trip, shows that he was happy to rewrite the
letter of the 25th to reflect the changed plans, even though it resulted in a text P never
saw. This demonstrates how potentially unreliable any of E's copy-letters are when
unverified by the texts of letters-sent.

[6] MS: replaces 'risking[?]' deleted, but reading uncertain.

[7] E, and his wife's family, had been drawn for engravings by Robert Nanteuil in Paris

perfecting my Collection, which is now as farr advanced as I thinke I can expect to carry it. I may possibly against I see you bee able to pay you in kinde, but with great disadvantages,[1] I haveing noe Nanteuil to helpe mee.

One thing more I must add on this occasion, that I am at a mighty losse for 2 or 3 other heads, the Market not being able to furnish mee therewith, vizt Old Admirall Nottingham's,[2] the old Duke of Buckinghams, my Lord Chancellor Clarendons,[3] and his Daughter the Duchesse of Yorke's.[4] Pray see whither you have ever a head to spare of these.[5]

I kisse my Lady's hands, I pray for both your healths, and am to both
                    Your most obedient Servant,
                              SPepys.

---

in 1651. The drawings survive and remain in the Evelyn family (see Bowle, 1981, *John Evelyn and his world*, London, plate 3).

[1] MS: 'dis advanges,'.

[2] Charles Howard, Lord High Admiral from 1585–1618.

[3] Edward Hyde, Lord Chancellor 1660–7, first Earl of Clarendon.

[4] Anne Hyde, first wife of James II as Duke of York.

[5] The collecting of prints was an important intellectual activity for a virtuoso. The acquisition of engraved portraits, and other works of art, was regarded as a useful adjunct to the collection of books. The prints were perceived as a visual record of the books and their contents. E's interest in the subject had begun early in his life and undoubtedly grew out of his relationship with Thomas Howard, Earl of Arundel. Arundel's highly-important collection of paintings and drawings was built in part out of his patronage of artists such as Wenceslaus Hollar and Hendrick van der Borcht. The latter painted E in 1641 (diary, 23 May 1641) but, as has recently been shown from an examination of correspondence, E had close links with both artists for some time acting as a patron to their careers (R. Harding, 'John Evelyn, Hendrick van der Borcht the Younger and Wenceslaus Hollar' in *Apollo*, August 1996 – the article includes full transcripts of a series of letters to E from van der Borcht and Hollar). P's print-collecting had also begun early and a number of references in his diary mention acquisitions and hanging them in his home. In later life he grew more interested in accumulating a major collection, pasting them into albums in various schemes such as portraits divided amongst royalty, noblemen, virtuosi, churchmen, lawyers, chirurgions, and others. This letter is one of a number in which the subject recurs; E's expertise in terms of subject material and sources was regarded by P as indispensable. His approach to the subject is usefully discussed in a 1984 paper showing that, despite his enthusiasm, P sometimes exhibited a strangely uninformed approach, for example failing to recognise Rembrandt's work unless it was signed, not identifying artists's monogrammed signatures, and even mistaking some prints for original drawings (Jan van der Waals, 'The Print Collection of Samuel Pepys' in *Print Quarterly*, Vol.1, no.4, December 1984, 236–57). Nonetheless P's print collection survives as the most remarkable and complete of the period (see E's compliment on P's diligence, p.237, below). Levis (1915) examined E and P's interest in prints and provides useful examples of related correspondence. It seems evident that P's interest was relatively passive, being in essence a customer, whereas E was active in encouraging artists, and in promoting the philosophy of collection.

D8. JOHN EVELYN TO SAMUEL PEPYS[1]

Advice to Pepys on perfecting his collection

For Samuell Pepys Esqr at his
house in York-buildings etc
With a small Rolle:

Deptford
Morning, 26 September 1690[2]

Sir,

Si vales, bene est[3] etc — Without more ceremonie then (and that my small excursion[4] be no impediment to the perfecting your Collection) To your quæries —— In the days of Queen Elizabeth (for before her time I hardly heare of any) came over one Crispin van de Pas, and in King James's (her successors) his Brother Symon (who calls himselfe Pasæus) and afterwards then, and in Charles the first's time, one Elstrack, Stock, De La Rœm, and Miriam; and of our owne Countrymen,[5] Cecil, Martine,[6] Vaughan, and especialy John Paine; (for I forbeare to honor Marshial, Crosse, and some other lamentable fellowes) who engrav'd the Effigies of the noblemen etc then flourishing: These prints were sold by George Humble and Sudbury, at the Popes-Head in Cornhill; by Jenner at the Exchange, one Seager[7] I know not where, and Roger Daniel; but who had the most Choice, was Mr Peake neere Holborn Conduict, and if there be any who can direct you where you may most likely heare what became of their Plates, and Works of this kind; I believe no body may so well informe you as Mr Faithorn (father to the Bookseller) who, if I am not mistaken, was Apprentice to Sir William Peake (for both He, and Humble, were made Knights), and therefore it may be worth your while, to enquire of him: There came after wards (you know) Lucas Vosterman, Hollar, Lombart and other excellent Artists, but these were of later times, which you do not enquire of the[re]in: They wrought after Van Dyke,[8]

---

[1] Source: PC MS.i.40. Endorsed, 'Septr.26.1690. Mr Evelyn to Mr Pepys in returne to some Enquirys of his about Prints.'

[2] MS: 'Deptford 26.7br:–90. Morning.'

[3] 'If you are well, it is good.'

[4] The projected short trip to Wotton, see the letters of 25 September (**D6**, and **D7**).

[5] De La Rœm (Delarem) was English but E appears to have assumed that the spelling of his name suggested he was French.

[6] Not readily identifiable but Howarth suggests Martin Droeshout, born in England of Flemish parentage and known only for engraving Shakespeare's portrait.

[7] Not identified. The name also appears spelled Segar.

[8] Hollar produced an engraving of Van Dyke's self-portrait and dedicated it to E, one of his patrons (British Museum Prints and Drawings: Etching P1393).

the Arundelian Collection,[1] and best painters, and now of late, the skillfull in Mezzo Tinto Masters, who for imitation of the life, sometimes exceede the burine[2] it selfe, never so accurately handled: But of this enough: ——

I send you Sir my Face, such as it was of yore, but is now so no more (*tanto mutata*)[3] and with it (what you may find harder to procure) the Earle of Notingham, Lord High Admiral, which, though it make gap in my poore Collection (to which it was glu'd) I most cherefully bestow upon you, and would accompanie it with the other two, were I master of them: I have Sir George Villars when a youth, and newly dignified,[4] in a small trifling print, not at all fit for you, who ought to have him when he was Duke and Admiral, and of such there are extant many, easily to be had: I am sure his Picture is before several flattering dedications, though at present, I do not well remember where; But this I do, that there is a *Taille douce* of that mighty favourite (almost as big as the life, and nothing inferior to any of the famous Nanteuils,) graven by one Jacob of Delph in Holand from a painting of Miereveld, that were well worth the sending even into Holand for, and for what ever else is of this kind of that incomparable workemans hand: I have once seene of it, and tooke this notice of it, to mention in a new edition of my *Chalcographie*,[5] when I have leasure to revise that trifle: Lastly ——

As to my Lord Chancelor Hide, though I have not his Effigies among the rest that I have huddld together (allways presuming to get it of my Lord Clarendon, but perpetualy forgetting to aske it) yet I can direct you where you may certainly come by it, and perhaps, already have it in your Library: If not, 'tis but inquiring where Sir William Dugdale's *History of the Lord Chancelors*[6] was printed, and there you'l find him; and the rest of the Long Robe, if you have a mind to them:

Thus Sir, in returne to youre Letter, I have given you a desultory Account of your Enquiries, as far as on the suddaine I am able, and shall (so soone as I am at liberty) be most ready to receive what other Commands you reserve for

Sir, Your most humble, faithfull servant,

JEvelyn:

Have you ben at Mr Baker's shop neere the old Exchange? Cannot Mr White furnish you? I am deceiv'd, if he has not graven most of the Chancelors since his Majesty's restauration

---

[1] That in the possession of Thomas Howard, Earl of Arundel and inherited by his son and friend of E, Henry Howard, afterwards sixth Duke of Norfolk.

[2] The engraving tool.

[3] 'So changed'. The portrait is that by Robert Nantueil, executed in 1651. It appeared in print in 1706 as the frontispiece of the 4th edition of *Sylva*, then spelled *Silva*.

[4] Villiers. In 1616 when he was made the Duke of Buckingham at the age of 24.

[5] *Sculptura*. Published in 1662 – no second edition appeared in his lifetime. In 1755 a second ʿ ʾition was published using E's annotations on his own copy of the first.

[6] *Origines Juridicales* ..., London 1666 by Sir William Dugdale (1605–86), historian.

D9. SAMUEL PEPYS TO JOHN EVELYN[1]

An unsuccessful auction visit and an exotic meal

[no place]
Thursday Morning, 13 November 1690

Sir,

I was very unfortunate in being abroad at your being here last night,[2] and more soe in comeing home so close after your goeing, that I had mighty hopes my Man (whome I sent to try) would have overtaken and brought you back. I was gone but to Covent Garden by Chaire, to try whither I could have layd out a little Mony well at an Auction of prints, upon the enclosed List thereof;[3] but fayled, there coming no Heads[4] in Play dureing my stay, which was not above ½ an houre. This was my errand, and the only one I remember I have beene out of Doors upon these 14 Dayes, but to dinner the last week to Mr Houblon's, where both hee and I dranke your health and earnestly wish'd you there, as believeing the Meale would have pleas'd you noe lesse then it did mee, as hardly consisting of one dish or glasse (besides bread and beere) of nearer growth than China, Persia and the Cape of Good Hope.

I would I could invite you to such a One to day; but you know my Stint,[5] and if it stand with your health and diversion to venture (as you have done) at it, I am told by the Coachmen I may bee in condition to begin to repay your visits some time the next weeke.

I have, indeed, a great deale to say to you, though most of it of one Sort, – I meane Thanks, but on a great many different Scores, and the last of them for that of your last Nights favour.

I am, Dear Sir,
Your most bounden and obedient Servant,
SPepys

---

[1] Source: BL Upcott Antiquaries II. Endorsed by E, 'Mr Pepys: 13: November 90. Account of an exotic Meale.'

[2] Not recorded in E's diary; however, on 23 December he took P's book to Godolphin (diary), suggesting that either P sent it on, or that they visited each other after the date of this letter.

[3] Not attached.

[4] I.e. engraved portraits.

[5] P was in prison in the Tower from May to July 1689, and again in June 1690 in connection with suspicions that he was involved in Jacobite plottings. On the second occasion he was bailed after five days but charges were not dropped until October shortly before the occasion of this letter.

D10. JOHN EVELYN TO SAMUEL PEPYS[1]

Pepys's apologies accepted

To Mr Pepys: etc

Sayes Court
12 June 1691[2]

Sir,

As I have allways endeavord, that my Conversation should be Easy to my Friends: so I think my-selfe the more obliged to those among them, who use me with your Freedome, and without Formality: I should have ben very uneasy, if your coming hither to morrow (in complyance of my fondnesse), and the satisfaction I receive in your company) should have ben to the prejudice of your weightier Concernements:[3] And there-fore I will not expect the favour of a Visite from you, 'til a necessity of some Relaxation, dispose you to take the fresh of the River[4] this way, and that you are at intire Leasure,[5] and I may have you wholy to my-selfe, who am wholy

Sir Your etc etc

---

[1] Source: BL CLBII.644. There is no means of verifying the contents of this copy-letter. In view of problems with dating other copy-letters dated in particular to January and June (see p.219, note 3) the date of this example should be regarded as suspect until proved otherwise.

[2] MS: 'Says Cot: 12 June –91'.

[3] P has clearly communicated to E an inability to keep a social appointment; if that was by letter, it has not survived. P seems to have been experiencing some financial discomfort; he wrote to Sir Robert Howard (the dramatist, see DNB) on 1 July 1691 to call in the balance of a loan made in 1676 (PC MS.i.52; Tanner 1926 no. 34).

[4] Deptford lies downriver from London. E probably means that P should catch the fresh water of the Thames, as it flows out to sea, to carry him to Deptford.

[5] E dined with P on 11 July 1691 (diary).

D11. SAMUEL PEPYS TO JOHN EVELYN[1]

No good conversation to be had all summer

[no place]
Thursday 8 October 1691[2]

Sir,

Thinkeing it long ere Mr Strickland[3] made good his promise of calling on mee when hee went next to Wotton[4] (in order to my thankeing you for the favour of your obligeing Letter thence) I went yesterday to Dover-Streete to enquire after you, where I was most wellcomely surpriz'd with the newes of your being come to Deptford in your way to your Winter-Quarters[5] (I hope) here. You may easily imagine what a summer I have had, that have not stirred one Mile out of Towne since I saw you,[6] nor had the pleasure of one hour's Conversation worth owneing since you left it, saveing our learned Doctor's, and his but since Bartlemtide,[7] which hee pass'd at the Waters.[8] But from that time I have had his Saturday-visitts,[9] in which Mr Evelin's Name and Excellencys have ever contributed to the best part of our Entertainment, and his Absence to the Worst.

Pray make mee certaine, some way or other, of your and my Ladys Healths, and when I may hope for the satisfaction of knowing it at the first hand, and receiveing your Commands in our Neighbourhood.   I am,

Your most obedient Servant,

SPepys

---

[1] Source: Princeton University Library (Robert H. Taylor Collection). No endorsement. Published by Braybrooke, using BL Upcott Antiquaries II. The letter seems to have been removed from the album some time between 1825 and the early twentieth century, but this is unverifiable. Braybrooke's transcription was accurate.

[2] MS: 'Thursd. Octb.8.1691.'

[3] See p.222, note 2.

[4] Altered, from London(?)

[5] E records in the diary that he arrived in Deptford on 5 October following an attack of the gripes and moved on into London for the winter on 3 November.

[6] E's diary records that they had dined together on 11 July 1691 with various churchmen.

[7] Dr Gale. Bartholomewtide: 24 August.

[8] Probably at Tunbridge Wells.

[9] It was Pepys's weekly custom to entertain his friends and associates from the Royal Society, the 'Saturday Academists', at his home in York Buildings, Villiers Street between 1689 and 1700. They sat in Pepys's immaculately organised and catalogued library to discuss whatever interested them.

D12. SAMUEL PEPYS TO JOHN EVELYN[1]

Mourning for Robert Boyle

[no place]
Saturday morning, 9 January 1692[2]

Sir,

I would have come at you the other night at St Martin's on that grievous Occasion,[3] but could not. Nor would I have fayl'd in attending you before, to have condoled the losse of that great Man, had I for some time beene in a condition of goeing abroad. Pray lett Dr Gale, Mr Newton, and my selfe have the favour of your Company to day,[4] forasmuch as (Mr Boyle being gone) wee shall want your helpe in thinkeing of a man in England fitt to bee sett up after him for our Peireskius, besides Mr Evelin.[5] I am sure I know what I think on't and shan't spare to tell it you. A happy New Year to you from

Your most faithfull and most obedient servant,

SPepys

Mr Evelin

---

[1] Source: BL Upcott Antiquaries II. Endorsed by E, 'Mr Pepys 9:January:91/2. Compliment on the death of Mr Boyle.' Tanner's source for this letter was a copy retained amongst the Pepys-Cockerell papers (MS.i.55; Tanner 1926, no. 37).

[2] MS: 'Saturday morning. January 9 1691/2'.

[3] The Hon. Robert Boyle, died on 30 December 1691; his funeral service was held at St Martin-in-the-Fields on 6 January. E provides an account of the occasion (diary).

[4] E has no diary entry for 9 January 1692.

[5] Nicholas Claude Fabri de Peiresc. Pierre Gassendi dedicated his translation of a biography of Peiresc to E. E was once described as an English Gassendi (by William Rand who dedicated his translation of Gassendi's *Life of Peiresc* to him – see Hunter 1995, 84–7, and n. 78) who, like him, had studied Epicurus, was dedicated to scientific study, and found no conflict with his own devout Christianity.

D13. SAMUEL PEPYS TO JOHN EVELYN[1]

Apologies for ruining Mr Evelyn's book

[no place]
28 March 1692[2]

Sir,

The last being Confession, this in all good conscience ought to bee Restitution-Week; and (as farr as I am able) the first act of it with mee shall be the acquitting my selfe honestly towards you in reference to that Treasure of Papers which I have had of yours soe many Yeares in my hands,[3] in hopes of that *Otium*[4] I have now for 3 yeares been Maister of, but on conditions (easy to bee guessed at) which have not allowed me the Company of more of my Papers than I was content to adventure being Visited and Disordered. From whence it has happened that it is not above 3 weeks that in all this time I have taken the liberty of remanding any of them within my reach.[5] But out of these I have, I hope, made shift to collect all that relate to the 2 Heads which I have ever beene most thoughtful of with respect to you, namely, Those of State-concernment in the Ministry of Sir Richard Browne, and those of your own growth towards the History of our Dutch Warr, 1665; Which, with that followed it in 1672, I wish to God I could live to see putt together by your hand, as greatly suspecting they will prove the last instances of the Sea-Actions of this Nation which will either beare telling at all or bee found worthy such an Historian as Mr Evelin to tell. Of which more when we meet; praying you in the meane time not to deny mee the Ayde of your Memory, touching what further Parcells I stand accountable to you for. That I may not only lay them by, as they Occurr to mee, but be the better directed to look out for such as may not otherwise so readily occurr.

Another piece of Restitution I have alsoe to make to you, but with some payne for the imperfection wherewith I must doe it, after several years laying-out for means of doeing it better; Which is your *Columna Trajani*;[6] Which out

---

[1] Source: BL Upcott Antiquaries II. No endorsement. Tanner's (1926, no. 43) and Braybrooke's source was a copy in the Pepys-Cockerell papers (MS.i.61; endorsed, 'returning him some books and papers therein mentioned, formerly lent him').

[2] MS: 'Easter Monday, 1692'.

[3] See letter, 6 December 1681 (**C10**).

[4] Freedom from responsibility.

[5] This suggests P's papers were already dispersed, perhaps explaining why those sold in the Davey Catalogue did not emerge until 1889, and Braybrooke's view that the Rawlinson manuscripts were papers left by P in London when he went to Clapham (see pp.15–16).

[6] Alfonso Ciaccono. As note 3 above.

of a desire of makeing the most use I could of, with greatest ease to my Eyes,[1] I took the Liberty of putting it out (but unfortunately) to an unskilful hand, for the washing its Prints with some thin Staine, in order only to the abateing a Little the too strong lustre of the Paper. In the execution whereof the former part of it has suffered such injury that, not knowing with what Countenance to return it you so, I determined upon making you amends by the first fair book I could meet withall, putting this into my own Livery, as what I could well enough content my selfe for my own private use. But with soe ill success, that not withstanding all my Industry, both at Auctions and otherwise, to furnish my selfe with a fayre one for you, I have not been able to this day to lay my eye upon one, either Fayre or Foule, saveing one that I have very lately mett with at Scott's,[2] greatly imperfect, as wholly wanting the Historical Explications referred to through the whole by figures from the Plates; Sir Peter Lilly[3] (whose booke it was) contenting himselfe with soe much of it, and no more, as touched the Profession of a Painter, without that of a scholler. Being thus therefore tought how great a Jewel your Booke (even with this Damage) is, I thought it more religious to restore it you now as it is then leave you to expect it in the same Pickle 7 years hence from God knows who; resting in the meane time upon your good Nature in accepting so ill a method of Payment of a Debt that for my life I know not how to discharge better.

But there is yet another which I have beene slower in the cleareing allsoe than (could I have governed the Workeman) I ought to have been, namely, my Promise to you a Mapp of Caxton's and a Sphære after Copernicus. Both which Trifles come herewith; and to shew you how little cost I am at for you in them, know that the Sphære is the very same you have often seene here: the Characters of whose Planets for distinguishing the orbs become of late less fit for my eyes, I have taken the opportunity of accommodateing myself with another of a more Legible Size and put you off with this.

I would at this time allsoe restore your admirable Magazine of *Taille-douces*; but I have yet some gleanings to come in which I would bee glad to see the most of, and have your assistance in the disposeing of the whole before I part with my sample, if you can spare it a little longer.

And thus finishing my Mint and Cummin Scores,[4] but leaving those of the most and most lasting consideration to bee payd when they can bee fully valued, which is never to be done by mee, I am very seasonably stinted of Roome[5] to say more but

Adieu

---

[1] Pepys's concern for his eyesight had caused him to give up his diary in 1669.
[2] Robert Scott of Little Britain, London.
[3] Lely (in fact pronounced 'Lilly').
[4] From *Matthew* xxiii.23.
[5] The last few lines of the manuscript are compressed at the bottom of the letter.

D14. JOHN EVELYN TO SAMUEL PEPYS[1]

Pepys is forgiven

To Samuell Pepys Esqr

Dover Street
12 April 1692[2]

Sir,

I have so much to say to you upon the account of favours, and retort[?] on the many obligations you are pleas'd to mention; that the[3] time I should be able to spend with you this Afternoone, were too narrow to expresse them in good for me: For what dos not he owe the generous person who is not satisfied to bestow a kingdom, but the whole[4] Universe upon his Friend, and then extenuate his munificence upon the receiving of a few Lacerated and insignificant papers not worthy his keeping? But do you think that this Impudence, or ill manners to suggest your bespeaking these things far more to your cost and trouble? No, you delight to overwhelme whom you favour with your generous Nature, and teach me to become more modest, by a method not to be learn'd by any moral precepts I have met with in all my Reading: You should not have ben solicitous about the *Columna Traiana*,[5] for any accident you mention,[6] if it had ben worthy your acceptance and retention; for I looke on it as an honor, that it stood so long, and kept its station where you plac'd it: But I am glad you have met with one so faire, as I doubt not must be that of Sir William Lelys,[7] to which the Notes may easily be supplied: In the meane time, I know not whether you have seene a Second Edition of that most noble Monument, with very elegant Cûtts, publish'd in Holland, one of which I saw in the hands of Mr Frazier;[8] but the designe indeede seemes not to compare with Villamenas:

I am asham'd at the Epithete you bestow on what I either have, or ever could have perform'd in the History, where I had no liberty of writing Truth, if I had ben ever so well able: Upon this Compliment, we must have more Discourse when we meete: Farewell deare Sir

---

[1] Source: BL CLBII.665.

[2] MS: 'Dover streete 12 Aprill –92'.

[3] MS: 'the' is repeated, perhaps for 'tho[ugh] the'.

[4] E's note: 'Copernicus Sphere in Grai'; Copernicus's theory of a heliocentric solar system, expounded in *De revolutionibus orbium coelestium* (1543) originated in the work of the Greek (Grai = 'of the Greek') Aristarchus of Samos (3rd century BC).

[5] See letters of 6 December 1681 (C10), and 28 March 1692 (D13).

[6] It had been damaged when being washed (ibid).

[7] MS: 'Willm'; a slip for Sir Peter Lely, the artist?

[8] This is Dr, Sir Alexander Fraiser, FRS, and former physician to Charles II.

D15. JOHN EVELYN TO SAMUEL PEPYS[1]

Evelyn is world-despising

Wotton
29 August 1692[2]

I have ben philosophising and world-despising in the solitudes of this place, whither I am retired to passe, and mourne the absence of my best and worthyest friend. Here is wood and water, meadows and mountaines, the Dryads and Hamadryads; but here's no Mr Pepys, no Dr Gale. Nothing of all the cheere in the parlor that I tast; all's insipid, and all will be so to me 'til I see and injoy you againe.

I long to know what you do and what you think, because I am certaine you do both what is worthy the knowing and imitation.[3] On Monday next will Mr Bently[4] resume his lecture (I think) at Bow-Church;[5] I feare I shall hardly get through this wildernes by that time: pray give him your wonted countenance if you can, and tell him how unhappily I am intangled. I hope however to get home within this fortnight, and about the end of October, to my hyemation[6] in Dover Streete. My son is gon with the Lord Lieutenant and our new Relation Sir Cyrill[7] into Ireland.[8] I looke they should returne wondrous states-men, or

---

[1] Source: Tanner 1926, no. 44 (PC MS.i.62), and BL CLBII.671. Endorsed, '[Mr Evelyn to Mr Pepys] from his solitude in the countrey'. Textual differences from the copy, despite the different date (9 September 1692) are minimal.

[2] Copy-letter is dated '9:Sepr:–92 Wotton'.

[3] E was at Wotton from early June but visited Hewer at Clapham on 25 July. He returned to Sayes Court on 20 August, his son and his family having left for Ireland on 10 August. On 27 August E went back to Wotton on his own to visit his brother George. Throughout the year he and his brother had been making the arrangements for Wotton to devolve to E and his heirs following George's son's death in 1691.

[4] Richard Bentley. E was named a trustee in Robert Boyle's will charged with selecting a minister to give sermons 'expressly against Atheists, Deists, Libertins, Jewes etc, without descending to any other Controversy whatever... we made choice of one Mr. Bently, a Chaplain to the Bishop of Worcester: Dr. Stillingfleete for our first preacher' (diary, 13 February 1692).

[5] St Mary-le-Bow. The plan decided on was that the lectures would take place on the first Monday of each month, beginning at St Martin-in-the-Fields in March 1692, then at St Mary-le-Bow in April and alternately thereafter (diary, ibid). E was therefore wrong here; the church due for the first Monday in September was St Martin's, a fact he corrected in the copy-letter.

[6] Winter lodging.

[7] Sir Cyril Wyche had married E's niece Mary on 15 May 1692.

[8] E's diary, 11 August 1692 'Went my Son, Wife and litle daughter, towards Ireland;

else they had as good have stayed at home:

I am here with Boccalini,[1] and Erasmus's *Prayse of Follie*, and looke down upon the world with wondrous contempt when I consider for what we keepe such a mighty bustle. O Fortunate Mr Pepys! who knows, possesses, and Injoyes all that's worth the seeking after. Let me live among your inclinations and I shall be happy.[2]

J. Evelyn.

There are none of my little family here by my selfe.[3]

---

there to reside one of the Commissioners of the Revenue: The Lord Jesus, accompany and blesse him, if it be his blessed will, and prosper him, and grant that I may yet see him in prosperity againe: ...'.

[1] Trajano Boccalini, his *I Ragguagli di Parnasso: or Advertisements from Parnassus... with the Politick Touch-Stone... now put into English by... Henry Earl of Monmouth*, 1656 (Evelyn Library Sale Lot 184).

[2] The copy-letter ends, 'O Fortunate and Happy Friend! who possesses and Injoys all that's worth the pursuite and injoying seeking: Let one still live among your Inclynations, and I shall be Happy too'.

[3] Absent from the copy-letter.

D16. SAMUEL PEPYS TO JOHN EVELYN[1]

Pepys recovering and longing to see his friend

[no place]
16 September 1692[2]

Deare Sir,

I mind your Doctrine about Despising the World, but at the same time am out
of Countenance for your soe soone forgetting it, in the fondnesse of your
Phrase towards soe abject a Clodd of it as that which you are preaching it to.[3]
And yet as abject as I know that liveing Clodd to bee; I could even referr you
to that (since you are setting up for such a World-Contemner) to take out a
new and higher lesson from, upon the same Subject. For such I take to bee
(and doubt not your allowance to't) the shutting my selfe up within this
lushious Towne a whole Summer long, with a clean Bartl'mew Fayre in it, and
a Country-house lying upon my hand at £30 charge within 4 mile of the town,
and but a bowshott off my friend James Houblon, and yet covering my not
being to bee found here even by the excellent Dr Gale or Madame Excellence
herselfe, Mrs Stewart,[4] under the disguise of being retired thither; and this

---

[1] Source: BL Upcott Antiquaries II. Endorsed by E, 'Mr Pepys, Lond, 16 September
92. Civility.' The retained draft/copy (on E's letter-sent, **D15**, at PC MS.i.62) is
endorsed, '[Mr Pepys to Mr Evelyn] giving him an account of his own late
sequestring of himselfe'.

[2] MS: 'September 16, 1692'.

[3] P came to share E's sense of detachment from the world. In a letter to a Mrs
Shellcrosse (or Shelcross), dated 18 November 1697 from York Buildings, he said of
melancholy, '...Not that I would lead your Ladyship from my owne calling it so, to
thinke it really Neglect, there being noe Lady upon earth towards whom I either
would or ought more to shun that Guilt then your selfe. But Indeed Madame the
World and I have been strangers a great while, even to the workeing my selfe as much
out of the Memory of that, as I have reason (if I could) to gett that out of mine... As to
other Matters, Madame, lett mee state them to you in one Stanza of Mr Burton's (I
thinke it is) – When I see a Discontent / Sick of the faults of Government / Whose
very Rest and Peace dis-ease him, / 'Cause giv'n by those that doe not please him /
Mee thinkes that Bedlam has noe Folly, / Like to the politick Mellancholly' (from
Robert Burton's *Anatomy of Melancholy*, 1621). Cited in The Rosenbach Company
catalogue, *From the Ninth Century to Today*, Philadelphia, 1937, Item 287, p.102. I
have not been able to trace any other reference to this letter and therefore the whole
passage quoted in the catalogue is provided here. Mrs Shellcrosse lived at Greenwich
(see Tanner, 1926, ii, 41, P to Dr George Stanhope, 11 August 1700).

[4] See the letter of 10 September 1688 (**C42**), p.183, note 3.

pursued, to what you of all the Liveing would last believe, namely, to the not so much as enquiring after the most desireable and to mee the most indulgent Mr Evelin, for fear of being discover'd too near him; without eating one Morsell (or but one) in that savoury place of your own makeing soe, since I had the pleasure of doeing it with my beloved *Duum-viri*;[1] and lastly, to the abstayning so long from Ayre and Exercize as to contract upon myselfe an Evill (by the falling of Humours into one of my Leggs) that has kept mee to one floore, without being able to draw on a Shoo, from a Month since to this day. This (I say) I take to bee another-gates proof of a Noe-Worldling than a man's being alone where hee would grudge any Body's being but himselfe; I mean, among Meadows, Woods, and Water, Dryads and Hamadryads. And yet this have I gone through, as unaccountable as I have described it to you, and all for the sake of a small peece of Worke that lay upon my hands which I had noe minde longer to trust futurity with, and lesse than such a sequestration as this I (after many attempts) had convinced myselfe would not suffice for.

But it is over, and my Legg (I bless God) soe amended as I hope to morrow to begin my March down stayres, where I have obtained Dr Gale's promise to meete mee, as I would despair of doeing yours, were you within reach. Which I shall now long to have; as hee allsoe will, and both of us joyne in the wish of, with the first glass wee lift.

What I have told you of my Lameness as well as Confinement will enough tell you that I have not been in the way of obeying you or gratifying myselfe about Mr Bentley.[2] But as it is the first, I trust it will bee the last of my Faylures of that kinde.

Hasten then to Towne, where wee have a whole Summer's cropps of Intelligence to gather, and seed to putt in the ground for another; but want the Ayde of your Weather-Wisdome towards judgeing what will come on't. Hasten then to Towne, and receive the longing Wellcomes of,

Your most affectionate servant and honourer,

SPepys

---

[1] *Duoviri*, an 'official' board of two men, i.e. E and Gale.
[2] See p.233, note 4.

D17. SAMUEL PEPYS TO JOHN EVELYN[1]

Evelyn's prints returned

[no place]
Tuesday Morning, 29 November 1692[2]

Deare Sir,

I returne you most thankfully, and I hope without the least prejudice, your Excellent Collection of Prints. To which mine (when ever it comes to bee put together) will shew how much it is beholden to, not only by helpeing it to what you saw the other day of Copyes of what the Towne could not furnish mee with Duplicates of the Prints, but to a[t] Times the Number of such as though the Towne could afford them, I had yet wanted, from my not knowing (but for this assistance) how to have sought for them. And hard it is to say, how much more of the little I have to bragg of of other kindes, I owe to that same Grace of yours Communicativeness.[3]

Pray take notice that the great and excellent loose Head of the Duke of Bucking[ham], comes safe to you againe, after haveing in particular enabled mee to look out for and procure a Fellow of it.[4]

You left me with a great Cold upon mee, and this Weather is not apt to render it better. I shall not therefore bee able to attend you at the Society to morrow. But if you will be soe good to eate a Dish of warme broth with mee on Thursday,[5] you shall have it without other trouble then the Company of

Your most faythfull humble Servant
SPepys

---

[1] Source: BL Upcott Book-Collectors I. No endorsement or address leaf. Content and location indicates E was the undoubtedly the addressee.

[2] MS: 'Tuesday Morning 29.Novr 1692.'

[3] E returned the compliment in *Numismata* while discussing the publication of engraved portraits of the learned: 'Among those of our Nation that have made this any part of their search, and for the same purposes, I know of none who merits more Regard, than my worthy Friend *Samuel Pepys* Esquire, (late *Secretary* to the *Admiralty*) as he is a diligent, and laudable Collector of *this*, and whatsoever else is Curious, and of solid Benefit to the Public; as it will undoubtedly find, if *God* spare him Life, Health, and Repose, for the perfecting of that Noble, and truly useful Work, the *Nautics*, under the Hand of the most Able to accomplish it, not only of *England*; but as I am persuaded, of any one in *Europe*' (*Numismata*, 1697, 291–2).

[4] See P to E, 25 September 1690 (**D7**), p.223, and p.225, note 4.

[5] 1 December 1692. Any such visit is not recorded in E's diary. However, they did meet on 30 December (diary).

D18. JOHN EVELYN TO SAMUEL PEPYS[1]

A letter of respect, news, and advice on Mrs Skinner's affair

*For Samuell Pepys Esqr: at his
house in
York-buildings.*

Sayes Court
6 July 1693[2]

I should never forgive my selfe, did I not as often Remember you, as I do any friend I value in the World: Every Day is Saterday with me as to that, whether in Towne or Country: This I should have told you 'ere now, at York buildings: had not my son Draper,[3] his wife, and Mother ben with us[4] 'til yesterday evening, that they return'd to London. Indeede sooner than I wish'd, for they are the most obliging, worthy, usefull, and ingeniously dispos'd Conversation I could ever have desir'd to place my Daughter among I think in England: I assure you, both the Mother and Son are perfect *Virtuosi*, and know, and (which is more) effect, a world of Ingenious things without Vanity, which you would be extreamely pleasd with: I Confesse I cannot but admire at the Encounter, and pronouncing my Daughter very happy upon all accounts, cannot but make so good a Friend part of my Contentment.[5]

Nor is my Son in Ireland[6] lesse unmindfull of you than his Father ——

Dublin, 27:June –93

Be pleas'd to Acquaint Mr Pepys that the Gentleman's Estate lies in Munster, and not in the North: That it is Considerable, but cost him a great deale of mony at law before he could be quietly possessd: He is (by all I can learn) esteem'd to be at his ease; has onely one Daughter; and is now one of the Commissioners of Inspection

---

[1] Source: PC MS.i.67. Endorsed, 'July 6th 1693. Mr Evelin to Mr Pepys. A Letter of Respect, of Newes, and some further advice touching Mrs Skynner's Affair in Ireland'.

[2] MS: 'Sayes-Cot: 6.July.–93.'

[3] William Draper, husband of E's youngest child, Susanna. They had been married on 27 April 1693 (diary).

[4] 'My Son in Law, his mother and my daughter, came now the first time to visite us at Says-Court' (diary, 1 July 1693).

[5] E will have had his second daughter Elizabeth's 1685 elopement and death shortly after from smallpox in the forefront of his mind (see letters of 29 and 31 July, and 3 August 1685, **C21–23**).

[6] Made a Commissioner for the Revenue there in 1692 (E's diary 20 March 1692).

into Forfaitures at £400 per Annum Salarie:[1] Mr Pepys's kind thoughts of me are a superaboundant Recompence for all the poore Services I can do him ———

He adds this News ———

We are now by the late arival of 5 men of War in this Harbour (viz., the *St Albans, Dover, Saphir,* etc.)[2] deliver'd from our feare of the French Corsaires, who had almost Circum-navigated our Island, to the damage of Trade and disgrace of our Victorious Navy: Some of these Frigats are to convey my Lord Lieutenant[3] on Monday next; one to go Northwards in quest of the privateers: I believe another to Cork, to Escort 400 Tun of crooked Timber;[4] the first fruite of Mr Nash and Knox: pourveyance of it in this Kingdom, which may be much Improv'd, if these two Industrious men be encourag'd and Convoys ready to waite on what they provide. Our Parliament was yesterday dissolv'd in Council, and proclamations expected to come out to day: Every-body complements my Lord Lieutenant before he leaves us; and I shall have the honor of his Company at dinner on Friday next at my house, and it is the least Accknowledgement I can make his Lordship for his constant favour to me, wherefore I embrace it with much satisfaction: It is not yet publish'd whom he will leave the Sword with 'til my Lord Capel and the rest arive, though 'tis likely either Mr Roberts[5] or my Lord Chancellor[6] will be joyn'd with Sir Cyril Wych,[7] who is so very kind, and friendly to me, that were he not a man of perfect Integrity, I might set up for Nepotissimo:[8]— I have 50 foote square behind my house and stables to practise your hortulan Instructions on, as far as may serve a Nose-gay and a still:[9]——

Thus far my sons Intelligence; and what I would have you to know more from me, is That I have as yet as good Beanes and Bacon, and (though but one Cow) as good Creame as ever one would wish to entertaine Mr Pepys and the Doctor[10] with if they durst shoote the Bridge,[11] and give a poore friend a Visite once a Yeare

---

[1] Tanner suggests that P's note on the letter indicates that the younger Evelyn was looking into the affairs of a prospective suitor for P's housekeeper, Mrs Skinner (Tanner 1926, i, p.68, n. 1).

[2] *St Albans,* 50-gun 4th rate, built at Deptford, 1687, and wrecked off Kinsale, Ireland, on 8 December 1693; *Dover,* 48-gun 4th rate(?), built at Shoreham, 1654, and rebuilt at Portsmouth, 1695; and, *Sapphire,* 32-gun 5th rate, built at Harwich in 1675, and sunk on 11 September 1696 by the French off Newfoundland (Colledge 1987).

[3] Henry, Viscount Sydney.

[4] Presumably timber with natural bends, of considerable value to ship-building.

[5] Uncertain but perhaps Sir Gabriel Roberts, godfather to E's son's daughter Martha Maria (diary, 4 July 1683).

[6] Sir Charles Porter, Lord Chancellor of Ireland 1686–7 and 1690–6.

[7] Appointed secretary to the Lord Lieutenant in 1692.

[8] Wyche had been married E's brother George's daughter Mary in March 1692.

[9] Probably for brewing.

[10] Dr Gale.

[11] That is, shoot the piers of London Bridge to come downriver to Deptford.

D19. JOHN EVELYN TO SAMUEL PEPYS[1]

On Eton College

To Mr Pepys

Dover Street
2 April 1694[2]

Sir,

I am ready for your Quæries about the dimensions of Eaton Schole, number of scholars etc: Dr Godolphin the (sub Warden)[3] would be a proper person you could discourse the matter with, unlesse you made a step to Sir Christopher Wren, who built the new schole (for so he did some years since) from the foundation: the old one being quite abandond and run to decay:[4] I Returne your Itinerary,[5] and am

Your etc

---

[1] Source: BL CLBII.693.

[2] MS: 'Dover streete 2 Aprill –94'. E seems to have been in London from 14 March, returning to Deptford on 2 April.

[3] Dr Henry Godolphin, then vice-Provost (1683–95).

[4] P's interest in Eton was probably in connection with his governorship of Christ's Hospital (since 1676; see R. Kirk, *Mr Pepys upon the state of Christ Hospital*, Philadelphia and London, 1935; also correspondence at BL Add. MSS 20732, for 1694–5). The 'new schole' is Upper School, built at Provost Richard Allestree's expense in 1665. There is no evidence that Wren was directly involved. It required rebuilding by 1689, payments for which were exclusively to Matthew Banks (Eton MS COLL/BA/40), a master carpenter who had worked for Wren at Whitehall for James II, and at Kensington Palace (Beard 1982, pp.36, and 42). It has been long believed at Eton that Wren worked there, so it is possible that this connection, however tenuous, gave rise to the story; even so, 1689 hardly amounts to having been 'some years since'. But, there is also a belief (likewise unverified) that Wren worked at Winchester College, so E may simply be confusing the two. P's account of Eton Lower School (diary, 26 February 1666) as being 'good' and 'mighty fine' rather conflicts with E's claim that it had been abandoned. As the subject does not occur in P's letter of 22 May (p.241), does not recur in any other of P and E's extant correspondence, and that this letter is known only as a copy suggests there is a possibility it was never sent in the form recorded.

[5] Presumably the list of queries.

D20. SAMUEL PEPYS TO JOHN EVELYN[1]

Pepys sends books on voyages to Evelyn

York Buildings
22 May 1694

Deare Sir,

What shall I say more (for introduction) then that wee Want you, Wish for your, Pray for you?[2]

The newest thing I have to send you is a small Collection of Voyages, which the Publishers,[3] in acknowledgement of what of them I have helped them to (namely, Narborough's, Wood's, and Sharp's)[4] have presented mee with 2 or 3 Copys of, as I doe you with one of them.

Least you should not remember where you left your Virginia-man's letter,[5] and hee thereby want the content, I dare say hee languishes for, of your answer[6] I thought it becomeing mee to send it you, (you haveing lent it mee to Copy,) and to tell you that his to Mr North[7] was safely delivered to his owne hand.

You won't be sorry (I believe) to finde, by the Præface left with me yesterday by Mr Chiswell, that Archbishop Laud's *Life* of his owne writeing, is now in the presse, with designe to bee fitted for the public against Michaelmas[8] Terme.[9]

---

[1] Source: BL Upcott Antiquaries II. Endorsed by E, 'Mr Pepys York Buildings. 22 May–94. Concerning Bookes etc.' With respect to the observation that some of E's letters which exist only as copies may never have been sent (above, p.20), it may be noted that this letter makes no reference to the content of the preceding letter (2 April 1694) though of course other, unknown, correspondence may have occurred in between.

[2] E had recently moved permanently from his home at Sayes Court, Deptford to the family estate at Wotton, Surrey (diary, 4 May 1694).

[3] *An Account of Several Late Voyages and Discoveries to the South and North...* by Sir John Narborough [and others], published by Samuel Smith and Benjamin Walford. It was dedicated to P.

[4] Sir John Narborough, John Wood(?), and Bartholomew Sharpe.

[5] Possibly Francis Nicholson, see letter of September 1686 (**C34**), p.171, note 2.

[6] MS: the comma is displaced thus: '...for of your answer, I...'

[7] Perhaps Roger North (1651–1734), the lawyer and historian. If P did indeed copy E's letter from Nicholson(?) it is not apparently amongst the recorded Pepys MSS.

[8] MS: 'Michms'.

[9] *The History of the Troubles and Tryal ... wrote by himself, during his Imprisonment in the Tower*, For Robert Chiswell, 1695. E's copy was Lot 882 in the Library Sale and carried marginal notes in the diarist's hand. See also p.244, note 1.

To these I adde a Sheete or 2 lately printed relateing to the sea, and aymeing at something good there. The Author seemes to have wit enough, and good Meaneing, and offers at something very bold in it (mee thinks) relating to Government. But, were it worth while, it were easy to shew him to bee but moderately instructed in the importance of the very Notion hee would advance, and which, indeed, wants to be more stricktly handled; I meane the Controversy (for Sea-Employment) between the Gentleman and Tarpawling.[1]

Sir, I kisse my Lady's Hands and your owne, and telling you once more that wee heartily Want, Wish, and Pray for you, I remayne,

Your most faithfull and obedient Servant,
SPepys

My Lord Clarendon asked mee the other day with great respect after you, and your work upon the Medaills, intimating (mee thought) his haveing something therein to pleasure you with. If you have any errand to bee delivered to him, on that or any other subject, pray lett mee bee your Messenger.[2]

I had a very kinde visit yesterday from our pretty Ætonian,[3] conducted by Mr Strickland, but could not get the Little Knave to dine with mee, as being elsewhere bound. But I hope he will make me amends another Day.

---

[1] I.e. 'Tarpaulin', a common sailor.

[2] The fruits of E's labours were published in 1697 as *Numismata, A Discourse of Medals, Antient and Modern. Together with some Account of Heads and Effigies of Illustrious and Famous Persons...To which is added A Digression concerning Physiognomy,* It was characterised by mistakes and typographical errors which caused E embarrassment and indicated that he had overreached himself.

[3] E's grandson, John, later Sir, Evelyn (1682–1763). He had entered Eton in June 1692 and was at this date a little over 12 years old. He had presumably been left at Sayes Court in the care of E's staff, though he moved on to Wotton (p.244).

D21. JOHN EVELYN TO SAMUEL PEPYS[1]

Evelyn has moved to Wotton

For Your Selfe, and with good Reason
for my boldnesse in giving you
this trouble

Wotton
30 May 1694[2]

My worthy Friend,

Mithinks Want, Wish and Pray, is like Cæsars *Veni, Vidi, Vici*; more could not be express'd in so few words, more needed not: But the Want is on my part, the Wish and prayer common, and reciprocal to both. I have at this moment in prospect of my exalted Museolum here, Water, Woods and Meadow with other Circumstances of Solitude: I have also a good Cart-loade of Books which I brought along with me: But there is no such thing as a Mr Pepys or a Dr Gale within 24 miles North of us; nor within thousands of any other point of the Compas:[3] for I have Travell'd to the Antipodes from Spitzbergen with the best Navigators in the World, by the pilots[4] you sent me; for which I returne you a thousand Acknowledgements, and for those two[5] other pieces which have Entertain'd me with greate Satisfaction: Whoever was the Compiler of the Journal was (I am perswaded) no Tarpaulin:[6] Sure it is not Sir John Narboroughs style: I wish we had more such Relations, and as faithfully, as I believe these are don. The Dedicatory Plate (which is my Friends)[7] is finely graven; The rest, (besides the Map) Tollerably; which makes me much long to see some of your fine Alumni of Christ-Church, come home, with their Draughts.

I cannot guesse at the Author of the New Model: The Man is brisk, I believe confident of his abillitie and a little conceited, and cuts a feather (as they say)

---

[1] Source: Princeton University Library (Robert H. Taylor Collection) MS. Endorsed by P, 'Wootton May 30 1694. Mr Evelyn to Mr Pepys'. Illustrated on pp.339–40.

[2] MS: 'Wotton 30:May–94'.

[3] P became equally frustrated by Gale's absence as Dean of York in 1699 and wrote to Gale on the subject, and E's declining health and visits (9 March 1699; see p.261, note 4). The letter, Pforzheimer MS105E, is published in the Pforzheimer Catalogue (1940, pp.808–10; copy in North Library, British Library).

[4] E adds a marginal note here on the copy-letter only: 'Sr J Narbor and Cap: Wood discoveries wh[ich] he sent me.' See P to E 22 May 1694 (**D20**), p.241, notes 3 and 4.

[5] A further marginal note on the copy-letter only adds: 'Mr Wharton Præface to AB: Lauds Life'. See p.241, note 9, and p.244, note 1.

[6] I.e. no ordinary sailor.

[7] Pepys.

in the Conclusion very gentilely: From Mr Whartons undertaking[1] I expect greate, and usefull things: You see what Time, and the providence of God brings every day to light; 'tis that we are to Waite, for more discoveries.

Thus you see how I live upon your Provisions, and how little I am capable else to returne you from the Desart I am in; Wanting in every thing but in a most gratefull Heart for these, and all your Favours to

Dear Sir,
Your most obedient faithfull
Servant   JEvelyn:

My Wife returnes you her most humble service, and the young Ætonian (who is with us) for your mention of him.

Give to Dr Gale all you can expresse of service and solemn Acknowledgements in the name of a most obliged Creature.

I beseech you when next you see my Lord Clarendon make my compliment for his kind Remembrance: I intend shortly to write to his Lordship upon the Account he mentions; and now by the deferrent you permit me to Employ, I am bold to intreate your assistance in conveying the Inclosd; having no other meanes to be just and civile to my known and un-knowne Friends in Virginia.[2]

When ever you, and the Doctor go downe the River, divert for a Moment to the young House-keepers at Says-Court,[3] and let me know in what fault you deprehend[4] them: They are I heare a family of 21: Mrs Tuke is Library-Keeper: The Rest Painters, Embroiderers, Carvers, Gard'ner *et Cætera p——a Campi*.[5]

The most certaine way of sending your Commands to Wotton, is by causing your Servant to deliver them to Mr Collins, at a Book-Sellers shop at the Middle-Temple gate,[6] (which is the Post-house) whence we have constantly the News-Letters and Gazzets twice every Weeke: The little Woman of the Shop is a Friend to the Family here, and takes particular Care of all that's directed hither.

We beg the favour that you will present our most humble Service to Mrs Steward, when you visite Lincolns Inn.[7]

---

[1] Henry Wharton's forthcoming *History of Dr William Laud*, published in 1695. See letter of 7 July 1694 (**D22**).

[2] A letter, see p.247, note 4.

[3] E's daughter Susanna and her husband William Draper (from May 1694).

[4] Obsolete form of apprehend.

[5] Sic, for *et Cætera pecora Campi*. See p.271, note 3, where the quote is repeated.

[6] Probably the Thomas Collins of the same address (or his son) who, with Gabriel Bedel, had published some of E's earlier works, for example Lucretius (1656).

[7] She lived in Portugal Row, on the south of Lincoln's Inn Fields (Howarth, p.140).

D22. JOHN EVELYN TO SAMUEL PEPYS[1]

The talents of William Wotton

Samuell Pepys Esqr
York-buildings

Wotton
7 July 1694

My worthy Friend,

It's now high time for me to make some apologie (if I had any besides your
wonted indulgence) for the trouble I lately gave you of a cumbersome packet;[2]
and (after I have enquired of your good health, with the rest of our Saturday's
Academists) to reiterate my thanks for the booke you sent me. You will not be
much inquisitive what I am doing whilst there's so much hay abroad and the
sun shines so bright; at least here is work enough for those who have leasure.
This is the style of the place, the season, and of my buisines, and must have
ben (for aught I know) my best employment, if some kind Genius had not in
pitty directed the most learned Mr Wotton[3] to give me a visit, and an
inestimable present too, his *Reflections upon the Antient and Modern
Learning*;[4] which in recognition of yours I should have sent you, but that I was
confident you must e're this have seene it, and ben entertained with as much
delight and satisfaction as an universaly learned, and indeede extraordinary
person is able to give the most refined tast. This is he whom I have sometimes
mentioned to you for one of the miracles of this age for his early and vast
comprehension.[5] Set him downe then in your *Albo*[6] amongst the Gales and
the Bentlys, as you will certainely do so soone as you know him. I assure you,
he is no lesse in the pulpit[7] and conversation than in his booke and writing
(with greate modesty). Judge you then what an unexpected blessing is befallen
me in the wildernes, and with what manna I am fed, when ever he dos me the
kindnes to come from Albery[8] (where he has the care of a hopefull young son

---

[1] Source: Tanner 1926, no. 62 (PC MS.i.86) and BL CLBII.707. Endorsed, '[Mr
Evelyn to Mr Pepys]. A letter of respect'.

[2] Referred to in the previous letter's postscriptum (**D21**), p.244, note 2.

[3] William Wotton.

[4] Published a few days earlier in June 1694. He also seems to have presented E with a
copy of the 1697 second edition (Library Sale, Lot 1597).

[5] E had been astounded by the 11-year-old Wotton in 1679 (diary, 6 July 1679).

[6] Album.

[7] E had heard him preach on 13 June 1694 (diary), just three weeks before.

[8] Albury, near Dorking. Heneage Finch, afterwards Baron of Guernsey and Earl of
Aylesford, had purchased it from Henry Howard in or around 1680 (de Beer, IV, 558,

of Mr Finch's) to Wotton, his name-sake as he calls it. And now you may well think I talke as famish'd and half-starved men are said to eate when they come to plenty of provisions; for so indeede I do, not having had such a *regalo*[1] since I went from York-buildings; nor should I have known what to write from this barren country had not this gentleman furnished me. I am told our friend Dr Lock has made addition to his excellent Essay, which may be had without a necessitie of purchasing the whole booke;[2] and a letter just now sent me from the Bishop of Lincoln[3] acquaints me that there is a little piece in duodecimo called *Religion and Reason* which he says he will give one an hour's good diversion;[4] for both which I am sending. That Mr Wharton's *Life* of the Archbishop (the preface of which you lately so kindly sent me) is by this time printed.[5] This is better newes than what we have here from Brest,[6] which I am astonished to find published, for the same reason that you and I would not that all the world should reproch our want of conduct as well as misfortunes.

My most humble service to the obliging Dr Gale. Receive you my wife's, who is at present become a water-bibber here, though we fetch it from Lingfield, almost 20 miles distant on the edge of Sussex,[7] and is stronger than the Spaw of Tunbridge.[8] If you or the Doctor come neere to Epshum this summer, I flatter myselfe you will make halfe a dozen miles step farther south to, Both your most humble and faithfull servant,

JEvelyn:

We drink Mr Bently's health, and wish his library finished, that we may have the sermons he has promised us, etc.[9]

---

n. 1). E had worked on the garden extensively for Howard. E's garden design for Albury, dated 1667, survives and is in the Pforzheimer Collection (MS 35C).

[1] Excellent entertainment.

[2] The second edition of John Locke's *Essay concerning Humane Understanding* (1st edition, 1690; 26 February 1690, **D2**); the additions also appeared separately in 1694.

[3] Dr Thomas Tenison, bishop of Lincoln 1691–4. His letter (19 June 1694) on this subject is published in Bray editions of E's diary and correspondence.

[4] See below, p.249, note 3.

[5] Of Laud (specified thus in the copy-letter), see letter of 22 May 1694 (**D20**).

[6] Lieutenant-General Thomas Tollemache had unsuccessfully assaulted the town in June, dying from his wounds. E had recorded the event in his diary, from a notice apparently published in *The London Gazette* of 18 June (de Beer, V, 184, n. 3).

[7] On the Kent border about halfway between Wotton and Tunbridge.

[8] 'Spa'.

[9] On 23 December 1693 Bentley was appointed King's Library Keeper at St James (see E's diary, 29 November 1694; de Beer, V, 196, n. 7). Further developments in the Library are noted by E on 17 November 1695 and 18 December 1697. Bentley wrote to E on the subject of expanding it on 22 February 1696, a plan which came to nought (Richard Bentley, *Correspondence*, ed. C. Wordsworth, 1842, i. 113–4).

D23. SAMUEL PEPYS TO JOHN EVELYN[1]

A family afflicted by the fever of the season

London
14 August 1694[2]

Dear Sir,

I have beene a good deale out of order my selfe, but much more soe in my family, for some time, and have 3 downe at this house of the feavor of the season; but I thanke God none Mortally, but on the Contrary well advanced in theyr Recovery. This however has kept me a great while under Care; and the more from the novelty of it (it being among all Domestick Evils that which by God's favour I have beene least exerciz'd with) and has sett mee (as one effect of it) greatly in arreare to all my friends, and to you at the head of them, for which I am now lookeing out for pardons, and with most concernment for yours. Which pray let this obtaine for mee.

I am owing to you for 2: the former in May, the other in July.[3]

Your Virginia-letter was delivered, immediately after my Receipt of it, to the Merchant's own hand from which you had yours.[4]

I earlily did your Commands to my Lord Clarendon, and since have had the honour of a visit from him, when your Name wanted not the mention due to it from all that I know it and themselves.

Dr Gale acknowledges himself your Debtor, as I am his, for all the Ease I have had a great While; the greatest Ingredient of which is, the frequent

---

[1] Source: BL Upcott Antiquaries II. Endorsed by E, 'Mr Pepys: Lond: 14:Aug:–94; Sending me a præface etc Answrd 2d: Sepr.' Tanner gives 10 August but had access only to a copy retained by P (PC MS.i.95; 1926, no. 63). Smith (1841, II, 265) had published the text of the letter-sent (then in Upcott's possession) but was unfairly criticised by Tanner for getting the date wrong. This is the only instance, in the correspondence with E, of P's copy bearing a different date from the letter-sent, but see note 2 below. There is no textual variation. Smith also published (ibid, 269) E's reply of 2 September (see **D24**) but almost certainly used E's scrawled draft which appears at the end of P's letter, thus explaining what Tanner described as Smith's 'inaccuracy' and 'considerable omissions' (1926, 99, n. 4).

A number of the persons and works referred to in this letter arose in E's letter of 7 July 1694 (**D22**) and are the subject of footnotes there.

[2] MS: 'London. August 14, 1694'. Copy dated the 10th (see note 1) but altered from '10'. Clearly both letter-sent and copy were made on the 10th but a delay in posting led to the letter-sent's date being altered, a correction omitted from the copy.

[3] See letters of 30 May 1694 (**D21**) and 7 July 1694 (**D22**).

[4] See letter of September 1686 (**C34**) and, above p.244, note 2.

Remembrance his Conversation starts occasions for betweene us of our distant friend Mr Evelin.

Mr Bentley is still (I believe) at Worcester, and a great man where ere hee is. But 'tis Winter only that will help us to any Tideings (I doubt) either of his Library or Lectures.

You have great reason to joy your selfe, as you doe, in such a Neighbour-hood as that of Mr Wotton's; whose incomparable Discourse[1] I read betimes, and was to blame I did not first doe right to it to you. Hee is indeed to bee reckoned among the leaders of the Age for Learning, through all the Dimensions of it, Length, Breadth, and Depth; and if hee lives a little longer (as I hope he will a great deale) hee will have nothing left him to doe but what Noe body but himself was, or possibly will ever bee, soe fitted to doe as hee; I mean, the reduceing into lesse roome what poor Mankinde is now to turn-over soe many cumbersome, jejune, and not seldom unintelligible volumes for; and when that's done, not have 5, perhaps not one year, to reckon-upon his whole life for the sedate applying and enjoying those sorry pittances of seemeing Knowledge that he possibly has beene 50 in collecting. What a Debt were this to lay upon mankind? and from what hand ever to be hoped-for but that of such an universalist as Mr Wotton, and one soe soon arrived at the being soe? I shall hope for the Honour and Pleasure of wayteing on him whenever the Season or Business shall bring you to Towne together.

I enclose you a paper new to me and soe (it may bee) to you: the inscription on the late venerable Bishop of Oxford's monument, which has something very awfull in it, and answering his Character.[2]

The Virtuosi there, are (you know) gathering and printing a generall Catalogue of what Manuscripts, publique or private, our country is possessed of. It is indeed a Worke that I have long wished. Not that I have ought of my owne to contribute to it. But I well remember how much I have been obliged to them that have, I mean, your selfe; and believe there are a great many other valuable things in ingenuous Men's hands, that (like you) would be glad to communicate them where they thought the Publique might be served by it; and this in all Facultys. I send you the freshest account I have had from Oxford of theyr Advance herein; and with it must give the Postscript of a letter I lately had on this Subject from our learned and most solicitous friend in this and all like virtous Undertakings, Dr Charlett (Maister of University-College) in his own few words, 'We must not forget Mr Evelin's MSS; and what became of Sir Richard Brown's?'[3] This hee meant but for a Text for me to enlarge on to

---

[1] See p.245, note 4.

[2] Dr John Fell, Bishop of Oxford 1675–86. His monument is in Oxford Cathedral. The inscription is a detailed record of his achievements. This and other enclosures referred to in this letter are not apparently with the surviving MS.

[3] Sic, for Browne. P's reply to Charlett on this matter (4 August 1694) is published (Howarth, no. 230). Browne had died in 1683 and the various historical manuscripts in his possession passed to E. Many of them are now in the British Library.

you. But it needs not; the Doctrine and Application of it being selfe-evident. Let me only adde my instance to his, that you would further this work with the Credit of what your Stocks will give it.

I take the liberty of sending you the newest French Toy that is come to my hand, which (if you have not seen) will not want some divertisement for you, if you may bee thought to neede any where you are soe well and variously employ'd as your Letters shew me.[1]

My Lady will (I hope) find her end in the use of the Waters, and ere this is return'd home possessed of it. I wish her steadinesse of health, and to you too, and with my most profound respects to both, remaine,

> Deare Mr Evelin,
> Your most faythfull and obedient servant,
> SPepys

Dr Lock has sett a usefull Sample for future Reprinters;[2] I hope it will bee follow'd, in books at least of value. I have read the little thing the Bishop recommended to you about Reason and Religion,[3] and found great satisfaction in it. Adieu.

---

[1] What the 'Toy' was is unknown but the word encompasses a variety of meanings including facetious or fantastic compositions.

[2] See p.246, note 2. Locke had supplied the additions for a second edition under separate cover for the benefit of owners of the first edition.

[3] It seems inevitable that this should be identified with Locke's *The Reasonableness of Christianity as delivered in the Scriptures* but as this was published in 1695 (DNB) it may have been seen in advance of formal publication.

D24. JOHN EVELYN TO SAMUEL PEPYS[1]

Evelyn overwhelmed with books

For Samuell Pepys Esqr
York-buildings

Wotton
2 September 1694

My worthy Friend,

Ecce iterum provocas me Beneficiis, neque habeo ullum ἀντίδωρον,[2] which plunges me and more into Debt; this last Packet of yours coming fruited with so many Favours at once, that I know not which of them first to give thanks for; All of them deserving a particular Acknowledgement:

I am extreamely pleas'd with these *Valesianus's*;[3] they are to me like those *Inter-messes* which are plac'd betweene the larger Dishes, not to make a Meale upon but to furnish Vacuities: I wish we had more of these Attic Nights,[4] and am glad to find they come so into fashion; Nor do I looke on them as scraps; but as *Bellaria*[5] and *Cupediæ*,[6] which refresh with their pretty Varietie when one has ben tir'd with moiling and turning-over the Rubbish you justly Complaine of to lie in the way: With you therefore I have a thousand times deplor'd that there has yet ben so little don toward the Ridding us of this monstrous Lumber: Honest Gesner[7] has yet don his part, and shew'd how fuisaible[8] it were by the example he has set and such as of late have taken paines in the Histories of Animals and Plants, etc: Dr Pell left a *Diatyposis*[9] of what he pretended to have performed in the Mathematics, and Bishop Wilkins[10] in his preliminaries to his Essay of a *Real Character*,[11] scor'd-out

---

[1] Source: Tanner 1926, no. 64 (PC MS.i.87), BL CLBII.715. Endorsed, '[Mr Evelyn to Mr Pepys] upon a late reflection of his upon the excessive number of books mankind is unnecessarily burthened with for the short time he has to worke therewith'.

[2] 'Behold! you are condemning me to an ordeal of favours, I haven't any protective clothing'.

[3] E compares P's last letter with Adrian de Valois' literary opinions expressed in his *Valesiana* of 1692.

[4] A reference to the works of Aulus Gellius, *Noctium Atticarum*, an educational compilation of references to various literary subjects and extracts from many authors.

[5] Dessert.

[6] Dainty dishes?

[7] Konrad von Gesner, the Swiss naturalist.

[8] Feasible.

[9] Dr John Pell the mathematician. The DNB states that he 'left nothing of moment.'

[10] John Wilkins, Bishop of Chester 1668–72.

[11] E's copy of *An Essay towards a Real Character and a Philosophical Language*

many very usefull Tables, preparatory to a more universal Worke than that of words alone: But so did my Lord Bacon before him with his caution concerning *Epitomies*;[1] and yet, I pray, what would the losse have ben if some of our tedious Historians were Contracted to so little detriment as Dio[2] has suffer'd by John Xiphilin, and most of the Fathers of the Church by the late Dupin?[3] I speake not this by guesse, having not long-since examined him, after I had first read Clemens Alexandrinus, which you know is a book of greate Varietie;[4] nor is he the only voluminous theologue I have compared him with of the primitive Writers without finding any material passage omitted or slightly treated: The *prolegomena* of the Polyglotte Bible[5] is another instance, etc. In the meane time, what a Benefactor were he that were able and willing to give us such a Catalogue of Authors as were onely, and absolutely, and fully Effectual to the attaining of such a Competency of Practical, Usefull, and Speculative knowledge too, as one might hope to benefit by within the ordinarie Circles of ones Life, without being bewilder'd and quite out of the way when one should be gotten home: I am still perswad'd this were not Impossible, and that lesse than an hundred authors, studied in proper Method, would go a greate way towards this End: I do not meane by Excluding any of the Classics, which in a very few yeares may all be read, together with all the Greeke and Latine Historians from Herodotus downwards: But I speake of the Subsidiarie Arts and other Faculties, as far as to Accomplish one who did not intend a particular Profession; or if he did, find the rest any burden to him: I know you have read Grotius's *Epistle* to Monsieur Maurerius; it is his first since *ad Gallos*:[6] What then might not a younger man, who sets out early hope to attaine by some such method? But I forget I am writing to one knowes all this so much better and is so ready to promote the Common good of Man-kind: I concurr with you therefore in all you say and think of Mr Wotton upon this Chapter; but 'tis now neere three-weekes since I saw him, about which time I understand he went to London, and whether he be yet return'd I have not heard: Onely a little before he went, he shew'd me a letter from Mr Bently Acquainting him that so much

---

(1668) was a presentation from the author (Library Sale, Lot 1579).

[1] Possibly a reference to Bacon's *Essay* 'Of Studies' (50) and the comment 'distilled books are like common distilled waters'; or to Book V, Chapter III of *The Advancement of Learning*, 'of all the methods [of notes] and common-place books... there is not one of value; as savouring of the school rather than the world...'

[2] Dio Cassius, the historian.

[3] E means recently published; Du Pin did not die until 1719.

[4] Clemens, *Opera Græce et Latine quæ extant... emendationes... a Fridirico Sylburgio*, Cologne, 1688 (Library Sale Lot 385).

[5] Walton's *Biblia Sacra Polyglotta*, 1657 (Library Sale, Lot 145), bound for E but carrying no annotation (pers. comm. Robert Harding, Maggs Bros Ltd, 1996).

[6] 'Consolatory Epistles to Monsieur Du Maurier and Thuanus', 1694; and *Epistolæ ad Gallos*, 1648–50.

buisinesse was likely to be his share (since he had undertaken the Library at White-hall,[1] besides other attendances) that he should not be able to continue his Lecture very long; and therefore most earnestly conjured him to take it up, there being no man so well furnish'd for it; giving him withall a short scheme after what method he intended to have proceeded: Since this, I lately receiv'd a Letter from the Bishop of Lincoln[2] intimating as much; and that if we must lose Mr Bently, he thought none more fit to supply his roome: But this will be referred to our meeting in the Terme, before which I hope to kisse my deare friend's hands at York-Buildings: As for Manuscripts, my stock is so trifling and this whole county (as far as I can possibly learne) so thin of scholars and libraries, that I fore-see little is to be expected from hence: What I have, consisting chiefely of Italian conclaves,[3] letters, and political matters, most relating to the late times, I send you a Catalogue of if I thought them suitable to the designe of those learned Editors, which I suppose chiefly consists in antiquities, critics, and other rare and valuable pieces:

And now let me not forget to Congratulate the Health, which I hope is by this time Confirm'd to You and Yours; with my hearty prayers for the perfection and continuance of it: My Wife (who is your humble servant) is after all her Water-drinking, in perpetual apprehension of some thing which makes her very Uneasy: For the rest, I thank God I beare-up tollerably as yet, and whilst I do so, and for ever, I am,

Deare Sir,

Your most fainedly,

[J E]

My most humble service to our Doctor:[4] There be many Doctors, but they are none of them so ours:

Aboundance of thanks for the Epitaph; it containes nothing but what is realy due to that worthy Prelate:

The Specimen of Tullie is in a most excellent letter, and the Account of the Books now published and in the presse at Oxon shewes they begin to make a better choice than they have some times don:[5]

I pray when you next write to Dr Charlett,[6] acquaint him with what I say concerning MSS, and his expectation from my poore stock:

Thanks for my Virginia conveyances:[7]

---

[1] See letter of 7 July 1694 (**D22**), p.246, note 9.

[2] Thomas Tenison. The letter is not identifiable.

[3] Cardinals in assembly for papal election.

[4] Dr Gale. In the copy-letter this paragraph appears at the end.

[5] Marcus Tullius Cicero (as specified in the copy-letter). This is possibly a sight of sheets of an edition of *De Officiis*, published from the MSS of 'Tho. Cockmouth' at the Sheldonian, Oxford, 1695. It also included a list of works in print.

[6] See P's letter to Charlett on 27 October 1694 (Howarth, no. 251).

[7] Copy-letter 'Virginia Correspondents' (see p.247, note 4).

D25. SAMUEL PEPYS TO JOHN EVELYN[1]

Plans for the Hospital at Greenwich

York Buildings
7 November 1694

Dear Mr Evelyn,

If (as old as you are) you fancy your selfe at liberty to do what you will with your selfe, you mistake; for I, and many more, have too greate a stock going in your Bottome, not to insist upon your taking more care on't than to be running out of a Warm roome into a cold Wherry in November, as you did from me on Saturday last: – for 'tis to it I impute your Cold, and would be glad I could as well ease you of it; but (God be thanked) you have a good Nurse.[2]

I thank you for your kind Message yesterday,[3] and in answer am to tell you, that the purport of my Motion to you the other day was, that, at your first visite to my Lord Godolphin[4] after his Returne from Newmarket, you would take occasion of letting him know, that in case he continues his Commands on me relating to Greenewich,[5] I have obeyed him in recollecting some of my old thoughts on that matter, so as to be in a Condition of applying them as soon as I shall be Master of the Plan I am to conforme myself to in it. Which his Lordship was pleased to say I should have, and is become the more necessary from Sir Christopher Wren's having (since his Lordship's going) been with me upon the same errand from Sir Stephen Fox,[6] and I with him at Greenwich; but under a view of a design very different from what his lordship gave me, as seeming Mr Surveyor[7] to be calculated only for turning the new building there into an Infirmarie for such Seamen as shall happen to be sent Sick and Wounded into the River for Cure, during the present War.[8] Not but that I have since had another Account of it from him: But that also of an Extent as much beyond my first Notion of it as this was short of it; namely, the raising another Wing of building answerable to that already there, with a

---

[1] Source: BL Upcott Antiquaries II. Endorsed by E, 'Copy: the originall I sent my Ld: Godolphin' (see overleaf). Upcott added: 'This copy is in the hand writing of John Evelyn, W. Upcott.' The manuscript is indeed in E's hand and therefore the spelling lacks P's characteristic usages such as 'hee' and 'bee'.

[2] The date would have been 3 November 1694. The visit is not recorded in E's diary.

[3] With news of E's 'exceeding greate Cold' (diary, 11 November 1694). Unknown.

[4] Sidney Godolphin, first Baron Godolphin.

[5] For the new Hospital. On 17 February 1695 Godolphin offered E the Treasurership, which he eventually accepted (diary; but for more detail see de Beer, V, 203, n.1).

[6] See E's diary, 6 September 1680.

[7] Wren.

[8] War of the League of Augsburg, 1689–97.

Gallery between both, and an Apparatus of every sort, as well for Elegancy as Bulk, within dores, as without,[1] that may render it an *Invalides* with us for the sea, suitable in some degree to that of Paris for the land, and so much more as it is to take in a provision for the widdows, orphans, and seamen slain, as well as for the persons of such as Age, Infirmities, or Wounds, shall have rendered incapable of further services; which as it is a Designe of a much higher Rate, so will it call for thoughts of a much greater compass than what I had any occasion of exercising upon the Scheme my unhappy Master[2] had layd for a work of like kind on the same Ground; or what his Lordship had now led me to with some Rapport to that: Nor dare I Encourage my Lord to expect from me upon a project of this Magnitude, what possibly he might not think too much for me, upon a Designe more within my reach: But, be it greater or lesse, if my Lord thinks I may have any Remaines of Observation worth his calling for: The work is too near akin to me, and to the Commands I have heretofore had concerning it, to let it want any degree of furtherance I can give it; besides, what my particular regard to my Lord Godolphin doe of right require from me: Whereof you may please to assure his lordship; but, withal to remind him of what, at his first opening of this matter, I took leave of observing to him: That no Fund or Method of Settlement other than Parliamentary will (I doubt) be found of Sufficiency for this Undertaking: And that therefore as its publickness renders it worthy thereof, and the Reason of it (when rightly opened) must be allowed to challenge it: Especially from a Parliament that seems as little disposd to deny, as any I ever sat in,[3] was to graunt ought that came handed to it from the Court: this very Session should not, me thinks, be let pass unapplyed towards it.

Forgive me this trouble, as on an errand you first brought me, and are (I am sure) a friend to, and remember that I am, most affectionately,

Your faithful and most obedient servant,

Sam Pepys

Copy of Mr Pepys to me
Concerning an Infirmary for Seamen etc
to be built etc at Greenewich
7:9br 94

---

[1] The Hospital at Greenwich, afterwards the Royal Naval College, is a complex structure. Its initial design was dictated by the King Charles Block (by John Webb, completed 1669). Wren's scheme utilised this block as one of two facing wings joined by a third block containing a central dome and entrance, similar to Blenheim Palace (Summerson 1991, 231, fig. 200). This scheme, dated 1695, is what P is describing. However, the presence of the older Queen's House beyond, and a desire to keep it visible from the river led to a revision, as executed, where the two wings were physically separate, incorporating two opposing domed halls (ibid, 273, fig. 235).
[2] The deposed James II.
[3] P was elected MP for Castle Rising in 1673, and for Harwich in 1679, and 1685.

D26. JOHN EVELYN TO SAMUEL PEPYS[1]

Manuscripts at Oxford

For Samuell Pepys Esqr

Dover Street
18 November 1694[2]

Sir,

It was, I assure you, upon a Letter of yours[3] sent me the last summer to Wotton, and another a little after, with the reiterated desires of Mr Gibbins;[4] that I was prevail'd with to Transcribe, and leave this Catalogue with him:[5] But by no meanes thinking it fit to take up any place among the Titles of MSS, which could be of any Use to the Designe of the University; and therefore intreated him to consider well of it, before he sent it to Oxford: And now I am heartily sorry to find it there, whilst I see none of Mr Pepys's, so much more worthy to be publish'd for the very greate Variety of the Choycest subjects, no where else to be found in England: If you persist to deney the Doctor's request (as it seemes til now, unknown to me, you have don) I shall almost beleeve you do it to Expose Me, with the Rest who are brought upon the Stage: Of this therefore Acquit your-selfe as you can; to be sure, I shall tell your story to Dr Charlett; unless you do justice to your Friends and to the Publique:

In the meane time, I returne you the Proofe you sent me, and should be glad it were Dissolv'd, rather than wrought-off,[6] unlesse I were assur'd of your Companie: But perhaps you are Asham'd of it; and indeede you have Reason, *Comparatis Comparandis*,[7] and in that case I have no more to say but ——
Your humble servant Sir

JE:

You dare not send this Letter to Dr Charlett, though you sent his to me.
9 a clock this night, before I came in, from visiting some of your friends and mine.[8]

---

[1] Source: PC MS.i.88. Endorsed, '18 November 1694. Mr Evelyn to Mr Pepys about Catalogues of their Manuscripts'.

[2] MS: 'Dover-streete 18th:IXbr–94.'

[3] See letter, 14 August 1694 (**D23**).

[4] Edmund Gibson, at this time librarian at Lambeth Palace (copies of letters to him from E at BL CLBII.707, 15 July 1694, and no. 721, 1 February 1695).

[5] *Catalogi librorum manuscriptorum Angliæ et Hiberniæ in unum collecti*, 1697.

[6] Printed.

[7] 'By comparing the things that need to be compared.'

[8] P wrote to Charlett on 20 November (Howarth no. 236), enclosing E's letter (evidently later returned as P requested), acknowledging his deserved chastisement.

D27. JOHN EVELYN TO SAMUEL PEPYS[1]

Evelyn stuck amongst the bumpkins

To Mr Pepys etc

Wotton
7 January 1695[2]

My Friend,

The desire I had that my Wife should be perfectly recover'd of her late and long Indisposition, hindred my motion from Says-Court[3] til a very fine warme day tempted us abroad; but since which here has fall'n so deepe a snow, accompanied with so severe a season of Frost and cold, that I hardly think has happend in many yeares, unlesse that when a Citty was built[4] upon the Thames, and we both rod over it in our Coaches: You will yet wonder when I tell you for truth that it has ben no Impediment from bringing to this hospitable place, neere upon 300 people of all the adjacent parishes, to devoure plum-pie, pottage, and Brawne all the Holy-days, without the least diminution of the antient and Laudable Custome of preparing and qualifying Suffrage etc for the Election of Knights of the Shire, Parliament-men and Legislaton:

Though we have very sorry Conversation among the Bumkins, we have yet Luculent Fires in most of the Roomes, which is no cold Comfort: For the rest, we live in Heathen-Darknesse, and unlesse you, the Doctor, and Mr Bently find us Missionem,[5] (Missives[6] your kind and frequent Letters, now and then, that may informe us how the learn'd and more civiliz'd world gos)[7] we shall become Barbares in a short time: The very Serapo[8] of your Saturdays Deipsonophisse,[9] would be delicious [coles?][10] to Sir

Your etc

---

[1] Source: BL CLBII.718. This letter was almost certainly never sent, probably due to appalling weather. P's letter of 15 February 1695 (**D28**) makes no reference to its contents and he implies that the two had not communicated since late 1694.

[2] MS: 'Wotton 7 Jan –95.'

[3] They went to Wotton 'for the rest of the Winter' on 29 December 1694.

[4] MS: 'bult'. For the 'Frost Fair', see E's diary for 9 and 24 February 1684.

[5] 'A release from captivity.'

[6] I.e. 'letters'.

[7] MS: the closing bracket is placed after 'civilised' which does not make sense.

[8] In this context, 'splendour'.

[9] Sic. A misspelling of 'Deipnosophisse' = 'a philosophical supper'.

[10] = Coals, i.e. ? MS scrawled and uncertain here.

D28. SAMUEL PEPYS TO JOHN EVELYN[1]

Deaths in Church and State

[London]
15 February 1695[2]

Dearest Sir,

The Sent,[3] as well as Noise, of Christmas is now over with you (I præsume) soe as a Man may treate you in the bas stile againe.

Wee have had 2 greate Vacancys fallen since wee last talked together;[4] that in the Church I am sure you and I shall thinke well fill'd;[5] while the other in the State fills it selfe.[6] *Fiat voluntas tua!*[7]

And with this Interjection, lett mee give way to an occasion that won't lett mee goe on, and I would not loose this Conveyance for the small prints that accompany this,[8] leaveing the rest to a further but speedy Day. I bid you Adieu and am as allways

Yours indefinitely
SPepys

---

[1] Source: BL Stowe 747, f.45. Endorsed by E, 'Mr Pepys: Lond: 15 Feb –94/5. Civilitie and Books lent me etc'. The letter is illustrated by Marburg (1935, facing p.60). When this letter was extracted from the Evelyn archive is unknown. Howarth published this letter (no. 238), surmising that it was probably to E but could not confirm the handwriting of the endorsement.

[2] MS: 'Febr.15th.1694/5'. No place, but probably London.

[3] I.e. 'scent'.

[4] This is a fairly clear implication that E's letter of 7 January 1695 (**D27**), surviving as a copy-letter only, was never sent (or at any rate was never received). Both 'Vacancys' preceded E's January letter. The atrocious weather which had confined E to Wotton House did not allow him to visit the nearby church until well into February (diary, 10 February 1695) so it seems likely that his letter of 7 January could not be posted.

[5] Tillotson, the archbishop of Canterbury, had died in November 1694 of what E calls a 'paralytical palsey' (diary, 22 November 1694). He was replaced on 8 December 1694 by Thomas Tenison, the former Bishop of Lincoln (de Beer, V, 198, n. 5).

[6] Mary II died on 28 December 1694 from smallpox. In being a joint monarch with her husband her death did not occasion a succession or coronation, hence P's remark.

[7] 'Thy will be done'.

[8] Referred to in E's reply, see 25 March 1695 (**D25**).

D29. JOHN EVELYN TO SAMUEL PEPYS[1]

The Archbishop of Canterbury's head

To Mr Pepys

Wotton
25 March 1695[2]

Sir,

'Tis a very pretty, as well as a very kind and wellcome Revenge, that for my not waiting on you to my Lord of Canterbery,[3] you should send his Grace to repruch and waite on me, whom in all his *pontificalibus*, I receiv'd on Saturday: as I still do a world of other things from my most obliging Benefactor: I assure you Mr White[4] has shew'd himselfe a Master, it is so very like the Original, and so tenderly ingrav'n, as he seemes to me, not onely to have express'd the Image of his Countenance, but the very *Icon Animorum* of our Bishop. And now that I am upon my Chapter of Heads;[5] I am vex'd at heart with my Negligence; that when I was lately with you, I did not beg a sight of that noble Assembly of them, which I am sure you have by the time gotten together. As to Bishops of Canterbury, the antienst[6] which I remember to have seene in stamp (that one may relie on for true resemblance) is the Effigies of Saint Thomas Becket, graven by Hollar from an Original of the Greate Earle of Arundel,[7] representing his Murder, by a sword struck into his Scull: Cranmers is Vulgar, and I believe most of the rest of the Arch Bishops and Bishops too; especialy, since the Reformation, and of late with more certainty (as to the Effigies) by the laudable Industry of Mr White, who has indeede given us the Icons of most of the famous Persons in Church and State of our Country, a Collection of which, I doubt not but you have more compleate, than any one else in England: I am for this, and infinite other Civilities

Deare Sir Your etc

---

[1] Source: BL CLBII.724.

[2] MS: possibly 'Wotton 25:Mar:90', presumably an error for '95' as the letter seems to be a reply to P's of 15 February 1695. It is also placed in the early 1695 copy sequence though, on its own, this would not be a verification.

[3] Tillotson (see **D28**) or the new incumbent, Dr Thomas Tenison (1694–1715).

[4] Robert White the engraver.

[5] 'Of *Heads* and *Effigies* in *Prints* and *Taille-douce*; their use, as they relate to *Medals*,' Chapter VIII of E's 1697 *Numismata*.

[6] I.e. 'ancientest'.

[7] Arundel was Hollar's patron (as later was E), discovering him in 1636 in Vienna and bringing him back to England (David Jaffé, 'The Earl and Countess of Arundel: Renaissance Collectors' in *Apollo*, August 1996, p.23).

D30. JOHN EVELYN TO SAMUEL PEPYS[1]

On the unhappy lot of kings

For Samuell Pepys Esqr
York-buildings

Wotton
3 December 1696[2]

I inquire not what you do, or think but how you do, because I am perswaded we think much alike; I onely wish I could do so too, for I should then be allways doing well. I am not yet altogether idle, for as often as the lame leg, which hardly carryed me out of towne into the country, gives me leave (which I thank God it begins to do), I take a walke in the gardens and a little grove I am planting; for all the world else is Deluge (no man alive remembring such a season)[3] and when I am confind, reade and scribbl, or build castles in the aer. To be serious, I have of late ben chewing-over some old-stories, and among others the Reigne of Lewes the XIth and Charles Duke of Burgundy, written you know by Philip de Comines 200 yeares since.[4] And whilst I contemplate your and my condition (*sic parvis componere*)[5] cannot but bemoane, pitty, and deplore the unhapynesse and misery of kings and princes (whilst either they are not born philosophers or philosophers kings) because they never take the Counsel of such honest, wise, and worthy persons as was the author of those *Memoires*.[6] If I were to be a prince's tutor, I would cause my royal pupil to reade Comenius[7] over once a yeare at least. Have you seen a little anonymus

---

[1] Source: Tanner 1926, no. 85 (PC MS.i.112) and BL CLBII.775. Endorsed, 'Mr Evelyn to Mr Pepys'.

[2] Date is (unusually) matched by the copy-letter ('Wotton 3d: Xbr 1696').

[3] 'So wonderfull and perpetual Rainy season without frost, but exceeding greate storms wrecking many at sea, has not ben knowne in any mans memory, so as hardly could they sow in many places' (E's diary, 15 November 1696), and 'There hapning so swiftly an exceeding firce frost after greate raines, and grew so very cold, that we had the office of the day at home' (ibid, 1 December 1696).

[4] E owned a copy of Commines' *Les memoires...* edited by Denys Godefroy, Paris, 1649 (Lot 405).

[5] *Sic parvis componere* [*magna solebam*]. Virgil, *Eclogues*, I.24. 'Thus [I used] to compare [great] with small.'

[6] E had expressed similar disdain for the lot of monarchs when he described the consequences of the Third Dutch War for an ordinary sailor who had a gangrenous leg needing amputation: 'Lord, what miseries are mortal men obnoxious to, and what confusion and mischiefe dos the avarice, anger, and ambition of Princes cause in the world, who might be happier with halfe they possesse' (diary, 24 March 1672).

[7] 'Comenius' would normally be taken to be Johan/Jan Amos Komensky, known as Comenius. This is a slip for 'Comines' which is supplied in the copy-letter.

piece intitled, *Discours sur les Reflexions ou Sentences et Maximes Morales?*[1] I am perswaded you'l not dislike it. The later part is written by a lady, another Mrs Astell;[2] you will find it thick of very noble thoughts. Amongst our owne small books but no small authors, I am well pleas'd with Nicolson's *English Historical Library*;[3] and exceedingly glad to find our learned Bishop of Worcester putting his hand so strenuously to the vindication of what has ben the faith of as wise and reasonable men as any of our bold and late blasphemous pretenders, reproching the lazinesse of the many concerned who, whilst they should defend the antient doctrine, worry and tare in pieces one another. By the way, you'l find some passages of Dr Locke civily discuss'd, and with his deserved eulogie.[4]

Were you at Gr[esham] College[5] on St Andrew's Day?[6] I have never before ben absent 'til this yeare, I thinke these five and thirty.

I feare to aske what progresse you make towards finishing your noble and most desierable work,[7] which none but you can pretend to. Will you never let us see it 'til perfect according to your scale? Remember the advise of a greate King that was such a philosopher as I spake of, *quicquid assequitur manus tua ut facias, pro facultate tua, fac.*[8] The rest is what you and I have often reflected upon. But why don't you give us a part or two, *ut ex pede Herculem?*[9] Time flies a pace, my Friend. 'Tis Evening with us; do not expect perfection on this side of life. If it be the very best, as I am sure it is, nothing can be better; no man out-throws you. And thus, partly, *demonstrativè* and partly *objurgativè*, whilst I entertaine my selfe at least with my worthy Friend, I hinder him perhaps from finishing the worke I am solicitous to se[e] published. God Almighty keepe you.[10]

> I am, Sir,
>> Your most faithfull, humble servant,
>>> JEvelyn:

---

[1] La Rochefoucald (see Tanner 1926, i, p.134, n.1).

[2] Mary Astell, a comparison with her *A Serious Proposal to Ladies*, 1694.

[3] William Nicholson/Nicolson. See the letters of 10 and 18 May 1700 (**E3** and **E4**).

[4] Dr Edward Stillingfleet, Bishop of Worcester. Locke's writings had been used by John Toland in his *Christianity not Mysterious* (1696) to contradict, with great controversy, the Trinity doctrine. Stillingfleet attacked Locke in his *Vindication of the Doctrine of the Trinity*, and they sparred in a series of pamphlets from 1696–9.

[5] MS PC: 'Gr Coll'; MS copy: 'Gressham Coll:'.

[6] The Royal Society: the date of the annual elections (30 November).

[7] The projected *History of the Navy* so frequently the subject of E's encouragement.

[8] A version (but not the Vulgate's) of *Ecclesiastes* ix.10, 'Whatsoever thy hand findeth to do, do it with thy might.'

[9] 'As Hercules by the foot'. Probably an allusion to Hercules' work in pacing out the Olympian stadium and quoted by Aulus Gellius, *Noctium Atticarum* I.1.

[10] Copy-letter ends: '...finishing the Worke I speak of'.

D31. JOHN EVELYN TO SAMUEL PEPYS[1]

The Battle of the Books, Errors in E's Numismata

For Samuell Pepys Esqr
at his house in
Yorke-buildings:
London: Wotton
                                                               3 April 1698[2]

Sir,

I have not ben so long in the Country without having often commanded my
Servant, to give me an account of your health, though I should be better
satisfied to see it confirm'd under your owne hand; together with your pardon
of my presumption, in making you so poore a present, as the Trifle I lately sent
you;[3] Not, I assure you, in the least Confidence of my meane performance; but
to shew my Respects, and rather to expose my failings, than to be wanting to
my Obligations, and Exercise your Charity and generous Nature, where my
Defects require them. In the meane time, I am, methinks, but halfe here, whilst
I am absent from Yorke-buildings, where my heart is so often:– [4]

   Be so perfectly kind, to let me understand, what you would have me Retract
in my Book; that in the Account, which will of course I heare, be publish'd in
the next Transactions, they may be reformd: I have already written to Mr
Waller (our Secretary)[5] of what through mistake and omission, I desird might

---

[1] Source: Houghton Library, Harvard University bMS Eng 9991 (119), and used by
permission. This letter is unknown prior to its appearance at Harvard. Endorsed,
'Aprl.3d. 1698. Mr Evelyn to Mr Pepys'. The MS bears a clear post-stamp impression
consisting of an outline circle 14mm in diameter, divided in half with 'AP' in the
upper part and '4' in the lower, for 'April 4th'. These are visible on some of the other
letters (see p.79, note 1) but this is the clearest example.

[2] MS: 'Wotton 3.Apr:–98'.

[3] This was undoubtedly a copy of E's *Numismata* (1697). In the diary (January 1698)
E states that he presented copies 'to divers noblemen'. See also p.237, note 3, for the
compliment E paid to P on his collecting.

[4] P's comments to Gale (overleaf, note 6) in a letter of 9 March 1699 (Pforzheimer
MS105E; see p.243, note 3, for publication details) on declining health and E's family
problems are enlightening: 'Mr Evelyn's Visits are still very kind and ever valuable.
But what with the Common Effects of Age, with the Addition of some late Domestick
Cares, and One of them now depending in Parliament upon an Unhappy
Misunderstanding between the 2 Brothers, are becoming less frequent and less lively
too, than you and I have known them.' See p.211 for the dispute.

[5] Richard Waller. Secretary of the Royal Society from 1687–1709. E calls him 'a
young modest, and most ingenious Gent:' (diary, 11 July 1683).

be rectified; but hearing since, that he is in the Country (and not knowing who supplies his absence) I feare it may come too late: The Chapter of *Taille-Douce* and *Heads*,[1] I added purely for your sake: for the rest, I am not much solicitous: Onely, let me intreate you (if Captain Hatton,[2] to whom I writ, did it not for me) to redresse the place in page 22 Line 3 — of a mixt, and Obrize sort[3] also: and Line 4 – *Constantinople*, as it certainely dos,[4] in that of Count Landus's *Valentinian*,[5] *Constantinopoli Obrizatum*: Others ——

My most humble service to all our worthy Friends, I hope the Deane of Yorke receivd my Answer to his last,[6] with the Ingagement which prevented my serving the worthy Dr in whose behalfe he wrot. I doubt not but you have seene, Mr Boyle['s] attaque[7] – and wish (with me) our concernd Friend[8] a good Deliverance:[9] I am Sir

Your most faithfull

humble and devoted Servant

JEvelyn:

---

[1] See p.258, note 5.

[2] Captain Charles Hatton.

[3] This phrase is a passage from *Numismata*.

[4] E means that in *Numismata* he had written that the letters 'Conob' on the coin in question 'some will needs have to signifie Constantinople; others, with good reason, some British Prince of ours [i.e. 'Cunob' for Cunobelinus]' (*Numismata*, 22, lines 4–6). Clearly he has decided that there is no doubt that 'Conob' represents Constantinople – the correct interpretation. E had raised the point earlier in letters to Dr Henry Godolphin on 8 February 1698 and Thomas Henshaw on 1 March 1698 respectively (see various Bray editions of the diary and correspondence).

[5] E's margin note: '*margin* in auro Numismata Valentiniani Cæsaris apud Constanzo Landum, Comitem nobillissime. Aldus Notari Expl p.Sor. Venet: CIƆ·IƆ·ICI.' This is Constanzo Landi, author of various sixteenth-century works on numismatics.

[6] Dr Thomas Gale, dean of York from 1697 until his death in 1702. Gale's letter of 19 January 1698 to E concerning his acquisition of *Numismata* is published in various Bray editions of E's diary. E's answer is not known.

[7] Charles Boyle (great nephew of Robert Boyle, and afterwards 4th Earl of Orrery), currently engaged in a literary war with Richard Bentley. The latter had exposed the Phalaris epistles, published by Boyle, as forgeries in an appendix to William Wotton's *Reflections upon Ancient and Modern Learning* (1697). Boyle responded in print in 1698 with his *Dr Bentley's Dissertation on the Epistles of Phalaris and the Fables of Aesop Examin'd*.

[8] Richard Bentley. In 1699 he published a revised version of *A Dissertation upon the Epistles of Phalaris*, which included... *an answer to the objections of the Honourable Charles Boyle*. He presented a copy to E (Library Sale Lot 127).

[9] In his letter to Gale of 9 March 1699 (see p.261, note 4) P discussed the affair. For Gale's response of 18 March see Tanner (PC MC.i.121; 1926, no. 104).

D32. JOHN EVELYN TO SAMUEL PEPYS[1]

Evelyn's family discomposed and dejected

For Samuel Pepys Esqr
at his house in
York buildings

Berkeley Street Saturday
14 January 1699[2]

Sir,

I should not know what Apology to make for having now ben so long from kissing your hands;[3] or tollerable Excuse for the Injury I have don my selfe, in the losse of a Conversation which I assure you, I Esteeme one of the greatest felicities of my whole life (and which I no where find so agreable and advantagious to me) had not some late Indispositions, and which yett (in part) continue, depriv'd me of coming to you, as this day I fully resolv'd to do, and to have brought with me my Young Man[4] to Acknowledge your favorable acceptance of his Small Essays: But we are all, (Male and Female) so discompos'd and dejected with Coughs, Defluxions, Sore-throats etc that we are fitter for Hospitals than for such Company, as ought to have nothing which may disturb it:[5] My hope is, that a few days will better fit us for that Blessing, and I am sure as I long for it, so will I take the first Opportunity of doing my

---

[1] Sources: Christie's (New York), Prescott Sale Catalogue, 6 February 1981, Lot 107 (plate), for text, and The Times of 18 February 1926 (p.15 column f; not 1927 as stated by Keynes, 1937, 274) for the address and endorsement. Endorsed, 'Janry 14th 1698/9. Mr Evelyn to Mr Pepys. A le'r of respect'. Braybrooke included it in his 1825 selection of Pepys's correspondence, stating its source to be the Pepys-Cockerell papers. It was probably removed shortly afterwards. A review of Tanner's 1926 *Private Correspondence of Samuel Pepys* in The Times of 26 January 1926 led to a series of articles by the librarian at Magdalene, O.F. Morshead. He printed various letters, including this one stated by that date to be in 'private possession'.

[2] MS: 'Berkley-streete Saturday' in E's hand and clearly all that was originally written; 'Janry 14th 1698/9' has been added below in what appears to be P's hand, and not E's, a fact which seems to have escaped the notice of Braybrooke and sale catalogue compilers. The 14th January 1699 was a Saturday so we can assume the added date is correct, and was inserted to aid P's records.

[3] He had attended the Royal Society Council Committee on 7 December preceding (diary) which is the last occasion noted on which he might have seen P.

[4] E's grandson, John, later Sir John, Evelyn.

[5] There is no record of any ill-health in E's diary.

selfe that honor:[1] In the meane time, I most heartily wish you an happy and prosperous New-Yeare; and in particular the Lady,[2] all the satisfaction of a Versailles, in the Cabinet she is adorning and worthy Mistris of, aboundantly Sufficient to gratify the Curiosity of those who having had the hapynesse to see it, think it not worth the going into France, so long as it is in more perfection at York-Streete I am Sir,

Your most humble
and most affectionate Servant
JEvelyn:

I thank you for the excellent[3] Booke you sent me to peruse,[4] There are many rare things, both in the Cutts, and discourse; but the impediment of plying the sheetes, so as to reade it as I desird, I shall beg the favour of another sight when 'tis bound up:[5]

---

[1] No visit is recorded.

[2] Mrs Skinner.

[3] MS: 'ex''.

[4] What this was is uncertain but P also sent Gale a book around this time. Gale wrote to P on 18 March 1699 to thank P for 'Dr Bentlye's booke' (Tanner 1926, no. 104; he suggests it was Bentley's *Discourse on the Letters of Phalaris*, see above p.262, notes 7 and 8). E certainly obtained his own copy eventually (Library Sale, Lot 127). In the same letter Gale also expressed his sorrow at any 'crosses' which had affected E, clearly an allusion to the dispute with his brother George (see p.211).

[5] The book had obviously been sent to E while still in uncut sheet form.

5 The 1700s

The quantity of surviving correspondence from 1700–3 is relatively substantial. This must be due partly to chance. Of 530 documents in the Pepys-Cockerell papers Tanner (1926, vol.i, p.vii) noted that 221 alone belong to 1700. Several letters, published by Braybrooke and Smith and now in private ownership, also came from this source. This is in contrast to the preceding four years. Conversely, there are no letters between the two at all for 1702.

Evelyn's prime interests were the maintenance of the Wotton estate, and his grandson's marriage and employment. So concerned was he for his grandson's security that he did not allow him to embark on a grand tour in spite of Pepys's urging that the advantages outweighed the risks.

Pepys was now more or less permanently lodged with his former clerk Will Hewer in Clapham. Evelyn visited him there in September 1700, finding a virtuoso living a life of dignified retirement. Evelyn himself continued to commute between London and Wotton as he could, but personal contact seems to have remained at best occasional.

It is evident that both men took an active interest in new books and in public events, at least when their circumstances or health allowed them. In August 1700 Pepys complained to Evelyn about the restrictions of his doctor's orders. Nonetheless, the appearance of the first parts of Clarendon's great *History of the Rebellion* was treated by both as an event of some moment. Pepys concentrated his efforts on refining his book and print collection, in particular sorting and binding the acquisitions John Jackson had been commissioned to make for him in Europe. By 1703 Jackson had been named as Pepys's heir, in favour of his elder brother Samuel who had made what his uncle considered to be an injudicious marriage. Pepys also remained loyal to his interests in Christ's Hospital, his library, and the rest of his family.

Ill-health became more significant as death approached. The merits of barley-water and 'nephretic powder' treatments were discussed. Their friends and contemporaries were steadily dying off and this compounded a natural preoccupation with settling affairs, and their own deaths. Neither expresses a sense of wasted opportunities and they combined this acceptance of the future with an invigorating sense of optimism. Evelyn remained professionally involved with the financial administration of Greenwich Hospital, prepared a fourth edition of *Sylva*, and a second edition of his translation of the *Parallel of Architecture* (published posthumously in 1706 and 1707 respectively). Pepys continued to organise his library, and left John Jackson with instructions for its completion and transference to Magdalene in perpetuity.

E1. JOHN EVELYN TO SAMUEL PEPYS[1]

Dogs in power

Dover Street,
1 January 1700[2]

Sir,

Remembring how my Credit lies at Stake to you and Dr Smith,[3] for the story of the Dog made Vice-roy of Norway. In reproch of that surly, and Currish nation: Saxo-Grammaticus in his History of that People,[4] is my Author: Nay, and tells us, he had a Court and Palace assign'd him at Nidrosia (now Drontheim);[5] wore a Chaine of Gold, and was carried (like the Pope himselfe) on Mens shoulders, when he went abroad:

Reflecting on the procession of the French King, which you shew'd us (so elegantly Ingrav'n by Miriam,) with two Dogs on each side of him (to say no more of our Charles IIs, which allways went before him) Masinissa King of Numidia, had constantly such a Guard; and so had the cruel Emperor Andronicus, and trusted more in them, than his Mercenarys as Nicetas relates: But Valentinianus was squir'd with Beares, which he afterwards honorably dismiss'd for their faithfull service: And now after all, why pray might not a King of Denmark as well make his Dog Vice-roy of Norway, as Caligula one of his Horses, a Consul of Rome, choosing him also into the Sacerdotal Order!

The Story of making an Asse a Doctor of Padoa, by the name of Dr Martin, was a wagish trick the Grizon students put upon the Rector, then you have in the Author of the journey to Naples: and since you are so much for Authors, see for this, and for the rest Dion Cassius: Arriani Κυνηγετικοῦ publish'd by Lucas Holstenius,[6] and more that I could name, where[7] it diversion so becomeing a New Yeares Gift as my Wishing Mr Pepys this an hapy-one, and many more, with the same to Mrs Skinner from our fire-side.

Sic Nuga[e?] feria[e?] ducunt[8]

JE

---

[1] Source: BL.1626 (draft). Endorsed by E, 'Copy to Mr Pepys'. The MS sent (not available) endorsed by P, 'Jan.1.1699/700. Mr Evelin to SP about a Dog of Denmark made Vice-Roy of Norway etc', was Houghton Sale Lot 204, Christie's 13 June 1979.

[2] MS: 'Dover-streete 1:Jan:–99/700'.

[3] Dr Thomas Smith.

[4] Saxonis Grammatici, *Danorum Historiæ*, various editions, for example Basle, 1534.

[5] MS: '(now Drontheim)' deleted. Drontheim is identifiable as Trondheim, Norway.

[6] Αρριανι Κυνηγετικος *Arriani de venatione L. Holstenius interprete*, 1644.

[7] Sic, for 'were'?

[8] 'Thus festive nonsense marches forth[?].'

E2. SAMUEL PEPYS TO JOHN EVELYN[1]

Thanks for a New Year's letter

[no place]
2 January 1700[2]

Dear Sir,

Your New-Year's guift is, of all, I have ever been favour'd with, the most acceptable; with this only abatement, that your knowledge is too extensive for mee to pretend to the answering you in kinde, and therefore must content my selfe with the doeing it in wishes, as I accordingly most faithfully do, that happiness of years may yet rest long upon you and my excellent Lady, and find no end in your illustrious family.

I thanke you againe and againe for the Letter you designed mee for my yesterday's entertainment and which I shall make a standing dish of, upon every Gawdy[3] Day, for a great while; remaining, most truly,

Your obedient and most affectionate servant,

SPepys

Mrs Skinner prays for you just in the terms I do.

I want your refreshing mee in the name of the author, (Morisson[4] I thinke, or something like it) of more than one Volume in folio, upon a subject I lately wished I knew where to reade something upon.[5]

---

[1] Source: Huntington Library, HM52160 (with: Maggs Catalogue 1920, no. 388, Item 676; and, Howarth no. 271, using Smith 1841). Endorsed by E, 'Mr Pepys 2:Jan—— 700/99'. Acquired by the Huntington in 1972 but not recognised until now as the Smith/Maggs MS (or even that it was to E). I am grateful to Mary L. Robertson of the Huntington for supplying revised readings as the MS was not easily available for reproduction. Howarth surmised this was a reply to E (1932, p.294) but was unaware of the existence of E's letter of 1 January 1700 (**E1**, above, p.266) to which P refers. This is the first time the two have been associated.

[2] MS: 'January 2 1699/700'.

[3] Sic, for 'gaudy', an occasion for feasting or entertainment.

[4] Not 'Mousson' (as Smith supplied). Perhaps Robert Morison's *Plantarum Umbelliferarum Distributio Nova* (1672) and *Plantarum Historiæ Universalis Oxoniensis* (1680) which E had bound in a single volume (Library Sale Lot 1048).

[5] On 8 January 1700 P wrote to his nephew, then on his European tour, telling him that the 'learnedst' of their circle, including E, would be attending on the 9th to hear Jackson's latest account of his adventures (Tanner, 1926, i, 268). E, however, has no diary entry for the day so if he attended, with the book requested, is unknown.

E3. JOHN EVELYN TO SAMUEL PEPYS[1]

Nicholson's request

For Samuell Pepys Esqr at Mr Hewers
house at Clappham
Surry:

Dover Street
10 May 1700[2]

Sir,

I do most heartily Congratulate the Improvement of your health, since your change of aire;[3] which acceptable Newes your Servant brought us this morning, and Returnes to you with our prayers and Wishes for the hapy progresse and full Restitution of it. — In the meane time, I take this Opportunity of Acquainting you, that a Worthy[4] Correspondent of mine (I am sure, not unknowne to you, Mr Nicolson, Arch-deacon of Carlisle)[5] being it seemes, about a Work in which he has Occasion to mention some Affaires relating to the Scotts;[6] and hearing from me that you were Indisposd,[7] writs thus to me:[8]

> I am troubl'd to heare of Mr Pepys's Indisposition: I heartily wish his Recovery, and the continuance of a restored health — When I was an Attendant on Mr Secretary Williamson,[9] above 20 yeares ago, I often waited on him at his House in Westminster: But I was then (as I still am) too Inconsiderable to be remembred by him:– Besides an Account of the Author (if known) of his MS. Life of Mary Queen of Scotts:[10] I very much desire to know, whether there be any Valuable Matters

---

[1] Source: Henry W. and Albert A. Berg Collection MS, The New York Public Library, Astor, Lenox and Tilden Foundations (the former Pepys-Cockerell papers MS used by Braybrooke). The letter bears a seal and is endorsed by P, 'May.10.1700. Mr Evelin to SP. a Letter of Respect after my Sicknesse, with a Request of Mr Arch-Deacon Nicholson's touching the use of Some of my Scotch Manuscrypts.'

[2] MS: 'Dover-Street 10:May—700.'

[3] P's health had been a source of concern: 'Mr Pepys is still Indisposd, though, I hope in no danger, yet keeps his bed'. E to his grandson, 21 March 1700 (BL.1652).

[4] 'Learned' here instead of 'Worthy' in the draft at BL.1658.

[5] William Nicolson/Nicholson.

[6] Nicolson's *English Historical Library* had appeared in 1696, a section covering Scotland followed in 1702.

[7] After 'hearing' the draft runs to this point 'you were not yet recovered'.

[8] This letter of Nicolson's was dated 25 March 1700 and is included in Bray editions of Evelyn's diary with correspondence, though Bray erroneously dated it to 1701.

[9] Sir Joseph Williamson.

[10] In 1681 (letter, 6 December 1681, **C10**), E lent P papers formerly in the possession

relating to the History of Scotland amongst Sir Richard Maitland's Collections of Scotish Pöems?[1] I Observe, that in the same Volume with Balfour's[2] *Practiques* (or *Reports*, as we call 'em) he has a Manuscript of the old Sea-Laws of Scotland? I would beg to be Inform'd, whether this last Treatise be the same with the *Leges Portuum*, which (tho' quoted by Sir John Skene, under that Latine Title)[3] is written in the Scotish Language, and is onely a List of the Customes of Goods Imported and Exported? If I may, (through your kind Intercession) have the favour of Transcribing any thing to my purpose, out of his Library; I have a young Kindsman (a Clarke to Mr Musgrave[4] of the Tower) who will waite on him to that purpose:

This Sir, is Mr Arch Deacon's Request,[5] and which indeede I should have communicated to you, when I was lately to kisse your hands:[6] But so was I transported with seeing you in so hopefull and faire a way of Recovery, as it quite put this, and all other things else out of my Thoughts.

I am now (God willing) about the middle of next Weeke, for a Summers Residence at Wotton;[7] where I have enough to do with a decay'd, and ruinous dwelling:[8] But where yet my Friends (or at least their Letters) will find me: And if I suspend my Answer to Mr Nicolson, 'til you are at perfect Leasure to Inable me what to write (without giving you the least disturbance) I am sure he will be highly satisfyed.

As I begun, so let me Conclude with the most hearty prayers for your Health and hapynesse, of Sir,

Your most faithfull
humble Servant
JEvelyn:

My wife presents her most humble service to you, and we both kisse Mrs Skinners hands:[9]

---

of Robert Dudley, first Earl of Leicester, which included letters from Mary.

[1] Sir Richard Maitland of Lethington.

[2] Sir James Balfour.

[3] *Regium Majestatem.*

[4] Possibly George Musgrave, at one time keeper of the ordnance at Chatham.

[5] Nicolson wrote to P (14 June 1700) with these queries (Tanner 1926, no. 238). He repeats them but addresses them to P in person, acknowledging E's role. The various documents were duly forwarded with receipts noted on Nicolson's 14 June letter, dated December 1700, and January 1701 (Tanner 1926, ii, p.363).

[6] The occasion is not recorded.

[7] 'I went from Dover Streete to Wotton for the rest of summer, whither I removed the rest of the goods from Says Court, to the House at Wotton' (24 May 1700).

[8] Repair work at Wotton was underway by 1702: 'My Wife going to Wotton for a few days, to see what the Workemen had don in repairing the house not yet finish'd' (diary, 26 April 1702).

[9] The last sentence of the letter and this postscriptum are absent from Braybrooke's version of the text.

E4. JOHN EVELYN TO SAMUEL PEPYS[1]

More on Nicholson, and building at Wotton

Dover-Streete
18 May 1700

What in the world could have come more acceptably and wellcome to me than the faire progresse of your health, confirmed under your owne hand! The continuance whereof, as I shall daily pray-for, so will it infinitly contribute to the satisfaction of my mind, and consequently to my body's health, whilst we are absent; such influence has the sense of a constant and generous friendship upon one who loves and honors you.

I shall have highly gratified the learned Arch-Deacon by inclosing your owne obliging letter in myne to him.[2] In the mean while, as to your inquiry whether he be like to come to towne this summer, I can onely tell you what he is about that may probably require it. 'Tis now above three moneths since he wrote thus to me:–

> I have had very pressing invitations from severall learnd men of Scotland to draw up another Historical Library for them, in somewhat of the same form with that of the English one; and the plentefull assistances which they have already given and promised have forced me into the attempt. I have made some considerable advances in it, and I hope (if God conserves my health) to finish and publish it the next summer. I designe it in one intire folio-volume, which (I guesse) will be about the bignesse of your *Numismata*. There are many pieces in our English Libraries that I must enquire after, etc.

It is from this passage one may conjecture he may looke this way. In all events he is well worthy your esteeme and the civilitys you expresse.

Vetruvius has said nothing of repairs, nor hardly remember I of any who repented not of an expense commonly greater than new-building, but at Wotton necessity compells me for the present, whilst I please my selfe with a *Castle in the Aire* which I have built in paper. I am sure I shall have enough to do this summer to settle our leale[3] œconomy there in any tollerable sort, as you will find if the sweete breath of our Surry downes tempt you to descend so low as your most faithfull, humble servants.

JEvelyn

My wife's to you, and both our most humble services to Mrs Skinner, Mr Hewers, wishing the circumstances of our migration hence alowed us the honour of comeing to kisse your handes at Clapham.

---

[1] Source: Tanner 1926, no. 219 (PC MS.ii.127). Endorsed, '[Mr Evelyn to Mr Pepys.] A letter of respect, and touching the worke the Archdeacon of Carlile is now upon, relateing to Scotland'.

[2] William Nicholson. See previous letter. P's 'obliging letter' is not known.

[3] Exact, or honest.

E5. JOHN EVELYN TO SAMUEL PEPYS[1]

Evelyn is a patriarch of old

Wotton
22 July 1700

I could no longer suffer this old servant of mine[2] to passe and re-passe so neere Clapham without a particular account of your health, and all your happy family. You will now inquire what I do here? Why! as the Patriarches of old, I passe the day in the fields, among the horses and oxen, sheep and cowes, bulls and sows, *et cætera pecora campi.*[3] We have, I thanke God, finished our hay-harvest prosperously. I am sewing[4] of ponds, lo[o]king after my hinds, providing carriage and tackle against reaping time and sowing. What shall I say more? *Venio ad voluptates agricolarum,*[5] which Cicero, you know, reckons amongst the most becoming diversions of Old-Age,[6] and so I endeavor to render it, though far from ever 'til now believing that this part of rustication should prove the compliment of my lemma,[7] Πάντα δοκιμάζετε.[8] But so it is, and, I thank God, in tollerable health. This without. Now within-dores. Never was any matron more buisy than my wife, disposing of our plaine country furniture for a naked old extravagant house, suitable to our imployments. She has a dairy and distaffs for *lac, linum, et lanam,*[9] and is become a very Sabine. But can you thus hold-out, will my friend say? Is Philosophy, Gresham College, and the example of Mr Pepys and agreable

---

[1] Source: Tanner 1926, no. 265 (PC MS.iii.12) and BL.1663 (draft). No reported endorsement. Addressed 'to Clapham'. The draft, dated the preceding day, bears a number of corrections which make the text correspond with the letter-sent. However, some minor differences remain showing that E continued to revise the text when writing the letter-sent.

[2] John Strickland. He had been left in charge of Sayes Court, which was now let to various tenants. He will have needed to travel via Clapham to see E at Wotton to discuss Sayes Court business.

[3] 'And the other flocks of the field.' Perhaps an allusion to Horace, *Odes* III.xviii.9 *pecus omne campo*. See also p.244, note 5.

[4] Draining.

[5] Cicero, *de Senectute*, xv.51. 'I am come [now] to the pleasures of farming.' E used part of Cicero's text, which follows this quotation, as a marginal note in *Sylva* (see *Writings* 1995, 192, n. 30). *De Senectute* was a text which E had used on several occasions in *Sylva*; it seems that the truth of Cicero's words was coming home to him now in his closing years in charge of the Wotton estate.

[6] Cicero, ibid, and also xvi.56–7.

[7] Subject of a piece of writing.

[8] 'You examine everything'.

[9] 'Milk, linen, and wool'.

conversation of Yorke buildings, quite forgotten and abandond? No, no. *Naturam expellas furcâ licet...*[1] Know I have ben ranging of no fewer than 30 large cases of books, destined for a competent standing library, during 5 or six days, wholy destitute of my young coadjutor;[2] who upon some pretence of being much ingaged in the Mathematics, and desiring he may continue his course at Oxon. 'til the beginning of August, I have wholy left it to him.

You will now suspect something by this dissordered character; and truely I was too hapy in these little domestic affairs when on the sudden, as I was about my books in the Library, I found my-selfe sorely attackt with a shivering, followed by a feavorish disposition, which forced me to lay-aside all other thoughts. But that which accompanyd it with most trouble and paine was a strangury which often hindred the passage of my water. Indeede, I have for these many yeares past usd to neglect making water, sometime[s] for a whole day together, not til now finding the ill consequence of it by weakning those spincters destined to retaine it any longer. I relate my present and naked case to you, who I am perswaded may have by you some excellent remedy; having hitherto consulted no other doctors than now and then a clyster,[3] an ounce of manna,[4] which greately relieves me, so as from having kept not my chamber onely but my bed 'til very lately, and with just so much strength as to scrible these lines to you. For the rest, I give God thankes for this gracious warning, my greate age calling upon me *sarcinam componere*,[5] every day expecting, who have still injoyed a wonderfull course of bodily-health for neere 40 yeares.

And now to give you some further account of your favorit, I will make you part of what he wrot to me from Oxon, though it come somewhat late as to what he acquaints me of the most unhapy catastrophy of that excellent poet and philosopher, Mr Creech.[6]

---

[1] A paraphrase of Horace, *Epist.* 1.x.23, *Naturam expelles furca, tamen usque recurret*, 'If you cast out nature with a pitchfork, she will soon return.'

[2] E's grandson.

[3] Injection.

[4] Laxative made of bark juice from the Manna Ash (from southern Italy). Constipation had become an occupational hazard of E's old age; he noted for early May 1702 that 'not having the benefit of natural evacuation for severall days, I was very ill, and feavorish, but by Gods mercy relieved, I began to be more at Ease' (diary).

[5] 'To settle my bag of woes.' E is more expansive in the diary, 'I was now visited with an attaque of a Feaver, accompanyed with the strangury [painful urination], which detain'd me in bed and house neere a moneth and much weakned me; But it pleased God, as to mittigate and allay my feavor, so to abate of my other Infirmity also; for which forever be praise ascribed to him by me, and that thereby he has againe so gratiously advertiz'd me of my duty, to prepare for my latter end which now cannot be far off, at this greate Age of mine' (7 July 1700).

[6] Thomas Creech.

June 17, in answer to a letter of mine:

Quod de Comitiis Oxon. in penultimâ scribis epistolâ, dubiam, ante opinionem negativa Convocationis suffragia jam confirmarunt. Captain Gifford non, ut promiserat, ad me ridendum divertit. Inexpectatum prorsus, et triste quiddam nuper hic evenit. Clarissimus ille Creech, Coll[egii] Omn[ium] Animar[um] socius, sibi ipse mortem conscivit. Cum enim paucis abfuisset diebus, suspensus tandum repertus est, quibus autem de causis hoc in se commisit nondum liquet. Jam ut de studiis academicis aliquid dicam: Varenii Geographiam Universalem, eo sub nomine physicæ considerationis multa complectentem, Tutor legit; et quotidie in quæstiones physicas disputamus. In Mathem[aticis], Geometriam practicam percurri, quid eo diutius detinuit quod undecimum et duodecimum Euclidis Librum non prius dedideram. Optica proximè discenda venit, et reliqua ad visionem pertinentia. Mathematicum nuper certamen erat in nostro Coll[egio], Doctore Gregory Professore judice, et viginti solidis sex præsta[n]tissimis præmio proposito, unum mihi adjudicatum est, quod in librum mathemat[icum] pro Bibliotheca donandum impendere statui, ne præmii magis gratiâ quam ut progressum ostenderem certasse videar. Vale![1]

And with much ado I have held out thus far. Your prayers I neede not beg, you are so charitable. But mine, my wife's, and all our most humble services to you, Mrs Skinner, Mr Ewers, I beseech you to present, and beare with the blotts and impertinences of this from,

> Dear Sir,
> Your most faithfully devoted servant,
> JEvelyn

---

[1] 'That decision, formerly in doubt, of the Oxford Council you wrote about in your last letter but one, has now been confirmed by Convocation's vote against. Captain Gifford has not been diverting me with merriment as he promised. Something tragic, and totally unexpected, has recently happened here. That illustrious Creech, associate of the college of all intellects, has committed suicide. After he had been missing for a few days, he was found hanging, but for what reason of his own he took this course is not yet clear. Now I will tell you something about my studies: the tutor chooses the Universal Geography of [Bernhard] Varenius with a view to embracing everything under the name of natural philosophy considerations; and we are debating daily natural philosophical questions. In Mathematics, I look through practical Geometry, which detains [me] for a long time because I hadn't already prepared books eleven and twelve of Euclid. Optical refractions come next, and the remaining parts relevant to vision. There was a Mathematical contest recently in our college, judged by Doctor Professor Gregory, with a proposed prize for complete pre-eminence of twenty six pounds. First prize will be awarded to me, which I have decided to spend on a gift of a mathematics book for the Library, so that I might not be seen to have competed [just] for the prize, [by] how much I demonstrated the achievement with thanks' (trans. R.C.A. Carey, and the editor).

E6. SAMUEL PEPYS TO JOHN EVELYN[1]

The properties of barley water

Clapham
7 August 1700

I have no herds to mind, nor will my Doctor[2] allow me any books here. 'What then,' will you say too, 'are you a doing?' Why truely, nothing that will bear nameing, and yet am not (I think) idle; for who can, that has so much (of past and to come) to think on as I have? And thinking, I take it, is working; though many formes beneath what my Lady and you are a doing. But pray remember what a clock it is with you and me; and be not now (by over-stirring) too bold with your strangury any more than I dare be with my stone; which too has been no less kind to me, in giving me my warning, than the other to you, and to neither of us, I hope, and through God's mercy dare say, either unlooked-for or unwelcom.

I wish, nevertheless, with the same sincerity I do it for my self, that I were able to administer any thing towards the lengthening that precious rest of life which God has thus long blessed you (and you, mankind) with. But I have been alwayes too regardfull of my own health to be a prescriber to others. This onely I must not omit, with thanks to God Almighty, to tell you; that I am at this day, and have been now longer together, under more ease in all things relateing to the passing and passages of my urine than I can remember my self to have been since the first of my being able to remember my self at all; and ow[e] it onely to the leaving off malt-drink and betakeing my self wholly to barley-water, blanched with a few almonds and sweetened with a little sugar.

How farr this may sort with your case I dare not determine, but this is what Dr Ratcliff[3] has most happily led me to; and if my Lady shall think it may be of any use to you, pray let me be told it, and I shall send her the method of its dressing with a little more exactness.

I cannot give my self the scope I otherwise should of talking to you now at this distance, from some care extraordinary I am at present under from poor Mrs Skinner's being suddenly fallen very ill here. But I trust it will not be long 'ere I am in a condition of makeing it up to you, when I may possibly venture at entertaining you with something from my young-man[4] in exchange (I don't

---

[1] Source: BL Upcott Antiquaries II. Dictated to a clerk with only the postscriptum in P's hand. No endorsement. Braybrooke and Tanner used the copy (PC MS.iii.28).
[2] See note 3 below.
[3] Dr John Radcliffe.
[4] His nephew, and eventual heir, John Jackson.

say in payment) for the pleasure you gratify me with from yours. Whom I pray God to bless with continuing him[1] but what he is, and I'll ask no more for him. And let this, with a double measure of my own respect (in the absence of Mrs Skinner's) to my most honoured Lady and your self suffice for this time from,

   Dearest Sir,
 Your ever most obedient and affectionate servant,
         S Pepys

My Eyes force mee to use another's Hand to you which pray forgive.[2]

---

[1] E's grandson.

[2] This line only in P's hand, absent from the PC MS copy/draft. P had spent much of his adult life fearing for his eyesight. This is discussed in detail in Latham and Matthews (X, 174–5), but briefly: after close work, typically reading and writing, P experienced watering of the eyes and pain leading him to assume he was going blind. For this reason above all he abandoned his diary in 1669. The medical advice which he received was, not unusually for the period, useless. It is now believed that he suffered from long-sight and a mild astigmatism. While this occasionally caused him discomfort he was certainly not going blind. As has been observed by Latham, his later handwriting, such as in the letters transcribed for this book, exhibits little difference from that of his earlier manuscripts.

E7. JOHN EVELYN TO SAMUEL PEPYS[1]

Death approaches

Wotton
9 August 1700

The confirmation of your health under your owne hand,[2] and that I still live in your esteeme, revives me. There could nothing come more wellcome to me. It brings me the tenderest instances of your friendship and, what I shall ever value, your counsel. Indeede, I am not a little sensible that more thought and lesse motion or stirring than usualy, had ben safer for me since I came hither; and though at present the indisposition I laboured under be much abated, yet the apprehension of its returne makes me take-hold of your kindnesse in offering me the receit of the barly water which you mention, and the method of preparing it. In the meane time, be assured I am not without those serious reflections you so Christianly suggest. The scantinesse, mutabillity, and little satisfaction of the things of this world, after all our reserches[3] in quest of something we think worth the paines, but are indeede the images onely of what we pursue, warne me (so much neerer my period as my sand[4] runs lower than yours)[5] that there is another and a better state of things which concerne us, and for which I pray Almighty God to prepare us both. Epictetus has an excellent and useful alusion to this readynesse.[6] When the master of the vessel (says he) calls on board the passengers he set on shore to refresh a little, etc, they should continualy be mindfull of the ship and of the master's summons, and leave their trifling and gathering cockleshells, nay all impertinences whatsoever, mind the signal, and run to the ship. The warning is in generall, ἐάν δέ γηράνῆς;[7] but if thou be a man in yeares, stray not too far, least thou be left

---

[1] Source: Tanner 1926, no. 279 (PC MS.iii.29). No endorsement. Addressed 'to Clapham'. The draft (at BL.1664) is endorsed, 'Copy to Mr Pepys. Wotton 9:Aug:1700', and bears a large number of amendments which correspond with the letter-sent indicating that it was a draft, rather than a true copy. However, not all the differences with the letter-sent are marked on the draft, showing that E continued to make alterations when he wrote out the letter to be sent.

[2] A strange comment as P's letter of 7 August (**E7**) was written by someone else for P, owing to his fears for his eyesight (see p.275, note 2). It is clear from the reference to the barley-water treatment that this is a reply to the letter of 7 August, so the possibility that E is referring to an unknown letter may be discounted.

[3] Draft gives 'recherces' (for recherches, an obsolete form of 'research') here.

[4] Draft: E has placed 'Glasse' here above 'Sand' to give himself a choice.

[5] E, now nearly 80, was about 12 years and 4 months older than P.

[6] E's note: '*Enchirid., Cap* XV.'

[7] 'If you should grow old.'

behind and lose thy passage. This alarme, Friend, is frequently in my thoughts, intent upon finishing of a thousand impertinencys which I fancy would render my habitation, my library, garden, collections, and the worke I am about, compleate and easy. *At si Gubernator vocavit ad navem,*[1] we must leave them all. Thus the philosopher. But we have better advice from the Divine Oracles themselves to be upon our watch and within call. Such was that which allwayes sounded, you know, in St Hierom's eares, *Surgite Mortui et venite ad Judicium,*[2] and this gives checque and allay to all the imaginary satisfactions we think to find in the things of this life. Let you and I therefore settle our necessary affaires, and pray we may not be surprizd. An easy, comfortable passage is that which remaines for us to beg of God, and for the rest to sit loose to things below. I have (I thank God) made my Will since I came hither,[3] and looke upon all other accessions with much indiference; and though I waite now and then upon an innocent diversion, and am not idle as to other improvements, *Inutilis olim ne videar vixisse.*[4] Let us both be ready to leave them when the Master calls. And with this meditation (by you so seasonably inculcated to your old friend) I returne the most humble thanks of,

Sir, Your most obliged, faithfull friend and servant,
JEvelyn:

I daresay we both very heartily condole the losse of my Lady Clarendon.[5] But the newes of the Duke of Gloucester's death is surprizing.[6] Where shall we once settle? This is indeed a subject of high speculation. My wife, who most humbly gives her service to Mrs Skinner, is extreamly sorry for her indisposition, of which yet you give us hopes of amendment. We both kisse her hands and yours.

---

[1] 'But if the helmsman has summoned [us] to the ship.'
[2] 'Rise up, ye dead, and come to judgement.'
[3] I.e. since he came to Wotton in 1694. He later revised it, for example in a will dated 25 February 1705 (quoted in H. Evelyn, *The History of the Evelyn Family*, 1915, pp.86–8).
[4] 'Lest one day I might appear to have lived unprofitably.'
[5] Flower Hyde, countess of Clarendon, wife of Henry Hyde, second Earl of Clarendon. She died on 17 July 1700. E had last dined with her on 6 March (diary).
[6] William, Duke of Gloucester, the only surviving child of Princess Anne, died of smallpox on 29 July. As a result the Hanoverian succession to the throne was confirmed in the Act of Settlement on 12 June 1701, in anticipation of the extinction of the Protestant line of descent from Charles I. See E's diary for July 1700, *passim*.

E8. SAMUEL PEPYS TO JOHN EVELYN[1]

LOST   19 August 1700

The Sotheby's Catalogue for 6 May 1919, Lot 3045 (3 letters, including one to Evelyn), reads as follows:

3045   PEPYS (Samuel) L. s. with initials, 1¼ pp. folio, *June 24th*, 1700, to Lord Clarendon, interesting letter, referring to the gift of second sight claimed by Scottish Highlanders; L. s. with initials, 1¼ pp. folio, *August 19th*, 1700, to John Evelyn; and A. L. s. 1 p. 4to, of Thomas Pepys to Lord Montague   (3)

This small group, sold to 'Suckling and Co' for £7 10s, has proved elusive. The letter of Thomas Pepys is included in the *Catalogue of the Collection of Autograph Letters and Historical Documents formed between 1865–82 by Alfred Morrison* (A.W. Thibaudeau, 1891), at Volume V, p.125. Neither of the others features in the Morrison Catalogue. However, the letter to Clarendon is referred to in Clarendon's letter to Pepys of 1 July 1700 (PC MS.iii.1; Tanner 1926, no. 252) which opens with 'Yours of the 24th past was doubly wellcome in bringing me the good news of the improvement of your health...'.

Unfortunately, no reference to the manuscript of the letter to Evelyn could be located in any other source prior to the Sotheby's Catalogue of 1919, or since. Its present whereabouts are unknown. The price for the Lot suggests the letters were not of great importance or interest, a probability emphasised by the fact that it was not acquired by Carl Pforzheimer; however, he purchased almost all the other Pepys and Evelyn lots in this sale.

Evelyn's letter of 25 August 1700 (**E9**) appears to be a reply to an otherwise unknown letter from Pepys received, as Evelyn describes, only the night before. The only possible candidate is this lost letter of 19 August 1700.

---

[1] Source: Sotheby's Alfred Morrison Sale Catalogue for 6 May 1919, Lot 3045.

E9. JOHN EVELYN TO SAMUEL PEPYS[1]

The wonders of a nephritic powder

Wotton
25 August 1700[2]

Your desire of having the Inclos'd return'd,[3] (and for which I cannot blame
you) must shorten something I had to offer in Excuse of my former
Impertinences (as I sometimes thought) for curiositye so much Inferior to
yours: Things, so discreetly and judiciously chosen, and as indeede it could not
be other; Mr Jackson, your accomplish'd Nephew, being the Collector of
them:[4] Had I leasure (for I receiv'd not yours 'til late the last night) I should
give you an Account of what I brought from Rome of this kind above 50
yeares past:[5] That so, if there could be any thing considerable wanting (as I
believe there's nothing) I might advertise you, whilst your Nephew is upon the
place: Had he onely furnish'd you with the stamps[6] of those excellent
Marbeax and Ribrati of the Persons mention'd in the Catalogue,[7] (which he
has inr[iched][8] with all that has past of Observable, since my peregrination),
they cannot but be worthy your Cabinet and Curiosity; And so much for that at
present:— And now (allowing all your Raillery on our Ignorance of Barly-
Water,) the hint you gave me first of an Emulsion of Almonds, before your
more perfect Receipt (for which I most humbly thank you) has not alltogether
faild of good operation —— But have you not taken any notice of an
Advertisment which you will find in yesterday's *Flying-post*,[9] describing the
Wonders of a Nephretic powder[10] lately brought into England, for its never-

---

[1] Source: PC MS.iii.39. Endorsed, 'Wotton. August 25th 1700. Mr Evelyn to Mr
Pepys'. No address leaf available, or reported by Tanner.

[2] MS: 'Wotton 25 Aug: –700:'.

[3] Presumably specified in the letter of 19 August 1700 (**E8**), and therefore unknown,
but probably prints as suggested at the end of the sentence, or E's grandson's poem.

[4] Letters from Jackson written at Venice in June had reached P by the end of the
month and he responded in a letter dated 1 July 1700 (Tanner 1926, no. 253). P was
particularly anxious that Jackson's print buying on his behalf was not going to result
in 'too many doubles'.

[5] E was in Rome from late 1644 to May 1645.

[6] Tanner supplies *stanzis* here (Italian *stanza*, for rooms, or locations of the prints).
However, 'stamps' is clear enough, probably meaning an inferior reproduction.

[7] Of his print purchases.

[8] Hole in MS.

[9] One of the newspapers founded after 1688. This publication was first issued on 7
May 1695 (see de Beer, V, 215, n. 3). E and his wife relied on them for London and
international news. Many of E's later entries in his diary were summaries of
newspaper stories (ibid, I, 90).

[10] Sic. Medicine for treating the kidneys.

failing Effects? Though I have very little faith in Emperics,[1] I am halfe perswaded to make tryal of a dose or two, and am therefore sending for some: Of this you shall have an Account, with some other Matters relating to my Condition, as a very errant farmer. A Dieu, Dear Sir

All our most humble Service, with continuance of prosperity to You, Mrs Skiner, Mr Hewers, etc

JE

My Young Scholar, buisy in his Mathematics, forgets not the greate Respects he owes you.

In Cimeliarchium D[octo]ri Pepys etc[2]

Epigram:

> *Romanas arcas nunquam vidisse doloris*
>> *Sæpe tibi causa, (ut fassus es ipse) fuit.*
> *Ne doleas, optata dies et attulit ultro,*
>> *Roma tuis oculis subjicienda venit;*
> *Utque olim Constantino sub Cæsare fertur*
>> *Mutasse Italiam sedibus illa novis: + Byzantio*
> *Sic terram petit Angliacam translata Nepotis*
>> *Egregii studio, et sedulitate tui.*
> *Ergo domi tutus maneat, quemcunque pericla*
>> *Deterrent maris, et tædia longa viæ.*
> *Londinum, atque tuas ædes modo disceat adire,*
>> *Hæ, quicquid jactat Roma superba, tenent.*[3]

Raptim.

JEvelyn.[4]

---

[1] The purveyors of treatments not founded on any scientific basis.

[2] 'In the jewel-house of Dr Pepys'. PC MS.iii.40 (attached to letter above).

[3]   'Never seen Rome', you mourn your luckless fate
>> Never – but don't despair, it's not too late;
> Your wish at last is granted: Rome lies
>> Submissive here before your very eyes.
> As Constantine, men say, in days of yore
>> Removed *Italia* to an eastern shore,
> So by his industry your nephew frames
>> now to transport her to banks of the Thames.
> Who dreads the long road's boredom or the deep's
>> commotion, let him find his way *chez Pepys*,
> For here in London safe and sound at home
>> He'll savour all the glory that was Rome. (trans. R.C.A. Carey, 1996).

[4] John Evelyn the grandson.

E10. SAMUEL PEPYS TO JOHN EVELYN[1]

On Evelyn's grandson

Clapham
19 September 1700[2]

Dear Sir,

Your Return of my Paper[3] would have been much more satisfactory to me (notwithstanding all the good Words you give it) had it come accompanyed with the List you have (I dare say) still by you of your own Marketings, when at the Place that came from;[4] for thereby I should have had the truest measure of judging what I have by learning from yours, what I want. Our Poet[5] too would have shortened[6] some of his flights, upon a subject he had so much more to say of his Own. But you have long since taught him to make all Mr Pepys's Geese Swans;[7] and let him go on in't, 'till (which will not be long first) his own Judgment will rectify him, though you won't.[8]

---

[1] Source: PC MS.iii.65. Endorsed, 'To Mr Evelin.' The MS is a draft and is in the hand of, perhaps, P's clerk Thomas Henderson (Tanner 1926, i, 382, n.2). However, the endorsement, corrections, deletions, and additions *are* in P's hand. Several letters of this exact date survive as P's retained copies only (this letter; P to Monsr Dégalénière, PC MS.iii.64; P to Charles Hatton, PC MS.iii.66; P to Thomas Smith, reference as Appendix 1.9, below, p.316, note 1), suggesting it was a day specifically set aside for correspondence. Hatton replied (Tanner 1926, ii, no. 316, PC MS.iii.69) which at least indicates that the letters were actually sent.

[2] MS: 'Clapham Septr 19th.1700.'

[3] With the previous letter, 25 August 1700.

[4] Rome.

[5] E's grandson had sent an epigram to P with E's letter of 25 August 1700 (**E9**), see previous page. He was shortly to contract smallpox (E's diary 5 November 1700) but survived.

[6] Replaces 'better known', deleted.

[7] I.e. 'geese into swans'.

[8] The last three words here replace 'if you will not', deleted. At this point the following substantial passage, constituting approximately half the letter as drafted is lightly deleted: 'In the mean time, I have nothing for want of something to requite this – his partiality to me as a Poet; I fancy I have something to do it with as a Mathematician, if the season would furnish him with a Sun-shine-day, and his Curiosity bear with the trouble of rideing over hither to see what I have been doing during my recess hither in refineing upon the common Experiment in Opticks of collecting the Rays of light in a dark Room; I having done it to a degree of pleasure and Ease in its Execution as much exceeds what I have ever seen, or is yet (I believe) to be seen, elsewhere. It will cost him (I am well aware.) the shifting of his Lodging

I give both my Lady and yourself Mrs Skinner's most humble services and acknowledgements and my own; greatly wishing for some fresh advices of your health,[1] and your proof[2] of the New-powder you speak so promisingly of.[3] I salute also most particularly your young Mathematician with the [just][4] Respect I truely bear him, and am,

Your ever faithfull and obedient servant,

[SP][5]

Pray indulge my Eyes by you excusing this in Another's hand[6]

---

for one night, but I am where you are sure he will be welcom, and not ill used. But Sun-shine be a *sine quo non* in the case as to the main end of his journey, and therefore I must recommend it to him to cast upon bringing that along with him, which (as late as it is) I shall not despair of within the time of my stay here, which probably will be all this Month; as not foreseeing my house's being in a Condition (after the Dust that has been long raised there) fit to receive me sooner.

It rests onely that I give both my Lády...' (and thereafter as per the remaining text).

[1] Instead of writing E visited P in person, recording on 23 September 1700 (diary), 'I went [to] visite Mr. Pepys at Clapham, who has there a very noble, and wonderfully well furnished house, especialy with all the Indys and Chineze Curiositys, almost any where to be mett with, the Offices and Gardens exceedingly well accomodated <for pleasure> and retirement'.

[2] 'Your proof' replaces 'the Effects of'.

[3] The 'nephretic-powder', see **E9**. As the two met shortly after this letter was sent it is unlikely that E replied on paper. In any case no such reply has survived.

[4] Deleted.

[5] No monogram visible though Tanner suggests there was when he saw it.

[6] See p.275, note 2, above in letter of 7 August 1700 (**E6**), concerning P's eyes.

E11. SAMUEL PEPYS TO JOHN EVELYN[1]

Pepys has not been out of doors

[no place]
Saturday, 7 June 1701

Dearest Sir,

In returne for the superlative Expressions of respect to mee and my (at the best) poore Conversation, when placed against yours; Lett mee, in one Word tell you, that I had but the Pleasure of that of yours, and some very few more, whome Time has now, one way or other, allmost quite separated; to make mee amends for the Benefitt I have for some time most sensibly quitted of the Ayre I am by my Physician's injunctions now hastening my returne to;[2] with some prospect of setting up my future Rest there: But 'tis in Surry, and soe not out of the reach of him (my most honored Mr Evelin) whom of all the surviveing World I Would last quitt the Neighbourhood of.

I have not yet made one stepp out of Doores since I came last thence, nor shall (I believe) now doe it before I goe thither againe, saving what I shall attempt to doe for the taking my due Leave of you, and two of my honour'd friends more, your Neighbours; and that I hope to doe in a few days. In the mean time, I am

Your most obedient and most affectionate servant,

SPepys

I am extreamly joy'd to hear of my Lady's being so well advanced in her recovery.[3]

I dare not expect to see you to-day, though the Day won't Lett me forgett to wish it.

---

[1] Source: A.W. Thibaudeau (1891), *Catalogue of the Collection of Autograph Letters and Historical Documents formed between 1865–82 by Alfred Morrison*, Volume V, p.125 – though not there recognised to be to E (and: Christie's 11 June 1980, Arthur Houghton Sale Part II, Lot 365, Sale Catalogue; Howarth no. 303, using Smith 1841). The letter was not included in the Morrison Sale of 1919 at Sotheby's.

[2] Clapham. Since December 1700 P had been back at York buildings.

[3] If this is a reference to a letter from E it is unknown. Mrs Evelyn had fallen 'into a Feaver and Pleurisy, of which she was hardly relieved to my greate sorrow' (diary, 23 April 1701). On 25 April E took Dr Hans Sloane to see her at Greenwich, staying with her until 1 May. By 11 May she was 'gathering strength apace' and on 24 May she was fit enough to act as godmother to her new grand-daughter (ibid, those dates).

E12. SAMUEL PEPYS TO JOHN EVELYN[1]

Pepys in perfect present ease

Clapham
19 November 1701[2]

Dear Sir,

as much as I am (I blesse God) in perfect præsent Ease here, as to my Health: 'tis little lesse, however, than a very Burriall to mee, as to what of all Worldly Goods I putt most Price upon, I meane, the few old and Learned friends I had flattered my selfe with the Hopes of closeing the little Residue of my life in the continu'd Enjoyment of, and at the head of them all, the most inestimable Mr Evelin. But Providence, that must not be repin'd at, has thought fitt to part us; yet not without a Reserve, I trust, of another place of meeting for us, and better, and more Lasting: for which God fitt us.

Not that I mean this for a finall God-b'-w'-you for one Way or other I hope we shall see one another before the Winter be over, and possibly a great Many other Sights that wee don't thinke of. In the time,[3] in return for your most kinde Enquiries after mee, I make this my Messenger on the same Errand after your health and my ever honour'd Lady's, which I shall never want a most particular concerne for.

'Twere endlesse to talke at this Time of Publiq matters, and not to much more purpose to thinke of them, if one could help it. But hee's a much abler Philosopher then I that can doe it under the Aspect they now seeme to bear towards both Church and State.[4]

Mrs Skinner is my Lady's most obedient Servant and yours; and my Nephew most dutifully the same; and all of us, Mr Evelin's, your grandson's and my friend, with all respect.

I am Dearest Sir,
Your most faythfull and ever most affectionate
humble servant,
SPepys

---

[1] Source: BL Upcott Antiquaries II. No endorsement.

[2] MS: 'Clapham, November 19 1701'.

[3] Perhaps 'meane' has been omitted before 'time'.

[4] Louis XIV had declared that his son was King of England, following the death of James II in September 1701 (see E's diary, 9 November 1701).

E13. JOHN EVELYN TO SAMUEL PEPYS[1]

Preparing for the inevitable

For Samuell Pepys Esqr
at Mr Hewer's house in Clapham, Surrey

Dover Street
10 December 1701

My deare, worthy, and constant Freind,

There could nothing have come to me a more gratefull present than what you lately sent me: the re-establishment of your health, and confirmation of the interest you still allow me in your friendship and kind thoughts. How accidents, and the vicissitudes of things in this life and world, puts Earth (as the Spainyard calls distance of place) betweene friends and neerest relations, and which interrupts their personal visites and conversations, no-body can be more sensible of and concerned for than myselfe; especialy since I am come to this smoaky, obstreperous Citty. In good earnest, Sir, I passe not by Yorke-Buildings without serious regret. Saturday, which was wont to be a Jubily,[2] and the most advantagious and gainefull, as well as the most diverting to me of the Weekely Circles, is from a real Sabbath and day of repose now become wholy saturnine, lugubrous, and solitary. What shall I say? There were nothing which could extenuate my losse and this dark eclipse, did not that self-love which renders us sorry for the decease and absence of those we most dearely loved (infinitely hapyer in a better world) come into and aleviate my drooping spirits; that (whilst I mourne your absence here) you are at Clapham, injoying better health, a purer aer, noble retreate, and (what's above all) are intirely your owne, and in your selfe (and with those you are worthily value for their virtue and accomplishments) in a state of blisse as greate as any person who (as you do) knows how to make a just and true estimate of things we call hapy (and to distinguish images from substances) can, I think, desire or wish for on this side Heaven. Let those who have written volumes *De Finibus*[3] define what it is they would call Hapynesse here which you are not in possession of, abating onely what's extrinsecal to a good and virtuous man; namely, those things Epictetus tells us are not in our owne power to avoyde (of which there are few concern you) and though by a philosophique, much more by Christian

---

[1] Source: Tanner 1926, no. 465 (PC MS.iv.86) and BL.1651 (draft, dated 9 December 1701; the substantial variations mainly concern the order). No endorsement reported.
[2] He means that generally, their regular Saturday meetings, amounted to one.
[3] 'On the ultimate limits of good and evil' – for example, Cicero.

fortitude, inabld to sustaine. Such I account the evil boadings which, without a miraculous and undeserved Providence, seemes to threaten a total dissolution of the Government and Constitution we are wrangling about. For as since the Incarnation, Europ has perhaps never suffered the like concussions, so never was this Nation (which is all the World to us) so atheistical, false, and un-steady; covetous, selfe intrested, impudently detracting and uncharitable; ingratefull, lewd, and luxurious; in summe, so universaly vitious, dissolute, and perverted; that I am not solicitous of being thought a visionary or enthusiast when as oft as I reflect on the prædictions of our B[lessed] Lord and his Apostles fore-tell shall be the præcursors of the last and worst of times I think are coming upon us. But which the World shall no more take notice of than of what is the farthest off their thoughts or concerns, and than the old *Rephaims*[1] and Gyants did whilst Noah was preparing the Arke, and the Universal Deluge came and swept them all away. This, worthy Friend, leads me to acknowledge your pious and seasonable Monition,[2] amidst these temporary and secular interruptions, of preparing *in occursum*[3] for that Day the vessel and the voyage which, through all these tempests and tossings here, shall (I trust) set us safe on shore in those regions of peace and love and lasting friendships, and where those whose refined and exalted nature makes capable of the sublimest mysterys, and aspire after experimental knowledge (truely so called), shall be filled; and there without danger tast of the Fruite of the Tree (which cost out unhapy parents so deare); shall meete with no prohibition of what is desierable, no serpent to deceive, none to be deceived. This is, Sir, the state of that Royal Society above, and of those who shall be the worthy members of it.

But how, deare Friend, am I fallen into a sermon instead of a letter, which should account for my having ben so long groveling in the country! Why truely, though too frequently interrupted in these contemplations, not altogether unthoughtfull of them, in the midst of those impertinencys which during this state of things we think necessary and convenient, and with such moderat circumstances as may render us innocently easy, to soften and compose those trist and meluncholy moments which the prospect and face of things present us with; referring the successe to, and casting all our other cares on, that Providence which determines all events according to His Divine Will and pleasure, who onely knows what is Best. Here then let us cast anker, and rest in attendance of more favourable gales.[4]

[*letter continues overleaf*]

---

[1] Lofty men, aboriginal inhabitants of mythical prehistoric Palestine, see *Genesis* xiv.5, II *Samuel* xxi.16.

[2] Warning.

[3] To meet.

[4] An allusion to *Acts* xxvii.29–30.

I left Wotton a few days before my wife, to avoyd the noise and contention of competitors[1] at Guilford, resigning the votes of my bumkins and dependants to their former choise, not well knowing where to mend it.

You heare my noble and boosum friend[2] has layd down his office, for which I am sorry, as I look on it an ill omen. I have as yet hardly seene any of our neighbours here, save C[aptain Hatton],[3] Lord Clarendon,[4] and Sir R[ichard?] Dutton,[5] who have prevented me.

Thus Sir, have you my history and my thoughts, but not all my wishes and my wants; namely, a participation of the cargo your accomplished nephew (Mr Jackson, to whom my *paraben*[6] and most humble service) has hapily brought home: I meane those ex[traordinary] and rare notices which, through your direction and addresses, his owne abillitys and application, must needs render his conversation infinitely agreable. This I might have hoped-for in York-buildings, and now almost envy you at Clapham, who am, Deare Sir, where-ever,

Your most faithfull, humble servant,

JEvelyn

My wife, just as I am now writing, is but come to Dover-Streete out of Surrey, and with my daughter[7] beg the acceptance of their most humble services to you and Mrs Skinner, whose hands I kisse, with my humble service to Mr Ewers.

I am to acknowledge the kind remembrance you sent me by a servant of mine lately passing by Clapham.[8]

The young scholar you so often favour and enquire after, replys thus to my last, and I give it you in his owne style:

Propter ejus quod scriberem inopiam (uti rectè conjicis), nullas ad te ineunte mense litteras dedi, etc – Ad methodum interim studiorum quod spectat, sic se habet. Dominus Keil[9] præter publicam lecturam, alternis diebus explicat Gnomonicam et Hydrostaticum, qui nuper etiam cursum Experimentalis Philosophiæ instituit, et me cum pluribus aliis ex Æde Christi auditorem habet. Hæ experientiæ multum, ut

---

[1] In the Parliamentary elections: 'very greate contention and competition about Elections, I gave my Vote and Interest to Sir R[ichard] Onslow, and Mr Weston.' (diary for December, undated, 1701).

[2] Sidney, Lord Godolphin. On 28 June 1701 he had been appointed a lord justice, a post he now resigned.

[3] Charles Hatton.

[4] Henry Hyde, presumably in residence in London for the winter too. He had lodgings in Whitehall in 1685 (diary, 29 May 1685).

[5] A Richard Dutton was a mourner at Pepys's funeral (Tanner 1926, ii, p.317).

[6] Comparable well-wishing.

[7] Susanna, Mrs William Draper.

[8] Presumably P's letter of 19 November 1701 (**E12**).

[9] John Keill, the mathematician and astronomer.

spero, confirmabunt, animoque fortius impriment, quæ de Motu et Mixta Mathemati[câ] prius didici. Horæ autem philosophiæ facem quasi præferent in veteris partibus; ultimâ Metaphysicâ scilicet versatur Tutor, quâ simul cum prædicto cursu sub ferias natalitias absolutâ, Academicam doctrinam et utilissimas Matheseos partes percurrero, nihilque discendum restabit quod alibi non melius discatur. Quo-circa, nisi aliter sentias, elapsum post mensem vasa colligere et Academiæ valedicere statuo. Vale. Oxon., 19 Novembris.[1]

You see how little ceremony we use. In the meane while, whether (having now been almost 3 yeares at Oxon.) I shall comply with his total leaving the University I am yet (though in no small neede of his assistance oftentimes, and believe him pretty well furnished, and inclyned to improve his studys where-ever he is) not absolutely determined.[2] He is now neere 20 yeares old, as I am of 80. And there are some polishings which I should rather he had learne here (and whilst I am here) than when in the country. By what I can judge, he is naturaly of a grave, serious temper, discrete without morosenesse.[3] Haveing already ben entred in the Civile Law, I intend he shall mix with it the Municipal, and acquaint him selfe well with our owne Constitution, without which I find gentlemen signify little in their country. Mr Finch[4] (my worthy neighbour, whose eldest son is a collegue of my grandson) purposes to breede him so. Your sentiments of all this will greately encourage my resolution; but I quite tire you, and writing by candle-light, afflict your eyes with a tedious scribble.

---

[1] 'Due to there being nothing about which I might write (as you correctly infer) I have given you no letters this month – all the same, because one strives after the process of learning, it follows one keeps to oneself. The master Keill, in addition to a public lecture, discourses on alternate days on measurements of time and hydrostatics. This man, who recently also instituted a course of philosophical experiments, has my ear, with many others from Christ Church. These numerous experiments, that I hope, will confirm, impress with reason and strength, which I have previously learnt of movement and mixed mathematics. However, these philosophers prefer things made as if in ancient times; evidently the Tutor is upset by ultimate metaphysics, so with an unqualified prediction that by the times of the anniversary celebrations of the course I shall have run through the academic teaching and useful mathematics. And, nothing will remain unconsidered because it is not taught better anywhere else. Therefore, unless you think otherwise, I propose to say farewell to the University and to collect my belongings in a month's time' (trans. R.C.A. Carey, and the editor).

[2] He left Oxford on 27 December 1701 (E's diary).

[3] An oblique reference to the boy's father, E's third son, who suffered from acute depression and melancholy in adulthood. He had died in 1699.

[4] Heneage Finch.

E14. SAMUEL PEPYS TO JOHN EVELYN[1]

Let your grandson travel

Clapham
24 December 1701

Dearest Sir,

Dover-Streete at the Topp and JEVELYN[2] at the Bottome had alone been a sight æquall in the pleasure of it to all I have had before me in my 2 or 3 Months by-Worke of sorting and bindeing together my Nephew's Roman Marketings: and yet I dare prædict that even you won't thinke 2 hours thrown away in over-lookeing them, whenever a kindelyer Season shall justify my inviting you to't.

What then should I have to say to the whole of that glorious Matter that was enclosed in your last? Why truly, neither more nor lesse than that it looks to mee like a seraphick *How d'you* from one allready entr'd into the Regions you talke-of in it, and who has sent mee this for a *viaticum*[3] towards my speeding thither after him: Which, as the World now is and you have soe justly described: and being bereft (as I now am) of the very uppermost of my wonted felicitys here, in your Conversation and that of a very few virtuous friends more, I should be in very good faith much rather choose to obey you in by leading, than staying to fallow you.

I am, for publick Good's sake, as truly sorry as you for your Friend's withdrawing; wishing only that I could as easily satisfy my selfe how he ever came-in as why he now goes-out.[4]

I fully agree with Mr Evelin (your excellent Grandson) in his thinkeing it no longer worth his while to stay where he is; and do the like with you too in your next thoughts concerning him; if (which I could not easily wonder at, hee being indeed a jewel) your and my Lady his Grandmother's tendernesses have determin'd against venturing him further from home. But since you aske it, I cannot but in faythfullnesse tell you that were hee mine, and (if it were possible) ten times more valuable than he is, I should not, even for his and my

---

[1] Source: BL Upcott Antiquaries II. No endorsement. The copy (Tanner 1926, no. 466, PC MS.iv.87) is endorsed 'in answer to his of the 10th ditto'. This is one of several letters also published by Braybrooke. Tanner justifiably reserved his most critical comments for Braybrooke's treatment of this text, describing it as a 'flagrant example of his editorial method'. It featured the wrong date (4 December) and various excisions and substantial recasting of passages.

[2] P has produced here a very reasonable facsimile of E's signature.

[3] Provision for a journey.

[4] Godolphin, see above p.287, note 2.

Family's sake, think the Hazard of sending him abroad (to morrow before next day, with a Passe) for 4 or 5 months, through Holland and Flanders to Paris and so home [A tour that by the Ayde of your Instructions I my selfe, when time was, and with a Wife with mee, dispatched in bare 2;[1] and to a degree of satisfaction and solid usefullnesse that has stuck by mee through the whole Cours of my Life and Businesse since][2] I say, I should not thinke it a Hazard fitt to be named with that of his being, when your and my Lady's Heads shall bee layd, and himselfe possibly engaged in Conjugal and Domestick encumbrances, tempted to doe, what the Deference which hee cannot but by this Time see payd to your selfes from all the politer World on the Account of the distinguishing Perfections eminently raised in you from your forreigne Education, in addition to your Native, must naturally, and therefore unavoydably, prompt him to; I mean, of Lookeing abroad, when (I say) his Home concernments may possibly much wors bear it.[3]

Nor have either of you (I trust) any ground to doubt a much longer continuance, through God's favour, among your Friends here than is necessary for your seeing this over, and him well returned (before Midsummer next) to prosecute (and all in very good time) the Cours you are now designeing him at the Common Law: thereby, with the Furniture you have already given him, to qualify himselfe for making another-gates[4] figures, upon the Bench, in Parliament, in the Ministry, and every other the most sublime Conversation, than any one among all that I have ever had the fortune to meet with, of those wee call *Country-Gentlemen* purely English; and this, as little as you are willing to see it in yourselves, I am sure you know to bee soe.

Nor doe I overlooke what you Note to mee of Mr Finch's thoughts herein in the Case of his Son, whom for my Lady his Mother's[5] sake, as well as his illustrious Father's,[6] I cannot but bee a most affectionate Well-Wisher to: but should rather joyne with him in them when I reflect upon my friend his Father-in-Law Sir John Bankes's unfortunate conduct upon the like

---

[1] Months, in September and October, 1669.

[2] The square brackets are P's.

[3] E's grandson was not apparently permitted by his grandparents to travel. All their sons were dead (four in childhood) and so were those of E's brothers. E's grandson was simply too important to the future of the Wotton estate to risk. He married Ann Boscawen on 18 September 1705. In the long-term E's efforts were in vain. His great-great-grandson, Sir Frederick Evelyn, died childless in 1812. The remaining descendants in the direct male line of descent, via E's grandson's younger son Charles, were of unsound mind; they inherited only the baronetcy which became extinct in 1848. In the meantime Sir Frederick's widow left the estate to descendants of E's grandfather's first marriage. Thus Wotton remains in the hands of the Evelyns but not descendants of the diarist.

[4] 'Gate' can mean a place of judicial assembly.

[5] Elizabeth Finch, Countess of Nottingham, née Banks.

[6] Sir Heneage Finch, Earl of Nottingham. He had been Lord Chancellor 1675–82.

Occasion;[1] were it not for my haveing been but too privy to the Occasions of it, and my being well assured of theyr being all abundantly provided against, in both your cases.

In a word, though it may look like a little Over-weening in mee, yet I know not how to mistrust the validity of a Doctrine that I have liv'd under more than 30 years' continued Proof of the Truth and Usefullnesse of; and that rays'd, not from borrow'd but my own immediate Notices of the different Grace as well as Reality of Performances in Persons of the highest Formes, noe lesse then greatest Eminence, in every of the stations above-mentioned; between those (I say) whose knowledge has been widen'd and refin'd by Travell and others whose Observations have been stinted to the narrow Practice of theyr own country. Nor am I without the satisfaction of being soe farr at least confirmed herein from the little Experiment I am just come from makeing upon your dutifull servant my Nephew Jackson: that though hee bee hardly yet at home after a near 2 Yeare's tour, through Flanders, France, Italy, Spaine, and Portugall, and through the Mediterranean by sea back, I shall struggle hard to give hime 2 Months' Leasure within the next summer to finish his Travaills with Holland, for the sake of the many eminent Particularitys to be mett with at this juncture: that were never to bee seene together there in any Age past, nor possible may ever againe bee in any to come: a Sight, in one Word, that, as late as it is, I should hardly thinke too late even for myselfe to covet, had I you to wayte on thither, for I am (in spite of this distance) with inseparable respect, My ever honoured Mr Evelin,

> Your most affectionately faithfull
>> and obedient servant,
>> SP

Mrs Skinner prays to bee thought noe lesse soe to my Lady; nor either my Selfe or Nephew Servants to the Young Gentlemen I have been here shooting my Bolt about; Nor Mr Hewer to you all; with wishes of a happy Christmas.

---

[1] What this means is unclear but E had been involved with the arrangements many years before when Bankes's son had travelled to France (diary, 25 August 1676).

E15. JOHN EVELYN TO SAMUEL PEPYS[1]

On an accomplished grandson, and Clarendon's History

For Samuell Pepys Esqr at
Clapham. Surry
Let this be Left at Mr Jones's house
in Villars-Streete, neere the Water-house,[2]
to be conveyd as above.

Dover Street
20 January 1703[3]

My worthy Friend,

I had not defer'd so long, either from Waiting on you, or giving you an Account of my impertinent Life, since I had last the hapynesse to kiss your hands at your Paradisian Clapham; had my owne health, and severall other uneasy Circumstances (since I came hither) permitted me to repay the many kind Friends, their Visits, for which I stand yet a Debtor:— In the first place, it did not a little grieve me; that coming so neere you, (when I past almost by your doore,)[4] it was so late; that with no small difficulty we got to Lambeth whilst it was tollerably light, and with much more; that when we came to the Water-side, neither of the Ferry-Boats were there, or could be gotten to returne, 'til it was dark, very Cold, and uncomfortable passing; Since I came to Dover-streete, I have scarsly injoyd three or fower days, without uncessant and pungent attaque, proceeding from Gravell lodged about my Kidnys,[5] disabling both my Body and Mind from some sort of Activity (till now competently enjoyd) considering my Age: I have yet at last, gaind now and then so much Relaxation, as to employ the very first opportunity, of sending you this

---

[1] Source: PC MS.iv.130. Endorsed, 'Janry 20. 1702/3. Mr Evelyn to SP.'

[2] The Water Tower by Villiers Street, on the site of the present Charing Cross Station was built in the 1690s. It stood close to York Buildings and the York Watergate. The latter is intact (see Barker and Jackson 1974, 178).

[3] MS: 'Dover-str:20 Jan:1702/3'. It is perhaps worth commenting that despite the considerable correspondence of 1700 and 1701 there is no trace of any for the year 1702, making a gap of around 13 months. E certainly implies that there had been a gap at the beginning of this, the last, letter of all. Other references, for example to the summer, indicate that there had been no letters during much of 1702. However E visited P at Clapham on 18 June 1702 (diary, exact date queried – see de Beer, V, 508, n. 3), leaving London for Wotton for the summer on 27 June.

[4] This is the 'faire journey' back to London from Wotton, stated in the diary to have taken place on Friday, 27 November 1702.

[5] MS: 'Kindys'. See particularly the diary for 10 January 1703.

Volant[1] Messenger, to let you know that in what ever place or state I am, you have a most faithfull servant:

I was continualy crazy in the Country all the late summer; yet with such Intervalls, as did not altogether interrupt my taking some satisfaction in the Improvement I had made, partly in the dwelling-house, and without doores, for Conveniences suitable to our Oeconomy, without reproch, among our Neighbours. My Tast for things superfluous, being extreamely alter'd, from what it was, every day call'd upon to be ready with my Packett, according to the Advise of Epictatus, and a Wiser Monitor, who is gon before to provide better places, and more lasting habitations: In the meane while, one of the greatest Consolations I am capable of, is the Vertuous Progresse which my Grand-son continues to make, in an assiduous cultivating the talents God has lent him: Having formerly seen his owne Country as far as Bristol, Bath, Salisbery, and the little Toure[2] about Oxford, he went this summer (with his Unkle Draper)[3] as far as to the Lands-End in Cornwall,[4] which was an Excursion of a Moneth and the next progresse, (if God continue health) is designd to be Northward as far as New Castle; in the interims perusing such Authors and Mapps, as may be assistant to the speculative part of these motions; and, to supply the present unfavourable period from travelling foraine Countrys; has learn'd the Italian toung, and intends to proceede to the Spanish etc (having already the French from a Child),[5] whilst both his Inclynations more Seriously leade him [to] History and Chronoloaelogy,[6] Mathematikes, and the study of the Civill Law, which he joynes with our Municipal Constitutions, without which, he finds a Country Gentle-man, makes but a poore figure, and very uselesse: He not onely keeps, but greately improves his Greeke, by diligently reading their Historys, and now and then among other Exercises, he turns some passages into Latine: Translates select Epistles out of Cicero, and Pliny; and letting them lie-by for some time, least the Impression of the style and phrase prepossesse him [not];[7] turnes them into

---

[1] Speedy.

[2] Not certain; MS may read 'Toun' for 'town'?

[3] The Drapers' house at Addiscombe (diary, 27 June 1702) was under construction so they had come to Wotton. It was demolished in 1863 (illustration in Weinreb and Hibbert 1983, 5). E's grandson returned around 6 September 1702 (diary, the only mention of the trip). He came back 'in health, for which I thank Almighty God.'

[4] The family seat of the Godolphin family was at Godolphin in Cornwall; as Sidney Godolphin was E's patron, subsequent source of employment for his grandson and brother of his future mother-in-law (diary 1705, *passim*) this was doubtless a pilgrimage of loyalty, perhaps also including a visit to Margaret Godolphin's grave at Breage Church near Godolphin House.

[5] E's wife Mary, had spent most of her childhood in France, and had perhaps taught her grandson.

[6] Sic.

[7] Apparently deleted.

Latine againe, the better to judge of his Improvement: He has his time for his agrestic[1] Flute in which (with his Tutor Mr Banister)[2] they spend a mornings houre together: He is likewise Mr Isak's[3] Scholar, and gos to the Fencing-Schole while here; and (when in the Country) takes as much pleasure with his hand-bill, and pruning knife about our Ground and Gardens; as I should do if I were able; sometimes, if weather and Neighbours Invite, he hunts with them; my worthy neighbour and Friend Mr Finch,[4] using that diversion, when he is in tollerable Health: In summ, finding him so moderatly and discreetly dispos'd, (studious, and mindfull of his owne Improvement,) I give him free Liberty; and I blesse God, have never yet found any Indulgence prejudice him, having taken a sort of Natural ply, which I am perswaded will be Lasting: 'Tis a greate Word, when I assure you, I never yet saw in him passion, or do a fault, for which he deserv'd Reproofe.

And now you will no more believe halfe this, than I do of what Zenophon has written of his *Cyrus*; However, it Entertaines an old dotarel,[5] and as such I Relate it. Now as for myselfe, I cannot but let you know, the Incredible satisfaction I have taken in Reading my Late Lord Chancellor's *History of the Rebellion*,[6] so well, and so unexpectedly well written; the preliminarys so like that of the noble Polybius, leading us by the Courts, Avenues and porches into the fabrick; and the Style masculine, the Characters so just, and temperd, without the least ingredient of passion, or tinctur of revenge; yet with such natural and lively touches, as shews his Lordship well knew not onely the persons out-side; but their very Interiors; whilst yet he treats the most Obnoxious (and who deserv'd the severest Rebuke) with a becoming Generosity and freedom; even where the Ill conduct of those of the pretended loyal party (as well as of the most flagitious)[7] might have justifyd the worst that could have ben sayd of their Miscarriages and Demerits: In summ, there runs through this noble piece, a thred so even, strong and without brace or knot in the whole Contexture; with such Choice and profitable Instructions naturaly emerging from the Subject, as persons of the sublimest Rank and Office, neede not be ashamed to learn their dutys, and how to govern themselves; And from the Lapses, and false Politiques of others, how the greatest Favorits, and men

---

[1] Rural/rustic.
[2] Not known.
[3] Possibly the dancing master 'Monsieur Isaac', mentioned in the diary as tutor to E's daughter Mary (7 February 1682). According to de Beer he was fashionable at the court of Anne and was still alive in 1727. However, de Beer also suggests that the name was an assumed one as others in the same profession seem to have adopted it.
[4] See previous letter, 24 December 1701 (**E14**).
[5] Dotard.
[6] Published in three parts, 1702, 1703, and 1704. Clarendon gave a copy of part 3 of his father's work to E on 9 February 1705 (diary), so this reference must be to part 1, and possibly 2, presented earlier as E states subsequently in this letter.
[7] Wicked, infamous.

in Grace, should be Examples of Modesty and Temperance; Un-Elated, Easy, and Accessible, without abusing their power; whilst being apt to forget themselves, and the slipery precipices they stand on, they too often study not so much how to make their Treading sure by the Vertue of Justice, Moderation, and a publique Spirit; as to raise themselves Fortunes, and purchase Titles and Adorations, by flattering the Worst, and most destructive, Inclynations of Princes, in the most servile Complyances and basest Offices: What I have written more in this style, and from my heart to my present Lord Clarendon, (who sent me his Fathers Bookes) I wish you had seene; for I acknowledge my selfe so transported with all the parts of this excellent History; That knowing (as I did) most of the person[s] then Acting the Tragedy,[1] and those against it; that I have no more to say, but much, very-much to Admire; not doubting but the Rest which follows, will be still matter of panegyrick, and justify the highest Epithete; and that by the time he has don, there will neede no other History or Account of what past during the Reigne of that suffering and unfortunate Prince, to give the World a piece equal to any thing Extant, not onely in our owne poorely furnish'd Historys of this, but of any Nation about us: To conclude, It requird no little skill, prudence and dexterity, to adventure so neere the heeles of Truth, without danger or just Resentment of those who deserv'd so Ill, as no Reflections could have ben severe enough[2]

But I have don; Let what I have written to his Lordship, speake the rest of my sentiments on this Author and noble work. Thus, What I would Wish for my selfe, and all I Love, (as I do Mr Pepys,) should be the Old man's life described in the *Distic*, to which you deserv'dly have attain'd:

> *Vita Senis Libri, Domus, Hortus, Lectus, Amicus,*
> *Vina, Repos, Ignis; Mens hilaris, Pietas.*[3]

In the meane time, I feede on the past Conversation I once had in York Buildings, and sterve since my Friend have forsaken it.[4]

My Wifes, and my most humble service to all with you, Mrs Skinner in particular, Mr Jackson, etc:

My Grandson humbly saluts you.

JEvelyn

---

[1] Though of course E was absent in Europe for much of the course of the Civil War.

[2] P shared E's views, writing to Clarendon on 4 August 1702 (Tanner 1926, ii, no. 482), 'I am but this morning come from the 3d reading of your noble Father my Lord Chancellor Clarendon's History with the same appetite (I assure you) to a 4th...'.

[3] 'The life of the free old man, home, garden, bed, friend, wine, relaxation, passion, sense of humour, piety.

[4] P had evidently suspended his weekly Saturday evening meetings since moving to Clapham, no doubt due to his deteriorating health.

Postscriptum

In March 1703 Evelyn broke his shin in Brompton Park. By 14 May he was well enough to make his way to see the ailing Pepys at Clapham who was 'languishing with small hope of recovery which much affected me' (diary). This was their last recorded meeting. Pepys had been told on 19 April that there was no hope of his recovering.

Samuel Pepys died at quarter to four in the morning of 26 May 1703. The event was recorded in some detail by his nephew John Jackson who had evidently been commissioned to make notes. Pepys's body was opened shortly after and Jackson wrote to Evelyn on 28 May to tell him the result (see Appendix 1.8). Pepys was buried on 4 June at St Olave's Hart Street beside his wife Elizabeth, who had died in 1669. Jackson proved a conscientious heir and Pepys's instructions concerning his papers, library, and other possessions were subsequently followed. The core, including the library, was transferred to Magdalene College, Cambridge, in 1724, the year after Jackson's own death. A large portion of the papers had already been acquired by Thomas Rawlinson but other papers remained in the possession of Jackson's descendants, who took the name Pepys-Cockerell, until 1931.

John Evelyn's final years were mainly concerned with making sure his grandson was employed and married. By the end of 1705 these had been achieved. He declined John Jackson's request to marry his grand-daughter (probably Evelyn's son's daughter Elizabeth, 1684–1760, afterwards Mrs Simon Harcourt) on the grounds that Jackson could not make a substantial enough settlement 'according to the Custome and Interests of this Age, and the satisfaction of Relations'.[1] Evelyn died on 27 February 1706 at his deceased son's former home of 14 Dover Street, London. His body was moved to Wotton and he was buried on 4 March at the church in which he had received his first school lessons in 1624. His wife followed him on 9 February 1709. They were outlived by only one of their children, Susanna, Mrs William Draper (1669–1754). Evelyn's papers and books remained in the family home at Wotton where, despite being used for scrap paper and occasional gifts, much stayed until the early twentieth century. They were subsequently placed on deposit at Christ Church, Oxford, until the books were sold in 1977 and 1978. The remaining papers were acquired by the British Library in 1995.

---

[1] E to Will Hewer, 16 September 1705 (for reference see p.316, bottom).

Catalogue of the Letters

I. ABBREVIATIONS (used throughout)

ABPC	*American Book Prices Current* (annual)
Bb	Braybrooke, Richard, Lord, *Memoirs of Samuel Pepys Esq. ... and a selection from his private correspondence*, 1825 and 1854
BL	British Library: CLBI (Evelyn MS 39a, 1644–79) and CLBII (MS 39b, 1679–98)[1] = Copy-Letter Books I and II (copies of letters *from* E); Up AnII (Evelyn MS 2) and Up BCI (Evelyn MS 3) = Upcott's Book-Collectors I and Antiquaries II (letters *from* P); BL.xxxx = Evelyn loose letters; S & W = Evelyn Sick and Wounded MS folders; Add. MSS = Additional Manuscripts
Blackwell	Blackwell's Rare Books, Catalogue A20, Spring 1981
Bod MS Rawl	Bodleian Library Rawlinson Manuscripts (microfilm available at Institute of Historical Research, Senate House, London)
Bray	Bray, W., *The Diary and Correspondence of John Evelyn*, various editions (principally 1852 and later for letters)
DC	*Catalogue of Historical Documents and Autograph Letters including A large and unpublished Correspondence addressed to Samuel Pepys... from John Evelyn... on sale by* Samuel J. Davey, London. Number 31, 1889 (copies at Pierpont Morgan Library, New York: 079 D24; and the Bodleian, Oxford: 25783 d.6)
DNB	*Dictionary of National Biography*
HL Harvard	Houghton Library at Harvard, Massachusetts
HM	Huntington Library Manuscript, Pasadena
HMCR	Historical Manuscript Commission Reports
Houghton	Arthur A. Houghton junior Sale, Christie's Part I, A–L, 13/14 June 1979 (inc letters *from* Evelyn); Part II, M–Z, 11/12 June 1980 (inc letters *from* Pepys)
HSP	Historical Society of Pennsylvania
Hw	Howarth, R.G., *Letters and the Second Diary of Samuel Pepys*, J.M. Dent and Sons, London, 1932 and 1933. Transcripts of letters previously published by Tanner, J. Smith, and Braybrooke, and unpublished letters in various libraries, e.g. the Bodleian
Hyde	Collection of Donald and Mary Hyde, Somerville, New Jersey
JJ	John Jackson, Pepys's nephew and heir
Library Sale	Evelyn Library Sale at Christie's, London 22–23 June, 30 November, and 1 December 1977, 15–16 March and 12–13 July 1978 (published in 4 volumes: A–C, D–L, M–S, and T–Z)
LC	*Catalogue of Interesting choice & rare Historical Documents &*

---

[1] There has been some confusion about these two copy-letter books (for exact details see *The Book Collector*, Summer 1995, 158). Also, CLBI (MS 39a) is one and the same as that sometimes known as 'Lord Camoys letterbook', in whose possession it was for a period; a microfilm of CLBI is at the Bodleian (MS Film 743).

	Autograph Letters offered for sale by Langham & Co, Successors to Mr S.J. Davey [see DC above]. No. 10, 1900 (copy in BL: 011904.ee). Previously featured in the Davey Catalogue (DC)
Marburg	Marburg, C., *Mr Pepys and Mr Evelyn*, University of Pennsylvania Press and Oxford University Press, 1935 (M = letters transcribed by her; A = letters noted as 'advertised')
Morrison	Alfred Morrison Sale, Sotheby's 1917–19 (in particular Part IV, 6 May 1919, Lots 2820, 2822, 3045; copies at BL and Sotheby's)
NMM LBK	National Maritime Museum, Letter Book 8. P's official copy-letter book 1662–79. Ex-Pepys-Cockerell family, sold Sotheby's 1 April 1931, Lot 19 (published by Tanner 1929)
OED	*Oxford English Dictionary*
PC MS	Manuscripts ex-Pepys-Cockerell family. Sold Sotheby's 1 April 1931 Lot 18 (some earlier, e.g. 14Jan99, **D32**), and resold at the Houghton Sale, Christie's, Part II, June 1980, Lot 363. Not at the Pepysian Library (PL) as stated by some authorities (published by Tanner 1926). Some made available for this book
Pforz	Carl H. Pforzheimer collection at the Harry Ransom Humanities Research Center, University of Texas at Austin. Mostly from the Morrison Sale, 1919, and before that the Davey Catalogue (DC)
PL	Pepysian Library, Magdalene, Cambridge
PML	Pierpont Morgan Library, New York
Prescott	Prescott Sale, Christie's New York, 6 February 1981
PRO S.P.	Public Records Office State Papers
PUL	Princeton University Library
Rosenbach	Dr A.S.W. Rosenbach of Philadelphia (in 1935, now sold)
Sm	Smith, J., 1841, *The life, journals and correspondence of Samuel Pepys*, Richard Bentley, London. Smith's edition of Pepys's diary contains some letters otherwise unknown, perhaps amongst the Pepys-Cockerell papers at the time. At least two (**E2**, and **E11**) seem subsequently to have surfaced in the private market
Tann	Tanner, J.R., 1926, *Private Correspondence... of Samuel Pepys*, London (1679–1703; PC MS), *and*
Tann	Tanner, J.R., 1929, *Further Correspondence... of Samuel Pepys*, London (1662–79; PC MS, now NMM LBK/8)

II. LETTERS BY DATE

The Catalogue lists by decade all letters in all versions traced for this book. Thus those of the 1660s are numbered from **A1**, the letters of the 1670s are numbered from **B1**, and so on. Abbreviated details indicate the present location of the manuscripts if known, and previously-published versions. Numbers with two or more entries, for example **A7**, indicate different versions of the same letter (letters-sent, drafts, and copies). Sometimes the dates of these differ, for a variety of reasons discussed in the Text note at the beginning of the book. Drafts and copies are specified as such. Dates in inverted commas, eg '07Jul80' indicates that the date as given is incorrect and is known to be wrong on the evidence of content or other versions of the letter.

L	manuscript lost but known to have existed, text printed or known from copies
L#	manuscript lost and no copies/previous transcriptions available
m	manuscript (or facsimile) <u>was</u> available for study
p	published/printed text of a version available only
xx	the exact date of the letter is unknown
→	primary and secondary source, e.g. (Bb → Hw 136) indicates that Howarth used Braybrooke's printed version, and not the MS
[]	date incomplete/absent on MS and inferred from content or copies/drafts

A. 1660s (29: 22E, 7P)

1.	P	27Apr65	m	NMM LBK/8, 199 (COPY)
2.	E	01May65	m	BL.1469[1]
3.	P	09Aug65	m	BL.1080
4.	E	23Sep65	m	PRO S.P. 29/133, f.28 (Marburg M1)
5.	P	26Sep65	m	BL.1081
6.	E	29Sep65	m	PRO S.P. 29/133, f.58 (Marburg M2)
7.	E	30Sep65	m	PRO S.P. 29/133, f.63 (Marburg M3)
8.	E	03Oct65	m	PRO S.P. 29/134, f.23–4 (Marburg M4)
9.	E	12Oct65	m	William H. Fern collection (Sotheby's 1995)[2]
10.	E	13Oct65	m	PRO S.P. 29/134, f.85 (Marburg M5)
11.	E	14Oct65	m	PRO S.P. 29/134, f.93 (Marburg M6)
12.	E	23Oct65	m	PRO S.P. 29/135, f.44 (Marburg M7)
13.	E	04Nov65	m	PRO S.P. 29/136, f.31 (Marburg M8)
14.	E	23Nov65	m	PRO S.P. 29/137, f.84 (Marburg M9)
15.	E	07Dec65	m	PRO S.P. 29/138, f.60 (Marburg M10)
16.	E	09Dec65	m	PRO S.P. 29/138, f.77 (Marburg M11)
17.	P	12Dec65	m	PML, no MS number (Marburg M12)
18.	E	13Dec65	m	PRO S.P. 29/139, f.11 (Marburg M13)
19.	E	31Jan66	m	PRO S.P. 29/146, f.73 (Marburg M14)
		03Jan66	m	BL CLBI.270 (COPY) (Bray → Hw 25)[3]
20.	P	17Feb66	m	NMM LBK/8, 369 (COPY) (Tann 1929, no. 92)
21.	E	17Feb66	m	PRO S.P. 29/148, f.51 (Marburg M15)[4]
22.	E	28Feb66	m	PRO S.P. 29/149, f.59 (Marburg M16)
23.	E	16Mar66	m	PRO S.P. 29/151, f.35 (Marburg M17)
24.	E	26Mar66i	m	Bod MS Rawl. A195, f.249 (Bray; Hw 26)
25.	E	26Mar66ii	m	Bod MS Rawl. A195, f.251 (Bray)
26.	E	20Jan68	m	Bod MS Rawl. A195, f.77 (Bb; Hw 29)
27.	P	08Feb68	m	NMM LBK/8, 526 (COPY) (Bb →? Hw 30)
28.	E	21Aug69	m	PL.2237.1–12 (COPY by P) (Bb; Hw 33; Marburg M18)[5]
29.	P	02Nov69	m	BL Up AnII (Bb → Hw 34)

B. 1670s (11: 4E, 7P)

1.	P	17Feb72	m	BL.1082
2.	E	27Aug72	m	PRO S.P. 29/328, f.114 (Marburg M19)
3.	E	20Sep72	m	PRO S.P. 29/329, f.33 (Marburg M20)
4.	E	07Oct72	m	PRO S.P. 29/329, f.94 (Marburg M21)

---

[1] Bought back by the Evelyn family at Sotheby's, June 1869 (Lot 364).

[2] Sale of 24 July 1995, Lot 487. The letter is illustrated in the sale catalogue.

[3] Copy-letter misdated by E and published by Bray under this incorrect date.

[4] Marburg supplies S.P. 29/146 in error.

[5] Carries amendments/insertions in E's hand; Bb/Hw published 1–2, Marburg 3–12.

5.	P	29Aug73	m	PL.2849.98 (COPY) (Marburg M24)
6.	E	04Sep73	m	PUL (DRAFT) (Maggs 1932; Christie's 1979)[1]
7.	P	08Sep73	m	PL.2849.118 (COPY) (Marburg M25)[2]
8.	P	15Oct73	m	BL.1083
		15Oct73	m	PL.2849.224 (COPY) (Marburg M26)
9.	P	15Jan74	m	PL.2850.37 (COPY) (Marburg M22)
10.	P	23Jan74	m	BL.1084
		23Jan[74]	m	PL.2850.55–6 (COPY) (Marburg M23)[3]
11.	P	01Mar77	m	BL Up AnII (Sm → Hw 55)

C. 1680s (49: 41E, 8P)

1.	E	30Jan[80]	m	HM25797 (DC2863; Marburg M27)
		30Jan80	m	BL CLBII.409 (COPY)
2.	P	31Jan80	m	Bod MS Rawl. A194, f.135 (COPY) (Marburg M28)
3.	E	27Feb80	m	BL CLBI.397[4] (COPY)
4.	E	15Jun80	L	unknown (DC2865; LC568)
		15Jun80	m	PL.2873.53–4 (COPY by P) (Marburg M29)
5.	P	25Jun80	m	Pforz MS 105B (DC2867 *as* C7)[5]
		25Jun80	m	PL.2873.61–2 (COPY) (Marburg M31)[6]
6.	E	25Jun80	m	PML (DC2866; HMCR XV; Marburg M30)[7]
		25Jun80	m	PL.2873.54–5 (COPY by P)
7.	E	07Jul80	m	Pforz MS 35D (DC 2867)
		07Jul80	m	PL.2873.65–89 (COPY by P) (Marburg M32)
8.	E	06Sep80	L	unknown (DC2868)
		06Sep80	m	PL.2873.56–9 (COPY by P) (Marburg M33)
9.	E	31Oct81	m	Maine Historical Society (DC2869)
10.	E	06Dec81	p	PC MS.i.29 (Bb; Tann 1926, no. 12 → Hw 113)
		06Dec81	m	BL.1533 (DRAFT) (Bray)
		05Dec81	m	BL CLBII.436 (COPY)
11.	E	xxDec81	L#	unknown (DC2870)
12.	E	28Apr82	m	PC MS.i.31 (Bb; Tann 1926, no. 13 → Hw 120)
13.	E	05Jun82	m	HL Harvard Lowell autograph 1925
		05Jun81	m	BL CLBII.430 (COPY) (Bray → Hw 129)
14.	E	10Jul82	m	BL.1537 (DC2871, LC572; Marburg A5)[8]
15.	E	19Sep82	m	BL CLBII.445 (COPY) (Bray)
16.	P	07Aug83	m	BL Up AnII (Bb → Hw 136)

---

[1] Maggs Catalogue 570, Spring 1932, item 160; Arthur Houghton Sale, 1979, Part I, Lot 203.

[2] Dated in error to October by Marburg.

[3] Text date has no year; attributed erroneously to 1673 by Marburg.

[4] MS dated 27Feb79 but is certainly 1680, see p.98, note 5.

[5] The date of this 'letter', consisting of various queries from P, and the sequence immediately following has been the subject of some confusion. E's principal reply was written on the 7th and 8th of July (**C7**). P's 'queries' are not dated. Marburg dated them to 7 July 1680. However, it is evident from E's letter of 25 June (**C6**) that he had seen the queries and that this letter (**C6**) was a preliminary reply. The confusion arose in part because the queries received by E were returned with his letter of 7 July. The two were kept together until they were sold as a single item in the Davey Catalogue (DC2867). Once they arrived in the Pforzheimer collection, not available to Marburg, they were separated and correctly dated.

[6] Attributed to 7 July erroneously by Marburg. See previous note.

[7] DC misdates to '23 June'. Reported in HMCR XV, 1897, 177, coll. of J. Eliot Hodgkin.

[8] Marburg supplies an extensive extract from the text but does not give her source. The Davey and Langham Catalogues carried no facsimiles or transcriptions.

		07Aug83	m	Bod MS Rawl. A190, f.8 (shorthand DRAFT)
17.	E	10Aug83	m	Bod MS Rawl. A190, f.10 (Bb; Hw 137)
		10Aug83	m	BL CLBII.460 (COPY)
18.	E	08Jun84	p	PC MS.i.32 (Bb; Tann 1926, no. 14)
		30May84	m	BL CLBII.479 (COPY)
19.	E	09Feb85	m	BL CLBII.492 (COPY)
20.	P	04Jul85	m	BL Add. MSS 29300, f.25[1] (Hw 46)
21.	E	29Jul85	m	Pforz MS 35E (DC2872a; Sotheby's 1919)[2]
22.	E	31Jul85	m	Pforz MS 35F (DC2872b)
23.	E	03Aug85	m	Pforz MS 35G (DC2872c)
		03Aug85	m	BL CLBII.502 (COPY)
24.	E	08Sep85	m	Guildhall Library MS 22425/8 (DC2873; Sotheby's 1968)[3]
25.	E	22Sep85	m	BL.1547 (DC2874; LC569)
		23Sep85	m	BL CLBII.507 (COPY) (Bray)
26.	P	02Oct85	m	BL Up AnII (Bray → Hw 153)
27.	E	03Oct85	m	Pforz MS 35H (DC2875)
28.	E	06Dec85	L#	unknown (DC2876; LC570)
29.	E	02Jan86	m	HL Harvard *bMS Eng 9991 (DC2877)[4]
		31Dec85	m	BL CLBII.512 (COPY)
30.	E	08Jan86	m	HSP (DC 2887; Marburg M34)
		01Jan86	m	BL CLBII.514 (COPY)
31.	E	01Mar86	m	BL.1549 (DC2878)
32.	E	[29?]Jun86	p/L	Rosenbach in 1935 (DC2880; Marburg M35)[5]
		29Jun86	m	BL CLBII.534 (COPY)
33.	E	21Jul86	L#	unknown (DC2884; LC571)[6]
34.	E	xxSep86	L#	unknown (DC2885)
35.	E	28Nov86	m	BL CLBII.552 (COPY)
36.	E	15Mar87	m/L	unknown (DC2879; Marburg's A19 misdated to 14 March)
		19Jan87	m	BL CLBII.561[7] (COPY)
37.	P	19Apr87	m	HSP (Marburg M36)
38.	E	20Jun87	m	BL CLBII.565 (COPY)
39.	E	03Oct87	m	Hyde Collection (DC2886)
		[03Oct87]	m	BL.1559ii (DRAFT)
40.	E	01Mar88	m	Bod MS Rawl. A179, f.8 (Hw 173)
41.	E	31Jul88	m	BL CLBII.581 (COPY)
42.	P	10Sep88	m	BL Up AnII (Bb → Hw 182)

---

[1] No addressee, content makes E the most likely. Howarth misdated it to 1675.

[2] **C21–23** were listed as a single item in the Davey Catalogue but were 'not offered for sale' because they referred to 'family matters' (Elizabeth Evelyn's elopement). How they subsequently came to be in the Morrison Collection (that sale, 5 May 1919, Lot 2822) from which they passed to Pforzheimer is therefore a mystery.

[3] Sotheby's Sale of 9 April 1968 (Lot 481). Presented to the Guildhall Library in 1987 by Lt. Col. C.D.L. Pepys, a descendant of Richard Pepys, a cousin of the diarist.

[4] Illustrated in *Catalogue of Union Art Galleries*, New York, 27 February 1934 (copy at HSP), and reported in ABPC 1945 (Vol. 51), both times misdated to 1685; see also '02Jun85' below under Phantom Letters (p.306).

[5] The Davey Catalogue dated the letter as 'June 1686'. Marburg saw no visible date. The BL CLBII version supplies an exact, though not necessarily precisely accurate, date.

[6] Langham Catalogue inexplicably gives 1697. The description, however, makes it certain that this is DC2884, with content confirming the year as 1686 (see text and p.306).

[7] The copy-letter's content differs little and also contains a reference to E's dismissal as a Commissioner of the Privy Seal on 10 March 1687, demonstrating that E misdated it.

43.	E	[11Sep88]	m	BL Up AnII (undated DRAFT reply on 10Sep88 **C42**)
44.	E	02Nov88	m	BL CLBII.592 (COPY)
45.	E	12Dec88	m	Bod MS Rawl. A179, f.84 (Bb; Hw 187)
46.	E	10May89	m	Bod MS Rawl. A170, f.64 (Bb)
47.	E	26Aug89	m	Pforz MS 35I (DC 2881)
		12Aug89	m	BL CLBII.616 (COPY) (Bray)
		26Aug89	m	Bod MS Rawl. A171, f.316ff (COPY by P)
48.	P	30Aug89	m	BL Up AnII (Bray; Bb → Hw 197)
		30Aug89	m	Pforz MS 35I (shorthand DRAFT on 26Aug89 **C47**)
		30Aug89	m	Bod MS Rawl. A171, f.326–7 (COPY by P)
49.	E	04Oct89	m	BL.1557 (DC2888)
		01Oct89	m	BL CLBII.619 (COPY) (Bray)
		04Oct89	m	Bod MS Rawl. A171, f.328ff (COPY by P) (Hw199)

D. 1690s (32: 21E, 11P)

1.	E	11Jan90	m	BL.1558 (DC2864)
2.	E	26Feb90	m	PL.2421[1]
		07Apr90	m	BL CLBII.625 (COPY)
3.	E	11Jun90	m	PC MS.i.36 (Bb; Tann 1926, no. 19 → Hw 207)
4.	E	17Jun90	m	PC MS.i.37 (Bb; Tann 1926, no. 20)
		20Jan90	m	BL CLBII.621[2] (COPY)
5.	E	14Aug90	m	PC MS.i.39 (Bb; Tann 1926, no. 22 → Hw 208)
6.	E	25Sep90	m	HL Harvard *64M–118 (Bb; Sotheby's 1891)[3]
		02Oct90	m	BL CLBII.633 (COPY)
7.	P	25Sep90	m	PL Pepys Ancill. MSS, file 25 (Bb → Hw 209)
8.	E	26Sep90	m	PC MS.i.40 (Bb; Tann 1926, no. 23 → Hw 210)
9.	P	13Nov90	m	BL Up AnII (Bb → Hw 212)
10.	E	12Jun91	m	BL CLBII.644 (COPY)
11.	P	08Oct91	m	PUL, ex-BL Up AnII (Bb → Hw 214)
12.	P	09Jan92	m	BL Up AnII
		09Jan92	p	PC MS.i.55 (COPY) (Bb; Tann 1926, no. 37 → Hw 217)
13.	P	28Mar92	m	BL Up AnII
		28Mar92	p	PC MS.i.61 (COPY) (Bb; Tann 1926, no. 43 → Hw 219)
14.	E	12Apr92	m	BL CLBII.665 (COPY)
15.	E	29Aug92	p	PC MS.i.62 (Bb; Tann 1926, no. 44 → Hw 220)
		09Sep92	m	BL CLBII.671 (COPY)
16.	P	16Sep92	m	BL Up AnII
		16Sep92	p	PC MS.i.62 (COPY) (Bb; Tann 1926, no. 46 → Hw 222)
17.	P	29Nov92	m	BL Up BCI
18.	E	06Jul93	m	PC MS.i.67 (Bb; Tann 1926, no. 50)
19.	E	02Apr94	m	BL CLBII.693 (COPY)
20.	P	22May94	m	BL Up AnII (Bb → Hw 228)
21.	E	30May94	m	PUL (HMCR III, 1872, 291a; Sotheby's 1937)[4]
		30May94	m	BL CLBII.704 (COPY)
22.	E	07Jul94	p	PC MS.i.86 (Bb; Tann 1926, no. 62 → Hw 229)
		07Jul94	m	BL CLBII.707 (COPY)
23.	P	14Aug94	m	BL Up AnII (Sm)

---

[1] Bound into P's copy of Locke's *Essay concerning Humane Understanding*.

[2] The copy-letter represents a curious discrepancy in date from the posted letter. See text.

[3] Sotheby's (T.S. Raffles) 29 June 1891, lot 185 (incorrectly dated; see HMCR, 1877, and Phantom Letters below). Also Parke-Bennet Galleries New York, 22 October 1964, Lot 309.

[4] Collection R.E. Egerton-Warburton, 1872; sale of 16 March 1937, Lot 488.

		10Aug94	p	PC MS.i.95 (DRAFT?) (Bb; Tann 1926, no. 63 → Hw 231)
24.	E	02Sep94	p	PC MS.i.87 (Bb; Tann 1926, no. 64 → Hw 232)
		02Sep94	m	BL Up AnII (DRAFT on **D23** 14Aug94) (Sm)
		02Sep94	m	BL CLBII.715 (COPY)
25.	P	07Nov94	m	BL Up AnII (COPY by E)[1] (Sm → Hw 234)
26.	E	18Nov94	m	PC MS.i.88 (Bb; Tann 1926, no. 65 → Hw 235)
27.	E	07Jan95	m	BL CLBII.718 (COPY)
28.	P	15Feb95	m	BL Stowe 747, f.45 (Hw 238; Marburg M37)
29.	E	25Mar95	m	BL CLBII.724 (COPY)
30.	E	03Dec96	p	PC MS.i.112 (Bb; Tann 1926, no. 85 → Hw 248)
		03Dec96	m	BL CLBII.775 (COPY)
31.	E	03Apr98	m	HL Harvard *bMS Eng 9991, 119
32.	E	14Jan99	m/L	unknown, ex-PC MS (Bb → Hw 255; Christie's 1981)[2]

E. 1700s (15: 8E, 7P)

1.	E	01Jan00	L	Horwood (Christie's 1979; Blackwell's 1981)[3]
		01Jan00	m	BL.1626 (DRAFT)
2.	P	02Jan00	p/m	HM52160 (Sm → Hw 271; Maggs 1920)[4]
3.	E	10May00	m	Berg Collection, New York (Bb → Hw 275)
		10May00	m	BL.1658 (DRAFT)
4.	E	18May00	p	PC MS.ii.127 (Bb; Tann 1926, no. 219 → Hw 276)
5.	E	22Jul00	p	PC MS.iii.12 (Bb; Tann 1926, no. 265 → Hw 278)
		21Jul00	m	BL.1663 (DRAFT)
6.	P	07Aug00	m	BL Up AnII
		07Aug00	p	PC MS.iii.28 (COPY) (Bb; Tann 1926, no. 277 → Hw 279)
7.	E	09Aug00	p	PC MS.iii.29 (Bb; Tann 1926, no. 279 → Hw 280)
		09Aug00	m	BL.1664 (DRAFT)
8.	P	19Aug00	L#	unknown (COPY) (Marburg A27; Sotheby's 1919)[5]
9.	E	25Aug00	m	PC MS.iii.39 (Bb; Tann 1926, no. 292 → Hw 281)
10.	P	19Sep00	m	PC MS.iii.65 (COPY) (Tann 1926, no. 313 → Hw 283)
11.	P	07Jun01	p/L	unknown (Sm → Hw 303; Morrison; Christie's 1980)[6]
12.	P	19Nov01	m	BL Up AnII (Sm → Hw 307)
13.	E	10Dec01	p	PC MS.iv.86 (Bb; Tann 1926, no. 465 → Hw 308)
		09Dec01	m	BL.1651 (DRAFT)
14.	P	24Dec01	m	BL Up AnII (Sm)
		24Dec01	p	PC MS.iv.87 (COPY) (Bb; Tann 1926, no. 466 → Hw 309)
15.	E	20Jan03	m	PC MS.iv.130 (Bb; Tann 1926, no. 511 → Hw 349)

---

[1] E notes he had sent the original to Godolphin; now lost.

[2] Prescott Sale, New York, 6 February 1981, Lot 107. Also printed in The Times, 16 February 1926 (p. 15f) when it was stated to be in 'private possession'.

[3] Christie's Arthur Houghton Sale, Part I, 1979, Lot 204; Blackwell's catalogue A20, 1981, Item 1, noting damage 'deleting approximately ten words'. Both give extracts, the latter with details of P's endorsement. The present owner was unable to locate the MS in 1996; thus, the text used here is that of the draft.

[4] Maggs Catalogue No 388, Spring 1920, Item no. 676. Howarth's source was Smith, 1841, using the same MS, then in Upcott's collection. Acquired by the Huntington, Pasadena, in 1972, bound in an antiquarian book given by one Mrs Irving Snyder, but not recognised there until now as being a previously-published MS or even that it was to E.

[5] Lot 3045 of the Morrison Sale, 6 May 1919.

[6] Morrison Collection Catalogue (ed. A.W. Thibaudeau, 1891, V, 125); Arthur Houghton Sale, Part II, Lot 365.

III. LETTERS BY LOCATION

(Where more than one version exists: a = letter-sent, b and c = drafts/retained copies)

Henry W. and Albert A. Berg Collection, New York Public Library
E: 3a

The Bodleian Library, Oxford
A: 24, 25, 26; C: 2, 16b, 17a, 40, 45, 46, 47c, 48c, 49c

The British Library, London
A: 2, 3, 5, 19b, 29; B: 1, 8a, 10a, 11; C: 1b, 3, 10b, 10c, 13b, 14, 15, 16a, 17b, 18b, 19, 20, 23b, 25a, 25b, 26, 29b, 30b, 31, 32b, 35, 36b, 38, 39b, 41, 42, 43, 44, 47b, 48a, 49a, 49b; D: 1, 2b, 4b, 6b, 9, 10, 12a, 13a, 14, 15b, 16a, 17, 19, 20, 21b, 22b, 23a, 24b, 24c, 25, 27, 28, 29, 30b; E: 1b, 3b, 5b, 6a, 7b, 12, 13b, 14a

William H. Fern Collection, Connecticut
A: 9

Guildhall Library, London
C: 24

Historical Society of Pennsylvania, Philadelphia, Pennsylvania
C: 30a, 37

Rosemary Horwood Collection, Seattle, Washington
E: 1a

Houghton Library at Harvard, Massachusetts
C: 13a, 29a; D: 6a, 31

Huntington Library, Pasadena, California
C: 1a; E: 2

Hyde Collection, Somerville, New Jersey
C: 39a

Maine Historical Society, Portland, Maine
C: 9

National Maritime Museum, Greenwich
A: 1, 20, 27

Pepys-Cockerell papers (J. Paul Getty, K.B.E.)
C: 10a, 12, 18a; D: 3, 4a, 5, 8, 12b, 13b, 15a, 16b, 18, 22a, 23b, 24a, 26, 30a; E: 4, 5a, 6b, 7a, 9, 10, 13a, 14b, 15

Pepysian Library, Magdalene College, Cambridge
A: 28; B: 5, 7, 8b, 9, 10b; C: 4b, 5b, 6b, 7b, 8b; D: 2a, 7

Pforzheimer Collection, H. Ransom Humanities Research Center, University of Texas, Austin
C: 5a, 7a, 21, 22, 23a, 27, 47a, 48b

Pierpont Morgan Library, New York City
A: 17; C: 6a

Princeton University Library, New Jersey
B: 6; D: 11, 21a

Public Record Office State Papers (Domestic), London
A: 4, 6, 7, 8, 10, 11, 12, 13, 14, 15, 16, 18, 19a, 21, 22, 23; B: 2, 3, 4

Letters whose whereabouts were unknown in 1996
C: 4a, 8a, 11, 28, 32a, 33, 34, 36a; **D**: 32; **E**: 8, 11

IV. UNKNOWN LETTERS REFERRED TO IN THE CORRESPONDENCE

The following letters are referred to in the known correspondence, but are themselves otherwise unknown. It is possible, but unlikely, that they will surface in due course.

17Oct65	P	Referred to by E in **A12** (23Oct65) as 'Yours of the 17th instant I found at my returne from Leades...' This or another referred to in P's letter to Coventry, 'I have since wrott to him to cause transcripts of these accounts to be sent to us...' (14 October 1665; Tanner 1929, no. 52 – see p.42 above)
07Dec65	P	Referred to by E in **A16** (09Dec65) as 'Your Letter of the 7th concerning our Prisoners in the Golden-hand and Prince...'
17Mar66	P	Requested by E in **A23** (16Mar66) as 'Be pleasd to returne me by this hand, the Particulars, on hand of the estimate I gave you of our proposd Infirmary...'
xxOct72	P	Referred to by E in **B4** (07Oct72) as 'I received the letter which was your reiterated exception...'
03Sep73	E	Referred to by E in **B6** (04Sep73) as 'my Last of yesterday'.
xxJun80?	P	Referred to by E in **C6** (25Jun80) as a letter clearly received that day or shortly before
02Aug83	E	Referred to by P in **C16** (07Aug83) as 'Your kinde summons of the 2d instant has overtaken me here...'
09/10Feb85	P	Requested by E in **C19** (09Feb85) as 'Sir, You will do me the favour to acquaint me by this bearer, What is resolv'd in this matter...'
ante 04Jul85	E	Implicit in P's **C20** (04Jul85) 'I have received your Commands'
30Jul85	P	Implicit in E's **C22** (31Jul85), 'You have rightly judg'd, and I concurr with you...'
02Aug85	P	Referred to by E in **C23** (03Aug85) as 'By what you were pleas'd to Communicate to me Yesterday...'
3–7Jan86	P	Referred to by E in **C30** (08Jan86), 'Now Sir as to the other part of your letter...'
xxMar87	P	Referred to by E in **C36** (15Mar87) as, ''til your Letter injoyn'd me to give you my thoughts upon them...'
xxFeb88	P	Referred to by E in **C40** (01Mar88) 'your Letter'.
06Nov94	E	Referred to by P in **D25** (07Nov94) as 'I thank you for your kind Message yesterday...'
12?May00	P	Implicit in **E4** (18May00), 'What in the world could have come more acceptably and wellcome to me than the faire progresse of your health, confirmed under your owne hand!'
xxJun01	E	Implicit in the general content of **E11** (07Jun01).

N.B. Some letters are now only represented by copies or drafts, for example 20Jun87 (**C38**). In theory it could be assumed that these were once matched by letters-sent which may one day turn up. However, as discussed above (p.18ff), in E's case it is likely that a number were never sent, and even those that were would often have borne different dates and had slightly or significantly different content.

V. PHANTOM LETTERS

The following are cited in various publications with incorrect dates or addressees:

1. 03Jan66   Bray editions of Evelyn's *Diary and Correspondence* based on Evelyn's misdated copy (CLBI.270) of 31Jan66 (**A19**)

2. 14Mar67   Marburg's A1 from the Davey Catalogue. A duplicated, but misread, reference to her A19 14Mar87 (correctly 15Mar87); also referred to by her as 'between two items dated 1686' and 'between items, 1686' making four entries (her A1, A14, A16, and A19). See **C36** above

3. 09Aug73   Marburg's (her M24) error for 29Aug73 (**B5**)

4. 08Oct73   Marburg's (her M25) error for 08Sep73 (**B7**)

5. 05Jun81   Bray editions of Evelyn's *Diary and Correspondence* based on Evelyn's misdated copy (CLBII.430) of 05Jun82 (**C15**)

6. 02Jun85   Marburg's A7 from 'ABPC 1930' (correctly 1930–1, p.692; the J. Fred Osterstock Sale at Stan V. Henkels, Philadelphia, 16 October 1930, Lot 369 – catalogue at the Grolier Club, New York). A misreading of 02 Jan 1685/6 (**C29**) from the MS where the 'a' of 'Jan' is not fully closed and the numeral '6' is written resembling a flourish beneath the '85'. Subsequently appeared as item 76 in *Catalogue of Union Art Galleries*, New York, 27 February 1934, now dated 2 Jan 1685 (copy of this catalogue entry at HSP). It was then listed in ABPC (1945), once more dated 2 June 1685. Happily the 1934 appearance was accompanied by an illustration of the MS confirming it to be the letter of 2 January 1686. It reached HL at Harvard in 1956 from the collection of C.R Richmond where it was correctly dated to January 1686

7. 23Sep85   Bray editions of Evelyn's *Diary and Correspondence* based on Evelyn's misdated copy (CLBII.507) of 22Sep85 (**C25**)

8. 14Mar87   Marburg's A19; a misreading of 15Mar87

9. 12Aug89   Bray editions of Evelyn's *Diary and Correspondence* based on Evelyn's misdated copy (CLBII.616) of 26Aug89 (**C47**)

10. 25Jul90   Correctly 25Sep90 (**D6**), E to P, Lot 185 T.S. Raffles sale at Sotheby's 29 June 1891 where it was erroneously dated 25 July 1690 due to the month on the MS being given as '7br' (HMCR VI, 1877, 473b, reporting the Raffles collection, gives the date of 25 September 1690)

11. 25Sep95   Marburg's A23; her misreading of HMCR VI, 1877, 473b (as previous), which says 1690, and thus also identifiable as **D6** above

12. 21Jul97   Langham Catalogue, Item 570; misprint for 21Jul86 (**C33**), as Davey Catalogue where it was sold before (Item 2884). References to Gauden and Dartmouth (both dead by 1691), confirms that 1697 is wrong.

13. 02Jan99   Marburg's A24; her misreading of Maggs Catalogue no. 388 (1920) where the letter is clearly dated 2 January 1699/1700 for 1700 (**E2**)

14. 19Nov00   Cited by Beal's *English Literary Manuscripts* (1987, Vol II, part II, 119) as Maggs Catalogue no. 449 (1924), item 343: Pepys 'to Evelyn'. Correctly, Pepys to John Jackson (copy at Tanner 1926, ii, no. 364)

15. 04Dec01   Braybrooke's error for 24Dec01 (**E14**)

16. Undated   Davey Catalogue, Item 2861, described as a letter and poem by Evelyn to Pepys. This is: HMCR XV, 1897, App. II, p.164, John Evelyn *junior* (where the poem is described as 'feeble'), and Lot 205 in the Arthur Houghton Sale (Part I, Christie's, June 1979) where it is described as 'EVELYN (JOHN, *Junior*): Autograph Letter signed, *no place, no date* [1680] TO SAMUEL PEPYS, sending him the manuscript of a poem to celebrate the recall of the Duke of York to England...' Now at PUL

Appendix 1: enclosures and other letters

Throughout the book various documents or letters are cited which are connected with the correspondence between Pepys and Evelyn, or which clarify events or topics. Where the material is published I have normally only supplied a reference in a footnote; brief items or excerpts, mostly unpublished, are quoted in the footnotes (see E to William Coventry, 2 October 1665, p.36; E to Richard Browne, 23 October 1665, p.45; E to Brouncker, 2 September 1672, p.80; E's description of an hour-glass, p.161; Mary, Lady Tuke, to P, 2 March 1687, p.176; Anne Fowler to P, 14 April 1688, p.181; James II to P, 4 December 1688, p.186; P to a Mrs Shellcrosse, 18 November 1697, p.235; P to Gale, 9 March 1699, p.261; and, E's grandson's poem for P, p.280).

The following consist of items enclosed with the original letters, and other letters or documents too long to be incorporated into the main text but of value to the reader. They include a letter to the Navy Commissioners as well as Pepys, and its associated enclosure. The priority is unpublished material but the previously-published (and recently rediscovered) letters, nos 8 and 9, are an important record of Pepys's death; they are provided here as a matter of convenience. However, those who wish to explore the subject in more detail should consult Tanner's volumes (1926 and 1929), Howarth (1932), and the Evelyn archive at the British Library.

1. **John Evelyn to Sir George Carteret**, 30 September 1665
   Enclosed with Evelyn's letter to Pepys of the same date (**A7**)
2. **Draft order**
   Enclosed with Evelyn's letter to Pepys of 14 October 1665 (**A11**)
3. **John Evelyn to Sir Richard Browne**, 14 October 1665
   Evelyn is franker about the problems facing him
4. **John Evelyn to the Commissioners of the Navy and Samuel Pepys**, 12 June 1673. On a shortage of clothing for prisoners
5. **Robert Birstall to John Evelyn**, 11 June 1673
   Enclosed with 4. above
6. **Samuel Pepys to the Commissioners**, 27 December 1673
   Royal instructions to place in quarantine soldiers sick with smallpox
7. **John Evelyn to Mrs Mary Evelyn**, [22] August 1685
   Concerning the elopement and illness of Elizabeth Evelyn
8. **John Jackson to John Evelyn**, 28 May 1703
   On the death of Pepys
9. **John Jackson to John Evelyn**, 5 June 1703
   On Pepys's funeral

1. JOHN EVELYN TO SIR GEORGE CARTERET[1]

Mr Vice Chamberlaine

Sayes Court
30 September 1665[2]

Right honourable

I could be very tender of importuning you with a repetition of my last so little
agreable if the straites we are in, and the necessities we are reduc'd to for want
of more considerable supplyes then we have yet touchd, did not even extort it
from me; I have here full 5000 sick wounded and prisoners who are not to be
fed without your care, nor can you expect from us more then the Constant and
most affectious informations which have been dues signified concerning our
wants; But are now arrivd to that height That perrishing reproach; and the
almost confation[3] will be the event thereof of not providing for us; The
Prisoners dieing for want of Bread and our Sick and Wounded for want of
harbour and refreshment, for these jealous times deprive us of quarters and our
lost credit and excessive debts of any meanes to recover it without speedyest
ayd whiles his Majesties subjects dye in our sight and at our thresholds without
our being able to relieve them, which with our barbarous exposure of the
Prisoners to the utmost of sufferings must needs redound to his Majesties great
dishonour and to the consequences of loosing the heart of our owne people
who are ready to exec[r]ate and stone us as we pass, Let not your honour
beleeve I have in the least exasperated[4] who report my-selfe to the principall
Officers that are witnesses of what I write nor is it the pettance[5] alsoe are
promised here, but have not yett toucht it, that can releeve us for any time
since wee shall have spent it before we receive it and when it may be to[o] late
to recover our-selves soe miserably lost as we are amongst a sort of wretched
people that starve if they be not dayly fed as your honour well knowes nor the
Prisoners who are of all other a trouble and an expence unsupportable. I
beseech your honour to lay the promises seriously to heart and then you will
soone set your hande to the worke that soe you may be deliverd from the

---

[1] Source: PRO S.P. 29/134, f. 63. Copy in P's(?) hand of a letter enclosed by E with
his to P of 30 September 1665 (A7); he seems to have experienced some difficulty in
reading E's writing. This copy was retained in the State Papers with E's original.
[2] MS: 'Says Court 30th: 7br 65'.
[3] A number of fates or consequences happening at once.
[4] Sic, perhaps a misreading for 'exaggerated'.
[5] I.e. pittance.

importunityes of us your servants or deliver us from this unspeakable servitude
which were either of them, the greatest favour you could accuelate[1] on of

> Your honours most faithfull
> And most obedient servant
> Eveling

2. JOHN EVELYN – DRAFT ORDER[2]

> *By the Deputy of the[3] Honourable his Majesties*
> *Commissioners for the Sick and Wounded Sea-*
> *men in the* Port *of   this*
> *day of   1665.*

*JEvelyn: By express *Order* from his *Royal Highness,*
You are to receive on *Board* these *Persons*
here under named, and to *Convey* them imme-
diatly to his *Majesties Fleet* with all Care and
Expedition; they having been of *those* who
have been *Recovered* of their *Wounds* and *Sick-*
nesses in the *Port* of   And you are
to send this *Certificate* to the *Lord Admiral,* or
Commander in *Chief* of the *Fleet.*

> *The Persons names are*

To the *Commander* or *Master* of the
now *Riding* in

---

[1] Sic, perhaps for 'aculeate'? from the Latin, meaning a sting or pointed remark. This,
however, does not make sense; P may, perhaps, have misread E's handwriting which
could have read 'you accord to one of' (Douglas Chambers, pers. comm.).

[2] Source: PRO S.P. 29/134, f.93. The text appears as a printed form attached by
Evelyn to his letter of 14 October 1665 (**A11**) and carries his signature in pen at the
point marked *.

[3] 'Deputy of the' struck out.

3. JOHN EVELYN TO SIR RICHARD BROWNE[1]

Sayes Court
14 October 1665[2]

Sir,

By this I acknowledge the receipt of yours from Oxon, and am amazed at your health: One would thinke I should much rejoice at His Majesties acceptance of my service: and realy I do so: But infinite is the mistake in the kindnesse of the supplies pretended me: for there is but barely £5000 assign'd me (the rest is for Sir William Doilys) which is totaly owing before I have touch'd one penny: Therefore to disabuse them I have written very plainely to the Greate-men or superiors, and whatever they say of it: I could not avoyd it: I will not make any repetition, but I desire you to ask Sir Philip Warrwick for a sight of mine of this late to you, Because it is a just prospect of my condition and there you will also see the extreme perill I have been exposd to since I saw you: I continue here in health (I thanke God) but in perpetual danger, we having now 5 houses of our Broomefield[3] atacq'd, wheroff Thomas Barn is at last one: a Guerl of his dying this night past: about 50 dyd this last weeke, there is almost no house cleere, and my Confusions continue so as if within one fortnight I have not ample supplies all will come to extreame confusion, and I must be forcd to see you at Oxon: however they take it, my charge being no less than £250 per diem, and my debt 4000 and more;[4] judge by this of my state, the Prisoners to be daily fed; I beseech you therefore make them sensible of it, and let you next informe me where I may safely lodge at Reading; as far as Oxon, I depend on your provision: Present my most humble service to my Brother; to Dr Charle[5] and Coll Reymes:[6] I left them all in health at Wotton on Tuesday and am

Sir, Your most obedient sonn
and servant

I received the warrant of Councill
Dr Wells[7] desires you to remember his Brother and begs of you to enquire

---

[1] Source: BL.1479.

[2] MS: 'Says-Court 14:Octr:65'.

[3] See Figure 5, p.338.

[4] P wrote to Carteret on 3 November 1665 (NMM LBK/8, 276–7) to tell him that E had been paid £2000 by Captain [Richard] Kingdon (Latham and Matthews, X, 214).

[5] Sic; probably Dr Walter Charleton.

[6] Colonel Bullen Reymes.

[7] Probably Dr Benjamin Wells.

which he has not of in a List of some [Books?] picked out for exchange in my Lord Arlingtons hands, if Sir I pray you make some enquiries for him, and do him what good you can.

4. JOHN EVELYN TO THE NAVY COMMISSIONERS AND SAMUEL PEPYS[1]

A shortage of clothes threatens disaster

Copy of my Letter to the Commissioners
of the Navy
To Mr Pepys Cleark of the Acts etc:[2]

Deptford
12 June 1673[3]

There being so vast an arreare due for the quartering of sick and wounded seamen within my precincts, (viz neere £10000), and I having in this present exigency of misery and [almost?][4] so incompetent supplies for them, that if I had Commission and power to do it (as you well know, I have not) I could not possibly comply with the wants of these naked and destitute Creatures; I think my selfe obligd in Christian Charity, to give your honourable Board an Account, how deeply the poor men (now set on shore at Gravesend and other places) are like to suffer for want of Clothes. It is not indeede the first time I have represented this sad case to you; but it is now ariv'd to that deplorable condition, that unlesse some speedy and effectull Course be taken in it, many of the poore wretches will be in danger of perishing, by exposd: For notwithstanding all the industry and credit I can possibly use (as circumstances

---

[1] Source: BL.1512. Endorsed, 'Copy of my Letter to the Commissioners of the Navy: Deptford 12 June: 1673. To Mr Pepys Cleark of the Acts etc:'. This letter appears to be addressed to the Navy Commissioners but via P. As it is thus not a letter specifically to P it has been placed here in preference to the main sequence of Pepys-Evelyn correspondence. E had received a letter from Gravesend which stimulated him to write to the Navy Commissioners. Neither are extant in the original; however, he copied both the letter received and the letter he composed on to a single sheet which he retained. Their order has been reversed here to reflect the order in which the Commissioners and P will have read them.

[2] Within two or three days P was elevated from this post to Secretaryship of the Admiralty.

[3] MS: as endorsement.

[4] MS: reading seems to be certain but the word is inappropriate.

are at present with mee, for want of monyes to discharge the Arreare)[1] they will not be received into quarters: I shall neede to exaggerate this no farther, after you have ben pleasd to peruse the inclosd,[2] wich[3] I just now receivd, who am   Sir Your etc:

Sir I have now in quarters in Kent above a thousand men, and the cry for cloths is so universall and intollerable that it deserves your pitty and redresse:

5. ROBERT BIRSTALL TO JOHN EVELYN[4]

News of an intollerable torrent

Gravesend
11 June 1673[5]

Honoured Sir,

Here be more from the *St Andrew* and the *London* 100 men put a shore in most unspeakable misery for want of Cloth[e]s which the people obstinately refuse to take in, if they be not allowd fresh Clothes and sweete shift without which they will not annoy themselves nor inspect their houses to the indangring of their lives etc.

Our number is already above 300 and before the fleete sayle, God knows what a multitude of such miserable Creatures they may be necessitated to impose and thrust upon us, to relieve the ships from the stench and taint of them aboard.

By fair words and large promises assumed upon our selves, they are taken in, but I cannot be at quiet day or night for the people, and if they have not

---

[1] E's diary entry for 12 June 1673 is so divergent from the tone and content of this letter that it bears quoting in full: 'Came to Visite and dine with me, my Lord VisCount Cornbery and his Lady, My Lady Francis Hyde Sister to the Duchesse of York, Mrs Dorothy Howard Mayd of Honour: We all went after dinner to see the formal, and formidable Camp, on Black-heath, raised to invade Holland, or as others suspected for another designe etc-: Thence to the Italian Glasse-house at Greenewich, where was Glasse blowne of finer mettal, than that of Muran ...'

[2] Not extant but E has copied it on the same sheet as this one. See next letter.

[3] Sic.

[4] Source: BL.1512. Copy by E on the same page as the copy of the previous letter. Original enclosed by E with the original of Appendix 1.4. Birstall was E's agent at Gravesend, in charge of pay and accounting for the sick and wounded. Subsequently he 'missbehaved himselfe' (diary, 22 March 1678; see de Beer, IV, 132, n.7 for references in official records).

[5] MS: 'Gravesend 11 June 1673'.

clothes for the men, without faile, and moneys very speed[i]ly in some competent measure, this intollerable torrent of the peoples out-crys will suddainly overwhelm me here, and extend farther than would be well thought of us, or be well-taken, and it cannot be anywise helped or prevented: I know Sir and am very sensible of your honest uttmost endeavours; but I humbly beseech you for Gods sake, the supply may be as speedy and as ample as possible may be, for I am not able any longer to endure this life, and it will be every houre much worse; but submitting to your Consideration, I crave to [....]¹

your honours humble servant
Robert Birstall:

6. SAMUEL PEPYS (for the King) TO THE COMMISSIONERS²

*To Our Commissioners for takeing care of
Sick and Wounded Seamen.*

27 December 1673

Charles R

Whereas we are informed, That Severall of Our Soldiers shipped on board the *Blessing*³ (to the Number of about fourty) now in the Downes, designed for Diepe, are Sick, and Severall of them of the small Pox, to the great indangering the Healths of the whole Ship's Company; Our will and pleasure is, that you doe forthwith find some meanes for the receiving and entertayning of the said Sick Persons in some convenient Quarters on Shore to be provided for that purpose, in the same manner as the Sick Men on board Our Fleete have or ought to have been taken care of; And that you alsoe give Order to your Officers at Deale to give notice to the Master of the said Vessell of the provision that shall be soe made by you herein, in Order to his conveying the said Sick Men on Shore to the Quarters that shall be by you provided for them. And for soe doing this shall be your Warrant. Given at Our Court at Whitehall this 27th day of December 1673.⁴

By his Majesties Command
SPepys

---

¹ Illegible.
² Source: BL Evelyn S & W folder II.
³ See p.88, note 4.
⁴ This order is the subject of a letter from E to John Conny the Chirurgeon dated 28 December 1673 (Marquess of Bath's *Portland Papers* II, f.210; microfilm at the Institute of Historical Research, Senate House, London).

7. JOHN EVELYN TO MRS MARY EVELYN[1]

I do not wish to see the Injurious Man

[no place]
Saturday morning [22] August 1685[2]

My Deare

Do not believe I abstaine from seeing this unhappy Child, either out of Indifference or implacable displeasure: If my coming may signifie anything besides trouble, and confusion as Circumstance may be: I will be sure to come; and therefore have dispatch'd John to bring me word in what Condition she is, and whether I should bring Mr Holden with me: I confesse I do not wish to see the injurious Man, who has (in great part ben the occasion of this redoubt'd Affliction, whether the poore Creature live or die; and truely that has ben the only cause of hindering me from being so often with her as I was with one who had never brought this sorrow and reproofe upon us. I have most earnestly besought Almighty God to be Mercifull to, and spare her life, if he think fit; and in all Events to accept of this severe Chastisement for all her errors, that she may be happy in another, and better World: Resigne (with me) therefore your selfe to his divine pleasure, and let me know what you want have me do, who am

Yours
JE

[1] Source: loose MS in the Evelyn Papers while on deposit at Christ Church, Oxford, 1992. Endorsed, 'From Mr Evelyn concerning poore Betty' in the hand of Sir John Evelyn(?). See letters 29 and 31 July, and 3 August 1685 (**C21–23**).
[2] Elizabeth died on Saturday, 29 August but E did not receive news that she had smallpox until Sunday, 16 August. The letter should therefore be dated to 22 August.

8. JOHN JACKSON TO JOHN EVELYN[1]

Tidings of Pepys's death

Clapham
Friday night, 28 May 1703[2]

Honoured Sir,

'Tis no small addition to my Grief, to be obliged to interrupt the Quiet of your happy Recess with the afflicting Tidings of my Unkle Pepys's death; knowing how sensibly you will partake with me herein; but I should not be faithful to his Desires if I did not begg your doing the honour to his memory of accepting Mourning from him, as a small Instance of his most affectionate Respect and honour for you. I have thought my selfe extreamly unfortunate to be out of the way at that only time when you were pleased lately to touch here, and express so great a desire of taking leave of my Unkle, which could not but have been admitted by him as a most welcome Exception to his general Orders against being interrupted: And I could most heartily wish that the Circumstances of your health and distance did not forbidd me to ask the favour of your assisting in the holding-up of the Pawle at his internment, which is intended to be on Thursday[3] next; for if the Manes[4] are affected with what passes below, I'm sure this would have been very gratefull to his.

I must not omit acquainting you, Sir, That upon Opening his Body (which the uncommonness of his Case required of us, for our own satisfaction as well as Publick Good) there was found in his Left Kidney a nest of no less than 7 stones, of the most irregular Figures your imagination can frame, and weighing together 4½ ounces; but all fast linked together and adhering to his Back: whereby they solve his having felt no greater Pains upon motion, nor other of the Ordinary Symptoms of the Stone: The rest of that Kidney was nothing but a bagg full of Ulcerous matter; which, irritating his Bowels, caused an irresistible Flux, and that his Destruction. Some Other lesser Defects there also were in his Body, proceeding from the same Cause: But his stamina in general were merveillously strong, and not only supported him under the most exquisite Pains, Weeks beyond all Expectations, but, in the conclusion, contended for near 40 hours (unassisted by any Nourishment) with the very

---

[1] Source: British Library MS (1996: Evelyn Correspondence, no number). Formerly Lot 208 Sotheby's 4 April 1955. Endorsed by E, 'From Mr Jackson upon the Death of his Unkle Mr Pepys Answerd 29th May:' The reply is not extant.
[2] MS: 'Clapham. May 28th. 1703. Fryd. night'.
[3] Corrected by JJ from 'Fryday'.
[4] The spirits of the departed.

Agonies of Death, some few Minutes excepted before his Expiring, which were very calm.

There remains only for me, under this affliction, to begg the Consolation and honour of succeeding to your Patronage, for my Unkle's sake, and leave to number my selfe with the same sincerity he ever did, among your greatest honourers, which I shall esteem as one of the most valuable parts of my Inheritances from him; being also with the faithfullest Wishes of health and a happy long Life to you,

Honoured Sir,

Your most obedient and most humble servant,

Jackson

Mr Hewer, as my Unkle's executor, and equally your Faithful Servant, joins with me in every part hereof.

The time of my good Unkle's departure was about ¾ past 3 on Wednesday morning last.

9. JOHN JACKSON TO JOHN EVELYN[1]

Clapham,
5 June 1703

Honoured Sir,

To what I troubled you with by Thursdays Post, I have, by this Messenger, only to add the Repetition of my humblest Thanks for the honours you have been pleased to do me; and to begg your own and young Mr Evelyn's Acceptance of the enclosed Memorials of my good Unkle Pepys; whose Body was last night interr'd in the Parish-Church of St Olave's Hart Street by the Navy-Office,[2]

I am, with profoundest respect, honoured Sir,

Your most faithful humble servant,

Jackson

[N.B. Further letters between Will Hewer, and John Jackson, with Evelyn concerning Jackson's thwarted plans to marry Evelyn's grand-daughter (see p.296) are published in Marburg 1935 (ref: BL Add MSS 15949, f.45-7).]

---

[1] Source: BL Deposit 9604 (an 1825 edition of P's diary with various MSS and engravings bound in; this letter was published by Smith in 1841 and presumably then was sold; acquired by the BL in November 1996). Endorsed by E, 'Mr Jacson [sic], 3d and 5 June, 1703 Sending me Rings, etc. for his Unkle Pepys' Funerall, who also sent me Mourning. Answered 5th.' This answer is lost.

[2] E had been unable to attend due to his 'present Indisposition' (diary, 26 May 1703).

Appendix 2: personalities

The information supplied here is basic and designed to serve as a very brief guide to the enormous array of personalities referred to in the correspondence and the notes. I have used a variety of sources, principally the *Dictionary of National Biography*, *Webster's Biographical Dictionary* (Springfield, Massachusetts 1933), Samuel Maunder's *Biographical Treasury* (6th edition, London 1847), de Beer's edition of Evelyn's diary and the Latham and Matthews edition of Pepys's diary.

The list is not exhaustive because some individuals defied reasonable attempts to identify them, caused in part no doubt by varied spellings and form. Space has also prevented the inclusion of classical personalities who are generally easily identifiable from almost any classical dictionary. I have, however, retained ancient literary figures. Each name is accompanied by an abbreviated indication of the letters in which their names occur; thus (01Jan00) indicates the letter of 1 January 1700.

ABBOT, George (1562–1633). Archbishop of Canterbury, 1611. (26Aug89)

ACOMINATOS (Cometas), Nicetas (11th cent). Byzantine scholar. (10Jul82; 01Jan00)

ÆTHELRED II. King of England 978–1016. (07Jul80)

ALBA, Duke of, *see* Alva

ALBEMARLE *see* Monck, George

ALBERTI, Leon Battiste (1404–72), architect and poet. (26Aug89)

ALDRICH, Henry (1647–1710). Scholar, divine, and musician. (31Oct81)

ALVA, Fernando Alvarez de Toledo (c.1508–83). Spanish military commander under Charles V. (26Aug89)

ANDREWES, Dr Lancelot (1555–1626), bishop of Winchester 1619–26. (31Oct81)

ANDRONICUS, probably Andronicus I, Byzantine emperor (1183–85). (01Jan00)

ANGLESEY, *see* Annesley, Arthur

ANNE OF DENMARK (1574–1619), Queen of James I of England. (19Sep82)

ANNESLEY, Arthur (1614–86), cr. first Earl of Anglesey 1661. Politician and writer; holder of various offices after the Restoration including Treasurer of the Navy, 1667–8, and Lord Privy Seal, 1672. (31Jan80; 26Aug89)

AQUINAS, Thomas (c. 1225–74). Italian scholastic philosopher. (26Feb90)

ARIOSTO, Lodovico (1474–1533). Italian poet. (26Aug89)

ARISTEIDES (AD129–189). Greek philosopher. (26Aug89)

ARISTOTLE (384–322BC). Greek philosopher. (26Aug89; 04Oct89)

ARLINGTON, *see* Bennet, Henry

ARUNDEL, *see* Howard, Thomas

ASCHAM, Roger (1515–68). Author and traveller. (26Aug89)

ASCLEPIADES (fl. 280BC), Greek poet. (06Sep80)

ASHLEY, Lord *see* Cooper, Anthony

ASHMOLE, Elias (1617–92). Antiquary, bibliophile and collector (see E's diary, 23 July 1678). (26Aug89)

ASTELL, Mrs Mary (1668–1731). Anonymous author of *A Serious Proposal to Ladies* (1694). The proposal was for an academic establishment of women run on religious principles. (03Dec96)

ATHENÆUS (fl. 200). Rhetorician. (30Jan80; 07Jul80; 06Sep80; 10Aug83)

AUGUSTINE, Saint (354–430). (07Jul80)

BACON, Sir Francis (1561–1626). (30Jan80; 07Jul80; 26Aug89; 02Sep94)

BACON, Roger (1214–94). Philosopher.

(26Aug89)

BAILLOT, Guil. de Baillou (1538–1616). French medieval writer. (07Jul80)

BAKER, –. Shipwright. (07Jul80)

BAKER, John. Printseller. Perhaps John Baker of St Paul's Churchyard. (26Sep90)

BAKER, Sir Richard (1568–1645). Historical and religious writer. He produced a history of the kings of England up to 1625. (07Jul80)

BALFOUR, Sir James (1600–57). Historian. (10May00)

BANISTER, Mr –. Tutor of E's grandson. (20Jan03)

BARBARO, Daniel (1528–69). Venetian diplomat and theologian. (26Aug89)

BARBOUR, William (c. 1640– post 85), clerk in the Navy Office; assisted E with the sick and wounded in 1666. (26Mar66)

BARLOW, Dr Thomas (1607–91) MA; Bodleian Librarian 1652–60; Bishop of Lincoln 1675. (26Aug89)

BATES, either William or George (1608–69). English physician and historian. (07Jul80)

BEAUMONT, Sir John (1583–1627). Poet. (26Aug89)

BECKET, Thomas à (1118–70). Archbishop of Canterbury. (25Mar95)

BECKFORD, Mrs –. An accomplice of Elizabeth Evelyn's during her elopement. Unknown but a Captain Thomas Beckford (d. 1685), known to P, was appointed slop-seller to the Royal Navy in 1666. Perhaps his wife. (03Aug85)

BEDE, 'The Venerable' (673–735). Monk, historian, scholar. (26Aug89)

BENNET, Henry (1618-85), cr. Baron Arlington, 1665; cr. first Earl of Arlington, 1672; Secretary of State 1662-74; served as Lord Chamberlain 1674-85. (29Aug73; 06Dec81)

BENTLEY, Richard (1662–1742). Scholar; appointed chaplain to Stillingfleet, bishop of Worcester, 1690; prebendary of Worcester, 1692; keeper of royal libraries, 1694. (29Aug92; 16Sep92; 07Jul94; 10Aug94; 07Jan95; 03Apr98)

BERKELEY, Sir Robert (1584–1656). Judge who supported Charles I's ship-money plans. (26Aug89)

BERTIE, Robert (1582–1642), cr. first Earl of Lindsey, 1626. Sailed with Buckingham (see Villiers); lord high admiral, 1636. (26Aug89)

BEZA, Theod (1519–1605). French religious reformer. (26Aug89)

BIDDULPH, Sir Theophilus, bt (c. 1615–83). Merchant who made his name in the 1650s as Master of the Drapers' Company and as an MP. (03Oct65)

BIRSTALL, Robert. E's Agent at Gravesend for sick and wounded. (App. 1.5)

BLUNDEL, possibly Peter (1520–91) or William (1620–98). Royalist and topographer. (26Aug89)

BOCCALINI, Trajano (1556–1613), Italian satirist. (29Aug92)

BOCHART (Bochartus), Samuel (1599–1667), French orientalist and divine. (30Jan80)

BODLEY, Sir Thomas (1545–1613). Diplomat and scholar, founder of Bodleian Library. (26Aug89)

BOHUN, Ralph (c. 1640–1716), E's son's tutor and later rector of Wotton. (10Aug83)

BOYLE, Charles (1676–1731), succeeded as fourth Earl of Orrery in 1703. Great-nephew of Robert Boyle. Scholarly opponent of Richard Bentley who exposed the Phalaris epistles, published by him, as forgeries. (03Apr98)

BOYLE, Hon. Robert (1627–91). Scientist, natural philosopher and theologian. E was an executor of his will. (26Aug89; 30Aug89; 29Aug92)

BOXHORNIUS (Buxhornius), Marcus Zuerius, (c. 1612–53). Scholar. (07Jul80; 19Sep82)

BRAHE, Tycho (1546–1601). Astronomer. (26Aug89)

BRAMSTON, Sir John (1577–1654). Judge under Charles I. (26Aug89)

BRIDGEMAN (Bridgman), Sir Orlando (c. 1606–74). Lawyer who sat on trial of regicides. Lord Chief Justice of common pleas, 1660–8, and Lord Keeper of the great seal, 1667–72. (26Aug89)

BRIDGEMAN, William (c. 1646–99). Introduced by E into the Royal Society in 1680. Among other posts he was a Clerk of the Council 1685-8, 1692-9, Secretary of the Admiralty 1694-5. (28Nov86)

BRISBANE, John (c. 1638–84). Secretary to

the lords commissioners of the
Admiralty, and judge-advocate of the
fleet. (06Dec81)

BRISTOL, *see* Digby, John

BROUNCKER (Broneker), William (c.
1620–84), second Viscount Brouncker
1645, mathematician, musician, virtuoso,
and first president of the Royal Society,
1662–77. Commissioner of the Navy,
1664. (03Oct65)

BROWNE, Sir Richard (1605–83), E's
father-in-law. Royalist diplomat, who
represented Charles I and II at the French
court before 1660. Master of Trinity
House 1672–3. (03Oct65; 2Nov69;
07Jul80; 06Dec81; 10Aug94)

BROWNRIG, Ralph (1592–1659). Bishop
of Exeter, 1641. (26Aug89)

BUCHANAN, George (1506–82). Historian.
(26Aug89)

BUCKHURST, *see* Sackville, Thomas
(26Aug89)

BUCKINGHAM, *see* Villiers, George

BUDÆUS (Budeus, Budé), Guillaime
(1467–1540). French expert in classical
literature. (07Jul80)

BURLEIGH, *see* Cecil, William

BURNET, Dr Gilbert (1643–1715). Bishop
of Salisbury, 1689-1715. Chaplain of the
Rolls Chapel 1680. His *History of the
Reformation of the Church of England*
was first (part one) published in 1679. E
contributed to the second edition,
published 1681–3. (06Sep80; 08Jun84)

BURNET, Thomas (c.1635–1715).
Opponent of James II and author of
various works of theology/cosmogony.
(08Jun84)

BURTON, Robert (1577–1640). Author of
Anatomy of Melancholy (1621).
(16Sep92)

BUTLER, Samuel (1612–80). Satirist and
author of *Hudibras* (1663). (26Aug89)

CABOT, John (c.1450– c. 1498). Explorer
and navigator. (07Jul90)

CABOT (Gabott), Sebastian (c. 1476–1557).
Explorer, son of John Cabot. (07Jul80)

CALVIN, John (1509–64). French
theologian and reformer. (26Aug89)

CAMDEN (Cambden), William
(1551–1623). Antiquary and historian.
(07Jul80; 10Jul82; 26Aug89)

CAMERARIUS, Joachimus *the elder*
(1500–74) and *the younger* (1534–98),
both German scholars. (10Jul82)

CAPEL, Henry (1638–96), cr. Baron Capel
of Tewkesbury 1692, appointed Lord
Justice of Ireland 1693-5 (see E's diary,
1 August 1693). (27Feb80; 06Jul93)

CARLISLE, *see* Howard, Charles

CARTERET, Sir George (d. 1680).
Treasurer of the Navy 1660-7, naval
commissioner 1673-9. (30Sep65;
29Aug73; App. 1.1, and 3)

CARNARVON, *see* Dormer, Robert

CARY, Lucius (c. 1610–43), second
Viscount Falkland. Royalist. (26Aug89)

CASAUBON, Isaac (1559–1614). Classical
scholar, his edition of Athenæus was
published at Lyons in 1600. (06Sep80)

CASTRUCCIO, Castracani degli
Antelminelli, Duke of Lucca
(1281–1328). Italian soldier and poet.
(26Aug89)

CATONEA (Catena), Girolama. (07Jul80;
06Sep80) *or* Biagio, Vincenzo di
(Catena) (1470–1530)

CATULLUS, Gaius Valerius (84–54BC).
Roman poet. (23Sep85)

CAVENDISH, Thomas (1560–92).
Circumnavigator and explorer.
(26Aug89)

CAVENDISH, William (1592–1676), cr.
first Duke of Newcastle, 1665. Royalist
and patron of playwrights. (26Aug89)

CAXTON, William (c. 1422–91). Printer.
(28Mar92)

CECIL, Thomas (*fl.* 1630), English
engraver. (26Sep90)

CECIL, William (1520–98), first Baron
Burghley/Burleigh. English statesman.
(26Aug89)

CHARLES II (1630–85; reigned 1660–85),
King of England. (17Feb66 both;
26Mar66; 27Aug72; 24Jan74; 06Dec81;
02Oct85; 14Mar87)

CHARLES V (1337–80), King of France
(10Jul82; 26Aug89)

CHARLES ('the Bold' or 'the Rash')
(1433–77). Succeeded as Duke of
Burgundy, 1467. (03Dec96)

CHARLETON, Dr Walter (1619–1707).
Royal physician but known as an
antiquary and founding member of the
Royal Society. (04Oct89; App. 1.3)

CHARLETT, Dr Arthur (1655–1722), master of University College 1692. (10Aug94, 02Sep94; 18Nov94; 15Feb95)

CHARLTON (Charleton) *see* Courten, William.

CHAUCER, Geoffrey (c. 1340–1400). Poet and writer. (26Aug89)

CHAUVEAU, François (1613–76), French engraver who produced primarily book illustrations. (21Aug69)

CHEKE, Sir John (1514–57). Classical scholar. (26Aug89)

CHIFFINCH 'Chiffings', William (c. 1602–88), page to Charles II until 1666, thereafter closet-keeper following his brother Thomas's death. (07Jul80)

CHILLINGWORTH, William (1602–44). Theologian and anti-Catholic. (26Aug89)

CHISWELL, Robert. Publisher. (22May94)

CHURCHILL, John (1650–1722), cr. Baron Churchill of Sandridge, 1685; cr. first Earl of Marlborough in 1689, and first Duke of in 1702. Shipwrecked with the Duke of York in 1682. (05Jun82)

CIACCONO (Ciaconius, Chacon), Alfonso (1540–99), a Spanish Dominican, his *Historia Utriusque Belli Dacici a Traiano Caesare Gesti*, Rome 1616. (06Dec81)

CICERO (Tullie), Marcus Tullius (104–43BC). Roman writer, politician and philosopher. (06Sep80; 04Oct89; 02Sep94; 22Jul00; 20Jan03)

CIFACCA, *see* Grossi, Giovanni Francesco

CLARENDON, *see* Hyde, Edward *and* Hyde, Henry

CLEMENS, Alexandrinus Clemens (3rd cent AD), Christian writer. (02Sep94)

CLEMENT, Saint (late 1st cent. AD). Third successor to St Peter as pope. His letter to the Corinthians. (26Aug89)

CLEVELAND, John (1613–58), royalist poet, educated at Cambridge and afterwards taught there. His poems appeared in various editions. (04Oct89)

CLIFFORD, Martin (E gives Matthew in error) (d. 1677). Author. (26Aug89)

CLIFFORD, Sir Thomas (1630–73), cr. first Baron Clifford of Chudleigh, 1672. Sub-commissioner for sick and wounded seamen from 1664–7, Treasurer of the Household 1666–72, Treasury Commissioner 1667–72, Lord High Treasurer 1672–3. Became a Roman Catholic in 1673, precipitating his fall. (27Apr65; 06Dec81; 28Apr82)

COCKE, George, Captain (c. 1617–79). A garrulous and bibulous merchant who held various official posts connected with customs and other naval matters including his post as treasurer for the sick and wounded seamen 1665–7. He was elected to the Royal Society in 1666. (23Oct65; 23Nov65; 07Jul80)

COKE, Sir Edward (1552–1634). Influential lawyer and judge. (26Aug89)

COLBERT (Colebert), Jean Baptiste (1619–83). French statesmen who encouraged literature, the arts, and building. (26Aug89)

COLEPEPER (Culpepper), Thomas (1635–89), second Baron Colepeper, owner of Leeds Castle, hired out to E in 1665. (03Oct65)

COLLIER, Frederick. Waterman at Deptford. (31Jul88)

COLONNA, Vittoria (1490–1547), Marchioness of Pescora. Poet. (26Aug89)

COLUMBUS, Christopher (c. 1446–1506). Navigator. (26Aug89)

COMENIUS *see* Komensky, Jan Amos

COMINES, *see* De Commynes, Philippe

CONDE, Louis II de Bourbon, Prince de (1621–86). French military leader who opposed Mazarin. (26Aug89)

CONNY, John (d. post-1689), surgeon to extraordinaries at Chatham from 1660 until (at least) 1679 (*see* P's diary 24 March 1669). (23Nov65)

COOPER, Sir Anthony Ashley (1621–83), cr. first Baron Ashley 1661, first Earl of Shaftesbury 1672. Chancellor of the Exchequer 1661–72, Treasury Commissioner 1667–72, Treasurer of the Commission for Prizes 1665–7. Supported Third Dutch War but opposed fund-raising. (23Sep65; 29Aug73)

COPERNICUS, Nicholas (1473–1543). Astronomer. (26Aug89; 28Mar92)

CORDESIUS, Balth., (1592–1650). Flemish theologian. (26Aug89)

CORTEZ, Hernando (1485–1547). Spanish conqueror of Mexico. (26Aug89)

CORVINUS, Matthew or Hunyadi (1440–90). King of Hungary. (26Aug89)

COSIN, John (1594–1672), chaplain to exiled Anglicans in Paris 1642–60, Dean of Peterborough, 1640–60 and Bishop of Durham, 1660–72. E knew him in Paris and once planned to buy his library (diary, 15 March 1652). (26Aug89)

COTTINGTON, Francis (c. 1578–1652), cr. Baron Cottington 1631. Diplomat. (26Aug89)

COTTON, Sir Robert (1571–1631), antiquary. (26Aug89)

COURTEN (self-styled, Charleton), William (1642–1702), of the Middle Temple. Natural historian and botanist. (26Aug89; 04Oct89)

COVENTRY, Henry (1619–86), Baron. Envoy and secretary of state. (29Aug73)

COVENTRY, Sir William, bt. (c. 1628–86), Secretary to the Lord High Admiral 1660–7, Commissioner of the Navy 1662–7, and Privy Councillor 1665. Kt. 1665. A colleague and close friend of P's. His reputation, and P's admiration, was founded on his efficiency and orderly administration. (9Aug65; 9Dec65).

COWLEY, Abraham (1618–67), 'that incomparable Poet, & Virtuous Man, my very deare friend' (E's diary, 1 August 1667). E dedicated editions of his *Kalendarium Hortense* to Cowley. (21Aug69; 26Aug89)

COWLEY, Thomas (d. 1669), brother of the poet. Clerk of the Cheque at Deptford 1660–5. (21Aug69)

COWS (Cowes), Mr –. Brother of Mrs Fowler. (01Mar88; 10 Sep88; 11Sep88)

CRANMER, Thomas (1489–1556). Archbishop of Canterbury, 1533. (26Aug89; 25Mar95)

CREECH, Thomas (1659–1700). Linguist and translator, 'an excellent Poet & Philosopher' (E's diary, 16 June 1700). Published a translation of Lucretius into English in 1682. E contributed a 22-line dedication to the 1683 edition (Keynes 129) recalling his own attempt with Book I of *De Rerum Natura* in 1656. His suicide was reputed to have followed a thwarted romance, and financial difficulties. (22Jul00)

CROMWELL, Thomas (c. 1485–1540), Earl of Essex. English statesman. (26Aug89)

CROSSE, Thomas (fl. 1632–82), engraver. (26Sep90).

CUPERTUS (Cuyper), Gisbertus

(1644–1716). (23Sep85)

DANBY, *see* Osborne, Sir Thomas

DANIEL, Roger. Bookseller in London and Cambridge. (26Sep90)

DARTMOUTH, *see* Legge, George

DEANE, Sir Anthony (c. 1638–1721). Master Shipwright, and business associate and friend of P with whom he was implicated in the Popish Plot. Much of their correspondence survives. (07Apr90; 11Jun90)

DE COMMYNES, Philippe (c. 1447–1511). Diplomat and counsellor at the court of Louis XI and Charles VIII. (03Dec96)

DEE, Jonathan (1527–1608). Mathematician and astronomer. (d. 1638) (07Jul80)

DE GROOT (Grotius), Hugo (1583–1645). Dutch jurist, theologian and author. (30Jan80; 02Sep94)

DE LA CASAS, Bartholomew (1474–1566). Missionary in America and historian. (10Jul82)

DE LAET, Johannes (1582–1649). Flemish geographer and physician. E possessed his *De Gemmis et Lapidus libri duo*, Leiden, 1647 (Lot 863) (04Oct89)

DE LA RŒM, (also Delarem) Francis (1590–1627). English engraver. (26Sep90)

DELFF, Willem Jacobszoon (1580–1638). Dutch portrait painter and engraver. (26Sep90)

DE LIONNE (de Lyonne), Hugues (1611–71), Marquis de Berny – Louis XIV's minister for foreign affairs. (06Dec81)

DE MASSUE, Henri (c. 1610–89), Marquis de Ruvigny. E's 'neighbour' – he came to England in 1686 and lived at the Queen's House in Greenwich (de Beer, IV, 523). (04Oct89)

DE MEDICI, Cosimo (1389–1464). Florentine statesman. (26Aug89)

DE MEDICI, Maria (1496–1533), Queen of France. (21Aug69)

DEMETRIUS PHALEREUS (d. 284 BC), pupil of Theophrastus. His writings on history and rhetoric are lost and only recounted by others, for example Cicero, *De Officiis*. (07Jul80)

DEMOSTHENES (385–322BC). Greek orator. (07Jul80; 04Oct89)

DE PEIRESC, Nicholas Claude Fabri (1580–1637), the French savant. (09Jan92)

DERBY, *see* Stanley, James

DESCARTES, René (1596–1650). French philosopher. (26Aug89; 26Feb90)

D'ESTE, Mary Beatrix Eleonora, *see* Mary, James II's Queen (Part 1).

DE VALOIS 'Valesianus', Adrian (d. 1692), his opinions. (02Sep94)

DEVEREUX, Robert (1566–1601), second Earl of. Soldier and courtier. (26Aug89)

D'EWES, Sir Simonds (1602–50), antiquarian. Associated with Selden and Cotton in the claim of Robert de Vere to the Earldom of Oxford. (26Aug89)

DE WIT (de Witesen), Johann (1625–72). Dutch mathematician. (30Jan80)

DIGBY, Lord, *see* Digby, John, Baron Digby

DIGBY, George (1612–77), second Earl of Bristol. Royalist. (26Aug89)

DIGBY, John (1580–1643), cr. Baron Digby, 1618, cr. first Earl of Bristol, 1622. Diplomat and statesman involved in marriage negotiations of Charles I. (26Aug89)

DIGBY, Sir Kenhelm (1603–65). Naval commander, writer, and scientist. (26Aug89)

DIO CASSIUS (Dion Cassius Coccelanus) (150–235). Roman historian. (02Sep94)

DIODORUS SICULUS (fl. 44BC). Roman historian. (30Jan80; 23Sep85)

DIOMEDES (5th cent. AD). Latin grammarian. (04Oct89)

DONNE, John (c. 1572–1631). Theologian, writer, poet and preacher. (26Aug89)

DORIA, Andrea (1468–1560). Genoese administrator. (26Aug89)

DORMER, Robert (d. 1643), cr. first Earl of Carnarvon 1643. Killed at first Battle of Newbury (1643). (26Aug89)

DORP, 'Admiral'. Perhaps Colonel Frederic van Dorp, governor of Ostend. (07Jul80)

DOYLY (D'Oily, Doily, Doolye, Doyley), Sir William (c. 1614–77), cr. baronet 1663. Commissioner for Sick and Wounded Seamen 1664–7, 1672–4. (27Apr65; 20Sep65; 23Oct65; 23Nov65; 7Oct72; App. 1.3)

DRAKE, Sir Francis (1540–96). English explorer and circumnavigator. (07Jul80;

06Dec81; 26Aug89)

DRAPER, Mrs – (d. 1701). William Draper's mother (E's diary, 28 March 1701). (06Jul93)

DRAPER, Mrs Susanna (1669–1754), née E. E's youngest daughter and husband of William Draper (married 27 April 1693). The only one of E's eight children born alive to outlive their parents. (01Mar86; 06Jul93; 30May94; 25Aug00; 07Jun01; 10Dec01)

DRAPER, William (d. 1718). E's son-in-law through his marriage to Susanna. Administrator of Greenwich Hospital project. (06Jul93; 30May94; 20Jan03)

DROESHOUT, Martin (1620–51), born in England of Flemish parentage and known only for engraving Shakespeare's portrait. (P's 25Sep90)

DRYDEN, John (1631–1700), 'the famous play-poet'. E thought his conversion to Catholicism 'no greate losse' to the Anglican church. (26Aug89)

DU BOSSE, Abraham (1602–76), French engraver. (21Aug69; 21Aug69)

DUDLEY, Sir Robert (1574–1649). Engineer and author of *Dell'Arcano del Mare* (1645–6), a compendium of naval knowledge. (30Jan80; 25Jun80)

DUDLEY, Robert (c. 1532–88), Earl of Leicester. (06Dec81)

DUGDALE, Sir William (1605–86). Antiquarian, historian, genealogist and writer. (26Aug89; 26Sep90)

DUILIUS (Duillius), Gaius Duilius Nepos (3rd cent BC). (07Jul80)

DU JON, François (1589–1677) philologist and antiquary. (04Oct89)

DUMMER, Mr Edmund (c.1650–*post* 1704). E's neighbour at Deptford who sought his help for promotion. Eventually became a surveyor of the navy and was falsely accused of corruption. (23Sep85; 06Dec85; 02Jan86; 08Jan86)

DUNS, Joannes 'John' Scotus (c. 1265–1308). 'Doctor Subtilis'. Philosopher and logician. (26Aug89)

DU PIN (Dupin), Louis Ellies (1657–1719), Doctor of the Sorbonne, His *New History of Ecclesiastical Writers* (French), translated into English variously from 1695 on. (02Sep94)

DUPPA, Brian (1588–1662). Bishop of

Winchester, 1660. (26Aug89)

DUTTON, Sir Richard, of Shelborne who was a mourner at P's funeral. (10Dec01)

EDGAR (944–75). King of England 959–75. (07Jul80; 19Sep82)

EDISBURY, Sir Kendrick[?], a relative? of Sir Ken[d]rick Edisbury (d. 1638) involved in Elizabeth Evelyn's elopement. Probably a navy commissioner. (03Aug85)

EGBERT. King of the West Saxons 802–39. (07Jul80)

EGERTON, Thomas (1540–1617), Baron Ellesmere and Viscount Brockley, Lord Chancellor. (26Aug89)

EGMONT, Lamoral (1558–90), Count of. Flemish soldier. (26Aug89)

ELLESMERE, *see* Egerton, Thomas

ELSTRACKE, Renold/Reginald (c. 1571). (26Sep90)

EPICTETUS (60 to post 118). Greek stoic philosopher. (09Aug00; 24Dec01)

EPICURUS (342–270BC). Greek philosopher. (26Aug89)

ERASMUS, Desiderius (1467–1536). (26Aug89; 29Aug92)

ESSEX, earls of, *see* Devereux, Robert, and Cromwell, Thomas

EVELYN, Elizabeth (1667–85). E's second daughter. Barely mentioned in the diary until she eloped in July 1685 with John Tippet's (q.v.) nephew, occasioning the most graphic series of E's letters to P. (29Jul85; 31Jul85; 03Aug85; 06Jul93; App.1.7)

EVELYN, John (1655–99), the younger. Gifted linguist and third son of the diarist, the only one to grow to maturity. In 1692 made a Commissioner for the Revenue in Ireland. Prone to ill-health and depression, dying in early 1699. His son, Sir John Evelyn (q.v.), became the diarist's heir. (01Mar77; 30Jan80; 28Nov86; 19Jan87; P's 25Sep90; 29Aug92; 06Jul93; 01Dec01)

EVELYN, Sir John (1682–1763), bart. Grandson of the diarist and heir to the Wotton estate. His progress at Eton and Oxford was a subject of great interest to E. P frequently expressed his own enthusiastic support in the letters. E proudly included excerpts from his letters

home. (01Mar77; 22May94; 30May94; 22Jul00; 25Aug00; 19Sep00; 19Nov01; 10Dec01; 24Dec01; 20Jan03)

EVELYN, Mrs Mary (c. 1635–1709), wife of the diarist. E met her father, Sir Richard Browne, in Paris in the 1640s. She was about 12 when he married her on 27 June 1647 in Paris. The marriage led to his purchase of his father-in-law's estate at Sayes Court in Deptford. Eight children (five sons and three daughters) were born. Only one, Susanna (*see* Draper, Susanna) outlived her parents. Mrs Evelyn's abilities are rarely mentioned by the diarist but even 19th century editors of the archive noted her skills as a correspondent. She was an able artist (*see* Hollar, Wenceslaus q.v.). In later life she suffered from recurrent ill-health and this is frequently mentioned in the letters. (17Feb72; 10Aug83; 19Apr87; 01Mar88; 10Sep88; 11Sep88; 11Jun90; 10Aug94; 07Jan95; 22Jul00; 19Sep00; 07Jun01; 19Nov01; 24Dec01; App. 1.7)

FAITHORNE (Faithorn), William (1616–91), engraver and painter. (26Sep90)

FALKLAND, *see* Cary, Lucius

FANSHAWE, Sir Henry (1569–1616). Remembrancer of the Exchequer. (26Aug89)

FANSHAWE, Sir Richard (1608–66) (*see* also Fanshawe, Sir Henry). Diplomat and friend of E's. Distantly related to E's mother-in-law Elizabeth, Lady Browne; ambassador to Spain 1664–6 but died in Madrid. (26Aug89)

FELIBIEN, André (1619–65). Architectural writer. (04Oct89)

FELL, Dr John Fell (1625–86), Bishop of Oxford 1675–86. He had received on behalf of the University the marbles formerly in Arundel's collection, a gift arranged by E. (31Oct81; 10Aug94)

FILLINGHAM, Bartholomew. Agent of E's during the Dutch Wars. (23Nov65)

FINCH, Elizabeth, Lady. Mother of Heneage Finch. (24Dec01)

FINCH, Sir Heneage (1621–82), cr. first Earl of Nottingham, 1681. Father of Heneage Finch. Lord Chancellor

1675–82. (24Dec01)

FINCH, Heneage (c. 1647–1719). Son of Sir Heneage Finch, and Elizabeth, Lady Finch, née Banks; purchased the Albury estate c. 1680–7 (de Beer, II, 77). Cr. first Earl of Aylesford 1714. (07Jul94; 10Dec01; 24Dec01; 20Jan03)

FISHER, Saint John (1469–1535). Bishop of Rochester, 1504. Opposed Henry VIII's divorce from Catherine of Aragon and was executed. (26Aug89)

FITZGERALD, Dr –, a contact of E's in Paris. (21Aug69)

FLAMSTEED   (Flamsted),   John (1646–1719). The astronomer. (06Jun84)

FLETCHER, John (1579–1625). Dramatist. (26Aug89)

FONTANA, Dominico (1543–1607). Italian engineer and architect. (07Jul80)

FOWLER, Mrs Anne. Wife of Captain Thomas Fowler (10Aug83; 01Mar88)

FOWLER, Captain Thomas (d. 1687?). Naval captain who died in debt. (10Aug83, 01Mar88)

FOX, Edward (c. 1496–1538). Bishop of Hereford, 1535. Assisted Henry VIII's divorce. (26Aug89)

FOX, Sir Stephen, (1627–1716), kt. 1665. Pay-master General of the army 1661–76 and Commissioner of the Treasury 1679–1702. He was a highly successful administrator and grew extremely wealthy. He proposed the Royal Chelsea Hospital with which E was involved (diary, 14 September 1681). E was impressed by his hard work (ibid, 6 September 1680). (30Jan80)

FRAISER (Frazier) Dr, Sir Alexander (c.1610–81). Physician to Charles II. (12Apr92)

FRANCIS I (1494–1547), King of France. (26Aug89)

FROBEN, Johann (c. 1460–1527). German printer and publisher, particularly of Erasmus's works. (26Aug89)

FROBISHER (Fourbisher), Sir Martin (c. 1535–94). Navigator and explorer. (06Dec81; 26Aug89)

FOURNIERE,   Georges   (1595–1655). French military writer. (30Jan80)

GALE, Dr Thomas (c. 1635–1702). Master of St Paul's School, afterwards Dean of York, 1697–1702). A member of P's and E's close social and intellectual circle and a cousin of P's by marriage. (02Nov88; 26Aug89; 08Oct91; 29Aug92; 16Sep92; 06Jul93; 30May94; 07Jul94; 02Sep94; 03Apr98)

GALILEO, Galileo Galilei (1564–1642). Astronomer   and   scientist.   (07Jul80; 26Aug89)

GARDINER   (Gardner),   Stephen   (c. 1483–1555). Bishop of Winchester, 1531. (26Aug89)

GASSENDUS, Pierre (1592–1655). French philosopher and scientist. (09Jan92)

GAUDEN (Gaudin), Alderman Sir Denis (d. 1688), kt. in 1667. Navy victualler 1660–77 for which he was rewarded by rarely receiving money from the crown and was bankrupted in consequence. He appears   frequently   in   P's   diary. (17Feb72; 07Jul80; 29Jun86; 21Jul87)

GELLIUS, Aulus (c. 130–180). Roman writer. (26Aug89; 02Sep94)

GESNER, Konrad von (1516–58). Swiss naturalist. (02Sep94)

GIBBONS, Mr, *see* Gibson, Edmund

GIBSON (Gibbons), Edmund (1669–1748). Librarian at Lambeth Palace, and chaplain to Archbishop Thomas Tenison from 1698. Subsequently Bishop of Lincoln, 1715. (18Nov94; 25Mar95)

GIBSON, Richard (d. *post* 1703). Friend and former clerk of P's. Served as Clerk of the Cheque at Deptford (1677–80), then chief clerk of the Victualling Accounts. Fowler's creditor? (01Mar88)

GIFFORD, Captain –. Merchant and adventurer friend of E's. In 1695 he lost everything on a trip to the East Indies when captured by the French (diary, 15 September 1695); however he recovered enough to be an associate of E's grandson at Oxford. Apart from the diary and letter reference he is unknown. (22Jul00)

GILBERT   (Gilber),   Dr   William (1540–1603). Royal physician and author of seminal work on magnetism. (07Jul80)

GIOVIO,   Paolo   (Paulus   Jovius) (1483–1552). Italian historian, author of *Historia   sui   Temporis*.   (10Jul82; 26Aug89)

GLAUBER, Johann Rudolf ('Polydor Virgil') (1604–68). German chemist and physician. (07Jul80)

GODOLPHIN, Dr Henry (1648–1733). Provost of Eton 1695–77. (02Nov88; 26Aug89; 02Apr94; 03Apr98)

GODOLPHIN, Margaret (1652–78), née Blagge. Former Maid of Honour, and close friend of E's. (04Sep73; 03Oct85; 26Aug89; 20Jan03)

GODOLPHIN, Sidney (1645–1712), cr. first Baron Godolphin 1684, Lord High Treasurer 1702–10. Patron of E's and husband of Margaret. (03Oct85; 11Jun90; 07Nov94; 10Dec01; 20Jan03)

GRAHAM, James (1612–50), first marquis and fifth Earl of Montrose. Royalist military commander. (26Aug89)

GRANDSDEN, Mr –. Stableman at Deptford dockyard. (03Oct87)

GREGORY, Professor David (1661–1708). Professor of astronomy at Oxford, 1691. Master commoner at Balliol, E's grandson's college. (22Jul00)

GREVILLE, Sir Fulke (1554–1628), cr. first Baron Brooke, 1621. Poet and statesman. (26Aug89)

GROSSI (known as 'Cifacca' or 'Cefache'), Giovanni Francesco (1653–97). The celebrated eunuch singer who deigned to appear at P's house. (19Apr87)

GROTIUS *see* De Groot, Hugo

GUICCIARDINI (Guichardin), Francois (1482–1540). Italian historian. (26Aug89)

HAKLUYT (Hackluyt), Richard (1552–1616). English naval historian. (07Jul80)

HALES, John (1584–1656). Linguist and theologian, fellow of Eton 1613–49 (at the time E would have been there had he been able to face the discipline: diary, 21 October 1632). (26Aug89)

HAMILTON, William Douglas (1635–94), third Duke of Hamilton. (26Aug89)

HANMER, Sir Thomas (1612–78), 2nd bart., E mentions him in *Numismata* as a coin collector. (26Aug89)

HANNIBAL (247–183BC). Carthaginian general. (26Aug89)

HARVEY, Dr William (1578–1657). Medical pioneer. (26Aug89)

HASCHENPERG, Stephan von. Military engineer. (07Jul80)

HATTON, Captain Charles (c. 1635– *post* 1701). Son of Christopher Hatton, first Baron Hatton (c.1605–70) and younger brother of Christopher, first Viscount Hatton (1632–1706). A dining companion of P's. He commissioned P's nephew, John Jackson, to buy biographical details of cardinals in Italy. Jackson was helped in his travels there by Hatton's sister, Lady Throgmorton. (03Apr98, 10Dec01)

HAWKINS, Sir John (1532–95). Naval commander and privateer. (26Aug89)

HENRIET, Israel (1590–1661), French engraver and tutor to Louis XIV. (21Aug69)

HENRIETTA ANNE, princess (1644–70), sister of Charles II and duchess of Orleans. (21Aug69)

HENRY IV (1553–1610), King of France. (07Jul80)

HENSHAW, Thomas (1618–1700). English scientific writer, and virtuoso friend and co-traveller of E's. (26Aug89)

HERODOTUS (c.484–420BC). Greek historian. (30Jan80; 07Jul80)

HERVEY, Jonathan (1616–79)? Catherine of Braganza's treasurer. (26Aug89)

HEWER (Ewer), Mrs –. Will Hewer's mother. (02Oct85)

HEWER (Ewer), William (Will) (1642–1715). P's clerk from 1660; rose to be deputy Judge Advocate of the fleet in 1677, then Treasurer for Tangier 1680–4, Commissioner of the Navy 1685–8. P lived with him from 1679. (30Jan80; 05Jun82; 10Aug83; 18May00; 25Aug00; 24Dec01)

HEYLIN, Peter (1600–62). Royalist historical writer. (07Jul80)

HIERO, King of Syracuse (d. 467BC). (07Jul80)

HIEROM, St., *see* Jerome

HIMILCO (Himilo). Carthaginian explorer. (07Jul80)

HOBBES, Thomas (1588–1679). Philosopher and writer. (26Feb90)

HOLBEIN, Hans (1497–1543), the Younger. Portraitist. (26Aug89)

HOLDEN 'Mr Holden', Rev Richard (c. 1627–1702), Rector of Deptford 1673–1702. Author of *The Improvement of Navigation* (1680). (15Jun80; 07Jul80)

HOLINSHED (Hollinshead/Hollingshead), Ralph/Raphael (d. *c.* 1580), historian. (07Jul80; 31Jul88)

HOLLAND, *see* Rich, Henry

HOLLAR, Wenceslaus (1607–77). E was one of his patrons. Some correspondence survives between the two discussing their financial relationship (BL Evelyn Letters 1318–1322). He produced the frontispiece for E's edition of Book I of Lucretius in 1656 (P's 25Sep90; 26Sep90; 25Mar95)

HOOKE, Robert (1635–1703). Experimental philosopher and architect; curator of experiments at Royal Society, 1662; secretary 1677–82. (Introduction; 25Jun80)

HOOKER, *probably* Richard (c. 1554–1600). Theologian. (26Aug89)

HOOKER, Sir William (d. 1697). Lord Mayor of London 1672–3. Mrs Fowler's landlord. (01Mar88)

HOSIER, Frank. Clerk of the Cheque, Gravesend, 1665; Clerk of Control at Deptford dockyard 1669–79. (27Feb80)

HOUBLON, Sir James (c. 1629–1700), kt. 1691. A Huguenot refugee merchant and later a banker. He was one of P's best friends as was his wife Sarah. E first met him on 15 January 1679 (diary). (02Oct85; 13Nov90; 16Sep92)

HOWARD, Charles (1526–1624), second Baron Howard of Effingham and first Earl of Nottingham, and Lord High Admiral from 1585–1618.

HOWARD, Charles (1629–85), first Earl of Carlisle of the second creation (1661). Former Parliamentarian, subsequently a diplomat under Charles II. (26Aug89)

HOWARD, Henry (1628–84), sixth Duke of Norfolk 1677. Friend of E's. (06Dec81; 09Feb85; 26Aug89)

HOWARD, Thomas (1585–1646), second Earl of Arundel. Aesthete and art collector. (26Aug89; P's 25Sep90; 25Mar95)

HOWARD, William (1614–80), Viscount Stafford. Executed for alleged involvement in Popish Plot. (26Aug89)

HUDIBRAS, *see* Butler, Samuel

HUMBLE, George, and his associate John Sudbury (*fl.* 1610–32). Print-sellers. (26Sep90)

HUS, John (c. 1373–1415). Bohemian reformer and martyr. (26Aug89)

HYDE, Anne (1637–71), duchess of York, first wife of James II as Duke of York, and mother of the Queens, Mary II and Anne. (05Jun82)

HYDE, Edward (1609–74), first Earl of Clarendon, and Lord Chancellor 1660–67. (03Oct65; P's 25Sep90; 20Jan03)

HYDE, Flower (d. 1700), countess of Clarendon. (09Aug00)

HYDE, Henry (1638–1709), second Earl of Clarendon 1674. Lord Privy Seale 1685. Lord Lieutenant of Ireland 1685–7. Like P he suffered under William III for his loyalty to James II and was imprisoned in the Tower where E visited him (diary, 17 July 1690). (09Feb85; 26Aug89; 14Aug90; 22May94; 10Aug94)

HYLIN, *see* Heylin, Peter

ISAAC (Isak), Monsieur – (fl. 1680–1712). Dancing teacher. (20Jan03)

ISABELLA of Castile (1451–1504). Queen from 1474. (26Aug89)

JACKSON, John (1673–1723). P's uninspiring but dutiful and conscientious nephew and eventual heir (by 1703). As E's grandson became the focal interest of E's later life so Jackson and his elder brother Samuel became P's. Jackson was sent abroad to explore Europe, something which P had not done but E had. P tried to persuade E to allow his grandson to do this too but it never came about, probably because E had too much invested in his grandson's future to take the risk. Jackson's dogged pursuit of his travels are recorded in letters to his uncle. (07Aug00; 25Aug00; 24Dec01; 20Jan03; App. 1.8, and 9)

JACKSON, Thomas (1579–1640). Author of various works including commentary on 'Apostles' Creed'. Dean of Peterborough 1639–40. (31Oct81)

JACOB, *see* Delff

JAMES II (1633–1701; reigned 1685–8), *as Duke of York* (12Dec65; 17Feb66; 26Mar66; 27Feb80; 05Jun82), *as James II of England* (09Feb85; 02Oct85; 31Dec85; 01Mar86)

JENNER, Thomas (fl. 1631–56), print-seller and publisher. (26Sep90)

JERMYN, Henry (c. 1604–84), cr. first Earl of St Albans, 1660. Guardian of Henrietta Maria. (26Aug89; 04Oct89)

JERMYN, Henry (c. 1636–1708), cr. Baron Dover 1685, Earl of Dover 1689. Nephew and heir of Henry Jermyn, Earl of St Albans. (04Oct89)

JEROME (Hierom), St., (c. 341–420). Theologian and writer. (09Aug00)

JEROME, of Prague (d. 1416). Follower of Huss in rejecting transubstantiation. (26Aug89)

JOHN 'Don John', of Austria (1547–78). Spanish general and illegitimate son of Charles V. (26Aug89)

JOVIUS, Paulus *see* Giovio, Paolo

JUNIUS, *see* Du Jon, François, *and* Young, Patrick

JUSTELL, Henry (1620–93). French royal bibliographer in England. (26Aug89)

JUSTINIANI, Bernhard (1408–89). Venetian diplomat and historian. (26Aug89)

JUXON, William (1582–1663). Archbishop of Canterbury, 1660. (26Aug89)

KEILL, John (1671–1721), the mathematician and astronomer, incorporated at Oxford in 1694 where he lectured on natural philsophy. (10Dec01)

KEN, Dr Thomas (1637–1711), In 1682 Dartmouth's chaplain but subsequently Bishop of Bath and Wells, 1685–91. (07Aug83)

KERSEBOOM (Causabon), Frederick (1632–90). Portrait-painter. Trained at Amsterdam but worked in England. Painted Boyle. (30Aug89)

KING, *possibly* Dr Edmund (1629–1709). Physician to Charles II. (30Aug89)

KINGDON, Captain Richard. Speculator, and commissioner at the Prize Office 1665–7. (23Sep65; App. 1.3)

KINGSTON, *see* Pierrepont, Robert

KIRCHER, Athanasius (1602–80). Jesuit mathematician. (07Jul80)

KNELLER, Sir Godfrey (1646-1723). Dutch painter who came to England 1675; kt. 1691, principal court painter of the period and of dignitaries. He painted E for P's collection of portraits of his best friends.

(26Aug89; 30Aug89)

KOMENSKY ('Comenius'), Jan/Johann Amos (1592–1670). Czech theologian. (03Dec96)

LAËT, *see* De Laet

LANDI, Constanzo (1521–64), Comte di. Italian numismatist and philosopher. (03Apr98)

LA PAULMERIUS, Jacques (Jacobus Palmerius) (1587–1670). French philosopher. (31Oct81)

LATIMER, Hugh (c. 1485–1555). Bishop of Worcester, 1535. (26Aug89)

LAUD, William (1573–1645). Archbishop of Canterbury, 1633. (26Aug89; 22May94)

LAUDERDALE, *see* Maitland, John

LAWRENCE (Laurence), Dr –. Dartmouth's physician to Tangier. (07Aug83)

LE BRUN, Charles (1619–90), French historical painter. (21Aug69)

LEGGE, George (1648–91), cr. first Baron Dartmouth 1682. Commander of the Tangier expedition 1683–4 which P travelled on. Admiral under James II but failed to prevent William of Orange's landing. As Lord of Lewisham manor he was a neighbour of E's. (07Aug83; 10Aug83; 29Jun86; 21Jul87)

LEICESTER, *see* Dudley, Robert

LELY (Lilly), Sir Peter (1618–80). Portrait painter at the courts of Charles I and II. Rival of Wright (q.v.). (26Aug89; 09Jan92)

LE TELLIER, François Michel le Tellier, Marquis de Louvois (1641–91). Louis XIV's minister of war. (15Mar87)

LINDSEY (Lindsay), *see* Bertie, Robert

LLOYD, Dr William (1627–1717), Bishop of St Asaph, 1680–92. One of the seven bishops tried and acquitted for seditious libel against James II in 1688. (14Aug90)

LOCKE, John (1632–1704). Philosopher. (04Oct89; 07Apr90; 07Jul94; 10Aug94)

LOMBART, Pierre (c. 1620–81). Working in England between 1650–72. (26Sep90)

LORRAIN, Paul (d.1719). Huguenot refugee. Publisher of the condemneds' confessions, and P's clerk. (19Sep00)

LOUIS XI (1423–83). King of France. (03Dec96)

LOUIS XIV (1638–1715). King of France.

(15Mar87, 19Nov01)

LOUVOIS, *see*, Le Tellier

LUCAR, Cyprian (fl. 1564–90). Mechanician. (07Jul80)

LUTHER, Martin (1483–1546). Theologian. (26Aug89)

LYDIAT, Thomas (1572–1646). Divine, chronologer, and writer. Contributed to Prideaux's *Marmora Oxoniensia.* (31Oct81)

MACHIAVELLI. Niccolo (1469–1527). Diplomat and writer. (26Aug89)

MACROBIUS, Aurelius Macrobius Ambrosius (fl. 395–423). (06Sep80)

MAITLAND, Sir John (c. 1545–95), first Baron Maitland. (26Aug89)

MAITLAND, John (1616–82), first Duke of Lauderdale, 1672. (26Aug89)

MAITLAND, Sir Richard (1496–1586), of Lethington. (10May00)

MALLETTEA, Alain Manessot (fl. 1670s). French writer on war. (07Jul80)

MANCHESTER, *see* Montagu, Edward

MARISHONS, *see* Morisot

MARSHALL (Marishal), William (fl. 1617–49), engraver for books. (26Sep90)

MARULLUS (fl. 160–180). Latin satirical poet. (26Aug89)

MAURICE, Prince of Orange (1567–1625). Liberated United Provinces from Spain. (26Aug89)

MAZARIN, Cardinal Giulio (1602–61). French statesman and cardinal. (21Aug69; 07Jul80)

MEIBONIUS *probably* Marcus Maybaum (1630–1711), German savant and author of edition of Greek writers. (30Jan80)

MELANCHTHON, Schwarzerdt (1497–1560). German theologian. (26Aug89)

MENNES (Minnes), Sir John (1591–1671), Comptroller of the Navy 1660–71, inappropriately promoted after an active naval career. Admiral, 1662. P regarded him as hopelessly ill-suited to naval administration. (03Oct65)

MERIAN (Miriam), *either* Matthias Merian (1593–1650), *or* his son Matthias Merian the younger (1621–87): mentioned by E in *Sculptura* (1662). Both born in Basle. (26Sep90; 01Jan00)

MICHAELANGELO (1475–1564). The painter and sculptor. (08Feb68;

26Aug89)

MIDDLETON (Midleton), John (1619–74), cr. first Earl of Middleton, 1656. Punished for corruption, but subsequently governor of Tangier. (8Feb67)

MIEREVELT, Michael Jansz van (1567–1641). Dutch painter. (26Sep90)

MIRANDOLA, Giovanni Pico della (1463–94). (26Aug89)

MIRIAM, *see* Merian

MONCK, George (1608–70), cr. first Duke of Albemarle 1660. Parliamentary general whose dissatisfaction with the crumbling government after Cromwell's death led to his serving as the catalyst which brought about the Restoration. Joint commander of the Navy, 1660. Administered prosecution of the Second Dutch War from London. (23Oct65; 8Feb67; 15Jan73; 10Jul82; 26Aug89)

MONCOMY, Balthadzar de (1611–65). French traveller. (06Dec81)

MONTAGU, Edward (1602–71), second Earl of Manchester. Parliamentary military commander but supported the Restoration. (26Aug89)

MONTROSE, *see* Graham, James

MOORE, Sir Jonas (1617–79), kt. 1663. Mathematician taught by Oughtred (q.v.), tutor to the Duke of York, Surveyor-General to the Ordnance 1669. His expertise brought him P's respect and ear. (07Jul80)

MORDAUNT, Elizabeth (c. 1645–87), Lady, née Johnson. Widow of Sir Charles Mordaunt, bart., (1) and Francis Godolphin (2). Sister of 'Mrs – Stewart' (q.v.). In the 1670s they became close friends of P's. (P's diary 11 December 1666; see Latham and Matthews, VIII, 403, n. 3, and X, 249–50). (25Jun80; 03Oct87)

MORE, Sir Thomas (1478–1535). Statesman and author. (26Aug89)

MORIN, Jean (1609–66), French engraver who emulated Van Dyck. (21Aug69)

MORISON (Morisson), Robert (1620–83). Botanist to Charles II. (02Jan00)

MORISOT (Morisotus), Claude Barthelemy (1592–1661), French writer and scholar. (07Jul80; 19Sep82)

MORLEY, George (1598–1684). Bishop of Winchester, 1662. (26Aug89)

MOXON, Joseph (1627–1700), Charles II's Hydrographer and draughtsman. (04Oct89)

MUSGRAVE, George (b. *post* 1671), second son of Sir Christopher Musgrave, 4th bart., of Hartley Castle. keeper of the ordnance at Chatham. (10May00)

MYTTENS, Daniel (1590–1642), the Elder *or* (1644–88), the Younger. Both Flemish painters. (26Aug89)

NANTEUIL, Robert, French artist and engraver (c. 1623–78). His portraits of E, his wife, and parents-in-law, made in Paris in 1651, are the finest visual record of E and his family to survive (reproduced in Bowle, 1981). E used his own portrait as the frontispiece for his 1706 edition of *Silva*, despite its being 55 years old. (21Aug69; P's 25Sep90; 26Sep90)

NARBROUGH, Sir John (1640–88), Admiral 1674 and Commissioner of the Navy 1680-7. He died of fever at Domingo trying to recover treasure. His journal is in the Pepysian Library. (22May94; 30May94)

NAUDÉ (Naudeus), Gabriel (1600–53). French writer. (26Aug89)

NEWCASTLE, *see* Cavendish, William

NEWTON, Isaac (1642–1727). Scientist and mathematician. (08Oct91)

NICANOR (fl. 127AD). Greek grammarian. (07Jul80)

NICETAS, *see* ACOMINATOS

NICHOLSON, Francis (1665–1728). Lieutenant-governor of colonies north of Chesapeake Bay, 1688; lieutenant-governor of Virginia, 1690-4; governor of Maryland, 1694, of Virginia, 1699, and held numerous other posts. (xxSep86)

NICHOLSON (Nicolson), William (1655–1727), made Bishop of Carlisle in 1702. He was generous about E's *Numismata* (1697) (see de Beer, V, 508, note 2). (03Dec96; 10May00; 18May00)

NORFOLK, *see* Howard, Henry

NORTHUMBERLAND, *see* Percy, Henry

NOWELL, Dr Alexander (c. 1507–1602). Clergyman. Dean of St Paul's from 1560. (26Aug89)

OCKHAM (Occham), William (d. c. 1349).

Controversial theologian who tangled with the pope. (26Aug89)

OLDENBURG, Henry (c. 1615–77). First secretary of the Royal Society, 1663–77, and publisher and editor of the *Transactions* of, 1664–77. (21Aug69; 06Dec81)

OPPIAN (fl. early 3rd cent. AD). Author of a poem on hunting (the 'Cynaegeticon'). (10Jul82)

ORTELANIUS, Jacobus Colius (1563–1628), Flemish-English Latin writer. (03Oct85)

OSBORNE, Sir Thomas (1632–1712), second baronet, cr. first Earl of Danby of the second creation, 1674, and marquess of Carmarthen, 1689. Joint-Treasurer of the Navy 1668–71, Treasurer 1671-3, Lord High Treasurer, and Admiralty Commissioner 1673-9. (04Sep73; 24Jan74; 06Dec81; 26Aug89)

OSORIO, Jeronimo (1506–80). Travel writer and explorer. (06Sep80)

OUGHTRED, William (1575–1660). Mathematician. (26Aug89)

OXFORD, Anne, Countess of, *see* Vere, Anne

PAINE, John (1606–47), pupil of Simon van de Pas. (26Sep90)

PAINS, Ferdinand (16th cent.). Military engineer. (07Jul80)

PALMER, Sir Geoffrey (1598–1670), cr. attorney-general, 1660. (26Aug89)

PANCIRELLA (Panciroli), Guido de (1523–99). Italian jurist. (07Jul80)

PANHEIM, Ezechiel (1629–1710). (26Aug89)

PASTON, Sir William (1610–83). His medal collection. (26Aug89)

PATIN, Guy (1602–72). French physician. (26Aug89)

PAUL III, Pope (1534–49). (07Jul80)

PAUSANIAS (f. 170AD). Greek historian. (07Jul80)

PEAKE, 'Mr', Sir Robert (c. 1592–1667). Royalist printseller. (26Sep90)

PEARSE (Pierce) James (d. c. 1693), Surgeon-General to the Fleet 1665, staying in this post till after the Third Dutch War. He and his wife Elizabeth, noted for her looks, were close friends of P's. (27Aug72; 07Oct73)

PEIRESKIUS, *see* de Peiresc

PELL, Dr John (1611–85), mathematician. (02Sep94)

PENSER, Edmund (c. 1552–99). Poet. (26Aug89)

PEPYS, Mrs Elizabeth (1640–69), née St Michel, wife of the diarist. She features hardly at all in the correspondence with E. Her death followed a trip to the continent and P never remarried though his housekeeper/ common-law wife, Mary Skinner, was sometimes known as Mrs Pepys, even by E. (02Nov69)

'PEPYS, Mrs' Mary, *see* Skinner, Mary

PERCY, Henry (1564–1632), ninth Earl of Northumberland. Soldier, and opponent of James I's anti-Catholic measures. (26Aug89)

PETRARCH (Petrarca), Francesco (1304–74). Italian poet. (26Aug89)

PETT, Peter (d. 1589). Deptford master shipwright. (07Jul80)

PETT, Peter (1610–72), Navy Commissioner at Chatham 1648–67. Master-Shipwright at Chatham 1664–7. Blamed partly for the success of the Dutch attack in 1667 which finished him though he escaped imprisonment. Elected a fellow of the Royal Society in 1662. (28Feb66; 26Mar66)

PEYTON, Sir Thomas (c. 1613–84), bart. An associate of E's during the Third Dutch War (Text note, p.22)

PHILANDER, William (1505–65). Writer on Vitruvius. (26Aug89)

PHILIP II (1527–98), King of Spain. (26Aug89)

PHILIPS, Dirk (1504–68). Dutch theologian *or* Fabian (1601–90). Royalist writer. (26Aug89)

PIERREPONT, Robert (1584–1643), cr. first Earl of Kingston, 1628. (26Aug89)

PIUS V, Pope (1566–72). (06Sep80)

PLATO (428–348BC). Philosopher. (26Aug89)

PLINY, Gaius Plinius Secundus 'the Elder' (AD23–79). Natural historian. (30Jan80; 07Jul80; 10Jul82; 10Aug83; 23Sep85; 20Jan03)

PLOT (Plat), Dr Robert (1640–96). Antiquarian and collector of curiosities which E admired in Oxford on 10 July 1675. (07Jul80)

PLUTARCH. Roman historian. (AD46–120). (30Jan80; 23Sep85)

POLE, Reginald (1500–58). Cardinal, 1555; archbishop of Canterbury, 1556. (26Aug89)

POLLUX, Julius (2 cent. AD). Greek historian. (10Jul82)

POLYBIUS (210–128BC). Roman historian. (20Jan03)

POLYDOR, Virgil *see* Glauber, Johannes

POMPONIUS (fl. AD150). Roman jurist. (30Jan80)

PORTER, Sir Charles (1631–96), Lord Chancellor of Ireland 1690–6. E had dealings with him over debts to the crown (de Beer, IV, 556, note 1). (06Jul93)

POVEY, Thomas (1615– c. 1702). Held several posts including secretaryship of the Committee for Foreign Plantations in 1661, Treasurer of Tangier in 1663. Unable to cope with all his duties he came to an arrangement with P to share the rake-offs if the latter administered the responsibilities for him. He was also a Fellow of the Royal Society. (31Jan80)

PRIDEAUX, Humphrey (1648–1724). Orientalist and writer. (31Oct81)

PRIESTMAN, Mr –. Co-conspirator in Elizabeth Evelyn's elopement. (03Aug85)

PRISCIAN (5th cent. AD). Latin grammarian. (04Oct89)

PUTEANUS, Hendrik van der (1574–1646). Dutch philosopher. (26Aug89)

RADCLIFFE (Ratcliff), Dr John (1652–1714). P's doctor. Earned 20 guineas a day in 1684; intolerant of hypochondria; legacies financed St Bartholomew's Hospital, London and Radcliffe Infirmary, Oxford. (07Aug00)

RALEIGH (Rawleigh), Sir Walter (c. 1552–1618). Courtier and (07Jul80; xxDec81; 26Aug89)

RAPHAEL, Sanzio da Urbino (1483–1520). Italian painter. (26Aug89)

REYMES, Colonel Bullen (1613–72). Co-commissioner of E's during the Dutch Wars. (27Apr65; App. 1.3)

RICH, Henry (1590–1649), first Baron Kensington and first Earl of Holland. Courtier and diplomat executed by Parliamentarians. (26Aug89)

RICHELIEU, Armand Jean du Plessis, Duc de (1585–1642). French statesman and cardinal under Louis XIII and XIV. (07Jul80)

RIDLEY (Ridly), Dr Mark (1560–1624). Former physician to the Tsar. Wrote on magnetism. (07Jul80)

RIPLEY, *possibly* George (d. c. 1490). Augustinian alchemist. (26Aug89)

ROBERTS, Sir Gabriel (c. 1629–1715). Deputy-governor of Levant Company from 1690. (02Jul93)

RODOGINUS, Caelius. (07Jul80)

ROWLANDSON, John, Marshall at Leeds Castle. (13Dec65)

RUPERT, Prince (1619–82), of the Rhine. His mother Elizabeth was sister of Charles I. Charismatic military leader on land and sea who made his name in the English Civil War, and the Second and Third Dutch Wars. (08Feb68)

RUVIGNY *see* De Massue, Henri

RYNGLEY, Sir Stephen. Military engineer. (07Jul80)

RYVES (Reeves), Sir Thomas (c. 1583–1652). King's advocate 1623. Judge of the Admiralty of Dover 1636. Author of works on law and naval history. (28Nov86)

SABELLICUS, Marcus Antonius Coccius (1436–1506). Italian historian and critic. (10Jul82)

SACKVILLE, Thomas (1536–1608), Lord Buckhurst and first Earl of Dorset. Poet and freeman. (26Aug89)

ST ALBANS, *see* Jermyn, Henry

ST ARMANT, Marc. Ant. de Gerard, Sieur de (1594–1661). French poet. (26Aug89)

ST MICHEL, Balthasar (d. *post* 1710). P's brother-in-law, and employed by him in various naval administrative posts out of loyalty. (23Jan74)

SALMASIUS, *see* Saumaise, Claude de

SANCROFT, Dr William (1617–91). Archbishop of Canterbury 1678–91. (04Oct89)

SANDERSON, Robert (1587–1663). Bishop of Lincoln, 1660. (26Aug89)

SAUMAISE (Salmasius), Claude de (1588–1653). French critic. (26Aug89)

SAVILE (Savill), Sir Henry (1549–1622); his edition of Chrysostom's works was published in 1610–13. (26Aug89)

SCALIGER 'both the': Giulio Cesare (1484–1558). Italian philosopher *and* Joseph Justice (1540–1609). French philosopher. (26Aug89)

SCOTT, Robert of Little Britain, book-seller and binder (see letter from him to P, 30 June 1688, Howarth, 189). (09Jan92)

SELDEN, John (1584–1654), jurist and orientalist. (30Jan80; 31Oct81; 26Aug89)

SENECA the Younger (c. 4BC–AD65). Philosopher and rhetorician. (26Aug89)

SEYMOUR, Jane (1509–37). Third wife of Henry VIII. (26Aug89)

SFORZA, Giacomuzzo Attendolo, 'the Great' (1369–1424). Italian general. (26Aug89)

SHAEN, Sir James (d. 1695), bt. A commissioner of Irish excise. (06Dec81)

SHAFTESBURY *see* Cooper, Anthony

SHARPE, Sharpe (fl. 1679–82) buccaneer operating in the Caribbean and South America. Acquitted of piracy. (22May94)

SHEERES, Sir Henry (d. 1710), kt. 1685. Engineer at Tangier 1669–83. His father was a member of E's parish in Deptford and E had heard the son expound on the size of African locusts, and how to deal with a scorpion (E's diary, 4 March 1675). Knighted July 1685, and around then made Master of the Ordnance. (07Aug83; 10Aug83; 08Sep85)

SHELDON, Gilbert (1598–1677). Archbishop of Canterbury, 1663. (26Aug89)

SHELDON, Ralph (1623–84), of Weston, Warwickshire. Brother of Mary, Lady Tuke, and coin and medal collector. (26Aug89).

SHELLCROSSE, Mrs –. Friend of P's at Greenwich. Probably widow of John Shelcrosse (P's diary, 22 July 1665). (16Sep92)

SHISH, John (d. 1686). E's neighbour and Master-Shipwright at Deptford dockyard. (03Aug85)

SHREWSBURY, *see* Talbot, Gilbert

SKENE, Sir John (c. 1543–1617). Scottish lord of session under James VI. (10May00)

SKINNER, Mary. P's housekeeper and common-law wife, 'Mrs Pepys'. (15Mar87; 06Jul93; 14Jan99; 01Jan00;

02Jan00; 18May00; 07Aug00; 09Aug00; 25Aug00; 19Sep00; 19Nov01; 24Dec01; 20Jan03)

SIDNEY, Sir Philip (1554–86). Poet. (26Aug89)

SILVESTRE, Israel (1621–91), French engraver, nephew of Henriet. (21Aug69)

SIXTUS V, Pope (1585–90). (07Jul80)

SLOANE, Dr Hans (1660–1753), MD. Secretary of the Royal Society. From 1689 his medical practice was in Bloomsbury Square. (07Jun01)

SMITH, Dr Thomas (1638–1710). Author of books on Turks, and Greek church. (01Jan00)

SOCINUS, Laelius Franc. (1525–62). Founder of Socianism. (26Aug89)

SOCRATES (469–399BC). Philosopher. (26Aug89)

SOUTHAMPTON, *see* Wriothesley, Henry, and Wriothesley, Thomas, Earls of

SPENCER, Anne (1646–1716), Countess of Sunderland. A close personal friend and correspondent of E's who had once sought his help in arranging her son's marriage (E's diary, 16 May 1681). (26Aug89)

SPRAT, Dr Thomas (1635–1713). Author of history of the Royal Society. Bishop of Rochester 1684. (26Aug89)

STAFFORD, *see* Howard, William

STANLEY, James (1607–51), seventh Earl of Derby. Royalist general. (26Aug89)

STATIUS, P. Papinius (c. AD45–100). Roman poet. (23Sep85)

STEWART (Steward), Mrs –. Sister of Elizabeth, Lady Mordaunt (q.v.). Both were friends of P, and were daughters of Nicholas Johnson of London. Mrs Stewart seems to have been godmother to E's grand-daughter Jane (E's diary, 12 January 1692). (10Sep88; 16Sep92; 30May94)

STILLINGFLEET (Stillingfleete), Dr Edward (1635–99). Dean of St Paul's, 1678–89. Bishop of Worcester, 1689–99. E possessed a number of his works. (02Nov88; 29Aug92; 03Dec96)

STOCK, Andreas (c. 1616–?). (26Sep90)

STRABO, Greek geographer. (63BC–AD24). (30Jan80; 10Jul82; 26Aug89)

STRADA, Famianus (1572–1649). Italian

Jesuit historian and poet. (07Jul80)

STRICKLAND, John (d. *post* 1710). E's servant at Deptford. De Beer (V, 98, n.3) notes the possibility that he served as E's messenger during the Third Dutch War. (P's 25Sep90; 08Oct91)

SUETONIUS, Gaius S. Tranquillus (fl. AD117–138). Roman historian. (23Sep85; 04Oct89)

SUIDAS (fl. 1100). Greek author of a Lexicon. (07Jul80)

SULIMAN (Solyman) 'the Magnificent' (1494–1566). (26Aug89)

SUNDERLAND, Countess of, *see* Spencer, Anne

SYDNEY, Henry (1641–1704). Cr. Viscount Sydney 1689, Lord Lieutenant of Ireland, 1692, Earl of Romney, 1694. (06Jul93)

SYLVIUS, Ann, Lady de (c. 1656–1730). Former Maid of Honour; a correspondent and close friend of E's and Margaret Godolphin's. Wife of the diplomat Sir Gabriel de Sylvius (1637–97). (08Sep85)

TACITUS, Publius Cornelius (c. 55–120). Roman historian. (10Aug83)

TALBOT, Alathea (d. 1654), Countess of Arundel. Married Thomas Howard in 1606. (26Aug89)

TALBOT, Gilbert (1552–1616), seventh Earl of Shrewsbury. (26Aug89)

TARTAGLIA, Nicolao (c. 1500–59). Italian mathematician. (07Jul80)

TASSO, Torquato (1544–95). Italian poet. (26Aug89)

TENISON, Dr Thomas (1636–1715), Bishop of Lincoln 1691–4, Archbishop of Canterbury. (06Jul93; 07Jul94)

THOMPSON, *possibly* John (fl. 1382). Carmelite. (07Jul80; 26Aug89)

THOU, Jacques Auguste de (1553–1617). French historian. (26Aug89)

THROGMORTON (Throckmorton), Sir Nicholas (1515–71). (07Jul80)

THUANUS, *see* Thou

THUCYDIDES. Greek historian. (469–391BC). (30Jan80; 07Jul80)

TILLOTSON, Dr John (1630–94). Bishop of Rochester 1683–4. Bishop of Ely, 1684–90. (02Nov88)

TIPPETS (Tippet), Sir John (c. 1630–*post* 1692) kt. 1675. Master-Shipwright at

Portsmouth 1660–8, Navy Commissioner 1668–72, Surveyor of the Navy, 1672–86, 1688–92. His nephew eloped with E's daughter Elizabeth in 1685 from Deptford. This may have been John or Robert Tippets, clerks in the Navy Office after 1677 who were presumably his relations. (03Aug85)

TITIAN, Vecellio Tiziano (1489–1576). Italian painter. (26Aug89)

TOLLEMACHE, Lieutenant-General Thomas (c. 1651–94). Opposed James II and joined William of Orange. Commanded fated expedition to Brest, 1694. (07Jul94)

TREW, John (16th cent). Military engineer. (07Jul80)

TRUMBULL, Sir William (1639–1716). Chancellor of the diocese of Rochester, 1682; appointed Judge-Advocate to travel with Dartmouth on the expedition to Tangier, 1683. Kt. 1684. (07Aug83; 10Aug83; 28Nov86).

TUKE, Sir Brian (d. 1545). Statesman and patron of learning. (26Aug89)

TUKE, Mary, Lady Tuke (d. 1705). Second wife of Sir Samuel Tuke and sister of Ralph Sheldon. (07Aug83; 10Aug83; 19Apr87; 26Aug89)

TUKE, Sir Samuel Tuke (d. 1674), bart. In his diary E calls him cousin (1 October 1649); de Beer suggests that he was a relative of E's mother-in-law Elizabeth, Lady Browne. E first met him on 1 October 1649 in Paris (ibid). (21Aug69; 2Nov69; 06Dec81)

TUNSTALL, Cuthbert (1474–1559). Bishop of Durham, 1530. (26Aug89)

TURNER, Mrs Elizabeth (d. 1685). Wife of Thomas Turner. A gossip who was friend, confidant, and correspondent of P's. She was not averse to his occasional sexual advances; features frequently in P's diary. (17Feb72)

TURNER, Francis (c. 1638–1700), Bishop of Ely 1684–90. (26Aug89)

TURNER, Thomas (c. 1620–81), appointed storekeeper at Deptford dockyard in 1668 following service in the Navy Office. P thought him a 'knave'. (17Feb79)

TWYNE, John (c. 1501–81). English teacher and writer. (07Jul80)

TYRELL (Tirrill), Sir Timothy

(1617–1701). (26Aug89)

USSHER (Usher), James (1581–1656). Archbishop of Armagh 1625. (26Aug89)

VAILLANT, Jean Fay (1632–1706). French numismatist. (26Aug89)

VALESIANUS *see* De Valois, Adrian

VAN DE PAS, Crispin (c. 1590), the younger. Engraver. (26Sep90)

VAN DE PAS, Symon (c. 1595), brother of Crispin (q.v.). Engraver. (26Sep90)

VAN DER BORCHT, Hendrick (1614– c. 1666). German artist. (P's 25Sep90)

VAN DYCK (Dyke), Sir Anthony (1599–1641). Painter. (26Aug89)

VARENIUS, Bernhard (1622–50). German/Dutch physician. (22Jul00)

VAUGHAN, Sir John (1603–74). Pro-Royalist judge, chief justice of the common please, 1668. (26Aug89)

VAUGHAN (Vaughn), John (1640–1713), styled Lord Vaughan 1667–86, then third Earl of Carbery. (04Sep73; 09Feb85)

VAUGHAN, Robert (fl. 1650). Engraver. (26Sep90)

VELLEIUS, Publius V. Paterculus (fl. AD20–30). Roman historian. (20Jun87)

VERE, Anne, née Cecil (d. 1588), Countess of Oxford married to the poet Edward Vere, 17th Earl of Oxford. (26Aug89)

VERE, Sir Francis (1560–1609). English general and military writer. (26Aug89)

VESPUCCI, Americus (1451–1512). Merchant and adventurer. (26Aug89)

VILLAMENA, Franciscus (c. 1566–1626). His engravings of Trajan's Column. (06Dec81; 12Apr92)

VILLIERS, George (1592–1628), first Duke of Buckingham, and Lord High Admiral 1619–28. (26Aug89; 29Nov92)

VIRGIL, Publius Vergilius Maro (70–19BC). Roman poet. (03Dec96)

VITRUVIUS, Marcus Vitruvius Pollo (late 1st cent. BC). Roman architect. (26Aug89; 18May00)

VOSSIUS, Isaac (1618–89). Editor of Catullus (1684). (23Sep85)

VOSTERMAN, Lucas Vosterman (c. 1578–1660), the elder. (26Sep90)

WALLER, Edmund (1606–87). Poet. (26Aug89)

WALLER, Richard (c. 1646–*post* 1714).

Royal Society Secretary, 1687–1709. (03Apr98)

WALSINGHAM, Sir Francis (c. 1530–90). English statesman. (26Aug89)

WALSINGHAM, Thomas (d. 1422). His *Chronicon Angliæ*. (07Jul80)

WALTON, Brian (c. 1660–61). Bishop of Chester, 1660, and editor of English Ployglot Bible. (02Sep94)

WARD, Seth (1617–89), bishop of Salisbury 1667–89. Theologian and mathematician. (07Jul80)

WELLS, Dr Benjamin (1616–78). Family physician of E's, related to E's wife. (App. 1.3)

WENDY, Thomas (c. 1500–60). Royal physician and benefactor of Gonville and Caius College, Cambridge. (26Aug89)

WESTON, Richard (1577–1635), first Earl of Portland. Lord High Treasurer 1628–33. (26Aug89)

WHARTON, Henry (1664–95). Divine and scholar, author of various works including his 1695 *History of Dr William Laud*. (30May94, 07Jul94)

WHITE, Robert (1645–1703), engraver. He specialised in portraits of the famous of his day. (25Mar95)

WILKINS, John Wilkins (1614–72), Bishop of Chester 1668–72. E had met him at Oxford in 1654 and seen his apiaries while he was warden at Wadham (see diary, 10 July 1654). (02Sep94)

WILLIAM, Prince of Orange (1533–84). (06Dec81; 26Aug89)

WILLIAM (1689–1700), Duke of Gloucester. Heir to the throne of England until his death in 1700. (09Aug00)

WILLIAMSON, Sir Joseph (1633–1701), kt. 1672. Secretary of State 1674–9. President of the Royal Society 1677–80. (25Jun80; 07Jul80; 01Mar86; 10May00)

WINNE, Roger, a messenger used by E to help with communications about the sick and wounded. (26Mar66)

WOLSEY, Thomas (c. 1475–1530). Cardinal, 1515. (26Aug89)

WOOD, John (fl. 1596). Medical writer. (22May94; 30May94)

WOTTON, Sir Henry (1568–1639). Diplomat and poet with an interest in architecture. (26Aug89)

WOTTON, William (1666-1727). Scholar and former child prodigy. E had come across him when he was about 13 years old in 1679 (E's diary, 6 July 1679) and subsequently corresponded with him. Wotton even offered to help E correct *Sylva* for a projected fourth edition (1706) (letter from E to Richard Bentley, 20 January 1697). (07Jul94; 10Aug94; 02Sep94; 03Apr98)

WREN (Mr Surveyor), Sir Christopher (1632–1723). Architect. Surveyor-General, 1661. (02Apr94; 07Nov94)

WRIGHT, John Michael (c. 1625–1700). Portrait painter and rival of Lely. (26Aug89)

WRIOTHESLEY, Henry (1573–1624), third Earl of Southampton. Literary aesthete, co-conspirator with Essex, diplomat and colonial adventurer. (26Aug89)

WRIOTHESLEY, Thomas (1607–67), fourth Earl of Southampton, Lord High Treasurer 1660-7. (17Feb66)

WYCHE, Sir Cyrill (1632–1707). Statesman and scientist. Husband of E's niece. (29Aug92; 06Jul93)

XENOPHON (Zenophon) (c. 430–355BC). Greek soldier and writer. (20Jan03)

XIPHILIN, John (fl. 1100). Professor of law at Constantinople and epitomiser of Dion Cassius. (02Sep94)

YOUNG, Patrick ('Patritius Junius') (1584–1652). Biblical commentator. Librarian at St James. (26Aug89)

ZENO (5th cent. BC). Italian philosopher. (26Aug89)

ZISCA, John Z. of Trocznow (c. 1376–1424). Bohemian general and Hussite leader. (26Aug89)

Figures

1. (p.4) John Evelyn to Samuel Pepys, 4 September 1673 (**B6**). Princeton University Library. Used by permission.

2. (p.336 top) South-East England showing the main ports and towns concerned with the Dutch Wars (the editor).

3. (p.336 bottom) Evelyn's design for the Chatham Infirmary (from a copy in Bray, W., *The Diary and Correspondence of John Evelyn*, London, 1854, vol. III, p.176).

4. (p.337) Copy of Evelyn's depiction of the Dutch Action at Chatham in June 1667 (actual original dimensions: 197mm by 305mm). This is the draft which accompanied his letter of 6 December 1681 (**C10**), confirmed by the fact that the letter states that the symbol for Saturn: ♄ , is on the MS (see p.126 above). The MS, now in the Pforzheimer collection (MS 35B), bears this symbol on the *verso* of the drawing as stated in the Pforzheimer Catalogue (1940, p.1209). That the drawing was sold in the Davey Catalogue (Item 2862), and the letter which it accompanied is amongst the Pepys-Cockerell papers is the strongest evidence that the Davey Catalogue Items were once amongst the Pepys-Cockerell papers.

The present reproduction was prepared by the editor from a copy in order to clarify the stained and faded original. Apart from selective boldening of outlines and excision of scratches, and extraneous marks it is faithful to the original. The second version of the drawing is more refined. Evelyn prepared it from the draft and sent it to P with his letter of 20 January 1668 (**A26**). It is bound with the letter at Bodleian (MS Rawl A195 f.77–8). An engraving, prepared from the drawing, was published in Braybrooke's editions of Pepys's Diary in 1825 and 1854.

5. (p.338) Plan of Evelyn's house and estate at Sayes Court, Deptford. A number of the letters make reference to problems with flooding and damage caused by activities in the Royal Naval Dockyard, and access to the mast dock (e.g. 29 June 1686, **C32**, and 3 October 1687, **C39**). This plan, based on a 1692 survey by Joel Gascoyne (British Library K.18.17.2), shows the relationship of the house to the Yard. The proximity of the house to the dockyard wall is particularly evident, despite Evelyn's acquisition of a triangular extension of his land in 1668. The house was given over to tenants in 1694 and after Evelyn's death the dockyard made inroads into the estate. The estate in 1753 is illustrated in Barker and Jackson (1991, 74–5).

6. (pp.339–40) John Evelyn to Samuel Pepys, 30 May 1694 (**D21**). Princeton University Library. Used by permission.

[Illustrations of some of Pepys's letters to Evelyn may be found in *The Book Collector*, vol.44, no. 2, Summer 1995, p.154 (2 October 1685); and, Clara Marburg, *Mr Pepys and Mr Evelyn*, 1935, facing p.60 (15 February 1695)]

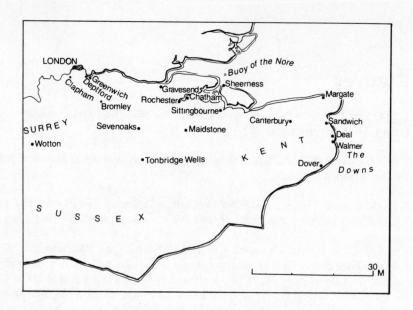

Fig. 2 South-East England

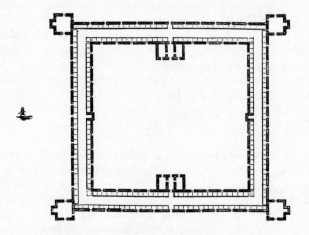

Fig. 3 Evelyn's plan for the Chatham Infirmary

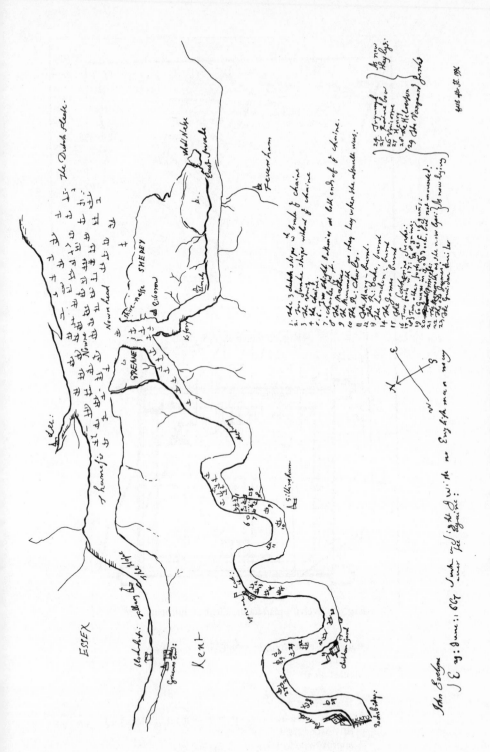

Fig. 4 Evelyn's drawing of the Dutch Action at Chatham 1667

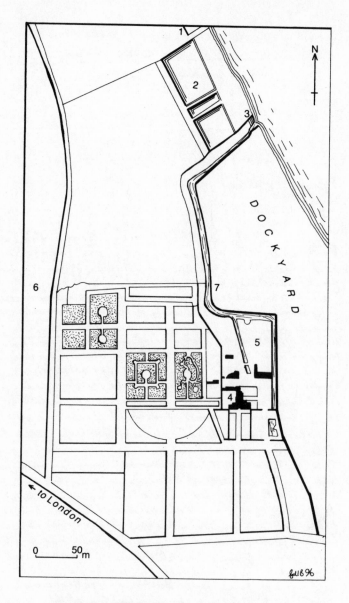

Fig. 5 Sayes Court and the Deptford dockyard
1. victualling stores
2. mast ponds
3. river stairs
4. Sayes Court house
5. land acquired by Evelyn in 1667–8 from the dockyard
6. the 'Broomfield'
7. approximate location of stables in 1753.

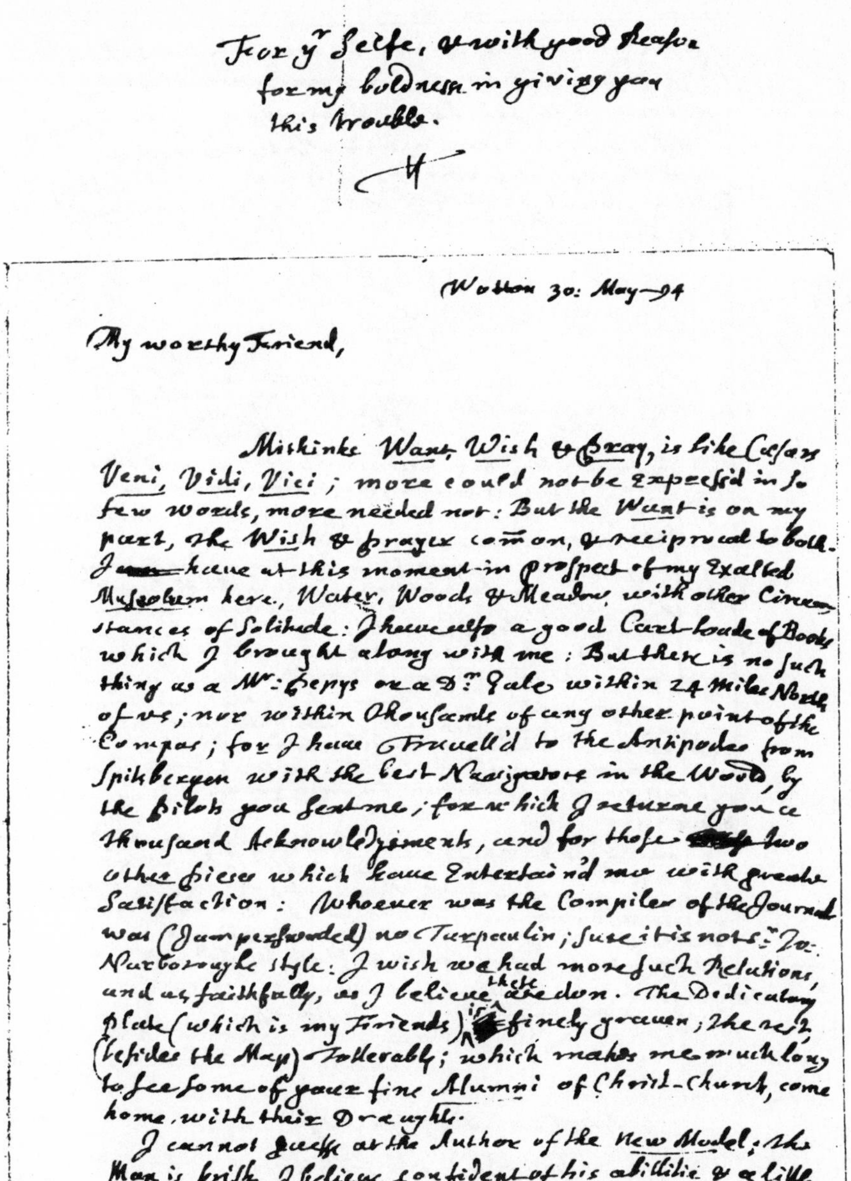

For y^r Selfe, & with good Reason
for my boldness in giving you
this trouble.

(Wotton 30: May—94

My worthy Friend,

Methinke Want, Wish & Pray, is like Cæsars
Veni, Vidi, Vici; more could not be expressd in so
few words, more needed not: But the Want is on my
part, the Wish & prayer common, & reciprocal to both.
I have at this moment in prospect of my Exalted
Mausoleum here, Water, Woods & Meadow, with other Circumstances of Solitude: I have also a good Cart-loade of Books
which I brought along with me: But there is no such
thing as a Mr Pepys or a Dr Gale within 24 Miles North
of us; nor within thousands of any other point of the
Compas; for I have Travell'd to the Antipodes from
Spitsbergen with the best Navigators in the World, by
the Bookes you sent me; for which I returne you a
thousand Acknowledgements, and for those two
other pieces which have Entertain'd me with greate
Satisfaction: Whoever was the Compiler of the Journal
was (I am perswaded) no Tarpaulin; sure it is not Sr Jo:
Narborough style: I wish we had more such Relations,
and as faithfully, as I believe these are don. The Dedicatory
plate (which is my Friends) finely graven; the rest
(besides the Map) tollerably; which makes me much long
to see some of your fine Alumni of Christ-church, come
home with their Draughts.
I cannot guesse at the Author of the New Model; the
Man is brisk, I believe confident of his abilitie & a little
conceited, & cutts a fesher (as they say) in the Conclusion very
genteely: From Mr Whartons undertaking I expect
greate, & usefull things: You see what Time, and
the

Fig. 6 John Evelyn to Samuel Pepys
30 May 1694 (D21) (see also overleaf)

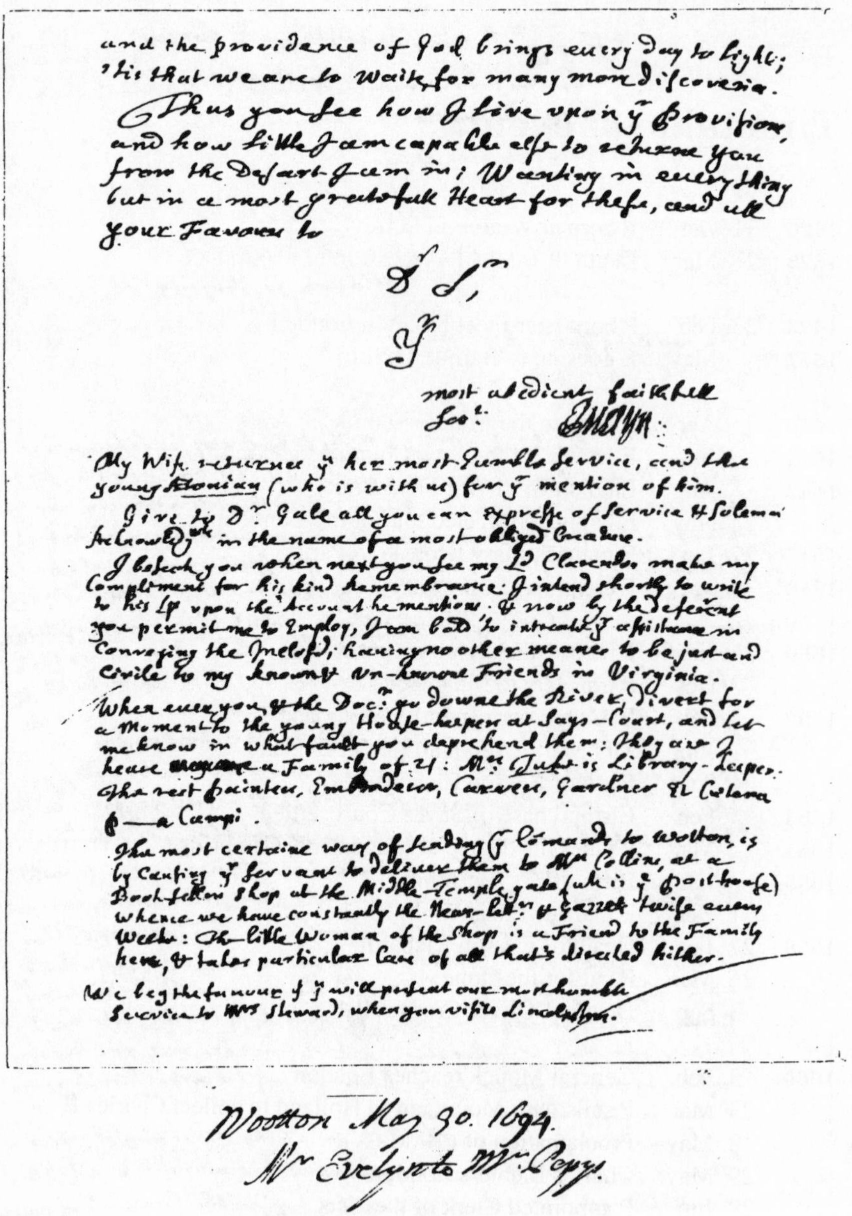

and the providence of God brings every day to light;
'tis that we are to waite for many more discoveries.

Thus you see how I live upon y Provision,
and how little I am capable else to serve you
from the Desart I am in; Wanting in every thing
but in a most greatefull Heart for these, and all
your Favours to

d S,

Y

most obedient faithfull
Ser: EVELYN:

My Wife returnes y her most humble service, and the
young Bostonian (who is with us) for y mention of him.

Give to D.r Gale all you can expresse of service & solemn
acknowledg.t in the name of a most obliged Creature.

I beseech you when next you see my L.d Clarendon, make my
Complement for his kind remembrance: I intend shortly to write
to his L.p upon the Account he mentions. & now by the defence
you permit me to Employ, I am bold to intreat y assistance in
Conveying the Inclosd; having no other meane to be just and
Civile to my knowne Un-knowne Friends in Virginia.

When ever you, & the Doc.r go downe the River, divert for
a moment to the young House-keepers at Says-Court, and let
me know in what fault you apprehend them: They are y
heare a Family of 21: M.rs Tuke is Library-keeper.
The rest painters, Embroiderers, Carvers, Gardiner & Colona
& a Campi.

The most certaine way of sending y Commands to Wotton, is
by Carting y servant to deliver them to M.rs Collins, at a
Book-sellers Shop at the Middle-Temple gate (which is y Post-house)
whence we have constantly the News-letters & Gazett twise every
Weeke: The little Woman of the Shop is a Friend to the Family
here, & takes particular Care of all that's directed hither.

We beg the favour y I will present our most humble
Service to M.rs Steward, when you visite Lincolnshire.

Wootton May 30. 1694.
Mr Evelyn to Mr. Pepys.

Fig. 6 John Evelyn to Samuel Pepys
30 May 1694 (**D21**) (continued)

Timetable of events

1620	31 Oct	E born at Wotton in Surrey
1625	27 Mar	Death of JAMES I /Accession of CHARLES I
1633	23 Feb	P born near Fleet Street in London
1637	May	E goes up to Balliol, Oxford
1640	Apr	E goes to the Middle Temple
1641	Jul	E leaves for the Low Countries and returns in October
1642	Aug	English Civil War breaks out
	Nov	E begins protracted tour of the Continent
1647	27 Jun	E marries Mary Browne in Paris
1649	30 Jan	Execution of CHARLES I
1650	Jun	P recorded at Trinity, Cambridge
	Oct	P transfers to Magdalene
1652	Feb	E returns permanently to England
	Jun	Mrs Mary Evelyn arrives in England
	24 Aug	Birth of E's son Richard
1653	Feb	E's purchase of Sayes Court settled
1654	Mar	P takes his degree at Magdalene, Cambridge
1655	Jan	Birth of E's son John
	1 Dec	P marries Elizabeth St Michel
1658	27 Jan	Death of E's son Richard
	26 Mar	P cut for the stone
	3 Sep	Death of Oliver Cromwell
1660	3 Feb	General Monck reaches London
	23 Mar	P sails with Mountagu to Holland to collect Charles II
	8 May	Proclamation of CHARLES II
	29 May	Charles II enters London
	29 Jun	P appointed Clerk of the Acts
1662	13 Aug	Royal Society charter approved and made a corporation
	20 Aug	E appointed to Royal Society council
1664	Feb	E's book *Sylva* published
	Oct	E appointed a commissioner for sick and wounded seamen and prisoners of war

1665	15 Feb	P elected Fellow of the Royal Society
	22 Feb	Second Dutch War begins
	1 May	P visits E's home for the first time
	20 May	P appointed Treasurer for Tangier
	1 Jul	E visits the fleet at Chatham
	5 Jul	P moves his household and staff to Woolwich and Greenwich to avoid the plague (until 7 Jan 1666)
	28 Aug	E sends his family to Wotton for the same reason
	Sep	E's management of sick and wounded reaches a crisis
	1 Oct	Birth of E's eldest daughter Mary
	27 Oct	P made Surveyor-General of the Victualling
1666	2 Sep	Great Fire of London breaks out
1667	30 Jan	E's son John goes up to Oxford
	11 Jun	Dutch attack English fleet in the Medway
	31 Jul	Second Dutch War over
	13 Sep	Birth of E's daughter Elizabeth
	22 Oct	P defends Navy Office before Commons
1668	5 Mar	P defends Navy Office before Commons
1669	20 May	Birth of E's daughter Susanna
	10 Jun	E takes P to see his brother Richard to demonstrate the advantages of being cut for the stone
	Jun	P leaves with Elizabeth for a tour of Holland, France, and Flanders
	10 Nov	Elizabeth Pepys dies
1671	May	E appointed a councillor for foreign plantations
1672	Mar	Third Dutch War begins
	16 Oct	E's pact of 'inviolable friendship' with Margaret Blagge, later Mrs Godolphin
1673	29 Jan	Seething Lane Navy Office destroyed by fire forcing a move to Winchester St
	Feb	Test Act enforced to exclude Roman Catholics from office
	Jun	P appointed Secretary of the Admiralty
	Oct	P elected MP for Castle Rising, Norfolk
1674	Jan	P moves to Admiralty Office, Derby House
	Feb	Third Dutch War ends
	Aug	E's *Navigation and Commerce* is suppressed
1676	1 Feb	P appointed a governor of Christ's Hospital
	26 Apr	E disovers Margaret Blagge's marriage to Sidney Godolphin
	22 May	P elected Master of Trinity House
1678	9 Sep	Death of Mrs Godolphin
1679	Mar	P elected MP for Harwich

1679	May	P resigns Secretaryship of the Admiralty and sent to the Tower
	Jul	P released
1680	24 Feb	E's son John marries Martha Spencer
	Jun	Case against P dropped
1682	1 Mar	Birth of John Evelyn (1682–1763), cr. bart., 1713, E's grandson and eventual heir
	5 May	Duke of York nearly drowned en route for Scotland. P in flotilla
1683	30 Jul	P leaves to travel with Dartmouth to Tangier
1684	Mar	P returns to England
	Jun	P reappointed Secretary of the Admiralty
	30 Nov	P elected President of the Royal Society
1685	Feb	Death of CHARLES II / Accession of JAMES II
	14 Mar	Death of E's daughter Mary from smallpox
	Apr	P elected MP for Harwich for second time
	Jul	P elected Master of Trinity House for second time
	6 Jul	Monmouth Rebellion crushed
	27 Jul	E's daughter Elizabeth elopes
	29 Aug	E's daughter Elizabeth dies from smallpox
	3 Sep	E nominated commissioner of the Privy Seal
	15 Sep	E and P accompany James II to Portsmouth
	3 Oct	P reveals to E Charles II's death-bed Roman Catholicism
1686	Mar	P appointed to Special Commission (dissolved October 1688) to repair the Navy
1687	19 Apr	E sees the eunuch Cifacca sing at P's
1688	Nov	William of Orange lands at Torbay
	Dec	James II flees
1689	Jan	P loses his seat at Harwich
	6 Feb	WILLIAM III and MARY II proclaimed
	20 Feb	P resigns Secretaryship of the Admiralty
	May	P imprisoned in the Tower (until July)
1690	Jun	P imprisoned once more
	1 Jul	Battle of the Boyne
	Dec	P's book *Memoires of the Royal Navy* published
1692	Mar	E's son made commissioner for the Revenue in Ireland
1693	27 Apr	Susanna Evelyn marries Will Draper
1694	May	E moves from Sayes Court to Wotton permanently
	Aug	P recovering from illness
	28 Dec	Death of MARY II
1695	Sep	E appointed Treasurer of Greenwich Hospital
1696	Jun	Greenwich Hospital begun

1697	Apr	P seriously ill
1698	Jan	E's *Numismata* is published
1699	Feb	E's grandson goes up to Oxford
	24 Mar	Death of E's son John
	Oct	P's nephew John Jackson embarks on his tour of Europe
	4 Oct	Death of E's brother George; E inherits Wotton
1700	May	P stays with Hewer at Clapham to recuperate
	30 Jul	Death of Duke of Gloucester occasions the Hanoverian Succession
1702	8 Mar	Death of WILLIAM III / Accession of ANNE
1703	26 May	P dies at Clapham
1705	18 Sep	E's grandson marries Anne Boscawen
1706	27 Feb	E dies at Dover St, London
1724		Pepys's Library transferred to Magdalene
1734		Bodleian Library acquires Thomas Rawlinson's manuscript collection which includes some Pepys-Evelyn letters
1813	Apr	Evelyn archive first visited by William Upcott at Wotton House
1818		First publication of Evelyn's diary and correspondence
1825		First publication of Pepys's diary and correspondence
1852		New edition of Evelyn's diary carries substantially extended correspondence
1889	1 Nov	Samuel J. Davey's Catalogue no. 31 appears with a major group of Evelyn's correspondence with Pepys for sale
1900	10 Nov	Some of the Davey Catalogue letters reappear for sale, in Langham Catalogue no. 10 (Davey's business successors)
1926/29		J.R. Tanner publishes much of the Pepys-Cockerell collections of Pepys's correspondence
1931	1 Apr	Pepys-Cockerell papers sold at Sotheby's
1932		R.G. Howarth publishes an extensive selection of Pepys's correspondence, including many to and from Evelyn
1935		Clara Marburg publishes some Pepys and Evelyn letters from the Public Record Office and various libraries
1940		Carl Pforzheimer Collection published
1955		De Beer's definitive edition of Evelyn's diary appears
1970		Latham's and Matthews' definitive edition of Pepys's diary appears
1995		British Library acquires the surviving Evelyn archive
1997		First comprehensive edition of Pepys's and Evelyn's correspondence published